Phillip Kerman

SAMS
Teach Yourself
Macromedia®
Flash™ 5
in 24 Hours

SAMS

201 West 103rd St., Indianapolis, Indiana, 46290 USA

Sams Teach Yourself Macromedia Flash 5 in 24 Hours

Copyright © 2001 by Phillip Kerman

International Standard Book Number: 0-672-31892-X

Library of Congress Catalog Card Number: 99-68175

Printed in the United States of America

First Printing: November 2000

03   02   01   4   3

Trademarks

Warning and Disclaimer

EXECUTIVE EDITORS
Randi Roger
Jeff Schultz

DEVELOPMENT EDITOR
Kate Small

MANAGING EDITOR
Charlotte Clapp

PROJECT EDITOR
Carol Bowers

COPY EDITOR
Bart Reed

INDEXER
Sheila Schroeder

PROOFREADER
Tony Reitz

TECHNICAL EDITOR
Lynn Baus

TEAM COORDINATOR
Amy Patton

INTERIOR DESIGNER
Gary Adair

COVER DESIGNER
Aren Howell

PRODUCTION
Tim Osborn
Gloria Schurick

Contents at a Glance

Appendixes 523

Contents

About the Author

PHILLIP KERMAN is an independent programmer, teacher, and writer specializing in Macromedia products. His degree in Imaging and Photographic Technology from the Rochester Institute of Technology was earned back when "multimedia" had a different meaning than today. One of Phillip's internships, for example, involved programming multiple slide projector presentations with dissolves synchronized to a sound track—the multimedia of the 1980s. In 1993 he found Macromedia Authorware a natural fit for his interest and skills. After getting his start at The Human Element, Inc., he moved back to Portland, Oregon, to work on his own.

Phillip has transitioned his expertise from Authorware to Director, and now, to Flash. Over seven years he has had to adapt to a total of 13 version upgrades—Flash 5 being the most significant of them all! In addition to retooling and building his own skills, Phillip finds teaching the biggest challenge. He has trained and made presentations around the world, in such exotic locations as Reykjavik, Iceland; Melbourne, Australia; Amsterdam, Holland; and McAlester, Oklahoma. His writing has appeared in such publications as *Macworld*, *Macromedia User Journal*, and his self-published *The Phillip Newsletter* (www.teleport.com/~phillip/newsletter).

In addition to showing others how to create multimedia, Phillip has had plenty of opportunities to get his hands dirty programming. Recently, Phillip programmed the all-Flash Web site www.m-three.com for Paris France Inc. This site was included in both *Communication Arts Interactive Design Annual* and the *British Design & Art Direction Annual* in 2000.

Feel free to email Phillip at flash5@teleport.com.

Dedication

Dedicated to my late grandfather, David A. Boehm, who inspired and supported me in addition to sharing countless books with the world. And to my wife, Diana, who listens, motivates, and challenges me and whom I love.

Acknowledgments

Most successful feats involve the efforts of many people. This book is no exception. I'm proud of the result, but I can't take full credit. Here is my attempt to acknowledge everyone.

First, the people at my publisher. When Randi Roger approached me, not only did she provide the faith that I could write this book but stressed the support I would receive from Sams Publishing. She wasn't exaggerating. The following people were professional and prompted me every step of the way: Jeff Schultz, Amy Patton, Carol Bowers, Mark Taber, and most notably Kate Small, who as development editor made this book flow. Plus all the editors listed in the front of this book.

When you look at other Sams books, you'll see many of these people acknowledged for a reason—they are great!

Macromedia is the most approachable software company I know of. Without the following Macromedia employees (and countless others I can't name), this book wouldn't be what it is (nor would the Flash 5 product be what it is): Brad Bechtel, John Dowdell, Gary Grossman, Peter Santangeli, Matt Wobensmith, Eric J. Wittman, and most notably Jeremy Clark and Erica Norton.

There are countless correspondents with whom I've learned a lot about Flash. Instead of naming several and inadvertently neglecting many, let me just say that participating in local user groups and online forums is a great way to expand your knowledge and build your business—they've helped me and helped this book. Of all the places I've learned about Flash, being in the classroom teaching has probably been the most educational for me. The students and staff of the Pacific Northwest College of Art and Portland State University deserve special recognition.

Tell Us What You Think!

As the reader of this book, *you* are our most important critic and commentator. We value your opinion and want to know what we're doing right, what we could do better, what areas you'd like to see us publish in, and any other words of wisdom you're willing to pass our way.

You can email or write me directly to let me know what you did or didn't like about this book—as well as what we can do to make our books stronger.

Please note that I cannot help you with technical problems related to the topic of this book, and that due to the high volume of mail I receive, I might not be able to reply to every message.

When you write, please be sure to include this book's title and author as well as your name and phone or fax number. I will carefully review your comments and share them with the author and editors who worked on the book.

Email: feedback@samspublishing.com

Mail: Mark Taber
           Associate Publisher
           Sams Publishing
           201 West 103rd Street
           Indianapolis, IN 46290 USA

Introduction

Macromedia is not exaggerating when it says that Flash is "the professional standard for producing high-impact Web experiences." You only need to visit a few sites that use Flash to understand how compelling it is. Using graphics, animation, sound, and interactivity, Flash can excite, teach, entertain, and provide practical information.

Literally hundreds of millions of users already have the free Flash player (needed to view Flash movies). The fact that Macromedia is continuing to distribute this software so effectively means the potential audience for Flash content is huge and continues to grow.

The tools needed to create Flash movies are within your reach. After you purchase Flash, the only investment you need to make is time spent learning. You can even download Flash from `http://www.macromedia.com` and use it for 30 days before having to purchase it. I find it exciting to watch people go from fiddling with Flash to making entertaining movies. Imagine a great musician picking up and learning an instrument in a matter of days. It really is that amazing. If you're motivated, with just a moderate time investment, you'll feel as though a powerful communication tool has been given to you.

Flash is so unique that sometimes the less experience you have, the better. If you have preconceived ideas about what Flash is or how you're supposed to use drawing tools, it might be best to try to forget everything and start fresh. This book is organized in such a way that you should start seeing successes very quickly. With each task, you'll prove to yourself you're acquiring knowledge and skills.

I don't need to give you a pep talk, because you'll see for yourself. In just a few one-hour lessons, you'll be creating drawings that you may have thought you weren't capable of. After that, in few more hours, you'll be making animations. Finally, after 24 one-hour lessons, you'll be unstoppable. I know this. I've taught Flash to hundreds of students and invariably even the those who don't have fire in their eyes at first will recognize the power Flash has given them and that they can hone their Flash skills over time. Where you take your skills is up to you, but you'll get a great foundation here.

You may not feel like a pro overnight, but you will feel that you have a powerful communication tool in your control. When you can't wait to show others your creations, you'll know you're on your way. Get ready to have some fun.

PART I

Assembling the Graphics You'll Animate in Flash

Hour

HOUR 1

Basics

The Flash environment is deceptively simple. It's possible to get started drawing and animating right away. However, Flash might not act the way you expect.

To make sure you get off on the right foot, it pays to first cover some basics. Although Flash is consistent with other types of software in several ways, there are many more ways in which Flash is different. Experienced users and novices alike should understand the basics covered this hour.

In this hour you will

- Become familiar with Flash's workspace
- Organize panels and learn how they're used
- Explore the Flash Movie Properties (global settings)
- Learn the common file types related to Flash

NEW TERM *Panels* are special tools in Flash (similar to what Macromedia calls *inspectors* in their other products) that give you access to see and change most any setting while editing a file. For example, the Character panel allows you to change the font style and size of any selected text.

Getting Your Bearings

The key to understanding Flash is always knowing "where you are." You're given the power to edit everything: static graphics, animations, buttons, and more. At all times, you need to be conscious what you're currently editing. It's easy to become disoriented about exactly what element is being edited. This section will help you get your bearings right away.

The Stage

The large white rectangle in the center of Flash's workspace is called the *Stage*. Text, graphics, photos—anything the user sees goes on the Stage. (See Figure 1.1.)

FIGURE 1.1

The Stage is the large white box in the center. It is on the Stage that all the visual components of your animation are placed.

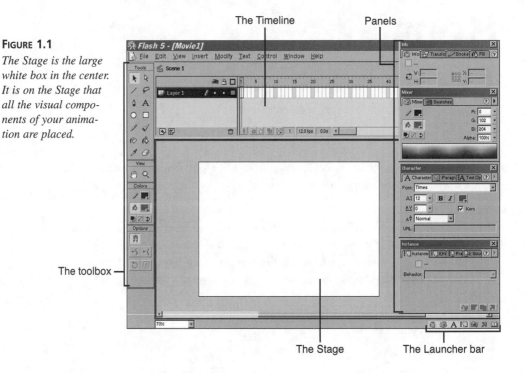

Let's take a quick tour of the Flash workspace.

- The Stage is your visual workspace. Any graphics placed in this area will be visible to the user.

- The toolbox contains all the drawing tools in Flash, of which there are many. These are covered in depth in the next hour.

1

- The Timeline contains the sequence of images that make an animation. The Timeline can also include many layers of animations. This way, certain graphics can appear above or below others, and you can have several animations playing simultaneously.

- Panels appear to float above everything else. They can be organized however you wish.

NEW TERM *User* is a general term to refer to the person watching your movie or visiting your Web site. Within this book, I'll refer to the user quite often. Occasionally, I'll call the user the *audience*. I've even heard the user referred to as the *witness*. It really doesn't matter which term you use—just realize that there's you (the author, creator, designer) and then there's the user (or audience, witness, or whatever term you like). As the author, you'll be able to make edits to the Flash movie, whereas the user will only be able to watch and interact with the movie.

Think of the Stage as the canvas on which a painter paints or the frame in which a photographer composes pictures. Sometimes you'll want a graphic to begin outside the Stage and then animate onto the Stage. Off the Stage is the gray area around the outside of the white area. You can see the "off Stage" area only when the View menu shows a check mark next to Work Area. (Selecting this option will toggle between checked and unchecked.) The default setting (Work Area checked) is preferable because it will mean you can position graphics off the Stage. Realize, however, any changes you make to the View menu only affect what you see. Changes here have no effect on what the user sees.

There's not too much to learn about the Stage—it's simply your visual workspace. However, two important concepts are worth covering now: Stage size and zoom level. By default, the Stage is a rectangle with the dimensions of 550 pixels wide by 400 pixels tall. Later this hour, you'll see how to change the width and height of your movie (in the "Movie Properties" section). However, the specific dimensions in pixels are less important than the resulting shape of the Stage (called the *aspect ratio*). The pixel numbers are unimportant because when you deliver your Flash movie to the Web, you can specify that Flash *scale* to any pixel dimension.

NEW TERM *Aspect ratio* is the ratio of height to width. Any square or rectangular viewing area has an aspect ratio. For example, television has a 3:4 aspect ratio—that is, no matter how big your TV screen is, it's always three units tall and four units wide. 35mm film has an aspect ratio of 2:3 (like a 4"×6" print), and High Definition Television uses an 11:17 ratio. In the case of computers, most screen resolutions have an aspect ratio of 3:4 (480×640, 600×800, and 768×1024). You can use any ratio you want in a Web page; just remember the portion of the screen you don't use will be left blank. A "wide-screen" ratio (as wide as 1:3, like film) will have a much different aesthetic effect than something with a square ratio (1:1).

NEW TERM   To *scale* means to resize as necessary. A Flash movie retains its aspect ratio
when it scales, instead of getting distorted. For example, you could specify that
the Flash movie in your Web page scale to 100% of the user's browser window size. You
could also take a movie with the dimensions 100×100 and scale it to 400×400.

Not only can you deliver your Flash movie in any size (Flash scales well), but while
working in Flash, you can zoom in on certain portions of the Stage for a closer look
without having any effect on the actual Stage size. Try the following task, where I intro-
duce a couple tools important to the Stage.

Task: Change Your View on the Stage

1. Open Flash. You'll be faced with a blank, unsaved document called Movie 1.

2. Instead of working from scratch, you're going to open an existing file. Select Help,
   Lessons, 01 Introduction. You'll effectively open an existing file. (Normally, you'd
   select File, Open…. However, several tutorial files are preinstalled, accessible
   through the Help menu.)

3. Notice the zoom control near the bottom of the Stage (see Figure 1.2). This control
   provides one way to change your current view setting. Other ways include using
   the View, Magnification menu and the Zoom tool (the magnifier button in the
   Drawing toolbar), which you'll see in more detail next hour.

FIGURE 1.2

*The zoom control
allows you to zoom in
on or zoom out of the
Stage. This has no
effect on what your
audience will see.*

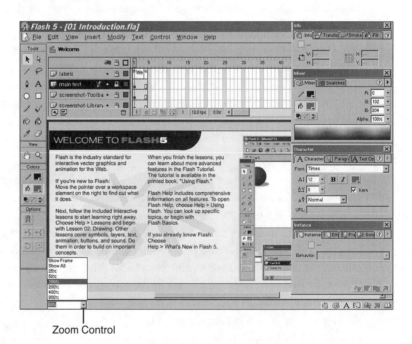

Zoom Control

4. Change the zoom control to 400%. Notice how everything is bigger. You haven't really changed anything, except your view of the screen.

5. Likely you can't see the whole Stage (unless you have a huge monitor). However, you can view the other parts of the Stage in one of two ways: by using the standard window scroll bars on the right and bottom or by using the Hand tool. The Hand tool is best accessible by simply holding down your spacebar. Go ahead and hold down the spacebar; then click and drag. You're *panning* to other parts of the stage without actually moving anything. It's important to understand that the Hand tool only changes your view port onto the whole Stage. The best thing about using the spacebar to select the Hand tool is that it's "spring loaded"—that is, the Hand tool is only active while you hold down the spacebar. Next hour, you'll learn about other spring-loaded tools.

6. Now change the View control to Show All. No matter what your screen size, Flash will scale the Stage to fit your window. Now you'll use another file to finish this task. Select Help, Samples, Keyframing.

7. Two interesting tools are available from the View menu: the grid and guides. Select View, Grid, Show Grid. Behind all the graphics onstage you'll see a grid (which the user won't see), as shown in Figure 1.3. You'll see next hour how the grid can help you line up graphics perfectly. Notice that from View, Grid you can select Edit Grid…, where you can edit the color and spacing of the grid. Turn off the grid now by selecting View, Grid, Show Grid (so that there's no check mark next to this menu item).

FIGURE 1.3

Turning on the grid will allow you to align objects.

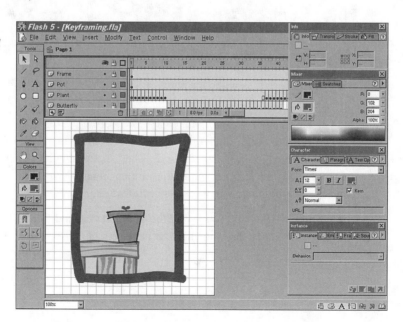

8. Guides are just like the grid, except you drag them into place where you wish. First, select View Rulers (so that there's a check mark next to this item). Now you can click either ruler and drag toward the stage to create and put into place a single guide, as shown in Figure 1.4. You make vertical guides by dragging from the left-side ruler and horizontal guides by dragging from the top ruler. To remove the guides, drag them back to the ruler. As with the grid, you'll find the option to edit the guide settings from View, Guides, Edit Guides... in addition to a way to lock the guides in place.

FIGURE 1.4

Guides are similar to the grid, but you can position the vertical and horizontal lines wherever you want.

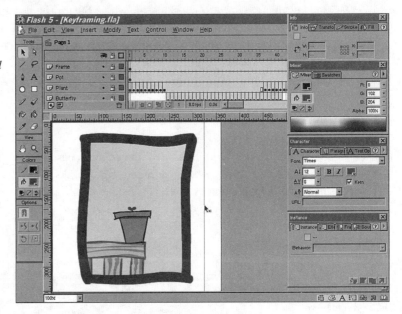

9. Close these files without saving.

Toolbars

Flash has five toolbars: Main (also called *Standard*), Status, Controller, the Launcher Bar, and the toolbox (also called *Tools*). The first four toolbars simply give you an alternative way to reach items found in the various menus—but through icon buttons. The Tools bar provides a way to insert and edit text and graphics.

From Window, Toolbars, you'll find the Main, Status, and Controller toolbars, as shown in Figure 1.5. Notice the Launcher Bar is present at all times.

Main (also called Standard)

FIGURE 1.5

*Additional toolbars can
be arranged however
you wish.*

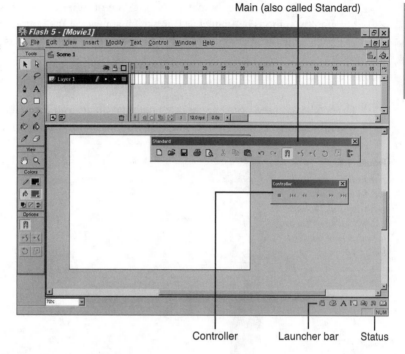

Controller   Launcher bar   Status

The Main toolbar includes buttons for common functions found under the File and Edit
menus—Open, Save, and Undo, for example. You can actually learn what each button
does by moving your cursor over a button and pausing there until a tooltip appears. The
Status toolbar simply displays the current status of your keyboard: Caps Lock and Num
Lock—that's it! (I usually leave the Status toolbar off because it takes so much screen
space and only provides information displayed already on my keyboard.) The Controller
toolbar resembles the controls on a VCR. When you create animations, you can use
Controller to play, stop, rewind, and step through your animations. Eventually, using the
shortcuts for these controller functions will become second nature to you, and you might
not use this toolbar at all.

The Main and Controller toolbars are *dockable*, meaning that they can appear to float
onscreen, or you can lock them to the Flash interface. This way, you can organize the
workspace however you wish. For example, select Window, Toolbars, Controller. The
toolbar should appear on top of everything else onscreen. If you drag the Controller
towards the Timeline at the top of the Stage, you'll be able to "dock" it—that is, lock it
to the interface. To "undock" it, click the line next to the stop button and drag. You'll see
other dockable windows in Flash, including the Timeline and all the panels, later this
hour. The Status toolbar is locked to its location at the bottom of the screen.

The Launcher Bar is one toolbar you can't drag or turn off—and it's so useful you probably won't want to. The Launcher Bar, which appears at the bottom of the Flash interface, gives you quick access to many of the most common panels, discussed later.

The toolbox is turned on and off by selecting Window, Tools. Like many toolbars, the toolbox is dockable. The default location is locked to the left side of the Flash interface.

The toolbox is used primarily to draw onto the Stage. You'll see it's actually broken into several sections: Tools, View, Color, and Options, as shown in Figure 1.6.

FIGURE 1.6

The toolbox has tools for drawing, editing, viewing, plus options that vary depending on the currently selected tool.

The Tools section enables you to create graphics and text (via the Line tool and the Text tool), to edit graphics (via the Eraser tool and the Paint Bucket tool), and to simply select graphics (via the Arrow tool, the Subselect tool, and the Lasso tool). You'll see all these tools next hour. The View section lets you change your view of the Stage (like you did in the preceding task). The Colors section gives you control over the color of objects drawn. Finally, the Options section is dedicated to additional modifiers for certain tools. Depending on the selected tool, you might not see anything in this section.

You'll look at these tools in detail in the next few hours (Hour 2, "Drawing and Painting Original Art in Flash," and Hour 4, "Applied Advanced Drawing Techniques," in particular). For now, go ahead and play with these tools. Be sure you understand how to dock the toolbars and what each tool's purpose is.

The Timeline

You'll look at the Timeline in depth when you start animating in Hour 7, "Animation the Old-Fashioned Way." Nevertheless, you'll take a brief tour of the Timeline now.

The Timeline contains the sequence of individual images that make up an animation. When the user watches your animation, he or she sees the images on frame 1 followed by frame 2, and so on. It's as if you took the actual film from a conventional movie and laid it horizontally across the screen, with the beginning on the left and the end toward the right.

Like many other windows, the Timeline is dockable, as shown in Figure 1.7. Docking is just one more way to organize your workspace. If you like, you can dock the Timeline under the Stage—or wherever you want. People with two monitors have even greater flexibility in the way the organize their workspace. Personally, I like to dock the Timeline above the Stage and the toolbox to the left. I use this arrangement for most of the figures throughout this book. If you close the Timeline to make more space (only possible when it's floating), you can always get it back by selecting View, Timeline.

FIGURE 1.7

The Timeline (and the toolbox) can be picked up and moved like any floating window. They can also be "docked" back in their original locations. This simply lets you customize your workspace.

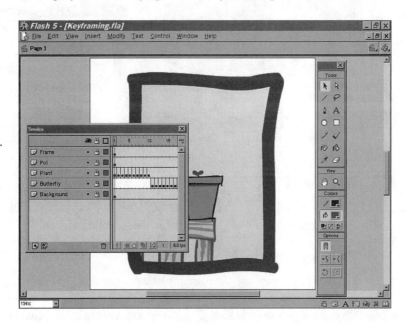

When you start to create animations, the Timeline will include many visual clues to help you. For example, you'll be able to quickly see the length of an animation simply by looking at the Timeline. Also, Flash uses a few subtle icons and color codes in the Timeline, this way you'll be able to see how the animation will play.

In addition to frames, the Timeline lets you have as many layers as you wish in your animations. As is the case with other drawing programs, objects drawn in one layer will appear above or below objects in other layers. Each layer will contain a separate animation. (You may have noticed in the "Keyframing" example, earlier this hour, that there were several layers.) This way, multiple animations can occur at the same time.

Using layer names and special effects (such as masking) you can create complex animations. Figure 1.8 shows the Timeline and layers of a finished movie. You'll learn more about layers in Hour 11, "Using Layers in Your Animation."

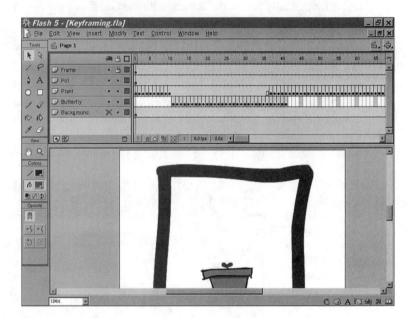

Windows

Certainly, you'll be faced with more windows in Flash than just the Stage, toolbars, and Timeline (although, these are the basic ones). In this section, you'll look at a few more.

Panels

Panels let you view and change properties of objects. For example, the Character panel that lets you view and change the font face and size. The Fill panel lets you control the fill color of any object. Although you'll only look at a few panels this hour, you'll eventually become familiar with them all. (You can see them all listed under Window, Panels.) Because there are so many panels, later this hour you'll learn how to organize them to suit your personal workflow.

As you'll see, using panels is simple. Panels operate in a very specific fashion. Although you can have a panel open while nothing is selected, making a change to the panel won't affect anything. To view or change properties of a particular object, you must first select it. For example, to change the font size of some text, you just select the text and then open the Character panel to make a change. The key is to keep the text selected while you open the Character panel. You can also change properties of several objects at once if you first select them and then open the appropriate panel. You'll see this in the following tasks.

Fill Panel

The Fill panel lets you view and edit the fill color of painted objects. You'll learn how to do this in the following task.

Task: Use the Fill Panel to Inspect and Change Colors

In this Task you'll use the Fill panel to inspect and change the fill colors of a finished animation. Here are the steps to follow:

1. To take a look at a finished file, select Help, Samples, Keyframing.

2. At the top of the Timeline, unlock all the layers by clicking the topmost padlock; otherwise, you won't be able to edit anything because each layer was locked before this file was saved. (See Figure 1.9.)

Lock/Unlock All Layers

FIGURE 1.9

All the layers can be unlocked (or locked) by clicking the padlock at the top of the Timeline.

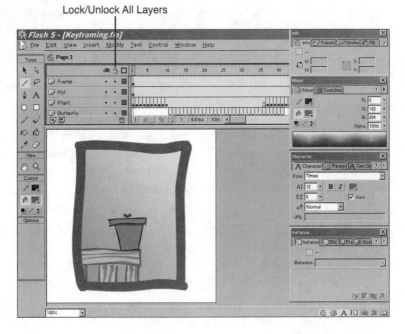

3. You'll now change the color of the frame. Select Window, Panels, Fill. (This is a toggle menu. If the Fill panel was already showing, you would have seen a check mark next to Fill in the menu, and selecting Fill would hide the panel. In that case, reselecting it from this menu would bring it back up.)

4. Click the Fill panel's tab and drag the panel to the middle of the screen, as shown in Figure 1.10. You can ungroup any of the panel groups this way.

FIGURE 1.10

The Fill panel can be dragged to the center of the screen to appear by itself.

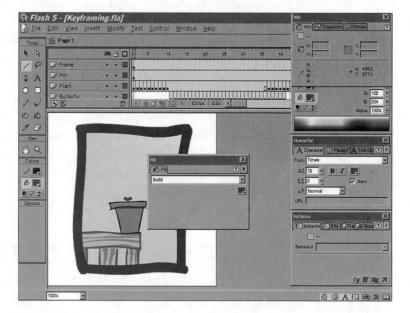

5. Select the Arrow tool at the top-left corner of the toolbox (also available by pressing V). Click the blue painted frame onstage. Notice that the Fill panel's swatch for Fill Color changes to match this color. Click and hold the swatch for Fill Color and select another color from the palette that appears. Using the Fill panel is only one way to change an object's fill color.

6. Click the potted plant. Notice that the Fill panel updates to a brown color. The Fill panel always reflects the properties of the currently selected object.

7. So far, using the Fill panel is pretty simple. Just for fun though, go ahead and note how it updates when you click the pale blue background inside the frame. You'll see that fill colors are sometimes gradients. You'll learn all about gradients in Hour 4.

8. Keep this file open. You'll do some more work with it in a moment.

Info Panel

The Info panel lets you see and manipulate visual properties of objects—namely, the width and height as well as horizontal and vertical position. The Info panel, like a few other panels, is used so often that Macromedia has placed a button for it on the Launcher Bar, as shown in Figure 1.11. You'll now explore the file you left open from the preceding task, but this time using the Info panel. Click the icon on the Launcher Bar to show the Info panel and then drag its tab to bring the panel into the middle of the screen.

FIGURE 1.11

The buttons on the Launcher Bar provide quick access to the most common panels.

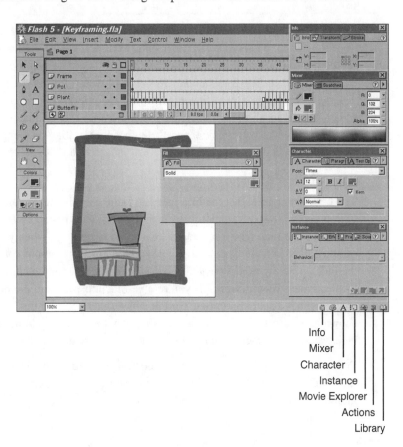

Info
Mixer
Character
Instance
Movie Explorer
Actions
Library

Make sure you still have the Arrow tool selected and then click different parts of the drawing onscreen. Watch how the Info panel updates the numbers displayed. Notice that the numbers at the bottom of the panel constantly update any time you move your mouse. Click the frame shape again and notice that the width and height are displayed in the Info panel. You should also note the location of the frame is displayed in the fields X and Y. X displays the number pixels horizontally from the left side of the screen, and Y displays the number of pixels vertically, counting from the top and moving down. Use the arrow keys on your keyboard to move the frame, and you'll notice that the X and Y coordinates change. In addition to letting you view properties, panels let you change properties. Therefore, if you type a higher number into the X field and press Tab, you'll see the frame shape move on the Stage. You can alter the width and height of any object the same way—for instance, you can make two objects the same width using the Info panel.

NEW TERM The *coordinate system* in all multimedia tools (including Flash) refers to locations by pixels in the X (horizontal) axis and the Y (vertical) axis. The very top-left corner of the screen (or Stage) is considered 0x,0y. As you move to the right, the X coordinate increases—for example, 100 pixels to the right has the location 100x, 0y. As you move down, the Y coordinate increases—the bottom-left corner of an 800×600 screen has the location 0x, 600y. Just remember that Y coordinates increase as you move down (not up, like you might expect). Here's an interesting challenge: What happens if you set the location of an object to –1000x? It's moved offscreen 1,000 pixels to the left.

Character Panel

The Character panel, like the Info panel, is quite useful. Create a new file (File, New or Ctrl+N) so that you can experiment with the Character panel. Select the Text tool, click the Stage, and then type a few words. Click the Arrow tool when you're done typing. Not only will you find the Character panel on the Launcher Bar, but you can also right-click the block of text you just created and you'll see a contextual menu appear with a section labeled Panels (control+click if you're on a Macintosh). From the menu that appears, you can select any panel appropriate for this object, including, in this case, Character (as shown in Figure 1.12). This is just another way to find the right panel. This feature is a nice way to find panels when you're not sure what panel is appropriate for an object.

From the Character panel, you can select a different font, change the font size, change the color, and control the text in many common ways. By the way, the Paragraph panel includes options related to alignment and margins. You'll explore these panels in depth next hour.

FIGURE 1.12

Accessing the appropriate panels for an object is simply a matter of right-clicking (or control+clicking on the Macintosh).

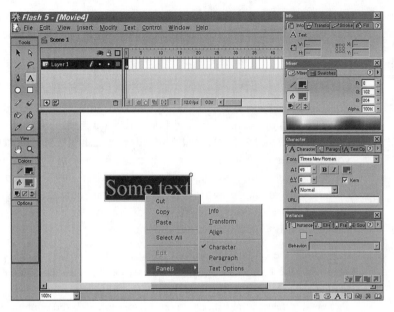

Organizing Panels into Sets

At this point you've probably explored enough to find that your panels are scattered all over the screen. This brings up an interesting point: You're given a lot of freedom with how you organize your panels. You can group and ungroup them in any way you see fit. You can even group them all in one wide "super panel" if you wish. The idea is that you can organize these panels to match your work style. If you're creating and positioning a lot of text, for example, you may want just the Character, Paragraph, and Info panels present.

> Depending on your screen size, you may find the panels are preventing you from viewing the Stage. A simple press of the Tab key will temporarily hide all the panels. Press Tab again to restore them.

You can always restore the "factory set" of panels by selecting Window, Panel Sets, Default Layout. In addition, you can save your own layouts. If you find an arrangement that works well for you, save it. Simply arrange the panels how ever you want and then select Window, Save Panel Set.... You'll be prompted to name the set. The name you give the set appears in the Window, Panel Sets menu. You'll also find a folder next to your installed version of Flash called Panel Sets, which contains a file for each set you've saved. These files can be shared with others or deleted when they're no longer needed.

Library

The Library is the best storage facility for all media elements used in your Flash file. There are lots of reasons why you'll learn to love the Library, which are discussed in further detail in Hour 5. Media that's placed in the Library can be used over and over within your file—and regardless of how many times you use that media, it doesn't significantly add to the file size! For example, if you have a drawing of a cloud and you put it in the Library, you can then drag 100 copies of the cloud onto the Stage (making a whole sky full of clouds), but deep inside the Flash file only one cloud exists. Using the Library is one of the ways Flash movies are kept small.

In practice, the Library is used in two basic ways: for editing and for maintaining (or accessing) the Library's contents. You may need to edit the contents of one library item (called a *symbol*), so in this case you'll be editing the contents of the Library. You may also need to access the Library to simply organize all the contents or to drag *instances* of the symbols into your movie. In such a case, you'll be maintaining the Library (as opposed to editing its contents).

NEW TERM A *symbol* is the name for anything you create and place in your file's library (usually something visual, such as a graphic shape). Although different types of symbols exist, the idea is that by creating a symbol, you're storing the graphic once in the Library. After it is in the Library, the symbol can be used several times throughout your movie without having a significant impact on file size.

NEW TERM An *instance* is one copy of a symbol used in the movie. Every time you drag a symbol from the Library, you're creating another instance. It's not a "copy" in the traditional sense of the word, because there's only one master, and each instance has negligible impact on file size. Think of the original negative of a photograph as the symbol and each print as another instance. You'll see that, like photographic prints, instances can vary widely (in their sizes, for example).

You can open the Library from the Launcher Bar or from Window, Library (also by pressing Ctrl+L). Notice how you'll see the names of every symbol in your Library, as shown in Figure 1.13. You can sort the list by name, date modified, kind, and so on—the same way you can sort a list of files when managing them on your computer. When one line is selected (just single-click), you'll see a preview of that particular symbol, and you can make changes via the Options menu (at the top-right corner of the Library window or a "mini" options menu when you right-click an item). Options such as Rename,

Properties… and Move To Folder… fall under the category of "maintaining" the Library. To use a symbol from the Library in your movie, simply drag it from the Library window onto the Stage. Finally—and don't try it yet—you can edit the contents of any symbol in the Library by either selecting Edit from the Options menu or double-clicking the symbol in the Library window (if you double-click the title of the symbol, you'll just edit the name). This is just intended as an introduction to the Library; it is covered in much more detail starting in Hour 5.

FIGURE 1.13

The typical Library contains many different symbols. The Library provides both access to all the media plus management tools for sorting, deleting, and renaming the different symbols.

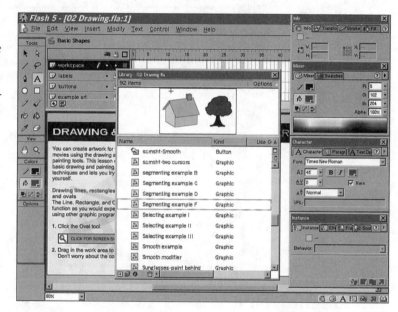

Getting Around

As mentioned, one of the important concepts in Flash is to understand where you are at all times. If you think you're in the Library editing the contents of a symbol, for example, you better hope you are really there. It can be confusing because, although it's always possible to figure out where you are in Flash, the clues are often very subtle. You'll now look at how you can determine where you are by reading the subtle clues in the interface.

Current Layer

Although there's just one main Timeline, earlier you saw how you can have several layers within the Timeline. Open a new file and add a layer so that you can explore it (Insert, Layer). One very important concept is that you can only be "in" one layer at a time. That is, if you draw or paste graphics, they are added to the current layer. The current layer is the layer with the pencil icon, as shown in Figure 1.14. Just single-click another layer to make it the active layer (notice the pencil moves to the layer you click). The key here is to always pay attention to what layer you're currently editing. For example, if the current layer is locked, you won't be able to affect it at all.

FIGURE **1.14**

Not only is the current layer highlighted (in black), but only the current layer has the pencil icon, indicating that this is the layer where anything drawn or pasted will go.

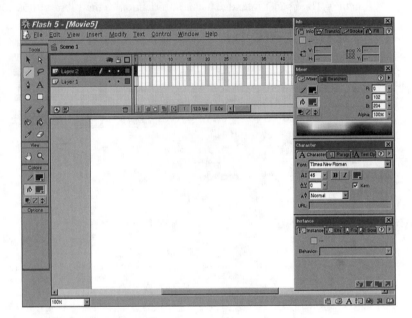

Current Frame

In the Timeline, a red marker indicates which frame is currently being viewed (see Figure 1.15). This red current-frame marker can be in only one frame at a time—and that's the frame you're currently editing. Right now, you'll find that you can't move the current-frame marker past frame 1 unless your file has more frames. You'll have plenty of opportunity to do this later; for now, just realize that the red marker indicates the current frame. If it helps, imagine a time machine. You can visit any moment in time, but only one moment at a time.

Figure 1.15

The red current-frame marker (on frame 11 here) can only be in one frame at a time. It's important to realize where this current-frame marker is located at all times.

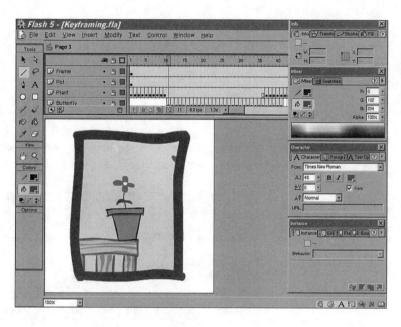

Current Scene or Current Symbol

By far, the most difficult concept for new users is this: In Flash, there's more than one Timeline! A large or complicated movie can be broken into several scenes. You can think of scenes as chapters in a novel. Deep inside Flash there's always just one long Timeline (just like a novel has one continuous story), but if you break your file into scenes, you can access them individually. This is a nice feature because you can easily change the order or sequence of the scenes. Without going into more detail, it should be apparent that at all times you should know in which scene you're currently working. The name of the current scene is always listed above the Timeline (if docked) or above the Stage (if the Timeline is undocked). I'll refer to this as the *address bar*. The default name is"Scene 1," and you should see this next to the icon for scenes—a movie "clapper" (see Figure 1.16).

Scene name and clapper icon

Figure 1.16

In the top-left corner of the Timeline you'll usually see the name of the current scene (Scene 1, by default). The "clapper" icon indicates that this is the name of a scene.

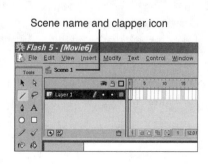

The address bar often includes more information than shown in Figure 1.16. As you'll see in Hour 4, when you start drawing, you can group graphics inside other graphics. When you learn more about the Library in Hour 5, you'll see how you can use symbols inside of other symbols. When you double-click a grouped graphic or an instance of a symbol to edit it, everything else on the Stage dims (indicating they're not editable). The best way to determine exactly which graphic you're currently editing is to look at the address bar. You might see "Scene 1: Group" (as shown in Figure 1.17). This means you're in a group that, itself, is in Scene 1. Sound pretty hairy? Well, it's not really so terrible because the address bar is very clear—you just have to remember to look there.

FIGURE 1.17

Here, the address bar indicates that you're in a group that, itself, is inside Scene 1.

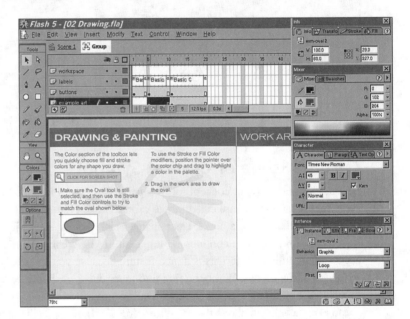

Navigating Through the Interface

You've seen how the interface gives you clues telling you where you are at all times. But how did you get where you are in the first place? And how do you get out? Navigating through your Flash file is very easy (maybe that's why it's so easy to get lost). Let's look at a few ways to get around.

The address bar not only contains the hierarchy of your current location, it also provides a means of navigation. Click the address bar. If, for example, you're inside a symbol within Scene 1, you should see "Scene 1: *SymbolName*." If you simply click "Scene 1," you'll be taken back to that scene (see Figure 1.18). Any time you see the address bar, you can navigate back through the hierarchy. Just realize that the address bar provides information and that it's clickable.

FIGURE 1.18

The address bar provides more than just information—you can click any name listed to jump "back." Here, you can click "Scene 1" to jump all the way back to the top.

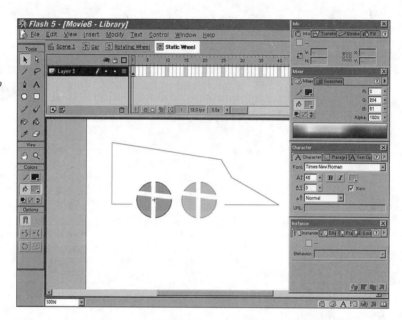

Finally, you'll notice two menus way off to the right of the address bar: Edit Scene and Edit Symbol (see Figure 1.19). From these two menus you can jump to any scene or symbol in the current movie. Of course, if you have no symbols and just one scene, using these menus won't be very interesting. However, when your files get bigger, these menus provide a quick way for you to get around. If you like, open one of the examples or lessons from the Help menu and try navigating through several scenes and symbols using these menus.

There are plenty more ways to get around in Flash, and you'll see them all. For now, try to feel comfortable moving around and be sure to notice all the clues that Flash gives concerning exactly where you are.

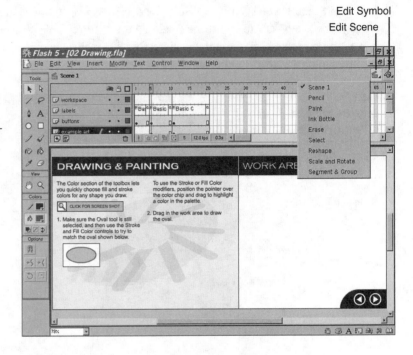

FIGURE **1.19**

The Edit Scene and Edit Symbol menus are always accessible on the right side of your screen. They provide the ultimate way to navigate to other scenes and symbols.

Movie Properties

You'll need to specify a few far-reaching settings early in the creation of any movie. Most of these are found in the Movie Properties dialog box, shown in Figure 1.20, which you access from the Modify, Movie… menu or by double-clicking the bottom of the Timeline (where you see "12.0 fps"). Access the Movie Properties dialog box now so that you can experiment with a few of its settings.

FIGURE **1.20**

The Movie Properties dialog box provides many global settings that should be determined at the beginning of every project.

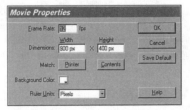

First of all, you should make sure Ruler Units is set to Pixels. This is the standard unit of measurement in multimedia and Web pages. It's important to set Ruler Units to Pixels because this will affect several other dialog boxes (including the previously mentioned Info panel). Next to Background Color, you'll see a white swatch that, when clicked, allows you to change the Stage color. This isn't actually as useful as you might think, because at the time you publish your movie to the Web, you can specify any background color you want—it will override this setting. So, feel free to change Background Color any time you want. Maybe gray will be easier on your eyes, or black will make selecting your white graphics easier. Do whatever you want—not only can you change this setting back later, but it only affects the Stage color while you're editing.

Two other Movie Properties settings are important to establish very early in any project: Framerate and Dimensions. Framerate specifies the rate at which Flash *attempts* to play—that is, how many frames per second. I say "attempts" because some of your users might not have a computer fast enough to keep up, so Flash just can't display as many frames in a second. Flash will not exceed the framerate you specify, but it could get bogged down and not keep up. Dimensions are only important insofar as they effect the aspect ratio of your Stage, as discussed earlier. Decide upfront on the shape for your Stage (sorry, it can't be round). Do you want a wide-screen "CinemaScope" look, or do you want a square Stage. You might even want a vertical rectangle if, for instance, you were building a button bar to appear on the left side of your Web page. You need to consider this early on because the Stage shape influences how you position graphics, and changing it later makes for a lot of repositioning.

People often confuse framerate with "speed," which is more of a visual effect. Animators can use tricks to make something appear to speed across the screen even while using a very low framerate. For example, if you see a picture of a car on the left side of the screen and then a fraction of a second later it's on the right side of the screen, that may tell your brain the car is moving fast. However, such a trick requires only two frames—and at a framerate of 4 fps, the second frame appears only a quarter second after the first! Frame rate controls the visual resolution. That is, how many chunks is each second broken into? Four frames a second may look "chunky"—each change occurs only four times a second. However, 30 fps (equivalent to the framerate of TV) is such a fine increment that you're not likely to see the steps between discrete frames (although, of course, that's what's really happening). By the way, you can still move a car across the screen in a quarter of a second using 60 fps—it would just involve 15 frames. You'll explore this topic in great detail in Hour 7, "Animating the Old-Fashioned Way," and Hour 21, "Advanced Animation Techniques."

File Types

Clearly, the most common use for Flash is to create interactive animations for the Web. Sifting through all the different file types involved can be a little confusing. At a minimum, you'll need to understand three types: source .fla files, exported .swf files, and HTML files (.htm or .html).

Source .fla Files

One of the two main file types in Flash is the source Flash Movie that you save while working. It uses the file extension .fla. You can open and edit any .fla file provided you own Flash. This is your "source" file. With the source .fla file, you can always restore the other file types—but nothing can restore an .fla file (except, maybe, doing all the work over again).

When sharing files with other workers who need to edit the source file, you share the .fla file. Anyone with Flash 5 (Mac or Windows) can open and edit the .fla file you create. However, you can't put .fla files into your Web page for people to view—they're just files containing your source content.

Exported .swf Files

When you're done editing your source file and ready to distribute your creation, you simply export an .swf "Flash Player" file. An .swf can be viewed by anyone with an Internet browser and the Flash Player plug-in. The audience can't edit the .swf—they can only "watch" it.

The process for creating a new .swf is simple. You open an .fla, select the File, Export Movie… menu, and specify the name and file location for the .swf. Although more details are involved, the important point to understand is that exporting involves creating a new file (the .swf file), but the .fla file remains untouched. It's similar to Save As or Save a Copy As, found in some other software programs (see Figure 1.21). Whatever you do, always keep a copy of your .fla. You can always create more .swfs from it—or make edits and then create more .swfs.

1

FIGURE 1.21

The Export Movie dialog box allows you to specify what type of file to export (most likely an .swf Flash Player file).

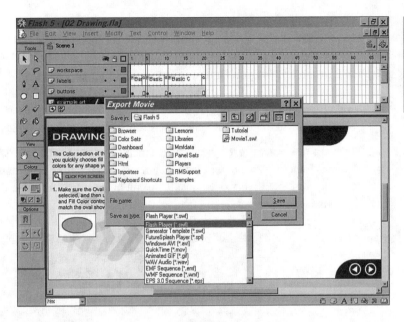

One last thing you need to understanding now, which applies if you work in a team environment or otherwise plan to exchange .fla files among different machines: Any .fla file you work on will open fine on anyone's machine with Flash installed (on a Macintosh, you may need to open Flash and then select the File, Open..., and on a Windows PC, you may need to ensure that the file is named with an .fla extension). However, there's one minor catch: The font choice for any text in the .fla file must be present on the machine attempting to create an .swf. It's not that you can't share a file if one person's machine is missing a particular font—rather, that person cannot edit the text and can't create an .swf. This is easy to avoid by properly installing fonts on everyone's machine or by simply creating the .swf on the appropriate machine.

HTML Files That Host the .swf File

If you have any experience creating HTML, the basic process of putting your .swf files in a Web page should be very simple. If you have no HTML experience, it won't hurt to learn a little HTML, but you really don't have to. For a quick review, when you "visit" a Web page, you're not really "going" anywhere. Rather, your browser software downloads a text file (usually with an .htm or .html file extension) to a temporary location on your hard drive. This HTML file contains not only the words you see on the Web page but additional instructions as well, including the font style and size. In addition, the HTML file contains details about any of the pictures that are supposed to be seen on the Web page—details such as the image file's name and where it should download to your hard disk temporarily so you, in turn, can see it. Putting a Flash Player file (.swf) in a Web page is almost as easy as putting a picture in a Web page. A few other details (in addition to the filename of the .swf) can be included, such as the background color, whether you want the movie to loop, and other interesting settings unique to Flash.

To make this process even easier, Flash includes a feature called *Publish* (discussed in Hours 17 and 24), which will walk you through the steps of creating both the .swf file and the .html file. Every detail available can be specified from the Publish Settings dialog box (see Figure 1.22).

FIGURE 1.22

From the Publish Settings dialog box, you can decide all the file formats you intend to distribute. Additionally, parameters for each can be specified through the tabs that appear (only the tabs for the file types you specify will appear).

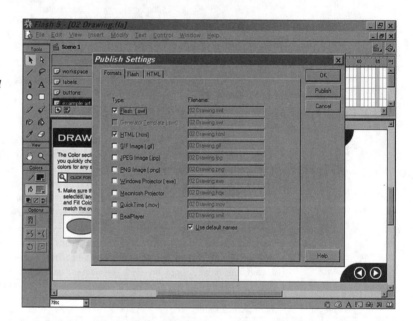

Summary

You sure covered a lot of ground this hour without actually *doing* anything. Don't worry, you'll get your hands dirty next hour. Besides, the information covered this hour should be useful throughout your Flash career.

You were introduced to Flash's main workspace, including the Stage, the Timeline, and the Drawing toolbar. You learned how to change the Stage size (through Movie Properties) and how to zoom in (with the zoom control). You got to see the toolbox (which you'll use next hour to create artwork) and some of the many panels that let you modify graphics onscreen. Although you didn't do much with the Timeline, you learned to pay close attention to clues, such as the red current-frame marker and the pencil icon, which indicates the active layer.

Other interface clues and navigation tools were introduced to help you track your current location at all times. The "address bar" at the top left always tells you where you are. Also, the two (rather cryptic) menus at the top right let you navigate to other scenes and symbols (provided you have some).

Finally, you learned about the file formats you'll likely create. It's important to take the time to understand all the files you create. You'll probably create a lot of files, so it's also a good idea to keep your files and folders organized so that you can track what's going on. The old saying is true: Haste makes waste. This is especially true when you have a million files to track. So, just take it easy, pay attention to how the Flash interface changes, and have fun.

Q&A

Q **When I hold down the spacebar (to get the Hand tool) and try moving my view over to the left or up, I can't go past the left of the Stage or the top of the Stage. Why is that?**

A Most likely the View, Work Area menu isn't selected (that is, it doesn't have a check mark next to it). Only when this is set can you (the author) see outside the Stage. (I recommend leaving this setting in the default "selected" state.)

Q **Somehow my Timeline has disappeared. How do I get it back?**

A It's really easy to get the Timeline back: Just go to the View, Timeline menu. The Timeline is the only window that you can turn on or off from the View menu. Other windows are found under the Window menu.

Q **While investigating some of the finished files in the Help, Lessons menu, I found the scene name (clapper icon) to be a useful way to get back to the main Timeline. For some reason, I've done something to make that scene name disappear from the address bar. How do I get back to the main timeline?**

A Usually, the address bar contains the "path" to where you're currently working, no matter how deep you go. However, if you edit one symbol and then edit another, you'll find that Scene 1 might not stay in the address bar. In this case, you'll see just the symbol name in the address bar. (This is still useful because it tells you where you are; however, it doesn't provide an easy navigation tool to get back to Scene 1—normally, you can just click the address bar.) For these situations, simply use the Edit Scene menu button at the top right of the interface.

Workshop

The quiz and exercise questions are designed to test your knowledge of the material covered in this hour.

Quiz

1. How do you open and edit an .swf file?

    A. You can't and unless you have a backup of the .fla file you're out of luck.

    B. Simply use the File, Open... menu.

    C. You can import it from the File, Import... menu.

2. How can you make your animation appear to play *really* fast?

    A. Crank up the framerate in the Movie Properties dialog box to 120.

    B. Trick the user by employing age-old animation techniques.

    C. Run the movie on the fastest computer you can find.

3. What is the standard unit of measurement for Web pages and multimedia?

    A. Inches

    B. Centimeters

    C. Pixels

Quiz Answers

1. A. Generally, you can't do anything but watch an .swf file. Truth be told, you can actually import an .swf (as in Answer C). However, this won't work if (when exporting the .swf in the first place) you specified Protect from Import in the Publish Settings, Flash tab. Also, when you *do* import an .swf file, just the sequence of frames are imported (no interactivity), so it's rarely very useful.

2. B. Although increasing the framerate to 120 fps (frames per second) will make Flash try to play quickly, the chances of it actually playing that fast are unlikely (depending on your computer). So, although Answer A is not entirely wrong, using age-old animation tricks (which are covered in Hour 7 and Hour 21) is the best way. Something doesn't actually have to move fast to appear to move fast.

3. C. This isn't an opinion. The standard is pixels.

Hour 2

Drawing and Painting Original Art in Flash

Believe it or not, Flash started life as drawing software. The creators of Flash intended to make a "more natural" drawing tool. Of course, Flash has evolved to become an animation tool, and, because you'll be animating images, it's convenient that you can draw these images right inside Flash.

This hour exposes you to the fundamental drawing concepts in Flash—think of it as your "basic training." There's a lot to cover, and you might find that it actually take a little longer than one hour to complete. Despite this lesson's length, you're not going to be creating anything particularly practical—it's more of a chance to play with all the tools.

If you have little or no background creating graphics on the computer, you're in luck! Flash is so unique that the less you know, the better—just let your mind act like a sponge and soak up all the information. If you have experience with computer graphics, try to forget everything you know about drawing software and get ready to learn the "Flash way."

In this chapter you will

- Learn how to draw and paint in Flash
- Understand the difference between lines and fills
- Learn how to draw geometrically perfect shapes in Flash

NEW TERM Graphics created in Flash are considered *vector* graphics (as opposed to *raster*, otherwise known as *bitmap*). Unlike bitmaps, for which the computer must store information on every single pixel, vector graphic files contain just the math to redraw the shapes. Therefore, a vector circle is described with the mathematical formula for a circle. Vector files are very small (and therefore download quickly), and they scale to new sizes easily (for example, the radius for a circle can be changed). Sometimes vector graphics tend to look too "computery," containing clean lines and solid colors. Not Flash. Once you get a feel for drawing in Flash, you should understand why Macromedia has called Flash "Vector Clay"—it's a vector format at heart, but it can be molded naturally like clay.

Drawing on the Stage

Remember from the last hour that everything your audience sees is drawn on the Stage. Sometimes, you'll want a graphic to start off the Stage and then animate into view. Drawing off the Stage requires that you leave the check mark next to View, Work Area. I recommend that you leave this setting checked, but realize that the gray area around the outside is considered "off the Stage" and will not appear in your finished movie. The Stage is the white rectangular area.

Tools

Your drawing tools should appear, by default, on the left side of the screen, as shown in Figure 2.1. If the tools aren't visible, use the Window, Tools menu.

FIGURE 2.1

Flash's drawing tool-bar may look simple, but because most tools have additional options, there's more than meets the eye.

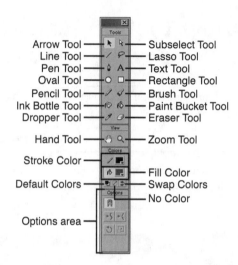

Arrow Tool —— Subselect Tool
Line Tool —— Lasso Tool
Pen Tool —— Text Tool
Oval Tool —— Rectangle Tool
Pencil Tool —— Brush Tool
Ink Bottle Tool —— Paint Bucket Tool
Dropper Tool —— Eraser Tool

Hand Tool —— Zoom Tool

Stroke Color ——

—— Fill Color
Default Colors —— Swap Colors
—— No Color

Options area ——

2

When you click a tool, it becomes selected. Alternatively, each tool can be selected by pressing its shortcut (or quick key). You can see each tool's quick key when you roll your cursor over the tool. In the tooltip that appears, you see both the name of the tool and a letter in parentheses. For example, when rolling over the Arrow tool, you'll see "Arrow Tool (V)." Pressing the V key will select the Arrow tool. (Try it out by first clicking another tool and then typing V).

It's time to look at how to draw with these tools. You'll learn about all of them in this hour, although the really advanced techniques aren't covered until Hour 4, "Applied Advanced Drawing Techniques." Keep in mind that, although some tools really do create artwork (such as the Pencil and Brush tools), others simply help you modify or view your artwork (such as the Arrow and Zoom tools). You'll learn how to create and how to edit artwork.

View Tools

Both View tools (Hand and Zoom) have no effect on your artwork. They are simply used to help you see your artwork. The following task walks you through a scenario in which you can use both tools.

Task: Use the View Tools to Help You See

In this Task you'll explore how to use both the Hand and the Zoom tools. Follow these steps:

1. Because you haven't drawn anything yet, you'll use one of the many sample files that ship with Flash 5. Select Help, Samples, Dice.

2. You can zoom in to critically inspect or change the artwork. Click to select the Zoom tool (it's the one that looks like a magnifying glass). Notice that, like many other tools, when you select the Zoom tool, additional buttons appear in the Options section of the toolbar. You should see two more magnifying glasses appear in the Options area, as shown in Figure 2.2.

FIGURE 2.2

The Zoom tool has two options: Enlarge and Reduce.

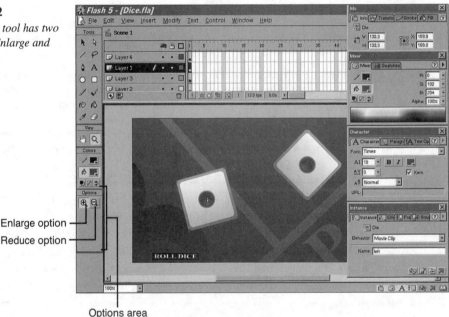

Enlarge option

Reduce option

Options area

3. Make sure Enlarge is selected (the one with the plus sign) and then click a red dot in one of the dies on the Stage. Click a few more times, and you'll keep zooming in.

4. While you're close up, chances are that most of the Stage is out of view. Of course, you can use the standard scrollbars on the left and bottom to change the portion of the (now huge) Stage. You can also use the Hand tool. Select the Hand and then click and drag to change your view.

5. Now you can zoom out. Just select the Zoom tool and make sure you remember to select the Reduce option (the one with the minus sign). Just click, and you'll zoom back out.

This task might have seemed pretty easy, but there's more you should know. Using any View tool will not affect your file but rather only your perspective on it. The View menu provides some of the same functionality as these tools (such as zooming in and zooming out). Similarly, none of the View menu options will have lasting impact on your file.

You used the Enlarge option of the Zoom tool by simply clicking on the Stage. Another way to zoom is to click and drag, and you'll see a rectangle as you drag. When you let go, that rectangle will define the viewable portion of the Stage. In the sample file, for example, you can click and drag with the Zoom tool and draw a rectangle around the ROLL DICE graphic to zoom in on just that portion. You'll always see the current zoom level displayed in the drop-down list at the bottom left of the Stage, as shown in Figure 2.3. If you click the Zoom control drop-down list, you can return to 100%. Another quick way to return to 100% is to double-click the Zoom tool (not the Enlarge or Reduce option, but the main Zoom tool).

FIGURE 2.3

The exact zoom control is always shown at the bottom left of the Stage.

Current stage zoom level

Speaking of quick techniques, both the Zoom and Hand tools have "spring-loaded" options. That means, for example, while you're using another tool, you can press and hold down the spacebar to get the Hand tool. Then, when you let go, it springs back to the tool you had. Holding down Ctrl+spacebar gives you the Enlarge option of the Zoom tool. Also, holding down Ctrl+Shift+spacebar gives you the Reduce option. These spring-loaded features provide very quick ways to temporarily select tools without actually going to the toolbar.

Creation Tools

Although the View tools prove very useful, they don't change your file. To create artwork in Flash, you either have to add to an image, change something you've already drawn, or remove some or all of what you've drawn. You're going to see how to add to your artwork first. This will, naturally, give you something to change or remove later. Let's go through each tool individually and then analyze how they can all be used together.

Drawing Lines

Two tools are available for just drawing lines: the Line tool and the Pencil tool. Lines can be given a stroke color, a stroke height, and a stroke style. It's interesting because the geometric definition of a line—the distance between two points—doesn't include mention of color, thickness, or style. It's best to think of a line this way: It's just an infinitely thin line that happens to be given a color, height (or thickness), and style (such as dashed, dotted, or solid). You can change any of the stroke attributes anytime and it won't affect the underlying line.

So much for theory of lines! In the following Task, you'll draw some.

Task: Draw and Change Lines

In this Task you'll begin to draw and manipulate lines. Here are the steps:

1. Start a new file. Lines can have different stroke attributes, so you should place the Stroke panel in a convenient place first. If your Stroke panel isn't present, select Window, Panels, Stroke. Then drag the tab in the Stroke panel and place the panel in a blank area of the screen, as shown in Figure 2.4.

FIGURE 2.4

*The Stroke panel lets
you set attributes of the
lines you draw.*

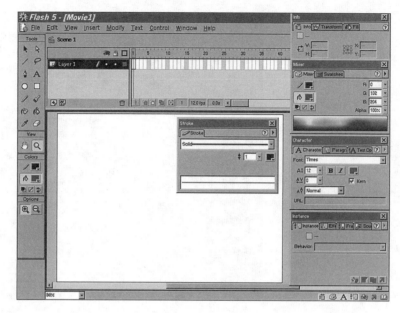

2. The Line tool draws straight lines. Select the Line tool. Your cursor (when on the Stage) changes to a crosshair. Click and drag to create a line. You may notice a dark ring that sometimes appears while you drag. This is Flash's way of assisting you while drawing. In the case of the line, you'll find drawing perfectly horizontal and vertical lines to be quite easy when the Snap to Objects option is selected in the View menu.

3. If you first set the stroke height or stroke color, this will affect subsequent lines you draw. Select a different color in the square swatch on the Stroke panel. Then change the stroke height, either by typing a number in the Height field or by clicking the arrow and dragging the slider. Now draw another line.

4. If you want to change the stroke attributes of a line you've already drawn, first select the Arrow tool and then click the line. While a line is (or lines are) selected, you can use the Stroke panel to affect its attributes.

5. Select the Pencil tool. Notice, first, that the Pencil tool has an option for Pencil Mode. Click the button that appears in the Options section to change the Pencil Mode, as shown in Figure 2.5.

FIGURE 2.5

The Pencil Mode is an option that affects exactly how the Pencil tool will behave.

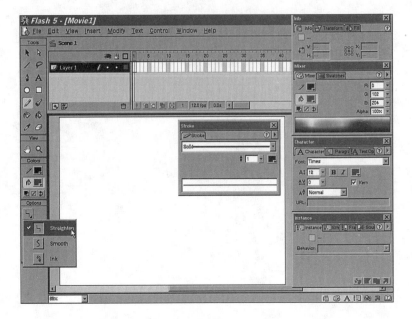

6. The Straighten option will attempt to straighten what you draw. Try drawing the letter *S*. It's likely to look jagged. Now try drawing the letter *Z*. It probably looks more like what you wanted. You'll learn to change the sensitivity later this hour, but drawing these letters should exemplify how the Straighten Pencil Mode works.

7. Choose the Smooth option and try drawing an *S* and *Z*. It's nice what happens to the *S*, but the *Z* has curves where there weren't any before. This option can come in handy if you find your hand-drawn images look too jagged.

8. Finally, the Ink Pencil Mode will draw *almost* exactly what you draw. Flash adjusts what you draw to reduce the file size. A simple line takes less data to describe and results in a smaller file that's faster to download.

All the attributes in the Stroke panel affect lines drawn with the Pencil tool the same as those drawn with the Line tool. The one attribute in the Stroke panel that you didn't experiment with is the stroke style. The drop-down list shows you a visual representation of each style. Solid (the default) is like Hairline, but Hairline effectively sets the stroke height to the lowest number possible. The other fancy stroke styles should be used with extreme caution. This is simply because the more random-looking ones tend to add to the file size. File size issues are addressed in Hour 20, "Optimizing Your Flash Site," but realize for now that you'll suffer a significant file size increase when using some stroke styles.

Finally, the little options arrow at the top right of the Stroke panel provides a way for you to create your own custom line styles. The dialog box that appears lets you control several attributes of your own custom line style (see Figure 2.6). These are fun, but be warned, they can significantly add to file size.

FIGURE 2.6

The Line Style dialog box (accessed from the Stroke panel) lets you specify every detail of a custom stroke style.

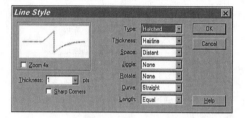

 As you begin to explore all the panels in Flash you should learn about the options arrow. Most of the panels have a supplementary menu accessible through this small arrow at the top right of the panel (shown in Figure 2.7) that will reveal a menu specific to that panel. I think of this as the "mystery arrow"—you'll never know what you'll find under it, but it often contains useful features. Throughout this book you'll be directed to select an item that appears in the menu "from the options arrow."

FIGURE 2.7

Many panels contain an options arrow that reveals a pop-up menu.

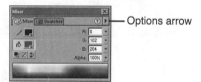 —— Options arrow

Painting Fills

In Flash, there can be only two components to any shape you draw: lines and fills. Some shapes are just lines (as you just saw), but some will be just fills (as you're about to see), and some shapes will contain both (as you'll see later this hour). Fills and lines are different. Lines have no thickness; only applied stroke attributes. Fills, on the other hand, have a left side, right side, top, and bottom. Think of lines as what you can draw with a sharp pencil and fills as what you can draw with a felt tip pen or crayon. This will become more obvious as you learn how to modify what you've drawn.

The two tools to create fills are the Brush tool and the Paint Bucket tool. You'll do a little experimenting with these tools in the following task.

Task: Painting Fills

In this Task you explore the basic features and some rather advanced features of fills. Here are the steps to follow:

1. In a new file use the Pencil tool to draw a few large circles. Make sure that at least one is totally closed, one is almost closed, and the other is obviously not closed, as shown in Figure 2.8.

FIGURE 2.8

Three hand-drawn circles that will be filled.

2. Select the Paint Bucket tool. Notice that the Options section has three buttons: Gap Size, Lock Fill, and Transform Fill (see Figure 2.9). For now you'll explore only Gap Size and see the others in Hour 4.

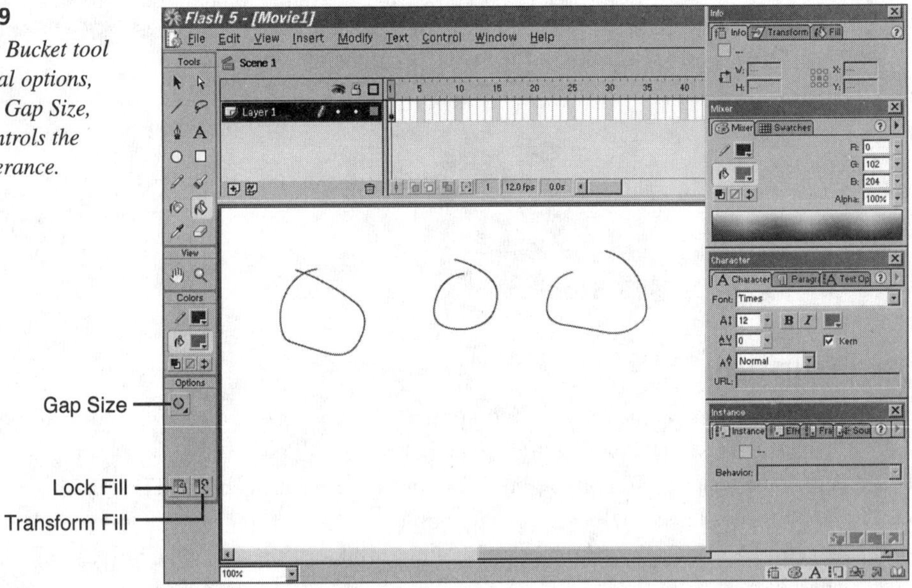

FIGURE 2.9

The Paint Bucket tool has several options, including Gap Size, which controls the tool's tolerance.

Gap Size

Lock Fill
Transform Fill

3. If you click with the Paint Bucket tool in an empty part of the Stage, nothing happens. The Paint Bucket tool fills closed shapes with the selected fill color (the swatch next to the small paint bucket in the Colors section of the toolbox).

It will also change the fill of any fill already created. Change the Gap Size to Close Large Gaps. Adjusting the Gap Size should enable you to fill all your circles—even if they are not totally closed.

4. Select the Brush tool and draw a quick line. Because you've used the Brush tool, it's really a fill (not a line) despite the fact it may look like a line.

5. Now, choose a new fill color by clicking and holding the color fill color swatch (from the Colors section of the toolbox). Then select the Paint Bucket and fill the shape you just drew with the Brush. Not only can the Paint Bucket change the colors of the filled circles you've already filled, but it can change the color of fills created with the Brush tool.

6. Now look at the Brush tool's Options area. The two drop-down lists that appear the same are actually quite different. The top one (Brush Size) controls the brush's tip size. On the other hand, the Brush Shape option controls the brush's tip shape. For example, you can have a calligraphy look with the angled tip, as shown in Figure 2.10). Lock Fill is covered in Hour 4, but the other option, Brush Mode, is very interesting and is covered in the next step.

FIGURE 2.10

The Brush Shape option affects the style of your drawings. Here's a calligraphy effect using the angled Brush Shape.

7. Figure 2.11 demonstrates each Brush Mode. You can try one now. Select the Paint Inside Brush Mode to experiment with it. Either use the closed circles you drew earlier or draw a few more with the Pencil tool. Make sure you have the Brush tool selected (notice that the Brush Mode remains where you last left it); then click and paint inside one of your circles. Try painting outside the lines. If you start painting inside the circle, the Paint Inside Brush Mode prevents you from spilling any paint outside the shape! With Paint Inside selected, if you first click outside the shape, nothing happens.

FIGURE 2.11

One Brush tool, several Brush Modes. In the Paint Selected example, I first selected the windows. The Paint Inside example worked only when I started painting inside the house graphic.

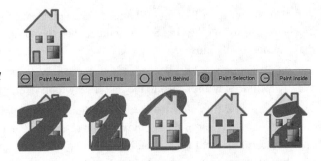

Let me recap just a few important points that are consistent for all the tools. First, certain tools have additional "options" that appear in the bottom section of the toolbar. If you can't seem to find an option that you've seen before, you might have to remember for which tool it was designed. This fact shouldn't be too frustrating because any attribute you need to change after drawing is available in various panels (which are hidden only if you choose to hide them). Only options for choices you need to make before you draw are in the Options section of the toolbox.

Another thing to notice is that sometimes the same tasks can be achieved different ways. For example, you saw the Zoom command in the View menu, the Zoom tool, and the Zoom setting on the Stage. The fill color swatch can be changed from the toolbox, the Fill panel, the Mixer panel, plus several other places! The fact that you can do the same task using different methods means you can find a work style that works best for you.

Drawing and Modifying Shapes with Lines and Fills

When you use either the Oval tool or the Rectangle tool, you'll create a shape with both a line and a fill. These shapes have a fill (of the current fill color) and a stroke with all the attributes in the Stroke panel. You can actually draw an oval or rectangle that has no fill by changing the fill to "no color" (the red line with an arrow pointing to it shown in Figure 2.12). Similarly, you can create a shape without a stroke by changing the stroke color to "no color." Realize that you can control both the fill color and the stroke attributes, but turning them *both* off means you can't draw anything. These tools are pretty self-explanatory. The only Rectangle tool option to take note of is the Round Rectangle Radius setting. This will make the rectangle you draw have rounded corners.

FIGURE 2.12

When using the Oval tool or Square tool, one option for the fill color is "no color" (shown as a red slash).

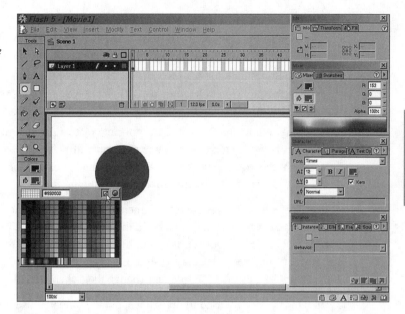

Creating ovals and rectangles is very easy. The following task walks you through a couple ways you can create and modify them.

Task: Draw and Modify Shapes

This Task combines what you've learned about fills and shapes, plus you'll learn a couple more tricks. Follow these steps:

1. Set the stroke height to something significant, such as 5 or greater.

2. Select any solid color for both the stroke and the fill—just not the "no color" diagonal red line.

3. Use the Oval tool to draw a circle. A *circle* is just an oval that happens to have equal height and width. To draw a circle, hold down the Shift key while you draw.

4. Now change the fill color and draw a square (holding down Shift while you draw with the Rectangle tool).

5. To change the fill color of the circle, select the Paint Bucket and click inside the circle you drew. The current fill color is applied to the circle's fill. The Paint Bucket is easy to understand—it either creates a fill or changes a fill.

6. Now you'll look at another tool—the Ink Bottle tool. Select the Ink Bottle tool and then pick a different stroke color. Now click the circle you drew. The stroke color

changes. What's really nice about this feature is that because the Ink Bottle tool only affects lines, you don't have to be particularly careful where you click. Usually you can just click anywhere on a shape and only the line portion changes.

7. The Ink Bottle tool doesn't just change the color of the stroke. From the Stroke panel, select a different height (say, 10). While you're there, pick a different stroke style. Now, click the circle again. You're affecting all the stroke portion's attributes.

8. Similarly to how the Paint Bucket tool can create a fill, the Ink Bottle tool can create a stroke where there wasn't one to begin with. Use the Brush tool to draw a quick shape. Now, select the Ink Bottle tool and click the fill you just created. You'll add a stroke to the fill, effectively outlining it.

This Task shows that there are two fundamental components to the shapes you create—lines (or *strokes*) and fills—and each has a different set of tools. The Oval tool and Rectangle tool can create both strokes and fills at the same time. To create a new fill or affect one that's onscreen, use the Brush tool or Paint Bucket tool. For lines, create them with the Pencil tool or the Line tool and change their characteristics with the Ink Bottle.

The Pen tool is primarily used to draw lines, but anytime you use it to draw a closed shape, the shape gets filled automatically. Later this hour you'll see how to modify drawn shapes (including removing the fill).

By simply clicking with the Pen tool, you can add sharp anchor points on straight lines. The Pen tool can also draw curves. Instead of just clicking to create a point, you can click and drag to create a curve. The direction you drag creates (what will become) a tangent to your curve. The distance you drag will determine how gradual or extreme the curve will be. If that makes perfect sense, I'm surprised. You'll just have to experience it to understand. Therefore, you'll experiment with these Pen tool basics in the following task.

Task: Use the Pen Tool

In this Task you use the Pen tool to draw controlled shapes. Follow these steps:

1. To begin, you'll draw a diamond. Select the Pen tool. Toward the bottom of the Stage, click and let go (this will be the bottom of the diamond). Then, up and to the left, click once for the left corner of the diamond. Click and release for the top and right corners as well. Finally, move your cursor near the first point you created. You should see the cursor change to include a little circle, as in Figure 2.13). You'll learn how the cursor frequently changes to provide you information later this hour. For now, it's enough to know that the little circle on the Pen tool indicates that if you click, you'll enclose the shape you started. Click to enclose the shape. It should automatically fill with the current fill color.

FIGURE 2.13

The Pen tool changes to include an extra circle, indicating a click will enclose the shape you're drawing.

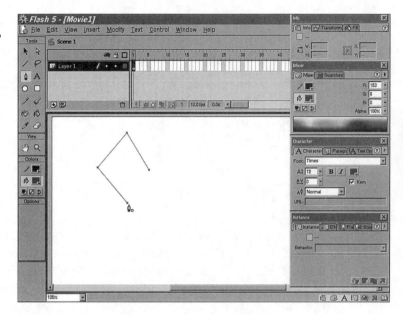

2. You can also draw a "V" shape. Click once for the top-left point of the V, click once for the bottom point, and then double-click for the third and final point (the top-right point). Double-clicking finishes the shape, even if it's not enclosed; if you click again elsewhere on the Stage, you'll be starting a new shape or line. Therefore, two ways to "finish" what you've started with the Pen tool include double-clicking and enclosing the shape (as you did in Step 1). Another way is to simply select another tool from the drawing tools.

3. Now you'll try creating a curved line. Click the Pen tool (to make sure you're starting a new line) and then click once, drag, and let go toward the left side of the screen.

4. Now you're about to lay down an anchor point on the curve you want to create. Therefore, click and drag before letting go. Up and to the right of the first point, click and hold the mouse down. While holding down the mouse button, if you move the mouse to the right, you'll see that your horizontal tangent causes a curve to appear that levels off, as shown in Figure 2.14.

FIGURE 2.14

When clicking to make an anchor point, if you drag (to the right in this case) you will establish a tangent for the curve that's created.

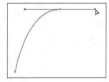

5. If you continue to hold down the mouse button while moving the mouse straight above the second point, you'll see that the shape of the curve is totally different because the tangent you're creating is different (see Figure 2.15).

FIGURE 2.15

Depending on the direction of the tangent (in this case, upward), the curve changes.

6. Finally, while still holding down the mouse button, you can increase or decrease the distance you're dragging (from the point you clicked). This affects the degree of the curve's arc. Before your hand gets tired, move the mouse to the right. Then double-click down to the right at about the same height as the first point to make an arc. Even though this curve has three points, only the middle one needs a curve to it—that is, when creating the first and last points, you didn't click and drag.

You'll see much more about the Pen tool (and its sister the Subselect tool) later in this hour when you start to modify what you've drawn.

Creating Text

Now for a graphic element that involves neither line nor fill, in this section, you'll explore creating text. To create text, you simply select the Text tool, click, and start typing. You can modify the font, color, and style for what you've typed after you create it. It makes sense to modify your text after it's typed in because only then will you be able to best judge how it looks.

Creating text in Flash has never been easier or more sophisticated. The following task walks you through a couple quick maneuvers.

Task: Create and Style Text

In this Task you'll explore using text in Flash. Here are the steps:

1. Select the Text tool, click on the Stage, and then type **Hello**.

2. This "click-and-type" technique expands the margin for the block of text to the exact width of whatever you type. The circle that appears at the top-right corner of your text block indicates that the margin will adjust in this automatic way

(see Figure 2.16). When you click and drag this circle (to adjust the width) it turns into a square (indicating the margins are fixed). You can double-click the square margin control to restore the automatic margin adjustment.

FIGURE 2.16

Creating text is easy. The subtle circle that appears is used to set the margins.

Margin handle

2

3. While editing the text block, you can set the margin. (Make sure the I-beam is blinking in the block—click inside the block of text, if necessary.) Grab the little circle at the top-right corner of the text block and widen or narrow this block of text. The circle margin handle changes to a square, which indicates that, from now on, any text you paste or type into this block will wrap when it reaches this margin. Go ahead and type a couple lines of text. You should see the text wrap without using the Enter key. By the way, if you had clicked and dragged with the Text tool to the right before typing (instead of clicking and then typing), you would have created a margin in one step. It doesn't matter which technique you use—just remember that grabbing the circle or square is the only way to change the margin.

4. Now that you've got some text into the block and set the margins, it's time to modify some attributes of the text. Click the Arrow tool to stop editing the text. Your text block should become selected. (If it isn't, just click it once, and you'll see a rectangle around it.)

5. With the block selected, access the Character panel. You can click the "A" icon on the Launcher Bar if the Character panel isn't already visible. The default panel set has the Character panel docked with the two other text-related panels (Paragraph and Text Options). For now, just modify the text's color, font, and font height from the Character panel, as shown in Figure 2.17. You'll find these options easy to understand and use. The font preview that flies out from the drop-down list is especially nice when you scroll through all your fonts.

6. Now you'll change the text style of just part of your text block to bold or italic. You need to first select just the characters you want to change. Double-clicking the text block automatically selects the Text tool. You can select the characters as you would in any word processor (just click and drag). While some text is selected, use the Character panel's settings to change just that text. If you want to change the font, the preview will include the text you have selected. Within any block of text you can change the properties of individual characters this way.

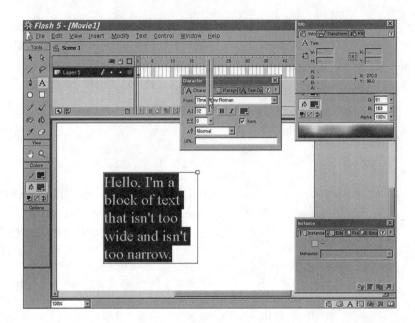

FIGURE 2.17
The Character panel allows you to change such text attributes as font size and color.

7. Select the Arrow tool and then select the block of text. Using the Paragraph panel, you can change the alignment to Center, as shown in Figure 2.18. Explore the other settings in this panel, which control such attributes as the margin padding and line spacing.

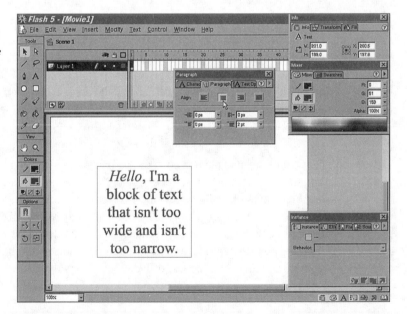

FIGURE 2.18
When the block of text is selected, you can use the Paragraph panel to change the alignment (to center alignment in this case).

The other text-related panel, Text Options, will be explored in Hour 15, "ActionScripting Applications for Advanced Interactivity." For now, always leave the Text Options panel set to Static Text. The text you type will never change, and your audience will see the same font you've chosen (even if they don't have that font on their machines). The option "selectable" will simply give your users the ability to select and copy the text.

In the preceding task, you learned how to create a text block and change attributes for either the whole block or select characters. Also, the concept of setting the margin width by dragging the small circle or square in the top-right corner of the margin box is very important. Later this hour, you'll learn how to scale objects onscreen, making them wider, taller, or both. If you scale a text block wider, the margins won't change. They may look wider, but all you'll have done is stretch the text wider. Changing margins as you did in the preceding task affects where word wrapping occurs.

Selecting and Modifying Objects

Now that you've seen how to create lines, fills, shapes (with both lines and fills), and text, it's time to explore how to modify them. The process is simple. Select the object you want to modify and then modify it. Selecting exactly what you want to modify is actually the most challenging part. This section looks at some of the fundamentals, and you'll see even more in Hour 4.

Selection Tools

The two basic selection tools are the Arrow tool and the Lasso tool. The Subselect tool (the white arrow) is for selecting and editing individual anchor points (in the same way the Pen tool created them). If you're familiar with controlling shapes using the Pen tool, this will be familiar to you. Otherwise, you should master the basics before working with the Subselect tool. You're going to concentrate on just the Arrow tool and the Lasso tool first.

The Arrow tool may seem so simple that it's not worth discussing, but it's actually quite powerful. You've already used the Arrow tool to select an object by clicking it once. The key to the Arrow tool is that the cursor changes to tell you what will happen when you click. You'll try out this tool on a couple simple shapes in the following task.

Task: Use the Arrow Tool to Select and Modify Shapes

In this Task you explore how the Arrow tool's cursor changes to inform you what will happen when you click. Here are the steps:

1. Use the Stroke panel to first set a very thick stroke height (5 or so). Then use the Oval tool to draw a circle and the Rectangle tool to draw a square.

2. Select the Arrow tool. Move the cursor to the middle of your square. The cursor changes to include the "move" symbol, indicating that if you were to click and drag, you'd start moving this fill (see Figure 2.19).

FIGURE 2.19

The Arrow tool's cursor changes when on top of a fill to indicate that a click will start to move the fill.

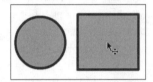

3. Click and drag, and you'll see that, indeed, only the fill of the square moves. Select Edit, Undo (Ctrl+Z) to restore the fill. Also, make sure nothing's selected (just click the white area of the Stage).

4. Now move the cursor near the outside edge of the square. The cursor adds a curved tail, as shown in Figure 2.20. Now if you click and drag, you'll bend the line. Go ahead and click and drag to the left, and you'll see that the line portion of the square bends. Notice that the fill bends with the line. (For this effect, remember to click and drag—don't just click and then click and drag.)

FIGURE 2.20

When the cursor is near a line, it changes to indicate that a click will start to bend the line.

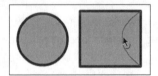

5. Make sure nothing's selected and move the cursor near another corner of the square. You'll see a corner shape added to the cursor, which means that if you drag, you'll be moving the corner point (see Figure 2.21). Try it. It's like you're bending the line, but instead you're just moving the corner.

FIGURE 2.21

When the Arrow tool is near a corner, it shows yet another cursor, this time indicating that you can extend the corner.

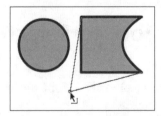

6. You've seen the cursor communicate what will happen when you click and drag. Now you'll use the Arrow tool to simply select something. For instance, select just the line portion of the circle by clicking it. It doesn't matter what the cursor changes to; it's telling you what will happen if you click and drag. Just click the line to select it.

7. With the circle's stroke selected, you'll notice that the cursor adds the "move" symbol (when you're near the selected line). Click and drag now, and you can move the circle's stroke. You can also just click Delete to remove the line portion. Do so now.

8. Deselect everything (by clicking a blank area on screen) and try selecting the square's stroke. If you just single-click one side, you'll just select that side. However, when you double-click the stroke portion, you'll select the entire stroke. At this point, you could move or delete the stroke. Just leave it for now.

9. Now select the entire square. You have several ways to do this. If you click the fill, you'll select just the fill. If you click the stroke, you'll select just one side. If you double-click the stroke, you'll only select the stroke portion. However, try to double-click the fill of the square. You'll find that the entire square is selected. Now you can move or delete the square.

10. Another way to select the square is to *marquee* it. With the Arrow tool still selected click outside the square and drag until you you've drawn an imaginary rectangle surrounding the square entirely. When you let go, the square becomes selected.

11. Sometimes the arrangement of other shapes onscreen makes the marquee technique difficult or impossible. Notice in Figure 2.22 that you can't marquee just the square without selecting part of the circle. In this case, you could simply double-click the fill of the square. However, there's another tool you can use to do this: the Lasso tool.

FIGURE 2.22

Sometimes using the marquee technique will select more than what you want.

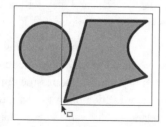

12. Select the Lasso tool and then click and drag around a shape to select it. The Polygon Mode option for the Lasso tool makes the tool act almost like the Pen tool. Select the Polygon Mode option, as shown in Figure 2.23, and click and let go. Then click and release in a new location to extend the selection.

Continue to extend the selection and then double-click when you're done. (In this case, double-clicking the fill would have probably been easier, but often when selecting several objects, you'll need to use this method.)

FIGURE 2.23

The Polygon Mode option for the Lasso tool lets you click for each corner of the selection you want to make.

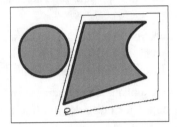

13. Finally, you can decide to select just a portion of a shape. Suppose you want to chop off the top of the circle. You can use either the Lasso tool or the marquee technique with the Arrow tool to select the portion desired (see Figure 2.24).

FIGURE 2.24

Using the Arrow tool to marquee just part of a shape chops off the top of the circle in this case.

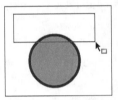

NEW TERM You use the Arrow tool to employ the *marquee* technique. If you click and drag an object, it will move or bend. However, when you click on the Stage where there are no objects, you'll see a rectangle appear while you drag (this is the marquee). You can draw that rectangle around other objects, and they will be selected when you let go. Often times, it's easier to use this marquee technique to select objects.

You'll learn how to modify what you've selected next, but for now, you have the fundamental selection techniques under your belt. More advanced techniques are discussed in Hour 4, but the best clue as to what will happen is to notice the cursor change. You'll find many places in Flash where the cursor is attempting to communicate information to you. For example, you can draw a line and see the same cursor changes you saw in the task you just completed.

Dropper Tool

One of the easiest ways to modify what you've drawn is to simply change the color. For example, the Paint Bucket tool can change a fill's color, and the Ink Bottle tool can change a stroke (its color and other attributes). This works fine when you make the effort to first select the fill color, for example, and then select the Paint Bucket tool and click a fill to change it. Sometimes, however, you'll want one fill to match the color of another. The Dropper tool lets you sample a color from an object already onscreen. It actually samples more than just color, though, as you'll see in the following task.

Task: Select Attributes with the Dropper Tool

In this Task you'll use the Dropper tool to select more attributes than simply color. Here are the steps to follow:

1. Set the stroke height to 10 and draw a circle. Change the stroke height, the stroke color, and the fill color. Then draw another circle. Finally, change both the stroke and fill color settings and draw a third circle.

2. At this point, if you wanted the second circle to have the same fill color as the first, you'd just have to change the fill color. If you remember the color, you're in luck. However, better than relying on your memory, you can select the Dropper tool. Notice how its cursor changes to include a brush when you're over the fill of the first circle, as shown in Figure 2.25. This indicates that if you click, you'll select the fill attributes of this shape.

FIGURE 2.25

The Dropper tool changes its cursor to indicate it will sample a fill when you click.

3. With the Dropper tool, click the center of the first circle. Not only does the fill color change to the sampled fill color, but the Paint Bucket tool becomes active. You can quickly go and fill the second circle. Do so now.

4. If you want to match the strokes on both circles, you could use the Ink Bottle tool, but you'd have to set all the attributes manually. Better than that, you can use the Dropper tool to sample all the stroke's attributes in the first circle. Select the Dropper tool and move it near the stroke of the first circle. Notice that the cursor changes to include a pencil (see Figure 2.26). This indicates that you'll be sampling the stroke (or line portion) of that shape.

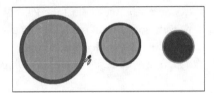

5. Click to sample the stroke, and you'll see the stroke attributes update in the Stroke panel. Also, the Ink Bottle becomes active, so you can click the second circle to change its stroke. The thing to remember is that the Dropper tool samples all attributes, not just color.

Modifying Scale and Rotation

Using the Arrow tool, you've seen how to bend, extend, and move shapes. Using the Ink Bottle and Paint Bucket tools, you've seen how to change shapes already onscreen. There are still more ways to modify the objects you've selected. Two common ways involve scale and rotation.

Basically, you just have to select an object and then select the Scale or Rotate option. These options are available anytime you're using the Arrow tool and have selected an object. You'll also find both Scale and Rotate under the Modify, Transform menu and on the standard toolbar (found under Window, Toolbars, Main). You'll now experiment with these option a bit in the following task.

Task: Scale and Rotate Drawn Objects

In this Task you'll explore the rotation and scale options. Follow these steps:

1. Use the Rectangle tool to draw a square. Select the Arrow tool and double-click the center of the square to select it entirely.

2. Click the Scale option (see Figure 2.27).

3. The selected object shows square handles in the corners and on the sides. Notice that the cursor changes when you roll over these handles. The corner handles let you scale both width and height equally and at the same time. The side handles let you change just width or just height. Click and drag a corner handle to change the scale. Drag a side handle, and you'll change just the width.

4. Make sure the square is still selected and choose the Rotate option. The handles change to circles. Corner handles rotate; side handles skew. Just roll your cursor over the handles to see the cursor change.

FIGURE 2.27

When an object is selected, you can choose the Scale option.

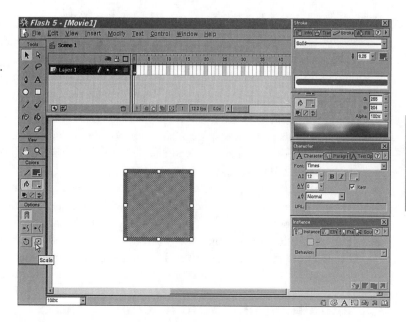

5. Click and drag a corner handle and notice that you can rotate the square. Actually, if the default Snap to Objects option is selected (that is, if the magnet button is pressed in, as shown in Figure 2.28), you'll find that the object will snap into place at 45-degree rotations (more about this later in the hour).

FIGURE 2.28

Provided Snap to Objects is turned on, when you rotate a object, it will snap to logical positions (such as 45 degrees).

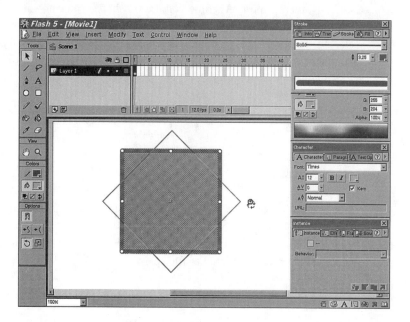

NEW TERM *Handles* are little white squares or circles that provide a way for you to stretch or rotate a selected object. When you select an object, it will either be highlighted or appear with a box drawn around its edges. When you select the Scale or Rotate option, for example, handles are added to the selection. Different handles often have different functions, such as the round Rotate handle and the square Scale handle.

In addition to the tools explored in the previous task, you can also control scale and rotation in two other ways. First, there's an option under Modify, Transform, Scale and Rotate that provides a dialog box to enter exact values. The other way to modify a drawn shape is with the Info panel and the Transform panel. Just select the shape and open the Info panel. You can type in new values for the width and height and press Tab. The Transform panel lets you rotate or skew any selected shape. You can also remove transformations from objects in this panel by pressing the Reset button. Finally, there's a really interesting button called "copy and transform" in the Transform panel. This button will duplicate the selected object and apply the most recent transformation every time you press it.

Smoothing and Straightening Shapes

You've already seen several ways objects can change their shape. When you drawing with the Pencil tool, Flash automatically adjusted everything you drew depending on the Pencil Mode. When using the Arrow tool, you saw ways to bend sides and extend corners. Finally, you saw how Scale and Rotate can change what you've drawn.

Naturally, there's more. Anytime you draw a shape, you can—after the fact—smooth or straighten what you've drawn. These two options are available when the Arrow tool is selected. The process is quite simple: Select a shape and click the option for Smooth or Straighten, as shown in Figure 2.29. Clicking repeatedly will continue to smooth or straighten whatever is selected.

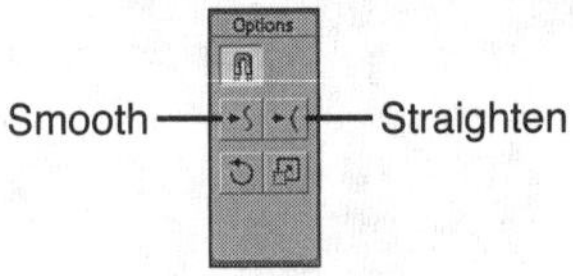

FIGURE 2.29

The Smooth and Straighten options for the Arrow tool will affect anything selected.

Smooth ———— Straighten

A couple before-and-after examples of smoothing and straightening are shown in Figure 2.30. Feel free to experiment with these options. Although the results will not always be what you might have in mind, Flash always makes the shapes less complicated, which results in a smaller file size.

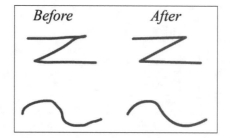

FIGURE 2.30

The shapes on the top were straightened, and the shapes on the bottom were smoothed.

2

Using Snap to Connect Objects

One of the most profound features in Flash is the way Snap to Objects helps you draw. By simply selecting View, Snap to Objects (or clicking the magnet button in the main toolbar), you can draw perfectly round circles, perfectly horizontal or vertical lines, and much more. The visual clue that Snap is helping you is the dark ring that often appears next to your cursor while you drag. When you see that ring, you know Flash is trying to help you draw.

You may already know (from using other software) that holding the Shift key will constrain your cursor similarly to Snap. But Snap can do much more. In addition to helping you draw perfect shapes, Snap will also allow you to connect two shapes. It's much more than simply making two shapes touch—they actually become bonded. In Flash, unless two shapes have been snapped together, they may look connected when they actually aren't. For example, you'll draw an arrow in the following task, but unless the arrow head is snapped to the arrow's body, it may not remain visually connected when you scale it larger. Once a shape is snapped to another, it's forever connected.

Task: Use Snap to Draw Perfect Shapes and Connect Objects

This Task walks you through some of the amazing ways Snap helps you draw. Here are the steps:

1. First, confirm that Snap to Objects is selected in the View menu. Select the Rectangle tool. While you click and drag, if you're anywhere close to drawing a perfect square, you'll see the dark ring appear near your cursor (see Figure 2.31).

FIGURE 2.31

While dragging with the Rectangle tool, a dark ring appears (provided Snap to Objects is turned on), which will help you create a perfect square.

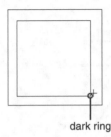

dark ring

2. Select the Line tool and draw a line at a 45-degree angle elsewhere on the Stage. This time you'll have to hold Shift as you draw the line to constrain to 45 degrees.

3. Now you're going to connect the top of the line to a corner of the square. Select the Arrow tool and make sure before you click and drag the end of the line that the cursor changes to show the corner tail. You can then click and drag to extend the line, and you'll see it snap to the square. Keep dragging and notice how it can snap to a corner or a side. (There are several different logical locations on the square.) Snap the line to a corner.

4. The last step probably changed the angle of your line, so select Edit, Undo (Ctrl+Z) and try again. This time, single-click the line to select the whole thing; then click the end of the line and drag to move it. You should be able to snap the end of the line to the corner of the square (this time without changing any angles). The only touchy part of this step is that, once the line is selected, if you don't "pick up" and drag the line from the end point or the middle, you won't see the dark ring. If you don't see the dark ring, let go and try picking the line up again.

5. Now draw two lines near the diagonal line that are almost parallel to it.

6. Use the Arrow tool to extend (by dragging) the endpoints of the two lines. Extend one end to connect to another corner of the square and the other end to the end of the 45-degree line, as shown in Figure 2.32.

FIGURE 2.32

You can extend lines to connect end points by dragging.

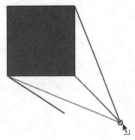

7. To prove that everything is truly snapped together, use the Arrow tool to drag the corner point where all three lines merge. If everything is snapped properly, all three lines will move at once and won't disconnect from the object to which they're snapped.

This Task provides you with just a taste of how perfect shapes can be created using Snap. Consider, for example, vertical and horizontal lines. If you select the vertical line and then pick it up from the center, you can snap it to the right end of the horizontal line. Then just drag the point of intersection to the right while remaining constrained to the same horizontal (which the dark ring will help you do). A perfect arrow is created! In Appendix A, "Shapes You Can Make Using Selection, Snap, and the Canvas Level," I show you how to create several sophisticated geometric shapes using Snap.

By the way, if you select View Rulers, you can click in a ruler and drag it onto your Stage to create horizontal and vertical guides. Provided View, Guides, Snap to Guides is selected, you can use the same Snap features to draw objects that are lined up with and connected to these guides. The guides are just for your use—they're invisible to your audience.

Finally, if you ever find Snap distracting, you can temporarily turn it off. Maybe you want to draw two lines really close, but you don't want them to snap together. Additionally, you can control the sensitivity of Snap (and other ways Flash tries to improve your drawings) through the Edit, Preferences, Drawing tab.

Summary

This long hour looked at practically every drawing tool in Flash. You saw how to create lines, fills, combination shapes, and text. After you created some objects, you found ways to modify their color, shape, size, rotation, and location. You even learned how to snap two shapes together. Even if you don't think you'll be creating artwork in Flash (maybe you're working with someone else who's the "artist" for your team), you should understand two important concepts: First, the simpler the shape, the smaller the file. Second, only shapes that are snapped together are truly connected. Of course, if you're going to create the artwork, this hour has exposed you to the fundamental drawing capabilities in Flash.

Q&A

Q The Paint Bucket tool appears to have stopped working and it looks like a regular pointer. What am I doing wrong?

A Most likely you've turned on the Paint Bucket option (called *Transform Fill*), in which case you can do nothing except change fill properties. This really only applies to gradient or bitmap fills, which are covered in Hour 4. For now, do not leave the Transform Fill button pressed in.

Q **Why does my Brush tool appear to be working when I click and hold, but as soon as I release, nothing's been painted?**

A You probably have the Brush tool's Brush Mode option set to Paint Selection, in which case only fills previously selected will be painted.

Q **It looks like there are a bunch of other tools (especially those under the Options section) that we haven't looked at. Are we going to go through each one in detail?**

A Many of the rest of the tools and modifiers will indeed be covered where applicable in Hour 4. However, given the foundation this chapter has provided, you should feel comfortable exploring some of the other tools. For example, the Eraser tool has a modifier called Eraser Mode that's strikingly similar to the Brush Mode and Pencil Mode of other tools. Try to apply the knowledge you've gathered in this hour, and I'll bet you can figure out most of the other tools on your own.

Q **Why do my lines have such bulky rounded ends no matter how short I trim them?**

A The endpoint of a line is indeed just a point; however, the radius of the point is half the thickness applied to the line. Therefore, an 8-point line has an extra 4-point curve on the tip. The only way around this is to draw a fill instead or convert your line to a fill and trim the end. You can convert lines to fills by using the Modify, Shape, Convert Lines to Fills menu.

Workshop

The Workshop consists of quiz questions and answers to help you solidify your understanding of the material covered. Try to answer the questions before checking the answers.

Quiz

1. What happens if you change both the stroke color and the fill color to "no color" and try to use the Rectangle tool?

   A. Shapes drawn will be black (the absence of color).

   B. You can try to draw, but nothing will appear onscreen.

   C. Flash crashes, and you'll learn never to try this again.

2. The quick-key for the Arrow tool is "A," the Pencil is "Y," and the Brush is "B." Where's the best place to find the quick-keys for the other tools?

   A. The front of this book.

   B. The Macromedia Web site.

   C. Just roll your cursor over the tool and wait, and the answer will appear under your nose.

3. Is there more than one way to set the fill color?

   A. Yes. Any place you see a swatch, you can set fill color.

   B. Yes. There are many places where the fill color swatch appears, and setting any of them affects all the others.

   C. No. You must set the fill color from the fill swatch in the drawing toolbar (the swatch with the bucket icon).

Quiz Answers

1. B. This is actually pretty unlikely to happen because only when the Rectangle tool or the Oval tool are selected can you set both the fill and stroke to "no color."

2. C. Although answers A and B may be true, the simplest way is to use the tooltips. By the way, although the default is "Show Tooltips," this can be changed under Edit, Preferences.

3. B. You don't need to memorize all the places where the fill swatch appears. Any fill swatch will do. Of course, you can't change the fill color by adjusting just any swatch. For example, the swatch in the Stroke panel only affects the stroke color.

Exercise

Try your hand at creating perfect geometric shapes, such as a cube. Use Snap to help you. If you want to see a few examples of interesting shapes, check out Appendix A, where you'll learn how to create some common shapes. Another idea is to try to copy a logo from a familiar brand-name product. This will force you to break down the task into geometric shapes.

HOUR 3

Importing Graphics into Flash

In the last two hours, we've seen how you can create very sophisticated custom graphics very quickly in Flash. Despite how powerful Flash's graphic creation tools are, eventually you may want to import graphics created elsewhere. Two good reasons are to use a photographic image or to use an existing graphic (instead of re-creating it from scratch). You can certainly use those other graphics in Flash—and that's what we're going to learn how to do this hour.

Specifically, this hour you will

- Import vector graphics into Flash
- Import bitmapped (raster) graphics
- Learn ways to avoid imported graphics
- Optimize and maintain the best quality possible when importing

Vector Versus Raster Graphics

Vector graphics have certain characteristics because of how they are stored by the computer. A vector graphic file contains the math to redraw the image onscreen. For example, a circle includes information such as the radius, the line thickness, and the color. All the graphics you create in Flash are vector based. Vector graphics have two advantages: the file size remains small (therefore it downloads fast), and the image can be scaled to any size without any degradation to image quality (a circle's still a circle even if it's a large circle).

Vector graphics are great, but it's important to realize their disadvantages. Vector graphics require the user's computer to work harder to display the image (it has to do a lot of math), and vector graphics often look "computery" or antiseptic because they tend to involve geometric shapes. Both disadvantages can be overcome, but you should be aware of them.

Bitmapped (also called *raster*) graphics are fundamentally different than vector graphics. A raster graphic file contains the color information for each pixel. If the image is 100 pixels by 100 pixels, that's 10,000 pixels each with a color value. As a result, raster graphics are almost always relatively large files. Raster graphics also can't be scaled very effectively. They tend to get grainy, similar to a photograph that has been enlarged. An advantage of raster graphics is that they will appear onscreen very quickly.

It might seem that vector graphics are obviously the better choice. However, the decision to use vector or raster graphics should be based on the nature of the image. If the image is geometric with clear delineations of color, vector is a good choice. If the image is a photograph of a person or a geographic location, nothing but a bitmap will do. Selecting which format to use is pretty easy; however, each type has its own set of considerations.

Reasons to Avoid Importing Graphics

Flash's capability to create nice vector graphics might be the best justification for this warning: Don't import graphics into Flash unless you have to! That's what we'll be learning to do this hour—but that doesn't mean it's always a good idea. If there's one way to make your Flash movie download slower or play slower, it's importing graphics unnecessarily. It's important to find ways to avoid importing graphics.

Wanting to import graphics is a natural tendency. If you show a graphics professional who's an expert with Illustrator or FreeHand how to draw in Flash, his first question will be how to bring his Illustrator or FreeHand files into Flash. This hour you'll learn the answer.

However, if we consider why a graphics professional would ask in the first place, we expose a problem. People can do some amazing (and complicated) things with other drawing tools. Some of the ways graphic files get more complicated include gradients, intricate text, and lots of individual objects. To use those complicated graphics in Flash causes two problems. First, Flash can't always handle all the intricacies in a complicated file, so the task becomes difficult. Second, a complicated file downloads slower and plays slower—so why would you want such a file in your Flash movie? The number-one consideration when deciding whether to import a graphic into Flash is if a simpler version can be re-created in Flash or can the graphic at least be simplified before importing into Flash. If you ask the graphics person to re-create the image in Flash, he might say that it doesn't enable him to do what he intended. If so, your solution lies in making the graphic simpler—not how to squeeze it into Flash.

Even so, you may still need to import graphics. Maybe you have a photograph (or other raster graphic) that you want to use, or perhaps you have a simple existing vector graphic (such as a company logo) that you don't want to redraw in Flash. We'll discuss raster graphics in the section "Using Bitmaps (Also Known as Raster Graphics)," later in this hour, but first let's look at vector graphics.

Importing Vector Graphics

There may be times when you have an existing vector graphic that needs to be included in your Flash movie. Typically, such a vector graphic is likely to be geometric—although not necessarily. Regardless of the exact form of the vector graphic, unless it's super complicated, you'll be able to import it into Flash.

From File

One way to incorporate other graphics into Flash is to import them from a file. It's as simple as selecting File, Import and pointing to the file you want, as seen in Figure 3.1. You will see several file types listed, but that doesn't mean they all work equally well. Not only are several image file formats listed (both raster and vector), but video and audio file formats also appear. Let's first look at the vector image formats available for import.

FIGURE 3.1

Importing images (or audio) is as simple as selecting the file you want to import.

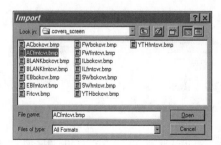

Although many file types are listed in the Import dialog, only four vector formats are worth considering: FreeHand (.FH9), Illustrator (.ai), Illustrator EPS, and Flash Player (.swf). Generally, the best option is FreeHand. Native FreeHand support is new to Flash 5 and it works great, as you'll see in a minute. The only Illustrator versions supported are 3.0, 4.0, 5.0, 6.0, and the older "88." Artists working in Illustrator versions greater than 6 simply need to save a copy and select version 6 or lower. Unfortunately, this occasionally means that certain visual elements are lost. The most important concern is that the artist always retain a copy of the source file matching the version of Illustrator he uses. The basic process is for the artist to create the graphics using his version of Illustrator, save a copy in version 6.0 when the graphic is finished, and then import that .ai file into Flash.

If you have an .ai file and you're not sure of the version (and you don't have Illustrator), you could try importing it into Flash. It will be painfully obvious if it doesn't work properly. The image will look nothing like what you expect, as you can see in Figure 3.2. This indicates that the version number is greater than 6, and Flash can't interpret the file. You must open the file in Illustrator (a new version) and then do the Save a Copy routine.

FIGURE 3.2

Upon importing an unsupported file format (in this case a version 8.0 Illustrator file), you're often left with meaningless graphics.

Importing FreeHand Files

Flash can seamlessly import FreeHand source files. If you're familiar with FreeHand, this is probably the best way to import vector art into Flash. It's simply a matter of selecting File, Import in Flash and selecting a FreeHand file to import. You'll be presented with the FreeHand Import dialog like in Figure 3.3.

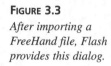

FIGURE 3.3

After importing a FreeHand file, Flash provides this dialog.

There are several options available when you import FreeHand documents into Flash. The Mapping choices let you specify how Flash deals with features unique to FreeHand. For example, if your FreeHand file has "pages," Flash needs to know it should handle them. All the options are fairly easy to interpret and are selected upon import into Flash. But there are a few things you can do (ahead of time) while in FreeHand to make the import smooth.

Here are some tips to help your drawings import into Flash. First, you should take advantage of FreeHand's symbols because these will translate directly to Flash's symbols so that graphics can be recycled. We'll discuss symbols and Flash's Library in Hour 5, "Using the Library for Productivity." Also, each object created in FreeHand should be separated into its own layer. Although you can easily put multiple objects on one layer, the file will import better if you create multiple layers.

There are many text effects that you can do in FreeHand that won't translate to Flash. For example, text attached to paths won't remain editable once in Flash. Also, because only FreeHand supports strokes on text, this effect will be ignored by Flash. Fine adjustments to font sizes (and kerning) are possible in FreeHand (but not as well in Flash), so often font spacing changes slightly once inside Flash. Sometimes text from FreeHand will automatically convert to paths (which means it won't be editable once inside Flash). I discuss converting to outlines as a solution to some text problems in the section "Steps to Maintain Image Integrity" because it can resolve some of these issues. These are just some general tips. To create the smallest, best-looking image that imports seamlessly into Flash might take some additional experimenting in FreeHand.

Importing EPS Files

Another vector format supported is Encapsulated PostScript (EPS). Unfortunately, there are many variations of this file format such as Photoshop EPS, but the only one Flash supports is Illustrator EPS. The best way to find out if your file works is to test it and see. Not only will your images look wrong if it's not working, but you'll likely see the dialog in Figure 3.4 telling you there is a problem.

FIGURE 3.4

Flash often warns you that there could be a problem with the file you're attempting to import.

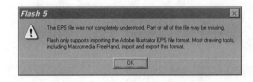

Of all the options that work, importing EPSs is the worst because it doesn't work reliably. It might work properly under one set of circumstances and then fail to work for another situation. If your testing involves truly representative samples, you'll be fine—but that's easier said than done.

Importing Flash Player Files

Finally, the most reliable option for importing vector graphics into Flash (besides, possibly, simply importing native FreeHand 9 files) is to import Flash Player files (.swf). Most graphics people don't think of .swf as a file format, but it's certainly a standard. Of course, an .swf is not like a FreeHand or Illustrator file because it's not fully editable. FreeHand 9, Illustrator 9, and Illustrator 8 (with the free Macromedia "Flash Writer" Plugin), will allow you to export your working files into the .swf format. They do it amazingly well. The proof can be seen in two measures: The final files are smaller, and the image retains all the details and quality of the original.

The best process is to create graphics in whatever program you prefer, and then open it in a program that exports .swfs and simply Export it as an .swf. You can then import it directly into your movie. Even if the graphics program you use doesn't support exporting .swfs, open the file in a tool that does and export an .swf from there. This means that the graphics tool you select must export files in a format that is supported by the tool you use to export .swfs.

If you have trouble with the process of exporting .swfs from the graphics program and importing into Flash, there are several remedies to try. First, investigate the export options in the graphics program. In Figure 3.5, you can see dialogs that appear when exporting .swfs. Without explaining each option, you should notice similarities among all three. Experimenting with these options is a good place to start.

In addition to the export to .swfs options, there are a few specific techniques you can try (covered in the section "Steps to Maintain Image Integrity," later in this hour). Ultimately, however, the solution *sometimes* involves making the graphic simpler—that is, reducing its complexity.

FIGURE 3.5

*When exporting an
.swf from FreeHand or
Illustrator, you're given
one of these dialogs.*

FreeHand 9 (via setup button)

Illustrator 9

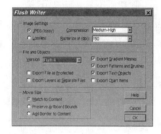

Illustrator 8

From Other Programs

The following technique works, but not very well. I mention it because it usually works well for simple graphics, and it's very quick. You simply open your graphics file in any graphics creation tool while Flash is open. Select and copy the contents (or some of the contents), effectively putting that image in your Clipboard. Go to the open Flash file and paste.

If you do use this technique, you should open the Clipboard tab in Flash's Edit, Preferences dialog (Figure 3.6). Additional preferences (namely, the gradient quality and editable text options) are available.

FIGURE 3.6

*Flash's Clipboard
preferences provide an
option to maintain
FreeHand text format-
ting.*

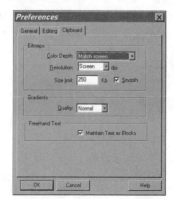

This sounds pretty simple compared to the previous section—but don't be fooled, it doesn't always work well. What actually happens is that the content of your Clipboard is converted to a particular file format. It varies as to what format, but it goes through a process similar to exporting an `.eps` then importing the `.eps`—it just happens automatically (and without your control). If it works, great. If not, go back to the other import options (exporting `.swfs`, `.ai`, or `.eps`) or better yet, draw it from scratch inside Flash.

Steps to Maintain Image Integrity

Despite how simple the export/import process may sound, it can be very frustrating when it doesn't work! Not to sound like a broken record, but the best way to maintain image quality is to create all your graphics inside Flash. For the times you must import an existing graphic or use a more advanced drawing tool, there are several things you can do to maintain image integrity. However, some of these tips are unnecessary when exporting `.swfs` from either Illustrator or FreeHand.

Font and text effects are usually the first things to go. Most drawing tools provide incredible font control, but Flash doesn't. The first consideration with text is whether the text must be editable within Flash. If you don't need to edit your text within Flash, you'll see the best results if your text is first converted to paths. You'll find an option to do this automatically when exporting `.swfs` from FreeHand, and it doesn't affect the source FreeHand file—just the exported `.swf`. FreeHand's Convert to Paths feature is the same as Illustrator's Create Outlines and is equivalent to Flash's Break Apart option under the Modify menu. Of course, you'll never be able to edit the text after you do this, so you should save a backup first. In addition, this can tend to make your file size increase. We'll look at file size issues in much greater detail in Hour 20, "Optimizing Your Flash Site."

If you use gradients, you should consider the Export `.swf` option. This is more important to keep the file size down and performance speed up (rather than simply retaining quality). A simple gradient, for example, will often include a separate circle for each step. Imagine hundreds of concentric circles, each varying only slightly in color and size. You can see this effect when you pick up and move an imported graphic with this characteristic, as in Figure 3.7. It's easy to see that such a gradient creates a larger file and one that plays more slowly—it's simply more complicated than it needs to be. When you export `.swfs` from Illustrator or FreeHand, the gradients are converted to Flash gradients. (Next hour you'll learn how to create and edit gradients inside Flash.)

FIGURE 3.7
Often an imported graphic is much bigger than it needs to be. This seemingly innocuous blend is actually lots of individual concentric circles.

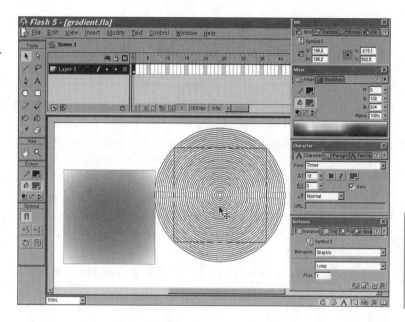

Going Back and Forth Between Flash and Other Vector Programs

Say you import a graphic created elsewhere, edit it in Flash, and then decide you need to touch it up again (in the original program). Doing so is not unreasonable or unexpected, but it doesn't work too well. Because it often fails to work, it's fair to question whether it's really necessary. Of course, if you just use Flash to create your graphics, this situation will be avoided—but the other drawing tool was probably chosen because it is more sophisticated. Because the other tool is so great, why not start over in that tool instead of trying to import the modified Flash graphic?

The best way to export an editable vector graphic from Flash is as an Adobe Illustrator .ai file. In the simplest case, you'll need to export just a still frame. For this, use Flash's menu File, Export Image and select Adobe Illustrator from the Save as Type drop-down list. This file can be opened in any drawing tool that supports .ai files (including Illustrator and FreeHand). No one can promise this will work without fail, but it seems to work better than other options.

If you just have a simple graphic, you can *try* the copy and paste technique. It usually works for simple graphics, although when you bring the graphic back to Flash, it will be different. For example, you might not be able to bend the line portions of a shape the way you could before it was taken to another program.

I've used a lot of techniques, and the only thing that is consistent is that you'll want to test several options until you find one that works well. The following summarizes the main points of this section:

- Try to create all your graphics inside Flash.
- If you use another program to create the graphics, try to refrain from making the file too complicated.
- If you must import files from another vector program, the best method is to allow the other program to export an .swf file (which, in turn, can be easily imported into Flash).
- A close second to the .swf option is to create your graphics in FreeHand and let Flash import the native FreeHand format. Although this might be the most convenient method, the files are not optimized automatically. So, you need to be familiar with FreeHand.
- If you need to export from Flash to another program then bring it back to Flash (which is really asking for trouble), the most reliable method is to select File, Export Image and make it an Illustrator .ai file.
- Finally, you're always best off testing your options to carefully determine the impact on file size and performance as we'll explore in depth in Hour 20.

Using Bitmaps (Also Known as Raster Graphics)

In this section we'll see how bitmapped (raster) graphics can be used in Flash. There are inherently unique characteristics of raster graphics that can't be created inside Flash. The only warning against this option is to make sure you really *need* raster graphics. Here is a summary of uses that require raster graphics:

- A photograph. The only time to consider a vector alternative to a photograph is when the picture is of a very geometric object.
- A series of still images extracted from frames of a video.
- An image with special effects that can't be achieved with a vector tool, such as clouds, fire, water, and other natural effects. (Of course, this is an invitation for a talented artist to re-create such an effect with a vector tool.)

If you're unfamiliar with the difference between vector and raster graphics, it can take some time to learn when one choice is better than the other. The file formats .gif, .jpg, .png, .bmp, and .pct are all raster graphic formats. However, just because a file was saved in one of these formats doesn't mean it was done appropriately. It's the nature of the image *in* the file that matters. If all you have is a .gif, for example, you need to first look at its contents to judge whether it's appropriate for raster graphics. Here's an easy way to decide: If you can trace or redraw the image in the file (with Flash's drawing toolbar, for instance), you're much better off redrawing it. If it's a photograph, you'd never be able to trace it (so leave it as a raster). If it's a picture of a plain box, maybe you could draw it just as well, and thus take advantage of all the benefits of vector graphics without even bothering with raster.

Importing Raster Graphics

Importing a raster graphic is pretty simple to do. Just select the menu File, Import and point to any raster graphic Flash supports: .jpg, .png, .gif, .bmp, or .pct. That's it.

However, importing not only places the graphic onstage but also places a master bitmap item into the library. If you import a raster graphic and then delete the object onstage, the master bitmap item will still be in the library (found with the menu selection Window, Library). It's called a bitmap item, and it has a little icon that looks like a picture of a tree (shown in Figure 3.8).

3

FIGURE 3.8

After importing a raster graphic, the bitmap item will appear in your library.

After a raster graphic is imported, you need to keep it in the library. This bitmap icon provides a way to specify how the image should be exported when you create a movie for the Web. If you leave it unchanged, your raster graphics will export using the default settings. You also can specify special settings for just that image. Let's import a raster graphic and explore some of these settings.

Task: Import a Raster Graphic

1. In a new file, select File, Import and select a `.bmp`, `.jpg`, or `.gif` file (`c:\Windows\` is a good place to look).

2. Click the graphic onstage and delete. Because it's a raster graphic, it's safe in the library.

3. Open your library with Window, Library (Ctrl+L).

4. Click the line in your library with the tree icon and the name of the file you imported.

5. From the library's Options menu, select Properties. The Options menu is inside the Library window at the top right. You should see the Bitmap Properties dialog shown in Figure 3.9. (This dialog may look slightly different depending on what type of file you imported.)

6. The Bitmap Properties dialog is where you can decide on the export settings for this graphic. Leave this dialog onscreen.

FIGURE 3.9

This dialog offers individual control over how bitmap items in your library will be treated during export.

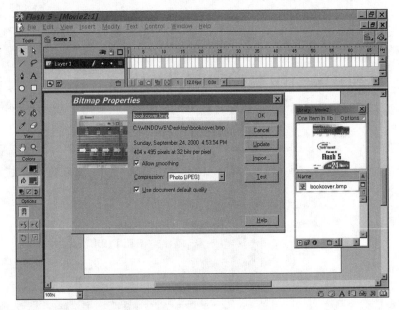

Adjusting Bitmap Properties

Flash imports all kinds of raster formats but only uses JPG, GIF, or PNG in the exported movie. Additionally, any raster graphic is called "bitmap" once inside Flash's library. This means that, no matter what file type you import, you must use the Bitmap Properties dialog to choose between JPEG (and its compressing level) and lossless

GIF/PNG for exporting. You can experiment with the Bitmap Properties dialog, pressing the Test button after each change to see the effects on both image quality (in the little picture at the top left) and file size (in the text information at the bottom of the dialog). See Figure 3.10. The process is one of experimentation where you make adjustments and view the corresponding results.

FIGURE 3.10

Selecting a low JPEG compression (10) and pressing Test will provide a preview of the resulting image and its file size.

Image window

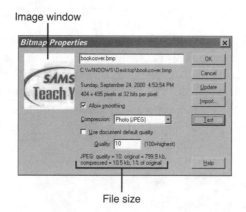

File size

JPEG compression is usually the most efficient option. Unless you import a `.png` or `.gif`, Flash will set the bitmap properties to JPEG by default. It's slightly confusing because if you import a `.jpg` file, Flash will "Use imported JPEG data" by default as shown in Figure 3.11. This option tells Flash to maintain the imported file's original compression. Leaving this option selected is generally desirable as it's a bad idea to re-compress (which will happen if you deselect this option).

FIGURE 3.11

Only imported `.jpg` files will provide the option to use the JPEG compression contained in the original file.

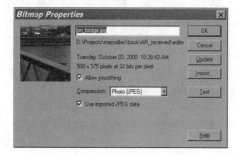

There are two suitable approaches to using raster graphics in Flash. One, start with the highest quality image you can (for instance, `.png`, `.bmp`, or `.pct`) and then experiment with Flash's JPEG compression to find the best compromise. Or, two, use an image editing software—like Fireworks—to

3

create a .jpg file with the best compromise (of filesize and quality) that gets imported into Flash. If you use this option, simply remember to leave the "Use imported JPEG data" option selected. If your image has already been compressed (using JPEG compression), you shouldn't allow Flash to re-compress. The result will be a poor quality image.

Importing other popular formats such as .bmp and .pct will also cause Flash to opt for JPEG compression by default. However, the Bitmap Properties dialog will display a different option: Use document default quality, as shown in Figure 3.12. Although this looks similar to the Use imported JPEG data option we saw earlier, it's a different option entirely. Leaving this selected will use a global setting to compress this file. The global settings are made when you publish your movie. This is discussed in more detail in Hour 24, "Publishing Your Creation."

FIGURE 3.12

Importing non-.jpg files provides the option to use the global (default) quality settings for the whole Flash file.

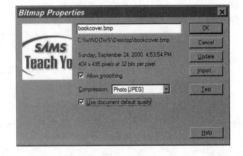

You can control the compression used on individual imported images by simply deselecting Use document default quality (or deselecting Use imported JPEG data for that matter—but understand the earlier caution). When this option is deselected, a field appears where you can type the JPEG compression level you desire. Instead of guessing what compression level is best, you can use the Bitmap Properties dialog to experiment. A lower number results in a smaller file, but also lowers the quality. Click Test after each change and you'll see a drastic difference between 100 and 1. After each change, click the Test button and you can review the effect on file size and quality as shown in Figure 3.13. Experiment until you get the best compromise of image quality and file size.

Additionally, the image portion seen in the image window at the top left of the Bitmap Properties dialog will show exactly how the image will look when exported. You can zoom into this window with a right-click and pan around to get a better view.

FIGURE 3.13

Setting the quality to 8 cuts this image size to less than 1/100 of its original, but the quality is visually affected.

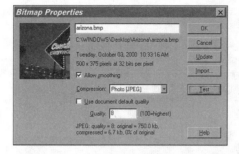

Figure 3.14 shows the results of several different compression levels on the same image. Notice the JPG 80 and JPG 100 are almost identical in quality, but the 80 is a much smaller file size.

FIGURE 3.14

The results of different compression settings on the same image.

JPEG 15   13kb

JPEG 50   28kb

3

JPEG 80   49kb

JPEG 100   204kb

Original BMP   697kb

Finally, the ultimate quality is the Compression option called Lossless (GIF/PNG). It is selected by default when you import .pngs and .gifs, but you can select this any time you want. The result is that Flash will leave the image in its original state. It's always going to provide the best quality—but not without a price. File size will always be highest with this option. This is a suitable alternative if you're making a movie that doesn't need to download from the Web—maybe you're just making a presentation you'll deliver on your hard drive. Otherwise, only use this option on images that you want to retain the best quality possible. If your imported image is a .gif that's already a small file size, it's perfectly suitable to select Lossless. And because even 100% JPEG compression causes *some* image degradation, Lossless is a suitable for images that are particularly important.

Converting a Bitmap to a Vector Graphic

Two common situations call for converting a bitmap into a vector graphic. The first is when you have a raster file that is more suitable as a vector graphic (so you'd like to take advantage of what vectors offer). The second is to create a special effect such as a "posterized" look or an outlined effect.

Let's convert a raster graphic to a vector. In Windows, import the pinstripe image that is provided as a desktop pattern.

Task: Convert a Bitmap to a Vector

1. In a new file, select File, Import and point to the file Pinstripe.bmp, found in the C:\Windows directory. (If you can't find this image try to locate a .pct, .gif, or .bmp that contains bold colors. Possibly, you'll find a .gif inside a subfolder of the Flash help files.)

2. Zoom in on the graphic so that you can see what a bitmap looks like close up. It should look grainy like the image in Figure 3.15. Obviously, it wouldn't scale well, which is a characteristic of bitmaps.

3. With the object selected, choose Modify, Trace Bitmap. In the resulting dialog, seen in Figure 3.16, enter 1 in Color Threshold field. This indicates how close two colors must be to be considered the same color. Minimum Area specifies how small the smallest vector shape can be. Set this at 10. Leave Curve Fit and Corner Threshold at Normal. Click OK.

FIGURE 3.15
A bitmapped image looks grainy when you scale it or zoom in.

FIGURE 3.16
The Trace Bitmap dialog lets you specify how tracing will occur.

4. The graphic is now all vector shapes. The stripes on the edge may be bent, and you may see some weird artifacts on the top or bottom (these can be fixed). Even so, the graphic not only looks as good as the original, it looks better—especially if you need to scale to a larger size.

NEW TERM An *artifact* is any unwanted or obscure result of a process. Static on the radio is an artifact of transmission. Moiré patterns in magazine pictures, color shifts on TV, raindrops on the camera lens, and typos in books are all examples of artifacts. Similarly, Flash's Trace Bitmap feature sometimes leaves artifacts. JPEG compression also has artifacts, which are most noticeable when you set the quality to a low number.

With its nice clear geometric shapes, the image I selected for this Task is particularly well suited to conversion to a vector graphic. Sometimes it's not easy for Flash to convert a graphic to a vector because the image is too intricate. There are other tools especially designed for this, such as Adobe's Streamline, that use more sophisticated processing methods. However, before you give up on this feature, experiment with the settings in the Trace Bitmap dialog. The Help button provides details about each setting.

The Trace Bitmap dialog (Figure 3.16) has several interesting options. The Help button provides more details about each setting.

- When tracing, Flash tries to lump areas of the bitmap into single shapes. Color Threshold specifies how different two colors can be (in RGB values) and still be considered the same. If you set this number high, you will end up with fewer colors and fewer areas.

- Minimum Area specifies the smallest area Flash will create. If you have a very detailed image, this number should be lower, unless you want a mosaic effect.

- Curve Fit affects how closely straight and curved areas will be copied. The Very Smooth end of the Curve Fit scale is like having a very large pen with which to draw a shape in one quick movement. If you could use a fine pencil and as many strokes as needed, that would be like the other extreme, Pixels or Very Tight.

- Corner Threshold determines if corners are left alone or removed.

- In addition to converting a bitmap to a vector graphic, you can "vectorize" a bitmap for an artistic effect. It just takes experimentation. Keep in mind that using Trace Bitmap sometimes results in an image that looks identical to the bitmap but with a larger file size. Consider this option only when the nature of the image is more suitable as a vector or when you want a special effect.

Figures 3.17–3.20 show several examples of bitmaps that have been converted to vectors using different settings.

FIGURE 3.17

Large smooth vector shapes that can be filled with any color.

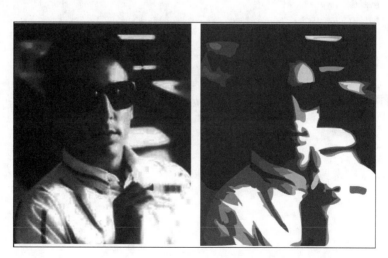

Color Threshold 100,
Minimum Area 100

FIGURE 3.18
Notice subtle differences in how the building windows are combined in the example on the right with a high color threshold.

Color Threshold,
10
Minimum Area
100

Color Threshold,
100
Minimum Area
100

FIGURE 3.19
With relatively small threshold and minimum areas this image looks "posterized."

Color Threshold 40,
Minimum Area 40

FIGURE 3.20
A large color threshold on the bottom left causes the sky to get "banded."

Color Threshold 110,
Minimum Area 10

Color Threshold 30,
Minimum Area 10

3

Bitmap Sequences

Although Flash doesn't import video, it does support the next best thing—a bitmap sequence, which is a series of still images. You may think you're watching a video, as many people were in a project I programmed entirely in Flash (see Figure 3.21 or visit www.m-three.com). Visitors to the site can watch bitmap sequences (of snowboard tricks) that are actually still frames extracted from a video. This isn't "video" because it doesn't have any synchronized sound. It was a rather simple process of using video editing software to export a bitmap of each frame, and then import it into Flash.

You might expect that it would take a long time to import one frame at a time. Luckily, Flash is smart when importing a series of graphics. If you have several images that contain sequential numbers in their filenames (pic_001.bmp, pic_002.bmp, pic_003.bmp, for example) and that are in the same folder, you simply import the first image. Flash will ask if you intend to import the entire sequence (as in Figure 3.22). Flash will do the additional work to create a frame-by-frame animation, as is discussed in Hour 7, "Animation the Old-Fashioned Way." With a little planning (mainly in naming the files correctly), you can import several images in one move.

Figure 3.21

*The Flash site
www.m-three.com
includes several action
sequences that simulate
videos. Screen shot
courtesy Paris France,
Inc., copyright MLY
Snowboards.*

Figure 3.22

*Flash will often recognize when you're
attempting to import
several images in
sequence.*

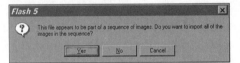

Summary

Create all the graphics that you can right inside Flash. If this hour taught you nothing
else, remember that it's always better to create graphics in Flash than to try to import
from outside.

Even so, there are times when you'll want to import graphics. This might be when you
have an existing graphic that would be impossible or difficult to re-create in Flash, or if
the graphic requires a raster file type (usually a photograph). When you're certain you
want to import, there are ways to do so. If it's a vector, you're best off using a graphic
tool that can export .swfs. Otherwise, there are a few file formats (such as Illustrator
.eps and .ai files) that are generally supported, albeit not very well.

A raster graphic is pretty easy to import. Flash has options for compressing on export.
Also, you can change the imported bitmap into a true vector graphic.

Q&A

Q **I have a photograph that must remain as a raster graphic. After I scan it into the computer and touch it up, what file format should I choose? There are so many.**

A Generally, you want to keep all your raster graphics in the highest-quality format possible before importing into Flash. Once inside Flash, you can compress it until you're satisfied. .bmp and .png offer the best quality. JPEGs are all right, but they always have some compression that may result in artifacts. GIF is not a good alternative because it can't have more than 256 explicit colors. Finally, simply changing the file format of an existing image will never make a graphic better—potentially, it will only make it worse. Start with the best quality possible, and then bring it down as the very last step.

Q **How do you determine how much one graphic is contributing to the final movie's file size?**

A If it's a raster graphic, you can explore the Bitmap Properties dialog, which tells you exactly. Vector graphics are more difficult. Ultimately, you should copy the graphic into a new file and export an .swf of that file (through File, Export). Look at the file size. Sometimes it's not so important how much one graphic is contributing, especially if it's an important graphic. However, your concern should always be to not add to the file size unnecessarily.

Q **I've imported a raster graphic and then used Trace Bitmap to turn it into a vector graphic. The result looks fine, but the file size has grown more than when the image was a regular bitmap. How can that be—vectors should be smaller than bitmaps, right?**

A Not necessarily. This is a very common misunderstanding. It's possible to trace every pixel of a bitmap so that there is a tiny vector shape for each pixel. This will take more file space than the original bitmap. You can convert bitmaps to vector (with Trace Bitmap) any time, but it only really makes sense when the nature of the image is appropriate or when you want a special effect. When Flash takes a very long time to execute a Trace Bitmap, it's a good indication the file size might actually grow. (The delay is because the process is so complex.)

Q **I have a fairly simple graphic (as an Illustrator file) that I'd like to import into Flash. It's impossible to redraw in Flash, so I *have* to import it, right?**

A It sounds like a contradiction to me: It's simple but impossible to draw in Flash. Make sure you're fully exploiting the potential of Flash (read Hours 2, "Drawing and Painting Original Art in Flash," and 4, "Applied Advanced Drawing Techniques," again if necessary). If you have to import it, do so. Of course, export it from Illustrator as an .swf, or at least try to simplify the image as much as possible.

Workshop

The Workshop consists of quiz questions and answers to help you solidify your under-standing of the material covered. Try to answer the questions before checking the answers.

Quiz

1. What's the most appropriate image file format to import into Flash?

    A. Raster.

    B. Vector.

    C. It depends on the nature or content of the image.

2. If you import a .gif image into Flash, what kind of compression will Flash use on this image when exporting the entire movie?

    A. It depends on the Compression setting in the Bitmap Properties dialog.

    B. Flash always uses JPEG compression, but it's up to you to specify what quality level to use.

    C. GIFs are exported as GIFs.

3. If you import an Illustrator file (.ai) and you get a clump of other graphics (including an upside-down graphic of the word ART), what happened?

    A. You broke the "keep it simple" rule.

    B. You tried to import a raster graphic by mistake.

    C. You tried importing an Illustrator file saved in a version number greater than 6.0.

Quiz Answers

1. C. Although a vector has benefits over a raster, it depends on the graphic. Photographs usually have to stay as raster graphics.

2. A. Each image imported can have a unique compression setting that is not depen-dent on its original format.

3. C. Figure 3.2 shows what you'll get, but it's pretty wild; if you drag all the pieces out, you get a ladybug, an arrow, the upside-down word ART. This results from importing an Illustrator .ai file that is of a version higher than 6.0.

HOUR 4

Applied Advanced Drawing Techniques

You've spent the last two hours acquiring basic drawing and graphic-importing skills. This hour, you're going to concentrate on gaining fine control of the features involved with these skills.

If you're an experienced Illustrator or Freehand user, it's unlikely this hour will make you drop those tools. However, in this hour, you'll see the power and ease of drawing in Flash. Flash may not replace your other drawing tools, but it's definitely the most appropriate tool for creating the artwork you include in your animated Web site.

In this hour you will:

- Create custom color swatches and gradients
- Select and isolate drawn objects
- Use and edit groups

Colors and Gradients

Choosing colors in Flash is a matter of personal choice. Although you must take into account some technical considerations when publishing to the Web, generally you can use any color or color combination you want. In this section you'll learn how to create and save color swatches to easily create customized color palettes for your movie. You'll also see how gradients can be created and used.

Creating Solid and Gradient Swatches

In Hour 2, "Drawing and Painting Original Art in Flash," any time you wanted to color a line or fill, you selected the swatch of your choice from the fill color or stroke controls in the toolbox. Clicking the fill color exposes all the swatches currently available. By default, only 216 "Web-safe" colors are available. For users whose computer's display can only show 256 colors ("8 bit") it is recommended that you only use colors within the selection of 216. The remaining 40 colors are used in the browser's buttons and menus for different platforms and may not display as expected. Most likely, your users will not be limited to 256 colors, so you can create your own colors.

Creating a custom color swatch involves two basic steps: create the color in the Mixer panel and then save the swatch. The process can involve up to three panels: Mixer, Swatches, and Fill. While performing this hour's tasks, you should have these panels visible. For the first task, you'll create a custom color.

Task: Create a Custom Color and Swatch

In this task you'll look at several ways to create colors and then save them as swatches for use later. Here are the steps to follow:

1. Make sure both the Mixer panel and the Swatches panel are visible. You can separate the docked panels by dragging the tab for one off to the side.

2. In the Mixer panel, click the color bar, shown in Figure 4.1, and drag as you move through all the colors. Although this choice of colors isn't infinite, there are much more than 216 combinations.

FIGURE 4.1

Selecting a color from the Mixer panel requires that you click the color bar.

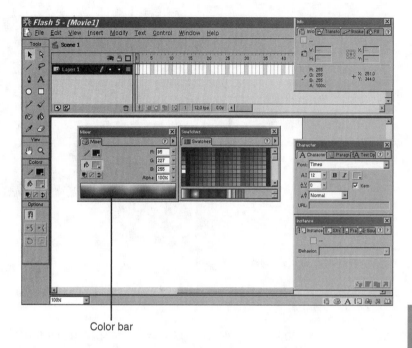

Color bar

3. You should notice as you move through the color bar that the numbers in the RGB fields (for red, green, blue) change. Colors are mixed from 256 "shades" of the colors red, green, and blue (with numerical values 0 to 255). These numerical values can be particularly useful. For example, a company that wants its logo colors to remain consistent can likely provide specific RGB values.

4. Another way to select a color is to sample it from somewhere else, even if it's outside Flash. Suppose you want to use the exact color of pink used in the Flash logo. Press F1 to launch the help files and position your Web browser and Flash application so that you can see both at the same time.

5. In the Mixer panel, click and hold the fill color and (as you drag) move to the "5" in the Flash logo screen in the help file (see Figure 4.2). The current fill color will change to the exact same color as the Flash logo.

6. Now that you've created a new color, you can use it immediately (just select the Brush tool and try it out). However, you'll now save it as a swatch so it can be easily selected later (without using the Mixer panel). From the Mixer panel's options arrow (top right, near the help question mark), select Add Swatch. This takes the current color and adds it to the bottom of the Swatches panel.

FIGURE 4.2

Sampling a color from outside Flash is possible. On the left side of the screen a Web page is positioned to sample.

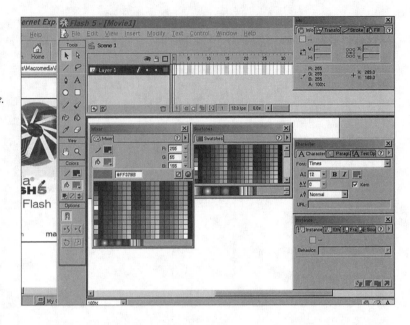

7. Scroll to the last color in the Swatches panel, and you'll find the new color. You'll also find this color any time you click to select a color for your fill color or stroke color (see Figure 4.3).

FIGURE 4.3

Once a swatch is added, it will appear almost everywhere—as the fill color, the stroke color, and the text color.

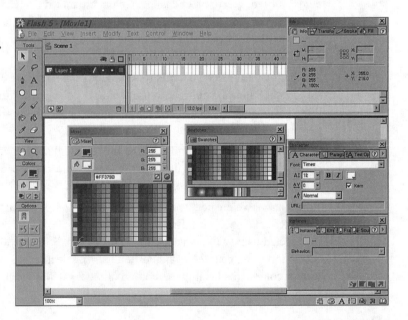

You've seen a couple ways to select colors and one way to save a swatch. Naturally, there are additional methods. For example, if you prefer to use a different color system instead of RGB, you'll find it under the options arrow of the Mixer panel. For example, you could use HSB (for Hue, Saturation, Brightness) or HEX (for hexadecimal), which refers to the way HTML uses 6 characters to describe any color. You'll probably also notice that for any color setting there's an option for the percentage of alpha. The lower this percentage, the more "see through" the color will be. You'll see next hour that there are other ways to control alpha. Generally, though, you don't need to set alpha in the creation of a color.

There are several ways to describe color. Your monitor has three color guns that project red, green, and blue respectively. Using RGB to describe a color tells each gun how much to project of its color. With 256 "shades" of color for each gun (0–255) means that practically any color can be created by mixing the three guns. (At least 16.7 million colors or so.) While RGB may be the most intuitive, other systems exist that are just as effective. Consider that the range of 0–255 used in RGE means 9 characters are necessary (three for each color since "255" uses 3 digits).

A system called Hexadecimal was developed that describes RGB using only 6 characters. Hexadecimal uses only 6 characters by extending our "base 10" numbering system (that has only 10 characters 0–9) to a "base 16" system (0–9 plus A,B,C,D,E,F). The result is that RGB each get two characters. For example, FF0000 is pure red (the highest value for red "FF" and no green or blue). Magenta is FF00FF (a mix of red and blue). HTML uses the hexadecimal system to describe colors.

There's no difference in resulting color. It's almost like the difference between English and Spanish: You can say "red" or "rojo" and the result is the same. I find Flash's Mixer panel a nice way to get a feel for the differences. Select a color and use the options arrow to change the setting from RGB to HEX then view the results.

Even though the process you just learned for creating swatches is time consuming at first, it can really help you down the line. For instance, although swatches are only saved with the current Flash file, once you've taken the time to create custom swatches, you can save them as a Flash Color Set file. From the Swatches panel's options arrow, select Save Colors…. The file that you save can be used with other files or other team members. To load colors that have been saved this way, select Replace Colors… from the Swatches panel's option arrow. (Notice the feature is called "replace" not "add"—so it will replace any custom colors you've already created.)

4

There are two other options that can appear to be the same—Load Default Colors and Web 216. The default colors that ship with Flash are the Web 216. However, if you wish, you can first create some custom colors (or use Replace Colors...) and then select Save As Default. Now every new file you create with initialize with these colors. Web 216 will always take you back to base colors that ship with Flash.

One other note about saving colors. The .act color table format is a standard file format. These color tables can be loaded into other programs such as Photoshop. For that matter, Photoshop can save .act files which can then, in turn, be loaded into Flash. The whole idea is to make consistent color control something you can share among files and team members.

No doubt you've noticed that the fill color can be a gradient. You'll see both radial and linear gradients in the default color swatches any time you click to specify the fill color. In the following task, you'll learn how to create our own custom gradient.

Task: Create a Custom Gradient

In this task you'll a create custom gradient. Follow these steps:

1. This task requires all three color panels: Fill, Mixer, and Swatches. Arrange them so they're undocked from each other and you can see them all (see Figure 4.4).

FIGURE 4.4

Creating a custom gradient swatch will involve three panels (Fill, Mixer, and Swatches).

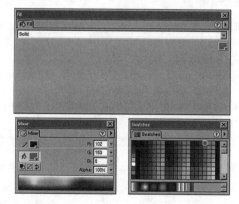

2. Click the first gradient in the Swatches panel. Notice that the Fill panel changes to reflect the new swatch. Select Duplicate Swatch from the options arrow of the Swatches panel. This will create a new swatch and make it the active swatch (indicated by a subtle white box around it). Now you can edit it without editing the default gradient swatch.

3. In the Fill panel, you'll see two pointers, one on each end of the gradient definition bar. Click the one on the left (the white side), and the pointer head changes to black (indicating this is the part of the gradation you're currently editing). In the Mixer panel you should also notice a pointer with the tooltip "Color Proxy." Use the Mixer to select a bright yellow color from the color bar. Notice that the swatch appears as a yellow-to-black gradation in both the Fill and Swatches panel, as shown in Figure 4.5.

FIGURE 4.5

With the left side of your gradient selected, you can use the Mixer panel to change the color.

Current gradation pointer

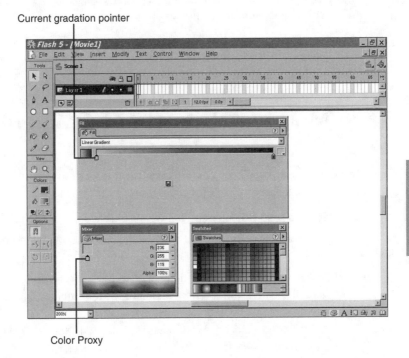

Color Proxy

4. In the Fill panel, change the fill style drop-down list to Radial Gradient, and you'll see the swatch change again.

5. Click the pointer on the right side of the Fill panel and then use the Mixer to select a bright blue color. You should now have a radial blend going from yellow to blue.

6. To add more colors to the gradient, just click underneath the gradient definition bar in the Fill panel (the wide sample gradient). New pointers will appear that can be moved, and their colors can be edited. To remove a color, drag the pointer down (not left or right).

7. You don't have to click the Save button in the Fill panel because this is effectively the same as the Duplicate Swatch feature in step 2.

Now that you have a custom gradient, you'll learn how it can be used in your movie.

Using and Modifying Gradients

Whether you use the default gradients or create your own (as you just did in the previous task), there's more to using gradients than simply selecting one of your choice from the fill color. It's important to understand the two options of the Paint Bucket tool: Lock Fill and Transform Fill.

When Lock Fill is selected, a white-to-black linear gradation will make one transition (from white to black) through several shapes. Without Lock Fill selected, each shape will have its own gradation from white to black.

Transform Fill gives you handles you can use to adjust the attributes of a gradation after it is used as a fill. The fall off, center point, rotation, and shape (for radial gradients) can all be adjusted. The following task uses these two features.

Task: Modify Attributes of Gradients Used in Your Movie

In this task you'll explore Lock Fill and Transform Fill to gain full control of gradients. Follow these steps:

1. Select a solid fill color and draw two squares close together.

2. Select the Paint Bucket tool and a radial gradient (the white-to-black default is fine).

3. Make sure the Lock Fill option is not selected, as shown in Figure 4.6. Click once in each square to fill it with the radial fill. Both squares have the entire radial effect—from white to black. This is the normal mode. Notice that the radial gradient centers around where you clicked. Click in different locations within each circle to move the center of the gradient.

4. Now click once near the edge of a square that borders the other square. Click Lock Fill. The last fill you made will define the start of all subsequent fills because Lock Fill has been turned on.

5. Click the other square, and you should notice that the gradient continues from where it started in the first square (that's the effect of Lock Fill). Also, if you click the first square again, the center point of the gradient remains locked.

6. Now click Transform Fill to allow you to edit the fills you've made. With Transform Fill selected, it may appear that the Paint Bucket tool isn't working because you can do nothing except transform fills.

FIGURE **4.6**
Lock Fill is not selected.

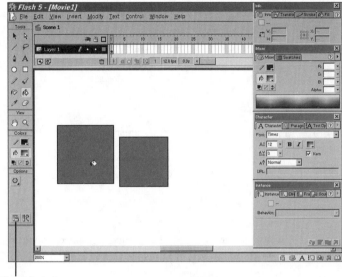

Lock Fill deselected

7. Click the fill of one of the squares, and several handles will appear, as shown in Figure 4.7. You can now move the gradient's center. The handles on the edge let you change the shape of the radial gradient, the fall off rate, and the rotation.

4

FIGURE 4.7

You can use Transform Fill on this gradient (which happens to span multiple shapes because Lock Fill is selected).

Reshape handle

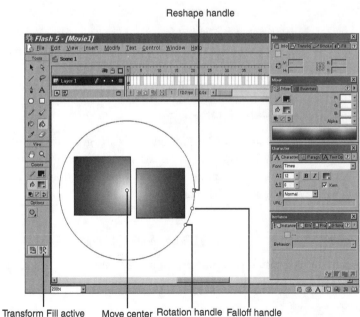

Transform Fill active   Move center   Rotation handle Falloff handle
                          point handle

8. You'll probably find these handles to be very intuitive but let's experiment with them a little bit.

9. Click and drag the Move Handle to change the center point of the fill. (Notice in Figure 4.8 your cursor changes to the move symbol when you're over the Move Handle.)

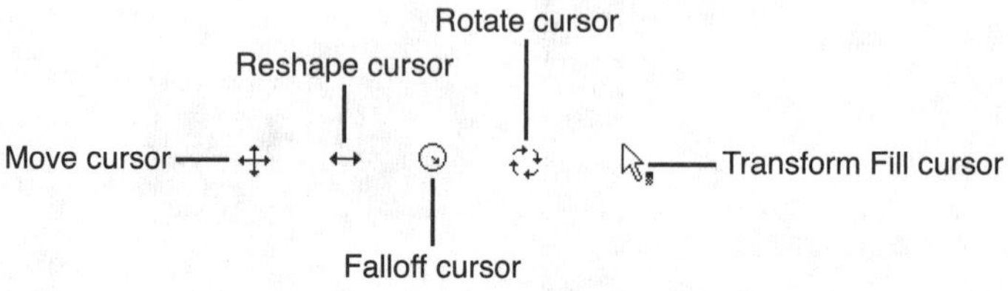

FIGURE 4.8
Cursors for the differ-
ent features of
Transform Fill.

Move cursor — ⊕   ↔   ⊙   ⟲   ▷ — Transform Fill cursor

Reshape cursor

Rotate cursor

Falloff cursor

10. Click and drag the Reshape handle to make the gradient an ellipse rather than a perfect circle. You'll notice in Figure 4.8 the reshape cursor is similar to the cursor when you scale an object.

11. Use the Falloff handle to change the rate that the gradient changes from white to black. You'll see a custom cursor for the falloff feature in Figure 4.8.

12. Now, adjust the rotation of the reshaped gradient. You'll see the same rotation cursor that we so from the traditional rotation tool in Figure 4.8. Also, realize that with radial gradients you'll have to first reshape the fill before the rotation handle will provide any results.

13. Finally, notice the entire time you have Transform Fill selected your cursor has a gradient icon (as shown in Figure 4.8). This is your primary clue that you need to turn off Transform Fill in order to continue using the Paint Bucket tool normally. (Click the Transform Fill button again to return to the normal mode.)

Filling with a Bitmap

Now that you understand using and modifying gradients, you'll take a look at a special feature—using bitmaps as a fill. Basically, any previously imported raster graphic can be used as a fill that will appear tiled in any shape in which it's used. The following task walks you through this special effect.

Task: Use a Bitmap As a Fill

In this task you'll experiment with using a bitmap as a fill. Here are the steps:

1. Import any raster graphic (.gif, .bmp, .pct, .jpg, or .png) as you did last hour.

2. Delete the copy on the Stage (don't worry, it's safe in your Library).

3. From the Fill panel, select Bitmap from the fill style drop-down list. You'll see a thumbnail of your imported graphic. Click the thumbnail to select it.

4. You'll notice a very small version of the graphic as your current fill color. Use the Brush tool and scribble some shapes on the Stage.

5. Now you can use the Transform Fill option under the Paint Bucket tool to adjust the tiled bitmap's size, scale, and rotation.

Text Effects

In Hour 2, you learned how to create text and make adjustments to its font, color, style, and so on. Now you'll learning some fancy ways to use gradients and bitmaps as fills. You'll quickly find out, however, that gradients and bitmap fills only apply to fills—not strokes and text. However, you can convert text to a fill. Once the text is a fill, you can use all the techniques exposed this hour.

The technique of converting text to a fill is quite simple. Just create a block of text and make sure the font, size, and style are set up correctly. Next, select the block of text and then select Modify, Break Apart. Once the text is broken apart, it can be treated as a fill. Be forewarned, however, that once the text is broken apart, you'll never be able to edit the words again! (That's why you set all the text's attributes first.)

Isolating Objects

So far, you've spent a lot of time drawing and modifying what you've drawn. Now you're going to learn how to pick up and move or remove specific portions of your drawings. The truth is, drawing shapes in Flash is so easy that sometimes it's just as easy to start over rather than try to fix a graphic. However, in this section, you're going gain the power to isolate parts of your drawings so you don't have to keep starting over.

The most basic isolation technique is to make simple selections. By now, you know that to move a line, you must click once (to select it) and then click and drag it. You may have noticed that if a line has any corners (or kinks) in it, a single click on the line selects just the portion of the line you clicked. For example, draw a rectangle (with a stroke) and single-click the stroke—only that side of the rectangle becomes selected. But when you double-click, you get the entire outline. This won't work with an oval because there are no kinks—you'll get the whole outline with one click. Similarly, if you click the fill once, only the fill is selected, but double-clicking selects both the fill and the outline.

If you think that's cool—just wait until you see some of the other ways you can select objects in Flash!

If You Can See It, You Can Select It

The first time I saw Flash demonstrated, the Macromedia representative presented it like a carnival barker, selling a device that "slices and dices." The most memorable and helpful thing he said was this: In Flash, if you can see it, you can select it. That's really true, and when you understand this concept, you'll find it easy to select portions of your drawings to modify them, move them, or delete them.

To see this in action, draw an oval and then take the Brush tool and paint a thick fill (in a different color) across the center, as shown in Figure 4.9. Because you can "see" the left section of the circle, you can select it.

FIGURE 4.9

Anything you can see, you can select. When this oval is bisected with the Brush, you can come back later to easily select any portion you can visually separate.

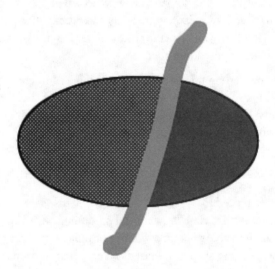

Using Levels

A related concept to "if you can see it, you can select it" is the fact that everything you draw is at the same "level." Nothing is really on top of or behind anything else. If you select and move the fill brush stroke from Figure 4.8, you'll find your oval is now missing its midsection—as if the Brush tool took a bite out of it. To use Flash terminology, everything you paint or draw is on the *canvas level*. Notice the word is *level*, not *layer*. Layers are something else entirely (and will be covered in Hour 11, "Using Layers in Your Animation"). Later in this hour, you'll see how to stack drawings on other levels, but for now understand these two points: The terminology is *levels* (not *layers*), and the seeming limitation that levels present can actually help you draw.

Up to this point, you've probably been frustrated by the fact anything you draw "eats away" at everything else. However, you can creatively use the fact that everything resides in the canvas level to your advantage to create some complex shapes. In the following task, you'll try this out as you create a crescent moon.

Task: Use Shapes on the Canvas Level to Create a Crescent

In this task you'll take advantage of Flash's single canvas level. Here are the steps to follow:

1. Make sure your stroke color is set to a solid color; then draw a perfect circle.

2. Double-click the fill of the circle to select the fill and the outline.

3. Select Edit, Copy (Ctrl+C) and Paste in Place (Ctrl+Shift+V).

4. While the duplicate is still selected, use the arrow keys to nudge it to the right, as shown in Figure 4.10.

FIGURE 4.10

When you nudge the duplicated circle across the top of the other, you'll be able to select and remove any area you can see.

4

5. Deselect everything (by clicking a blank area on the Stage), and the shapes will "eat away" at each other.

6. Now you can selectively click and delete the excessive portions: the fill and extra outline of the second circle. You should have a crescent shape remaining onscreen.

If you think this last task was interesting, you'll find several more examples like it in Appendix A, "Shapes You Can Make Using Selection, Snap, and the Canvas Level." It's amazing how you can use a little bit of geometry theory to make all kinds of shapes.

Grouping Objects

Despite my promise that you can learn to love the way everything's on the canvas level, you'll eventually need to stack graphics without them effectively trashing each other. Imagine that you place a client's logo on top of another graphic, as shown in Figure 4.11. As long as you draw this three-circle logo second and position it in the right place on the first try—everything looks fine.

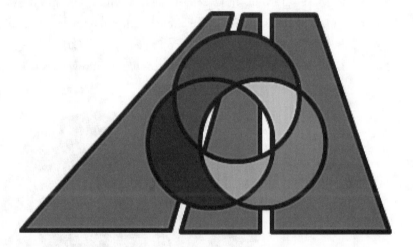

FIGURE 4.11

As long as you draw this three-circle logo second and position it in the right place on the first try, everything looks fine.

If your clients are unlike mine, they will be satisfied where you placed the logo the first time. However, it's likely they'll want to move it around to see what it looks like in other locations. As you see in Figure 4.12, this causes problems because it "eats away" at the other graphic.

FIGURE 4.12
Try picking up and moving this three-circle logo, and you'll become painfully aware of the fact everything's drawn on the same level.

4

Finally, images with graphics stacked as shown in Figure 4.13 are next to impossible to create—given what you know so far. But that's just because you haven't learned the effects of grouping.

FIGURE 4.13
Without the effects of grouping, such tricks with levels is practically impossible.

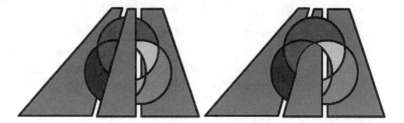

Effects of Grouping

Grouping has two effects:

- The most obvious is that it takes the grouped objects into a level of their own (above the canvas), allowing the group to be stacked above or below other groups without eating away at them.

- It locks the images together, allowing them to move, rotate, and scale as a group, while preventing individual colors and lines from being accidentally edited.

You'll now take a look at both effects. First, here's an example of how the stacking effect works. Draw a rectangle and then draw an oval directly above it. Select both objects and group them together by selecting the Modify, Group (or Ctrl+G). Now, draw another rectangle, select the rectangle fill and stroke (remember, Flash treats these as separate objects), and group it. Grouping something by itself is a way you make an object exhibit the properties of a group. Now you have a couple of groups that can be placed in the same space without eating away at each other.

Notice, too, that the second group you created is "on top of" the other. Each group has an effective level in which it resides—you won't see "level 1" and "level 2" anywhere, but these levels do exist. You can change the stacking order by selecting Modify, Arrange, Send to Back. If you have three or more groups, the rest of the Arrange menu makes more sense. Move Ahead and Move Behind will move the selected group one level at a time. Send to Back moves the group behind all other groups, and Bring to Front moves the group in front of all other groups.

The other effect of using groups is that the objects are "locked together." If you move the grouped circle and square, it's pretty obvious that they stay together in the same relative location. Until you either ungroup or edit a group (which is covered next), moving, scaling, and rotating will affect the group as a whole.

There is an exception to the rule that everything is in the canvas level until it's grouped. This exception involves text. Unless you break it apart, text isn't really a line or a fill. As such, text is an exception to the canvas level rule as it will remain above objects in the canvas level. When you break it apart and make it a fill, text will act as if it's grouped from the start.

Editing Groups

Individual groups can be moved, rotated, and scaled with little effort. You can also change the stacking order of multiple groups through the Modify, Arrange menu. But what if you want to change the fill color of an object in a group? Clicking with the Paint

Bucket tool does nothing. If you want two objects within a group to be closer together, the only obvious way to do this is to first ungroup them (Modify, Ungroup), make the edit, and group them again. However, while these objects are ungrouped, they could easily eat away at other objects in the canvas level. The answer to this dilemma is to "take a trip inside the group." The following task takes you on such a trip.

Task: Edit the Insides of Grouped Objects

In this task you'll learn how to temporarily enter a group to make edits to its contents. Here are the steps to follow:

1. Make sure View, Snap to Objects is selected. Draw a perfect square. Select the fill and stroke and then select Modify, Group (Ctrl+G).

2. Rotate the square exactly 45 degrees.

3. Change the fill color swatch and draw a perfect circle.

4. Select the entire circle (by double-clicking its fill) and drag it by its center to snap it to the top corner of your square, as shown in Figure 4.14. Because the square is grouped, neither object will eat away at the other. Notice that the circle shape is stacked behind the square group. Remember, groups are automatically stacked at a higher level than the canvas level.

FIGURE 4.14

Selecting the circle and then dragging it by its center will allow you to snap it to the corner of the square.

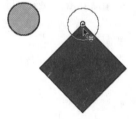

5. At this point, you'll make a fundamental change to the square. You don't want to ungroup it because it will eat away at the circle. Instead, you can temporarily enter the group without affecting anything else. Simply double-click the square, and you'll be taken inside the square's group.

6. Notice that the address bar at the top of the screen reads "Scene 1:Group" (see Figure 4.15). Also notice that the other contents of the Stage are dimmed slightly. These are your clues that you are inside the group. Anything you do here will only affect the square's group.

Address bar

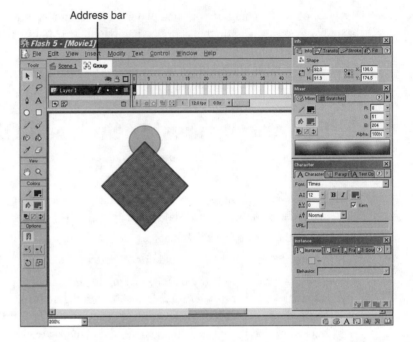

7. While in the group, deselect everything by single-clicking outside the shape. Then bend the two lower sides of the square inward to make a wing-like shape, as shown in Figure 4.16.

FIGURE 4.16
*When inside the
square's group, you can
make fundamental
changes to its shape.*

8. You can make other changes to the square (such as changing the fill or stroke color). Once you're done, return to the main scene. You can return in two ways. The most deliberate way is to simply click "Scene 1" in the address bar. The other way is to double-click an empty part of the Stage. Save this file or leave it open— you'll be using it again.

The address bar changing and the contents on the Stage dimming (in step 6) are critically important. These are your only clues that you're inside a group. For instance, if you start adding shapes and then return to the scene, the shapes you added to the group will move and change with everything else in the group. There are certainly times when you need to add to a group, but it's important you do so deliberately. Overlooking the address bar change happens to be one of the most common mistakes made in Flash, so pay close attention when you see it change.

One last thing about groups: There's no rule that you can't have groups within groups. Take the square and circle from the previous task, select the entire circle, and group it. Then group the square and the circle groups. The interesting thing about such nested groups is that you can take a trip inside any level of the hierarchy. Double-click the circle/square group, and you'll be inside that group. Double-click the square, and you'll be inside that group. The entire hierarchy is displayed in the address bar to help you from getting lost. See Figure 4.17 for such an example.

FIGURE 4.17

Both the circle and the square are grouped and then grouped together (and duplicated a couple times). You can double-click the group. Double-click again and you can edit a nested group.

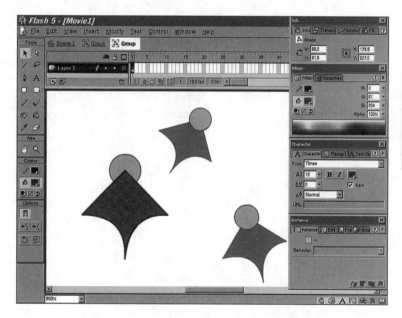

4

Summary

You've acquired a lot of skills now. Refining those skills and applying them to whatever challenges you encounter is just a matter of practice.

In this hour, you created and used swatches and custom gradients. You saw how fills—whether gradients or bitmaps—can be transformed using the Paint Bucket tool's options. Grouping shapes has two main benefits: First, it isolates shapes from the other shapes so that they don't eat away at each other. Second, it allows you to stack the shapes.

Finally, the fact that every ungrouped object exists on the same level can actually help you draw some unique shapes.

Q&A

Q I set the Paint Bucket tool's option to Lock Fill, but when I fill a shape with a gradient, I just see a solid color. What's going on?

A If you think you're looking at a solid, it's possible you're just seeing one end of the gradation. The best way to use the Lock Fill feature is to first fill a shape with Lock Fill turned off and then turn it on and continue to fill other shapes. Otherwise, what often happens is that the gradient's transform handles are set so that the fall off is extremely large. If this happens, try setting the Stage zoom level to 25 percent and select Transform Fill. You may see the handles for the gradation way off the Stage.

Q What is the best color specification system to use: RGB, HSB, or HEX?

A Whichever one you prefer. No one system is better than the other. For every color onscreen, there's a corresponding color value for any of the systems. If your client provides its trademark colors in RGB, you should use RGB. If someone provides you with the hexadecimal values for color, use that system. They are practically the same.

Workshop

This Workshop consists of quiz questions and answers as well as some activities to help you solidify your understanding of the material covered. Try to answer the questions before checking the answers.

Quiz

1. How do you know that you're editing a grouped shape?

   A. Everything else on the Stage is dimmed and you see "Group" in the address bar.

   B. You first selected Modify, Ungroup.

   C. You held down Ctrl+Shift when double-clicking an object.

2. When creating a gradient swatch, which panel do you use?

   A. The Swatch panel and the Gradient panel

   B. Just the Fill panel

   C. The Swatch panel, Fill panel, and the Mixer panel

3. How many shapes do you need to create a group?

A. One.

B. Two or more.

C. Zero. You can only group gradients.

Quiz Answers

1. A. The address bar is really your best clue. Watch this area.

2. C. It's possible to create a gradient with just two of these panels, but really you need all three (and besides, answers A and B are just plain false).

3. A. Grouping a single shape is useful for preventing it from eating away at other shapes. Also, you can change the stacking order of objects once they're grouped.

Exercises

Now that you have some pretty sophisticated drawing skills, try these activities:

1. Explore the ways you can use text. For example, regular text can be skewed by grabbing the side handles when rotating. Therefore, you should be able to create a shadow effect by duplicating a small block of text and skewing the copy. Change the color of the duplicate, send it to the back, and see how believable the effect is.

2. Other text effects can be created when you break apart the text (remember, you won't be able to edit the text again after breaking it apart). As a fill, text can have a stroke added. If you try one of the special stroke styles, you can create interesting effects by stroking text.

3. Try to create geometric shapes using Snap and the fact everything on the canvas level eats away at everything else. For example, you can turn a square into a triangle by simply dragging one corner to snap to an adjacent corner. There are more examples in Appendix A. Either look at the examples in the appendix or try to create your own basic shapes, such as a semicircle, a 3D pyramid, or a flower.

4

Hour 5

Using the Library for Productivity

Flash's Library is so fundamental that it's almost impossible to create a Flash movie *without* it. If you don't use the Library, it's fair to say you're doing something wrong. Using the Library as much as possible is your key to productivity and efficiency. Productivity because you'll have "master" versions of graphics that, with one edit, will reflect the change throughout your movie. Efficient because graphics stored in the Library—despite how many times they're used in your movie—are stored and downloaded only once, in the Library.

This hour we'll explore the Library. By far, the Library is the most important feature to understand and use, so after this hour be sure to use the Library whenever you can.

In this hour you will:

- Create symbols
- Use the Library to minimize work
- Identify clues in the interface to help keep your bearings
- Use multiple symbol instances without increasing your movie's size

NEW TERM *Symbols* are what you put in the Library. Anything created in Flash (shapes, groups, other symbols, even animations) can be placed in the Library and will be called a *symbol*. There are several symbol types that you can choose from—each with unique characteristics. In addition, the Library also contains two media types that can only be imported into Flash (not created in Flash): bitmaps (like you saw in Hour 3, "Importing Graphics into Flash") and Audio (as you'll see later in Hour 10, "Including Sound in Your Animation"). However, symbols created in Flash are surely to be the Library items with which you'll become most familiar.

NEW TERM *Instance* is the term given to a symbol any time it's used outside the Library. As you'll see, there's only one "master" of any symbol (and that's the one *in* the Library). However, you can drag as many instances of that symbol out of the Library as you like. Each instance is like a copy of the original. However, as you'll see this hour, instances aren't really copies because they don't add to the file size (the way extra copies would).

The Concept of the Library

The process of using the Library involves creating symbols and then using instances of those symbols throughout your movie. You always have one master version of a symbol stored in the Library. You can drag multiple instances of that symbol from the Library to any other part of the movie (even inside other symbols). This may seem like a meaningless procedure, but it has two valuable benefits. First, it means your file size remains small because only the master symbol adds to the file size, and each instance just "points" to the master (not unlike how a *shortcut* in Windows or an *alias* on the Macintosh points to a master file). The second benefit is you can make a visual change to the master symbol and that change will be reflected in each instance. This is similar to using styles in a word processing document—make a change to the style, and each instance where you used that style will reflect the change. You'll see these benefits in a minute, but let's first go over the basics of how to create and use symbols.

How to Create and Use Symbols

You can use two methods to create symbols. You can either convert a selected object to a symbol or make a symbol from scratch. Let's look at both methods.

Task: Create a Symbol by Converting Selected Objects

In this task we'll create symbols the way I prefer to—that is, using the "Convert to Symbol" feature.

1. In a new file, draw a circle with the Oval tool. Select the Arrow tool and make sure the circle is entirely selected (you can double-click the center, marquee the whole thing, or do a Select All).

2. Select the Insert, Convert to Symbol... menu item (or press F8), and Flash will force you to specify the name and default behavior for this symbol (shown in Figure 5.1).

FIGURE 5.1

When you convert to symbol you must specifying a name and behavior.

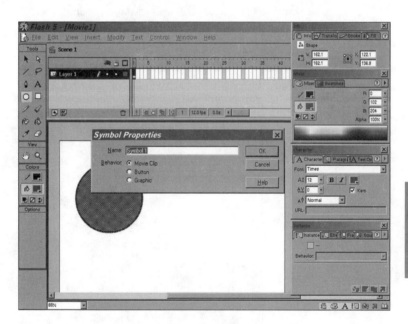

5

3. You should always name your symbols logically (for example the default "Symbol 1" may seem logical, but when you have 35 symbols all named in this manner it can become unwieldy). So, let's name this one "Circle." Regarding the default behavior, we'll look at all three types eventually, but for now just consider Movie Clip the best choice when you're not sure which behavior is best. Button is only necessary when you're creating buttons, and Graphic is primarily used for synchronization applications like lip synching. Leave it set to Movie Clip and click OK.

4. Open your Library window using the Window, Library menu item, and you should notice one symbol, Circle, in the Library. You just did two things in one move: You took your selected shape and put it in the Library, and you caused the "object" remaining onStage to become an instance of the symbol. If you drag more instances from the Library window (by single-clicking and dragging the picture of the circle from the Library window onto the Stage), they will all be equivalent to the instance already onStage. (If you double-click by accident, you'll see "Scene 1 : Circle" in your address bar, indicating you're editing the master version of the symbol. Simply click "Scene 1" to get back to the main Stage.)

5. After you've dragged a few instances of the Circle symbols onStage, it may look like you have several copies of the master, but actually you have multiple *instances* of the master. You're about to make a change to the master version (in the Library), and you'll see that change in each instance onStage.

6. You have several ways to edit the contents of the master version of your Circle symbol. One way is to single-click it in your Library window and then from the Options menu of the Library, select Edit (see Figure 5.2).

FIGURE 5.2

The Library's Options menu includes several choices including Edit.

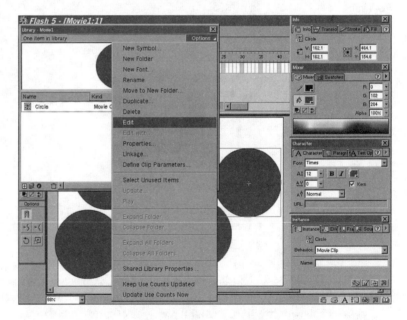

7. It may appear that nothing has happened, but behind the Library window the screen has changed—the best indication being the address bar, about which you learned in Hour 1, "Basics" (see Figure 5.3). In addition, you'll only see one copy

of your circle (the original) in the center of a Stage that appears to have no borders. You are currently inside the master version of the Circle symbol, about to edit it.

FIGURE 5.3

You'll know you're editing the contents of a symbol from the address bar.

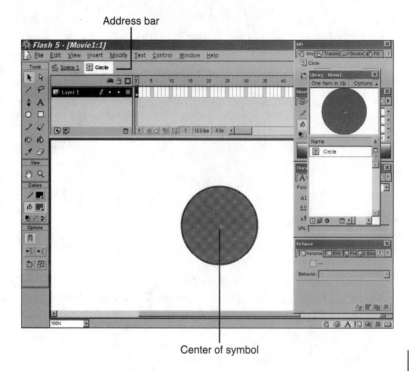

Address bar

Center of symbol

8. Before that, let's get out of the master version and we can re-enter another way. Click "Scene 1" from the address bar and you'll return to the main scene (with multiple instances of Circle). Now enter the master version of your symbol by double-clicking an instance. Do that and you should see the address bar change (which is always your best clue) and all the other instances will dim slightly. This is similar to how you could edit the contents of a grouped shape last hour. This time we will edit the Circle.

9. Take a "bite" out of the master graphic of the circle (using the Marquee tool), as shown in Figure 5.4. This is a drastic edit (not something subtle such as changing the color).

5

FIGURE 5.4
The edits we make to this symbol will affect each instance.

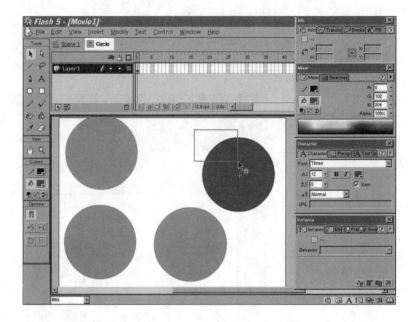

10. Now you can go back to the main scene by clicking "Scene 1" in the address bar. You should notice that all the instances of the Circle symbol have the same bite taken out of them! Also, any new instances you drag from the Library will have the same effect.

In the last example, you took a selection and converted it into a symbol. This left behind, onStage, an *instance* of the symbol you created. The other way to create a symbol is to simply decide you want a new symbol and create it. One method isn't better than the other, and you end up with the same result.

Task: Create a New Symbol from Scratch

In this task we'll make a symbol using the feature "New Symbol".

1. In the file containing the Circle symbol (or a new file), make sure nothing is selected and choose Insert, New Symbol…. (Note that the Convert to Symbol… option isn't active because nothing's selected.)

2. You'll be faced with the same Symbol Properties dialog you saw when Convert to Symbol was used. Name the new symbol "Square" and leave the Behavior setting Movie Clip. This time when you click OK, you'll be taken inside the master version of the Square symbol (yet to be drawn) as shown in Figure 5.5. You should see the address bar change accordingly. Think of it this way: Convert to Symbol

just takes your selection and puts it in the Library (end of story), whereas New Symbol (after you name the symbol) takes you to the master version of the symbol so you can draw something—effectively saying, "Okay, you want a new symbol? Draw it."

FIGURE 5.5

Selecting New Symbol will take you into a blank symbol so that you can draw its contents.

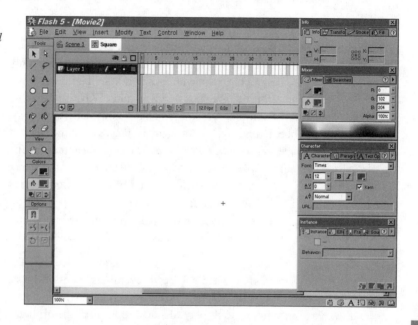

3. Now that you're in the master version of the Square symbol, you can draw the square. You'll probably want to draw it in the center, indicated by the plus sign in the middle of the Stage (shown in Figure 5.5). This will become the axis around which rotation and scaling occur in each instance used of this symbol. But how do you get the square you draw in the center? Surely by now you've discovered the Paste in Place command from the Edit menu. This lets you paste anything in the same location from which you copied it, unlike the "Paste" command which centers whatever you paste onStage. However, this time the regular Paste function will be useful. Make sure you first select View, Magnification, Show Frame (which basically centers the screen). Then just cut and immediately paste your square. Presto! It's centered. By habit, I quite often cut and paste everything inside my master Library symbols for just this centering effect.

4. When you're done creating the Square symbol, go back to the main scene (by either clicking "Scene 1" in the address bar or selecting Scene 1 from the Edit Scene menu). Where's the square? Well, New Symbol just creates a symbol and keeps it safe in the Library. Let's drag a couple instances out onStage. Open the Library and then drag as many instances of the Square symbol onStage as you like.

5

How Symbols Help You

You may already be thinking of some ways symbols can help you, but likely there are many more you haven't even imagined. Let's go over the two fundamental advantages of storing symbols in the Library: reducing the movie's file size and minimizing your work.

Reducing File Size

Believe it or not, you can have one graphic in a Library symbol and 100 instances of that symbol onStage, and your file will be no larger than if you had only one instance. Here's how it works: The graphic, movie clip, or button in the master symbol contributes to the file size. Therefore, if the graphic is 1KB, it adds 1KB; if it's 100KB, it adds 100KB. It just depends what's in that symbol. No matter how many times a symbol is used, it's only stored once. Even as you drag many instances onto the Stage, the symbol is still only stored once. A tiny bit of data is saved inside Flash that specifies how each instance is different (for example, their positions), so I suppose each instance does actually add to the file size. However, it's just such a *tiny* bit of information that it's almost not worth mentioning (but I'd hate to lie). Imagine what would happen if it didn't work this way— a 100KB graphic used 10 times would make your movie balloon to 1MB! Instead, 10 instances of a 100KB symbol might make your file grow to, say, 101K (if even that much).

Symbols may seem great when you need several instances of the same shape. However, using symbols is actually powerful because each instance can appear very differently. So far, we've used symbols to display identical replicas of the original. The only way each instance has varied was in its onscreen position. However, that tiny bit of extra data telling Flash where each instance is positioned onscreen can also contain how each instance is scaled or rotated differently. This way each instance can look different. You'll learn more about this later in the hour, but for now realize if you have three instances onStage and have each one scaled to a different size, you haven't added to your file size in any significant way.

Minimizing Work

In addition to reducing file size, the Library can reduce the amount of work you do. For example, say you have a block of text that's used in several places within your movie (maybe a title). If you first put the text in the Library, each time you need the text onscreen, you drag an instance from the Library. Then later if you want to change the text, you can edit the master version in the Library and see the change in every instance. This advantage requires only that you invest a little bit of time and planning.

Using the Library

You've already used the Library to do the preceding exercises. However, we didn't take time to really explore all the details of the Library. Let's do that now so you're sure to take full advantage of the Library's offerings.

Getting Your Bearings

The first hour discussed the importance of "knowing where you are" at all times. In the Library, this point becomes even more important. It's very confusing if you don't pay attention to subtle clues. Before you select a tool from the drawing toolbar, you should ask yourself, "Exactly where am I, and what am I doing here?"

Here are a few clues to help you get your bearings:

- Although the address bar may not always show you a clear hierarchy (path) to the symbol you're currently editing, you'll always see an icon indicating whether you're in a scene or symbol. The last item listed will have either the scene "Clapper" icon or one of the three symbol icons. For instance, in Figure 5.6, we're editing the "Circle" master symbol, as indicated by the address bar and icon.

FIGURE 5.6

The address bar displays whether you're editing a symbol or scene.

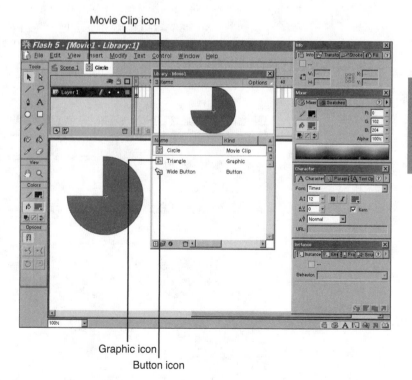

Movie Clip icon

Graphic icon
Button icon

- Any time you're in the Library, you'll see a plus sign in the center that indicates the axis around which rotation and scaling occurs. You won't see this if you're editing the contents of a regular scene.

- In addition to the plus sign, while editing a symbol you'll never see edges to the Stage because there isn't a Stage. When dragging instances onStage you'll need to place them within the Stage borders (if you want the users to see the objects). Symbols simply don't have a Stage.

- You have many ways to access the contents of a master symbol:

    First of all, from the Library window, select the symbol and then choose Options, Edit. Alternatively, you can just double-click the symbol (double-clicking the symbol name let's you rename it).

    Second, you can simply double click any instance onscreen and you'll be taken in to edit the master symbol. The difference in doing it this way (as opposed to using the Library window) is while editing you'll see the rest of your onscreen contents dimmed out—but in position.

    Third, any symbol can be accessed from the Edit Symbol menu. Recall, the two buttons at the top right of your screen: the clapper button is for Edit Scene and the circle-square-triangle button (that looks like a graphic symbol's icon) is the Edit Symbol button (shown in Figure 5.7). This menu provides a list of all the symbols in your movie. Also, the Edit Scene menu is your easiest way to get back to your scene.

FIGURE 5.7

The Edit Symbol menu gives you quick access to all the symbols in your file.

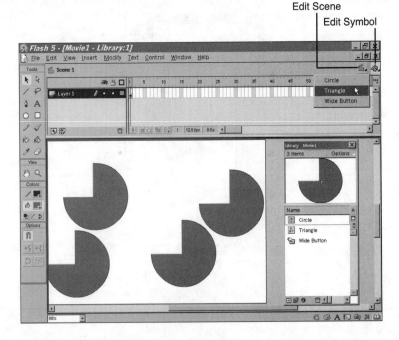

Managing the Library with Names, Sorting, and Folders

The Library is so great that you'll use it all the time. As the total number of symbols in the Library grows, you'll want to develop ways to keep them organized. You can manage the Library however you wish, but we're going to look at three ways in particular: naming, sorting, and using folders.

Because every symbol must have a name (and they're easy to rename), it makes sense to name them consistently. How to best name symbols is subjective, but there are some standard practices worth following. First, be clear and concise. If you have an image of a circle, call it "Circle." There's no need to be cryptic and call it "Cir." However, a name such as "Red Circle with No Line" might be a bit much. Say what you have to, but nothing more. Also, realize that the Library can be sorted alphabetically by symbol name, so you can develop a naming strategy to plan ahead. For example, if you have several symbols all being used in a particular part of your movie, you could precede each name with the same text prefix—for example, "game_." Therefore, you might have symbols named game_background, game_piece, game_scorecard, and so on. You could even use a similar method when an entire team is working on the same file. Have each person precede symbol names with his or her initials so it's easy to see which symbols were created by which team members. In Hour 22, "Working on Large Projects and in Team Environments," you'll learn more about such naming conventions.

As mentioned, the Library automatically sorts symbols alphabetically by name. If you widen the Library window, you can explore the additional sorting options. (You can either resize the window by dragging a corner of it or click the Wide View button on the right side of the Library, as shown in Figure 5.8). Take a look at this figure to familiarize yourself with the Library window. Note that you can sort by Name, by Kind (all the Graphic symbols are listed separately from the Button symbols, for example), by Use Count (meaning how many instances you've dragged from the Library) or by Date Modified.

5

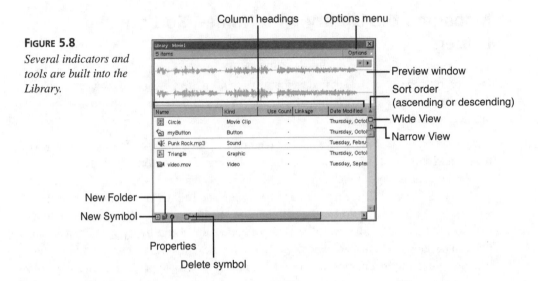

FIGURE 5.8
Several indicators and tools are built into the Library.

- The preview window gives you a thumbnail view and preview of any animation or audio).

- Column headings do more than just explain what's listed in the column. If you click a column heading, your Library will be sorted by the attribute you select (Name, Date Modified, Use Count, or Kind).

- The tiny arrow can be clicked to toggle between ascending or descending alphabetical sorting.

- New Symbol... is the same as selecting Insert, New Symbol....

- New Folder lets you create a new folder to hold several Library items.

- Properties... will give you access to the original Symbol Properties dialog box you saw when creating a symbol.

- Wide View stretches the window for you. Narrow View changes the window to a narrower view.

- The Options menu provides all the options available (just don't forget it's here).

Finally, you can organize your Library with folders. It's almost identical to using files and folders on your computer's hard drive, except in the Library you have symbols and folders. Creating a folder is as simple as selecting New Folder from the Options menu (or clicking the orange New Folder button at the bottom of the Library). You can name the folder immediately after creating it or you can name it later, the same way you rename symbols (double-click the name or select Rename from the Options menu).

Organizing folders is pretty intuitive, but let me mention a couple maneuvers now. You can put symbols inside folders by simply dragging a Symbol's icon (which appears to the left of its name) on top of the folder. You can open a folder (to reveal its contents) by double-clicking the Folder's icon. You can even put folders inside of folders.

It isn't as if organizing the Library is difficult to figure out. Most of the material we just covered on the subject are general "good organization" skills. If you know how to rename Library items, sort, and use folders, you'll be fine.

Using Symbols from the Library

So far, the concept of dragging a symbol from the Library to create as many instances as you want of the symbol has been pretty straightforward. It's powerful, but easy to use. For a simple example imagine you made one symbol of a cloud. You could create many instances of the cloud symbol to make a cloudy sky. But you can do much more. Each instance onStage can be more wild than the next. One could be large and another one could be stretched out and darkened. In the upcoming task for example, you'll see how multiple instances of one symbol can vary in size, scale, and rotation. And later this hour you'll make a symbol that contains instances of another symbol. Such nesting means not only can you have many instances onStage, but you can recycle symbols to be used in the creation of other symbols. One step at a time, but I wanted you to have an idea of some of ways you can use symbols.

Placing Instances of Symbols Onstage

This discussion may seem like repeated material, but the concept and process are very specific. One master symbol in the Library can be dragged onStage as many times as you like. Each one onStage is called an *instance*. You'll see how each instance can vary in a minute, but first let's review a couple points. If you copy and paste an instance already onStage, you are simply creating *another* instance. Not only is this okay, but it's sometimes preferable to the alternative—simply dragging an instance from the Library—because all the properties of the instance being copied will be in the new instance. Remember the "copy" is just another instance.

There's one other way to get an instance onStage (in addition to dragging it from the Library or copying one already onStage). Maybe you'll think I'm cheating, but as a review, consider that you can draw a plain-old shape, select it, and use Convert to Symbol. This procedure puts the symbol in the Library but also leaves behind onstage an instance of the symbol. If this doesn't make sense, try repeating the exercise "Create a Symbol by Converting Selected Objects."

5

Modifying Instances of Symbols

Believe it or not, by simply dragging two instances of the same symbol onStage, you've created two instances with different properties, because they vary in position. In other words, each instance is in a different location onStage. Each instance can be made different in other ways, too. For example, you can change the scale of any instance onStage (and you won't be adding to the file size in any significant way). You can rotate each instance separately, as well. Here's a task that explores how to vary the properties of separate instances in regard to their position, scale, and rotation.

Task: Change the Location, Scale, and Rotation of Instances

1. In a new file, draw a rectangle and then use the Text tool to type your name. Try to position the text and resize the rectangle so they're about the same size. Change the text color so it's legible on top of the rectangle.

2. Select everything you just drew and then choose Insert, Convert to Symbol. Name this symbol "My Name." Leave the default Movie Clip behavior and then click OK.

3. Onscreen you now have an instance of the My Name symbol you just created. Create more instances of this symbol however you want—either copy and paste the one onscreen or drag instances from the Library.

4. For each instance onStage, make a change in its position by simply moving the instance to a different location. With some of the instances, change their scale (remember from Hour 2, "Drawing and Painting Original Art in Flash," you can scale width or height or both at the same time). With other instances, change their rotation (remember that rotation includes "skew" when you select the non-corner handles). You can go pretty crazy here like Figure 5.9, yet your file will only be as "big" as the master symbol.

FIGURE 5.9

Many instances of the same symbol each scaled, skewed, rotated, and positioned differently.

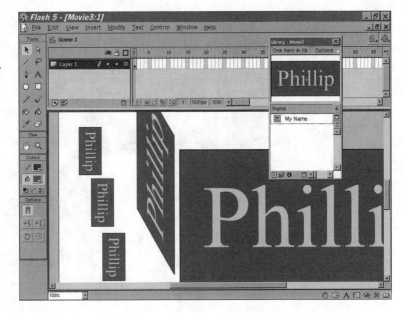

Instance Effects

You may think varying each instance's position, scale, and rotation provides for a lot of combinations—and it does. However, there's more. Each instance onStage can have an effect applied to it. Effects include tinting the color of an instance and changing an instance's alpha property (that is, its opacity). Similar to how each instance can have a different location, each instance can have different effects. To move an instance, though, you just pick it up and move it. To apply an effect you'll use the Effect panel.

Using the Effect panel

To change an instance's effect, simply select the instance onStage and open the Effect panel. You'll find the Effect panel from the Window menu and in the context sensitive menu when you right click an instance as shown in Figure 5.10. While the instance is still selected you can specify any effect you wish.

5

FIGURE 5.10

*The context sensitive
menu provides all the
panels appropriate to
the selected object.*

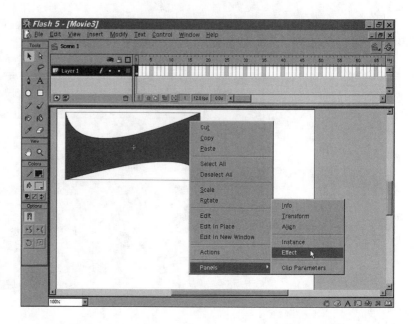

The Effect panel contains a drop-down list that allows you to select which color effect
you want. Take a look at Figure 5.11 and the following list to familiarize yourself with
these effects (then you can proceed to the task, which steps you through many of the subtleties of several effects).

FIGURE 5.11

*The Effect panel pro-
vides several ways to
change an instance.*

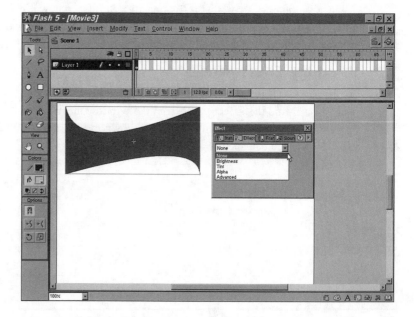

- *Brightness* allows you to effectively add black or white to the instance—similar to turning the lights out or turning them way up.
- *Tint* is similar to brightness, but instead of causing the instance to be more white (or more black), it tints the instance any color you want.
- *Alpha* (same as *Opacity*) lets you specify how "see through" the instance will be.
- *Advanced* lets you combine Tint and Alpha (although later this hour you'll learn a trick to figure out the eight sliders).

Task: Change Effects on Several Instances

1. Open the file you created in the last task with the many instances of the My Name symbol. (Redo the exercise if necessary.) Make sure you have at least four instances onStage.

2. Select one instance by single clicking it (if you double click you'll be taken inside the master symbol and will need to return to the main scene). Open the Effect panel while the instance is selected.

3. From the Effect panel's drop-down list, select Brightness. The Brightness percentage will appear on the right of the panel, as shown in Figure 5.12. Click and hold the arrow to the right of the percentage and you'll be given a slider. Adjust the slider until the percentage reaches 80%. Alternatively, you can just type the percentage "80" into the field.

FIGURE 5.12

The Brightness Effect can be applied to one instance.

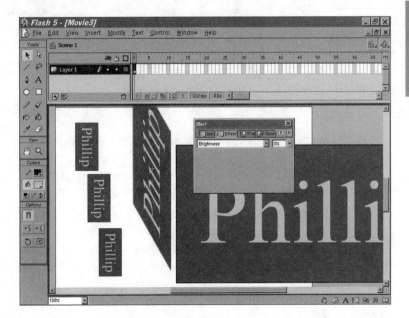

5

4. Keep the Effect panel open and select another instance. This time, select Tint from the drop-down list. The Tint effect is pretty straightforward: you just select the *hue* that you want to tint the instance with (as in Figure 5.13). But notice the 100% in the first field (which designates the amount of tint). If the original symbol contained several colors, the entire instance will change to the color in which you tint it. However, tinting less than 100% causes the colors to mix. For example, if your original symbol was yellow and white, tinting it 100% cyan would cause everything to turn cyan. However, tinting it 50% cyan would cause the white parts to become a faded cyan and the yellow parts would turn green.

FIGURE 5.13

The Tint Effect changes the color of an instance.

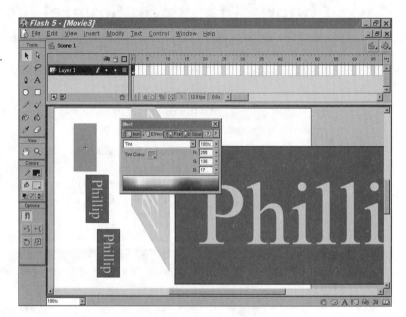

5. Now for Alpha. Set the effect of another instance onStage to Alpha. Set the Alpha slider to 40%. Unless the instance you selected is on top of something else, you're not likely see much of a semitransparent effect. Therefore, go ahead and position the instance onStage to be on top of another instance. Remember that you can use the Send to Back control and similar stacking controls from the Modify, Arrange menu.

6. Finally, let's look at the Advanced Effect. This setting lets you combine Alpha and Tint. It's next to impossible to figure out the eight sliders in the Advanced Effect panel, so here's a trick to avoid using them. Let's try tinting something yellow and making it semi-transparent as well. First, select an instance and choose Tint from the Effect panel. Then select a yellow from the mixer area of the Effect panel.

Now, change the Effect drop-down to Advanced. Notice the pairs of numbers next to Red, Green, Blue have already been filled in (with something other than 0) like Figure 5.14 shows. These are based on the tint you just specified. Now you can select the Alpha slider at the bottom of the Effect panel (while Advanced is still selected). The trick was that by first selecting Tint we had a nice way to choose a color. Had we first selected Advanced we would have had to select a color in a less intuitive manner (namely, via the six sliders shown in Figure 5.14).

FIGURE 5.14

When you select Advanced after first tinting the sliders will be initialized with the same color.

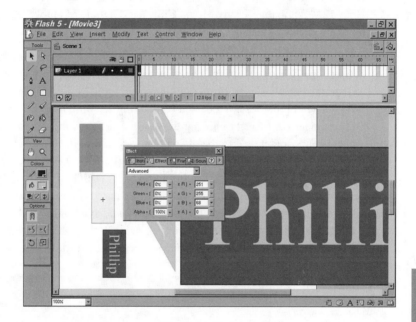

7. Go wild and bring out a bunch of instances onStage. Adjust the Alpha, Tint, Brightness settings. Do anything you want. Again, note that your file is basically the same size it would be with just one instance.

NEW TERM One way to describe color is by specifying the three factors hue, saturation, and brightness. If you want to explore, change the Mixer panel's option arrow from RGB (red green blue) to HSB (hue saturation brightness). *Hue* is the base color. Moving from left to right in the Flash color mixer, you'll see Hue change from red to yellow to green to blue and to red again (with every shade of color in between). *Brightness* is how much white is included in the color. Imagine a paint store with a bunch of hues of paint. They could mix in white paint and create other colors. In the Flash mixer the brightness is shown vertically—at the top the colors are all white and at the bottom all black. Finally, *saturation* is the amount of color. For example, if you were staining a wood fence the more stain you use the more saturated the color could become. In Flash the saturation is varied by the amount percentage scale.

How Each Instance Behaves Differently

You've already seen how each instance onStage can be uniquely positioned, scaled, rotated, and colored. There's one more way in which instances can be different from one another: Namely, they can behave differently. Remember the Behavior choice for creating a symbol? You have to decide between Graphic, Button, and Movie Clip. So far, I've suggested just using Movie Clip (the default). Later, we'll spend a whole hour on the Button and Movie Clip options (Hour 13, "Making Buttons for Your User to Click," and Hour 12, " Animating Using Movie Clips and Graphic Symbols") For now, we'll discuss how this relates to instances onStage.

When you create a symbol, you must select a behavior. You'll learn the differences between the behaviors, but for now they're not terribly important because you can change the behavior later. From the Library window, you can change any symbol's behavior via Properties... (accessed by clicking the little blue "i" button, from the Options menu, or by right-clicking the item). The Symbol Properties dialog box appears, which is almost identical to the dialog box used when you created the symbol in the first place (this one, though, has an additional button labeled "Edit," which takes you into the master symbol to edit it as shown in Figure 5.15). Think of this setting as the default behavior—any instances dragged out of the Library while the symbol is, say, a Graphic will start "life" as a Graphic. Changing the master symbol to another default behavior will have no effect on instances already "spawned." Therefore, you can change the default behavior and only affect new instances dragged from the Library.

FIGURE 5.15

The Properties dialog lets you change the default behavior for a symbol.

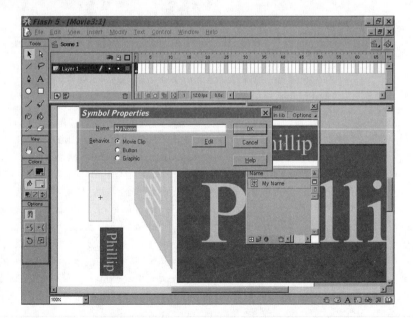

Not only does a master symbol have a default behavior, but each instance on screen has its own behavior. You can use the Instance panel to see and change the behavior of any instance or instances. For example, you can use the Instance panel to see that the instances we used in the last two exercises have the Movie Clip behavior. That's because the master symbol was created as a Movie Clip at the time. You can change any onscreen instance by simply selecting it and changing the Behavior drop-down in the Instance panel. You can actually control several instances using this technique as shown in Figure 5.16.

FIGURE 5.16

Just like any panel, you can use the Instance panel to change several instance's behavior.

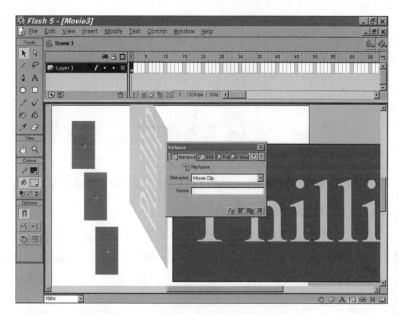

Using Instances of Symbols in Symbols

You can drag a symbol from the Library and create an instance any time. You can even use instances of one symbol in the creation of another symbol! This means you could draw a bunch of houses (as shown in Figure 5.17) with just one line. Sure, there's a "House" symbol, but that was drawn with several instances of another symbol, Box, and a few instances of a symbol called Line. Actually, the Box symbol was created with four instances of the Line symbol. This case shows an excessive use of hierarchy, but it does prove a point: Instances of symbols can be used in the creation of other symbols.

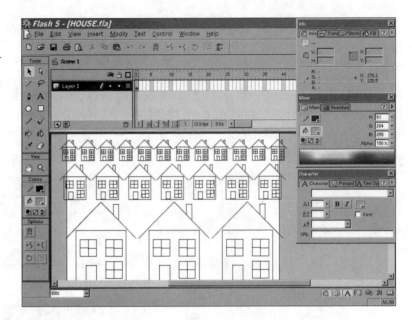

FIGURE 5.17

The house, duplicated and modified, was created with several instances of a "line" symbol.

Task: Make a Symbol Using Instances of Another Symbol

1. In a new file, draw a circle and fill it with gray.

2. Select the entire circle and then choose Insert, Convert to Symbol.... Name it Circle and click OK.

3. At this point you'll make an eyeball from two instances of Circle. One way you *could* do this is to create a new symbol and then, while inside the master "Eyeball" symbol, drag out instances of Circle. Instead, you'll do it another way, which might be more confusing at first, but I think it'll be easier. There's two ways to get stuff in the Library (either create a new symbol and draw or convert an item to a symbol). Here, you'll use the "convert to symbol" method.

4. To make the Eyeball symbol, notice that you already have one instance onStage (Circle). Copy and paste this onStage (or drag another instance from the Library). Change the Brightness Effect on one instance to –100% (using the Effect panel, select Brightness from the drop-down list and set it to –100%). The other instance should be set to 100% Brightness. It might help at this point to change your Movie background color to any color except black or the default white (choose Modify, Movie... and then click the Background Color path and select another color). This will help you see the all-white instance of Circle.

5. Now arrange the two instances so the black one is on top, scaled smaller, and set near the edge of the white instance, as shown in Figure 5.18.

FIGURE **5.18**

Two instances of the same Circle symbol with different scales and brightness effects.

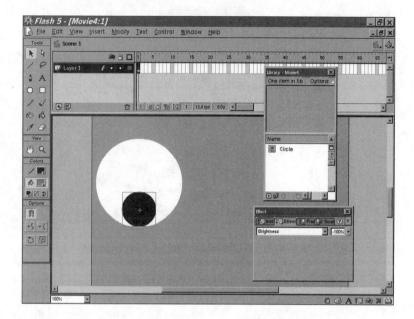

6. Select both instances and then choose Insert, Convert to Symbol…. This will take what's selected—a couple instances—and put them in the Library. Name this symbol "Eye Ball" and click OK.

7. Left behind, onStage, is an instance of the Eye Ball symbol you just created. If it's really big, scale it down a bit and then copy and paste it to make two instances exactly the same size. You can rotate one instance of Eye Ball if you want.

8. Drag an instance of Circle onto the Stage. Send it to the back (right now it's on the top level) using the Modify, Arrange, Send to Back menu. Make it large enough to be the "face" for the two Eye Ball instances. Change the Tint color effect of this instance of Circle to bright yellow.

9. Now you'll make the entire face a symbol. First, though, draw a smile with the Brush tool. You might think it's not working because anything you paint on the yellow face disappears. This is because you're painting on the canvas level, and any symbol is like a grouped shape in that it's above the canvas level. You can still draw a smile though. You could draw it off to the side and then group it, or, if you think you've already drawn one that's hiding behind the face, try carefully marqueeing just the area where the smile is, as shown in Figure 5.19, and then grouping the selection (using Modify, Group). If you have several smiles due to failed attempts, just delete this group and try again.

5

FIGURE 5.19

Using the marquee technique we can select the smile on the canvas level.

10. Finally, when your symbol looks like the one shown in Figure 5.20, select everything, choose Insert, Convert to Symbol…, name the symbol "Face," and click OK. You now have a Face symbol that can be used over and over again throughout your movie. It's nothing more than recycled circles and a smile. By the way, there's no need to put the smile in the Library by itself (unless you needed to use it independently with other faces) because it's really in your movie only once—inside the master version of the Face symbol.

FIGURE 5.20

Our completed Face symbol.

There comes a point where too much hierarchy affects file size negatively. In the case of the house in Figure 5.17, all I had was one line recycled many times. Previously I said Flash stores the original data in the Library, plus information concerning how each instance varies. Usually the original data is the big portion and instance information is insignificant. However, if you take the instance information to an extreme, it can actually work against you. To prove this point, suppose you make a one-pixel dot, put it in the Library, and then use it millions of times to create all kinds of graphics (tinting each pixel instance individually). The extra data for those millions of instances would indeed outweigh the dot in the Library. It's a balance. You should combine convenience with efficiency. In the case of the house, I found that by creating the box from scratch (not with four instances of the line), I cut my exported movie size in half!

Summary

There's more to the Library than you might expect. You learned the basics of managing the Library as well as some of the ramifications of using the Library. Getting shapes into the Library can be achieved by either selecting New Symbol... or by selecting Convert to Symbol.... Remember that converting to a symbol leaves behind an instance of the symbol you just created.

Once you have some symbols in the Library, they can be used anywhere in your movie. These instances of symbols don't significantly add to the file size. Plus, each instance can be modified as to its position, rotation, scale, and its tint, brightness, or alpha from in the Effect panel. Therefore, you can "recycle" the same graphic. Finally, you learned that instances of symbols can be used in the creation of other symbols. As you begin to understand the hierarchy of symbols you'll be unstoppable.

5

Q&A

Q When I try dragging a symbol from my Library to the Stage, my cursor changes to the international "No" symbol. It used to work. Why not now?

A You can drag symbols from the Library onto the Stage provided you have an open layer into which to drop them. This happens because the current layer (with a pencil in it) is locked, the current layer is invisible, or the red current frame marker is in an interpolated frame (as discussed in Hour 8, "Using Motion Tween to Animate," and Hour 9, "Using Shape Tween to Morph").

Q **Libraries seem like they can save a lot of time and keep the movie sizes down. Is there any way to use these benefits among several files?**

A As a matter of fact, Flash 5 added a really powerful feature called Shared Libraries. You'll create and use shared libraries in Hour 22, "Working on Large Projects and in Team Environments."

Q **I dragged a symbol from the Library onto the Stage and then made a visual change to the master version of the symbol. When I returned to Scene 1, I was in a different file! I selected the movie in which I was working from the Window menu, but now the instance of my symbol onstage is the same as before I edited it! What's wrong?**

A The Library can sometimes fool you—in this case, by letting you drag a symbol from one file's Library into another file. The Library window will turn a darker gray when it is a Library from a different file. If you open the Library and then start a new file, the first file's Library will remain onscreen (and turn darker gray). However, it's the Library from the first movie (each movie has one Library of its own). If you drag symbols from one movie's Library onto the Stage of another movie, Flash copies the symbol into the new file's Library. If you just keep the Library closed at all times, you won't run into problems. Also, consider saving your movies as you work because the title bar of the Library will contain the file to which it's linked.

Workshop

The Workshop consists of quiz questions and answers to help you solidify your understanding of the material covered. Try to answer the questions before checking the answers.

Quiz

1. If you don't see a symbol listed in Library window (one that you know you've created), what is the likely cause?

    A. You have an outdated version of Flash and should get the upgrade.

    B. You're either not looking at the Library window for the current file or the symbol is hiding in a folder.

    C. You forgot to name the symbol; therefore, it isn't listed.

2. What are the clues that you are currently editing the master version of a particular symbol?

   A. The address bar will contain your symbol's name and a big plus sign appears in the middle of the screen.

   B. The Effect panel is grayed out.

   C. The symbol is highlighted in the Library window.

3. Should you consider another Color Effect setting instead of Alpha when you simply want an instance to be faded back?

   A. No, nothing beats Alpha.

   B. Yes, never use Alpha.

   C. If the instance is not on top of anything else, then, yes, you should consider Brightness or Tint instead.

Quiz Answers

1. B. A Library from another file can fool you, and putting symbols in folders can effectively hide them from your view. Consider, too, that answer C can't be correct because all symbols must have a name.

2. A. The address bar is the main clue you're in the Library.

3. C. If the Alpha color effect is used, it's only effective (and therefore "worth it") when it's on top of something that can show through it. Brightness and Tint can be used for the same effect, and both will perform better on slower machines.

5

PART II
Animating in Flash

Hour

HOUR 6

Understanding Animation

There's nothing like animation. It can inspire, educate, and entertain. It's memorable, too—no doubt when you hear the name Disney, images pop into your head immediately. You are on the verge of gaining the power to communicate with animation. Before we jump right into animation, there are several concepts worth studying first. This hour we'll discuss animation in general and, as applied to Flash, to ensure that you understand exactly where we're headed. If the goal is clear, it will be easier to acquire and apply the technical animation skills discussed in the next several hours.

This hour you will

- Learn the fundamentals of animation
- Cover the common terms of animation
- Familiarize yourself with the basic Flash components related to animation
- Find out the common misconceptions of animation (and how they're overcome)

How Animation Works

Animation is made from individual images. However motion is created in an animation, it's still a collection of fixed images. Suppose you see a car drive by. You see the car throughout the entire time it's within sight, but you'll probably blink. Your brain covers up the fact that you missed part of the action. When you watch a movie or television, the screen is blinking very fast—sometimes it shows an image, and other times it's black. The fact that the black moments are so short makes you *think* you're watching full motion.

The image projected onto the retina of your eyes remains even after the light stops. If you close your eyes, the last thing you saw remains imprinted for just an instant, and then it fades. This *persistence of vision* is why you don't notice the blank spots between frames of a movie, assuming they are short enough.

Components of Animation

Now that we know a little bit about how animation works, we can discuss how it applies to Flash. There are several general animation terms that have a specific meaning in Flash. You'll want to understand both the general meaning and how the term applies to Flash.

Frames and Framerate

As I've said, animation is a series of still images. Each image is called a *frame*. In movies, frames are the individual pictures on the film itself. In Flash, frames are the little rectangular cells in the Timeline. They're numbered at the top of the Timeline, and every fifth frame is gray; the rest are white with a gray outline. The Timeline will display all the frames, but you can look at the contents of one frame at a time. The red current frame marker can be in only one place at a time—the frame you're currently viewing. You don't draw into a frame on the Timeline—you draw onto the stage. The current frame marker indicates the frame whose contents are currently onscreen. Figure 6.1 shows the Timeline in its initial state. Until this movie's duration is extended, you can't move the red current frame marker past 1, and only frame 1 is enclosed by a solid white box with a black outline.

By default, your Timeline will be one frame long. The current frame marker will be unmovable because it can be placed only in a frame of your animation, which so far has only one frame. Let's look at an animation with more frames, but instead of building an animation, let's view one of the samples that come with Flash. Select Help, Samples, Spotlight Mask. Now you can click in the numbered area of the Timeline on frame 25. The current frame marker moves to where you click (be sure to click in the numbered area towards the top of the Timeline—not in the cells). (See Figure 6.2.)

FIGURE 6.1

The Timeline with its many cells is actually only 1 frame long initially.

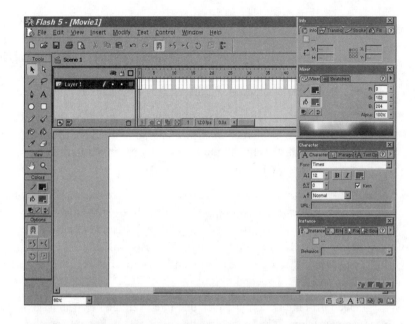

FIGURE 6.2

A 50-frame Timeline is shown, with the red current frame marker on frame 25. You can move the current frame marker to any frame within the 50 frames by dragging (in the numbered area).

6

The Spotlight sample illustrates a few important concepts. First, if you click and drag the current frame marker in the number area above the frames all the way from frame 1 to 50, you will see a quick preview of the animation. This is called *scrubbing.* The preview you're given is dependent on how fast you scrub. Naturally, the *framerate* is locked when the user watches an animation. Select Control, Play (or just click Enter), and you'll see this animation play at its correct *framerate*. (To stop, click Enter again.) You should also notice the status area near the bottom-left of the Timeline. The three numbers are the current frame, the *framerate*, and the current time elapsed (see Figure 6.3).

NEW TERM *Scrub* is a term used in all kinds of animation software. It's a technique to preview your animation. You simply grab the red current frame marker and drag it back and forth (through all the frames of your animation). You move your mouse in a scrubbing motion, hence the name.

NEW TERM *Framerate* is the rate at which frames are played back for the user, measured in frames per second (fps). A framerate of 30fps means that 30 frames will be displayed every second. It is easy to confuse framerate with speed, but they're not necessarily the same. If an entire animation uses 10 frames (at 10 frames per second), it might look identical to the same movement using 20 frames if the framerate is set to 20fps. They both take 1 second to finish.

Speed isn't the reason you pick one rate over another. The issue is the capability of your user's machine. The framerate you specify should really be called "maximum framerate." Your movie will never exceed this, but on a slow computer it may play slower.

FIGURE 6.3

The status area in the Timeline contains three important numbers related to timing.

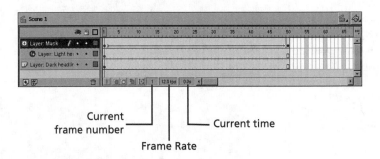

Current frame number — Frame Rate — Current time

The current frame number (on the left) indicates the location of the red current frame marker. It changes while playing or scrubbing, reflecting that you can be in only one frame at a time. The framerate (the middle number) normally indicates the framerate for your movie as you last specified (from menu Modify, Movie Properties). However, the number shown will be reduced if, after playing the movie, Flash estimates it can't actually keep up with your "requested" framerate. It's not entirely accurate but does provide a good estimate.

Let's change the framerate to something very high and see what happens. With the Spotlight Mask sample file open, access the Movie Properties dialog by selecting

Modify, Movie. (You also can open this dialog with Ctrl+M or by double-clicking the framerate number on the Timeline.) Change the framerate to 60 and click OK. Click Enter to play the movie and notice that as the red current frame marker moves through Timeline, the framerate changes to show how fast Flash is actually playing. It wants to go 60fps, but it can't keep up. Now the status shows a more realistic framerate, one that your computer can maintain. In reality, however, the framerate shown here is not particularly accurate, because it shows only how fast Flash plays while authoring—not in the actual exported movie. If you were to export this movie and play it in a browser, it will likely play slightly differently.

Current time (the third number) indicates how long it takes to reach the frame you're viewing from the start of the movie. For example, how long it takes an animation to play 50 frames depends on the framerate. At 24fps, it should take about 2 seconds. At 12fps, it will take about 4 seconds. The duration of the movie is based on the framerate.

Framerate Versus the Number of Frames

The numbers in the status area are very important. When you design your animation, you want to pick a framerate and stick to it. When you change the framerate, you're changing it for the entire movie. For example, say I have an animation of a character walking, running, jumping, and sitting still for a few seconds. If the portion where he's walking is too slow and I try to speed it up by increasing framerate, that portion might look better. But then he'll run extra fast, his sitting time will go by quicker—everything's faster! It's best to leave the framerate alone and find another way to increase the speed.

There are other ways to change the *effective speed*. Suppose you have an animation of an airplane moving across the sky. You need to decide the effective speed of the airplane according to the size of the airplane and how much sky you're showing. If you move the airplane all the way across the screen in 36 frames, you can't determine if that's the right speed unless you consider the framerate. At 12fps, the airplane takes 3 seconds to move across the sky.

NEW TERM *Effective speed* is how fast something seems to move. Actual speed, in comparison, is absolute and can be measured. If an animation uses 12 frames (at 12fps), the elapsed time of 1 second is its actual speed. It's your psychological impression that determines effective speed. Therefore, we can use illusions to increase or decrease an animation's effective speed. If a lot of action and changes occur in those 12 frames, it's effectively fast. If only one slight change occurs, the effective speed is slow.

If an airplane in the sky travels completely through my view in 3 seconds, it's probably pretty close. If the plane is at 20,000 feet, it would take about 15 seconds (or longer) to move across the sky. If 3 seconds is too fast for the airplane in your animation, you can

6

make it appear slower by slowing down the framerate or by increasing the number of frames in the Timeline. If you slow the framerate to 2fps, it will take 18 seconds for 36 frames, but the animation will be very jumpy. If you extend the animation to take 240 frames, the airplane takes 20 seconds to complete the motion. We'll learn how to do these things in the next few hours, but for now it's only important to understand the difference between framerate and total frames.

Framerates of Different Types of Animation

To put the animation we're about to embark upon in perspective, let's compare some traditional animation media. In a motion picture, the framerate at which the images appear is 24 frames per second (fps). Even at this relatively slow rate, you don't notice the moments when the screen is black. Television plays at 30fps.

In computer animation, we don't put a black screen between frames, but we do have a choice as to what framerate to use. Technically, the user's monitor will flicker as much or as little as he has it set, but in any case it will be much faster than an animation's framerate. In computer animation, framerate affects how frequently the onscreen graphic changes or, conversely, how long it pauses before advancing to the next frame. In practice, if you go much below Flash's default setting of 12fps, your user will start to notice jumpiness, and if it is any faster he will think it's as smooth as real life. Remember that traditional movies use 24fps and look quite smooth.

It may seem that you should always crank up the framerate as high as you can, which would address the issue of jumpiness. However, it's not that easy. First of all, more frames can mean your movie has a bigger file size. Also, it often requires a computer that can display images quickly. If your user's machine can't keep up, it slows down the animation and makes it not only jumpy but slow.

Finally, creative animation techniques enable you to fool the user in ways other than relying on persistence of vision and a fast framerate. We'll see examples in Hour 7, "Animation the Old-Fashioned Way," when we create an animation that uses only three frames. In Hour 21, "Advanced Animation Techniques," we'll look at even more techniques. For now, just remember that framerate is important, but it isn't everything.

Keyframes and Blank Keyframes

A keyframe is simply a frame in which you establish exactly what should appear onstage at that particular point. This might include an image, or it might be blank. A blank keyframe is still a keyframe; it's just one in which nothing appears onscreen.

In traditional film animation, every frame is a keyframe—something new appears onscreen each frame. In Flash you can make every frame a keyframe, but you can also take some shortcuts. If the first keyframe occurs on frame 1 and the next keyframe doesn't occur until frame 10, there won't be change onscreen during frames 2–9. The keyframe in frame 1 establishes what will appear in frame 1, and it won't change until the keyframe in frame 10, which establishes what appears then. This is totally appropriate for something that doesn't need to change every fraction of a second. When you create a keyframe, it's as if you're telling Flash "put this stuff onstage and keep it here until you reach the next keyframe." The next keyframe says the same thing: "put this new stuff onstage...." There are two things to decide when creating keyframes: when you want them to occur (in the Timeline), and what you want to appear onscreen at those moments.

Establishing a keyframe is simply a matter of clicking the cell in the Timeline exactly where you want a keyframe to occur. When you've clicked a single cell in the Timeline, select Insert, Keyframe (F6). A couple of things happen when you select this option. Flash places a keyframe in that frame (indicated by either a white square or a solid circle), and it copies the onstage content from the previous keyframe. If at the previous keyframe you have nothing onscreen, a blank keyframe is inserted. If at the previous keyframe you have something drawn onscreen, that shape or symbol instance is copied onstage at the new keyframe. This can be convenient because a keyframe is your chance to specify both when you want an onscreen change to occur and what the onscreen contents should change to. Often you want just a small change. This enables you to start with a copy of the previous keyframe's content instead of redrawing it from scratch.

Whatever you draw in a keyframe will continue to be displayed until the Timeline arrives at the next keyframe. If keyframes are placed one after another, the screen will change with every frame. If the framerate is 10fps, you'll see 10 keyframes in one second.

However, keyframes don't have to occur one after another. If you insert keyframes at alternating frames, changes appear 5 times per second (still at 10fps). For any frames between keyframes, you will see the content of the previous keyframe, either an image or a blank screen. Say you want a box to appear onscreen and remain still for one second before it moves. In one keyframe draw a box, then 10 frames later (1 second at 10fps) insert a new keyframe in which you can move the box to a new location.

6

Task: Analyze a Finished Animation

In this Task we'll view a sample animation and make some edits so we can better understand keyframes.

1. In Flash select Help, Samples, Keyframing. Press Enter to watch the animation. (See Figure 6.4.)

FIGURE 6.4
*This Timeline has
many clues as to what
kind of animation is
taking place.*

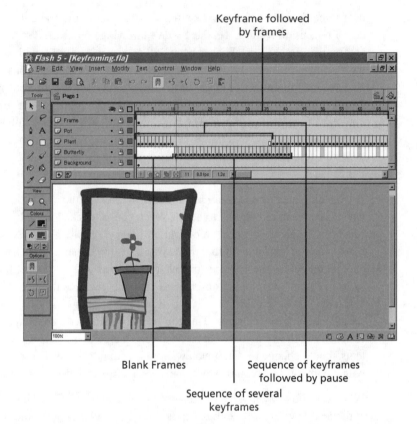

Keyframe followed
by frames

Blank Frames

Sequence of several
keyframes

Sequence of keyframes
followed by pause

2. You should notice there are separate named layers (Frame, Pot, Plant, Butterfly, Background). We'll look at each separately. You may need to resize the height of the Timeline to see all the layers (as illustrated in Figure 6.5.) (In Hour 11, "Using Layers in Your Animation," we'll cover layers much more extensively.)

3. The layers Frame, Pot, and Background all behave the same. They appear initially in frame 1 and remain unchanged onscreen for the duration of the animation. Notice that each has a keyframe in frame 1, followed by many regular frames. (You can extend or reduce the length of the Timeline by dragging the box at frame 81 in any one of these three layers.)

4. Scrub frames 1 through 10 by dragging the current frame marker in the numbered area of the Timeline. Notice the animation of the plant growing. In the Plant layer, you'll notice a keyframe in each frame from 1 to 10. Onscreen, a different drawing

of the plant appears for each frame. Scrub past frame 10, and the plant stops moving for about 15 frames. That's because in the Plant layer, there are no keyframes between frame 10 and frame 37 (when the plant pounces on the butterfly).

FIGURE 6.5

You can resize the height of the Timeline to see all layers.

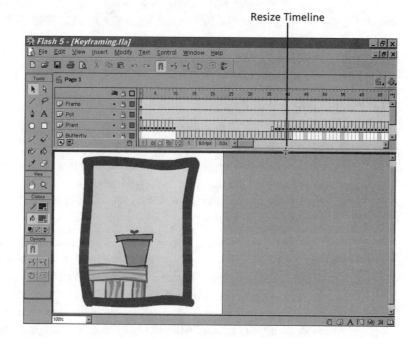

5. The Butterfly layer is probably the most interesting. During the initial growth of the flower (frames 1 through 10), the butterfly isn't just off screen—it doesn't exist! Frame 1 of the Butterfly layer is white (indicating a blank keyframe—a keyframe with nothing drawn onstage). The next keyframe appears in frame 10, where the butterfly starts moving. Notice that there aren't any frames following the keyframe in Butterfly at frame 41. (There are still vertical lines making cells—like the Timeline in a new file.)

6. Let's see the result of adding frames after frame 41 in the Butterfly layer. Click the cell at frame 81 and select Insert, Frame (F5). When you play the animation now, the butterfly never disappears. The new regular frames extend the duration of the contents at keyframe 41. One way to remove the frames following the keyframe in frame 41 is to drag the box now at the end of the Butterfly layer to the left (see Figure 6.6).

7. Close this file without saving.

6

FIGURE 6.6

Once we add frames to the end of a layer, we can reduce the duration by dragging this box to the left.

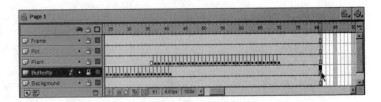

This practical example is a great chance to see keyframes, blank keyframes, and regular frames in a working file.

Tweening

You can put whatever you want in keyframes. The space between two keyframes effectively "holds" the onscreen contents from the first keyframe. Alternatively, you can tell Flash to interpolate the change. For example, suppose that in one keyframe there is an airplane on the left of the stage. The next keyframe shows the airplane on the right side of the stage. Flash can calculate how to move the first image to the second. It does this through the process of *tweening*.

NEW TERM   *Tweening* is the process of interpolating two keyframes. Tweening will smooth out a big change by breaking it into little steps. If a circle at the bottom of your screen jumps to the top of your screen 1 second later (at 10fps), the change appears abrupt. If the two frames are tweened, you'll see the circle move a little bit (about 1/10 of the total distance) 10 times. The coarse movement is smoothed out with small changes in the in-between frames. Flash will calculate these tweened or interpolated frames so you don't have to do all the work.

The word "tweening" is from the word "between," and it is used in conventional animation as well. If you look at the credits on any full-length animated feature film, you're likely to see the names of both the principal artists and the tweeners. The principal artists draw the keyframes, and the tweeners fill in the blanks. Similarly, in Flash you draw the keyframes, and Flash creates those in between.

Just so you can see what it looks like, check out the tweened frames in Figure 6.7. It really is as simply as drawing two frames and making Flash tween the difference. We'll do tweening in depth during Hours 8, "Using Motion Tween to Animate," and 9, "Using Shape Tween to Morph." For now, just realize that Flash will help us by doing the tedious work.

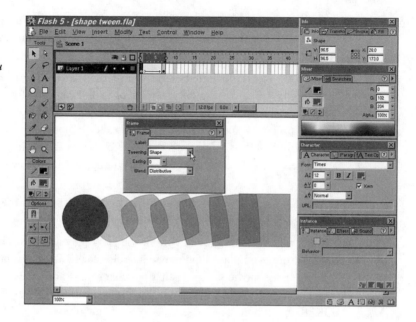

FIGURE 6.7

After you have two keyframes separated by several frames, you can tell Flash how to get from one to the next.

Summary

Although we didn't actually create any animations this hour, we did look at a couple. The concepts we discussed, however, prepared us for the next few hours. We discussed familiar media like television and film, including how persistence of vision makes the illusion of animation work. This general discussion was applied to Flash in several of the terms we learned.

In particular, we discussed framerate, keyframes, and tweening. Framerate is how fast Flash attempts to display the contents of each frame in sequence. Keyframes are where you establish what will be onstage at a particular time. Finally, tweening is Flash's way of filling the spaces between keyframes. These three concepts (and many more) will become almost second nature as we practice during the next three hours.

Q&A

Q What is the best framerate to use?

A There's really no right answer. The framerate you specify is a maximum—your animation will never play faster, but on some machines it could play slower. Ideally, you pick a very high framerate, around 30fps, but not so high that you user's machine can't keep up. Remember two concepts: First, you should pick a rate and stick to it. Second, you can make something appear to move quickly by using fewer frames instead of increasing framerate.

6

Q My monitor's refresh rate is 75Hz, meaning it blinks 75 times per second. However, I can crank the Flash movie's framerate all the way to 120fps. What's the value of doing that?

A First of all, you'll likely find that if you set the framerate to 120fps, Flash won't keep up. If you're playing only a frame or two, it can actually go much faster than 30fps. It can reach 120fps only in theory, and you certainly won't see anything different. In Flash 4 this caused scripting to execute more frequently (we'll discuss this in Hour 14, "Using Actions to Create Non-Linear Movies"). In Flash 5, however, there are better ways, so such high framerates are usable only on super-fast computers.

Q I've set my movie properties to 24fps, but the display on the bottom of the Timeline changed to 18.2fps. How do I change it back?

A First of all, this is a sign that your movie can't play at 24fps. The 18.2 indicates that last time you played the movie it could reach only that framerate. The framerate set in the movie properties has not changed. If you really want to change the display number, access the movie properties again (double-click the 18.2) and click OK. Keep in mind that just because you set the framerate to 24fps doesn't mean Flash will play that fast. It will try, but it might not succeed.

Workshop

The Workshop consists of quiz questions and answers to help you solidify your understanding of the material covered. Try to answer the questions before checking the answers.

Quiz

1. What is the visual effect of a movie that has a keyframe in every frame?

   A. It'll appear very smooth.

   B. It will appear jumpy.

   C. It may have no visual effect.

2. If you set the framerate to 2 frames per second, what is the visual result?

   A. The animation will look jumpy.

   B. You'll see the blank (black) pauses between frames.

   C. Subliminal messages can be seen between each frame.

3. If your movie properties are set to a framerate of 60fps, how long will it take to reach frame 90?

    A. 1.5 seconds exactly.

    B. 1.5 seconds or more.

    C. None of the above.

Quiz Answers

1. C. There are many factors besides how frequent your keyframes appear that affect how an animation looks. First, the nature of the content has more impact than how many keyframes you have. You could have very similar or very different content onscreen for each keyframe. Also, framerate affects how an animation appears.

2. A. A framerate of 2 frames per second is slow enough for you to notice the still frames, but the visual effect is jumpiness. The pauses between frames are just that, pauses, not black frames.

3. B. It's very unlikely your computer can actually display 60 frames a second. It will probably take longer than 1.5 seconds to display all 90 frames. (If your computer *could* keep up with the framerate of 60fps, it would take slightly less than 1.5 seconds, because it only has 59 frames to travel from frame 1.)

6

HOUR 7

Animation the Old-Fashioned Way

It's finally time to animate! You've assembled the graphics that will be animated, and last hour you learned the basic components of an animation (frames, keyframes, frame rate, and tweening). Now you're ready to create your own animation.

Instead of starting with the two ways Flash can tween *for* you (motion tween and shape tween), we're going to begin by animating each step in the animation frame by frame. We'll get to shape and motion tweening in the next two hours (Hours 8, "Using Motion Tween to Animate," and 9, "Using Shape Tween to Morph") but for now, we're going to animate the old-fashioned way, frame-by-frame.

This hour you will

- Learn how to make a frame-by-frame animation
- Learn to use the Onion Skin tools for assistance
- See some tricks that can make you more efficient with this otherwise cumbersome technique

Understanding the Brute-Force Technique

If you've ever made a flip-book, you already know how to make a frame-by-frame animation. Each page in a flip-book contains a slightly different image so that, when you fan through all the pages, the image is animated. That's what we're doing this hour. However, instead of drawing something different on each page of a book, we'll be drawing a different image in each keyframe of the Flash Timeline.

This hour we will learn features and techniques of Flash that make the animation process easier. However, frame-by-frame animation isn't a "feature" of Flash, it's a technique that you will implement using Flash's features. I mention this because you won't find "frame-by-frame" anywhere in the Flash manual or help files.

Task: How to Make a Frame-by-Frame Animation

Enough talk! Let's make a quick animation, and then we can discuss what we've built. We'll make the animation "Stick man takes a walk."

1. Draw a stick man using only lines (no fills) and make sure everything is snapped together, as in Figure 7.1.

FIGURE 7.1

A stick man drawn with lines. Lines are used for these exercises because they are easier to modify.

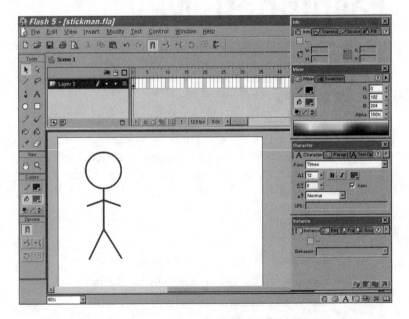

2. Single-click just to the right of the keyframe dot in Layer 1—that is, click in the second cell of Layer 1.

3. Select Insert, Insert Keyframe (or press F6), which inserts a keyframe in frame 2 with a copy of the stick man graphic.

4. To make a slight change to the stick man in frame 2, first assure that you are editing frame 2. You should see the red current frame marker in frame 2. If it's not there, click in frame 2 of the Timeline.

5. Now, we'll make a slight change—namely, bend one leg slightly and change the end point of the arm so it looks like it's swinging (as in Figure 7.2).

FIGURE 7.2

In the second keyframe, bend the stick man's leg in preparation for taking a step.

6. If you want to preview what you have so far, use the scrub technique. Grab the red current frame marker and drag it back and forth. Okay, there's not much yet, but you can see stick man beginning to take a step.

7. We're ready to create the third frame, so click in Layer 1 right after frame 2 and select Insert, Insert Keyframe, which copies the contents of frame 2 into the new keyframe in frame 3.

8. Make a slight change to the stick man (bend the leg more and swing the arm more).

9. Continue to insert keyframes one at a time. Make an edit to each new frame to keep the arms and legs moving, and then select Insert Keyframe again.

7

Previewing Your Animation with Test Movie

There are three ways to watch the entire animation: Scrubbing, Playing, and Testing. Scrubbing the red current frame marker is a good way to preview as you work. The only problem with scrubbing is that the speed won't be consistent, it will only be as smooth as you scrub. The second way is with the menu selection Control, Play (which is also available from the Controller toolbar). However, as we'll see later (in the chapters on buttons, layers, and Movie Clips), Play doesn't always show you *exactly* what your viewers will see, so let me strongly recommend that you not get into the habit of previewing with Play. The best way to view your animation is with the menu selection Control, Test Movie.

Test Movie exports a .swf file into the folder where your file is saved, names this file the same as your file with a .swf extension, and then launches the Flash Player program for you to view the results. You'll see how this works when you first save your source .fla file into a new, empty folder. After a Test Movie, your folder will have an additional .swf file.

NEW TERM   .swf *Files*. As you recall from Hour 1, "Basics," a .swf file (pronounced "swif") is an exported Flash file. This is the kind of file you put in your Web pages. It differs from the source Flash file (.fla) in that it is not editable. The critical concept is that your source file is an .fla file, and that's the file you need to keep. You can always export again to create a .swf (from an .fla) but you can't get an editable .fla from a .swf.

You may have noticed that when testing a movie, your menus change. That's because you're actually running the Flash Player, which is a different program than Flash. Also, the movie loops by default, which is something we'll address later when we publish the movie to the Web (in Hours 17, "Linking Your Movie to the Web," and 24, "Publishing Your Creation"). The only thing weird about testing the movie is that you must close the Flash Player program to return to Flash. The good news about Test Movie is that you will see almost exactly what your viewers will see!

Editing One Keyframe at a Time

The frame-by-frame technique is simple. You just put a keyframe on each frame. An entirely different image appears on each frame—sometimes drastically different, sometimes only slightly different. The beauty is that you can put anything you want in one keyframe, because it doesn't matter what's in the other keyframes.

Although frame-by-frame animation is a simple concept, it can be a lot of work. Imagine conventional animation in which an artist must draw each frame even when only a slight change is necessary. It's detailed, meticulous work and, unfortunately, not really any easier in Flash, though you have functions such as Undo that help. Just realize that this technique is for situations that require it—something with lots of details such as an animation of someone walking. No other technique gives you this level of control to change each frame.

Changing Frame View

Just because frame-by-frame animation is a lot of work doesn't mean you can't use a little help. One way to make the process a little easier is by changing the Frame View setting. In Figure 7.3 you can see the Frame View pop-up menu. If you select Preview, each keyframe in the Timeline will be displayed as it appears onstage. Figure 7.4 shows the stick man animation with Frame View set to Preview. Preview lets you see all the frames of your animation without actually stepping through them. The Preview in Context setting draws the preview in the correct proportions (including blank whitespace), so the stick man would likely appear smaller.

FIGURE 7.3

The Frame View pop-up menu is available to change the size and character of the Timeline. You can make each frame larger or include a visual preview of the contents onstage in each frame.

The Frame View settings don't actually affect your animation. For example, if you set Frame View to Large, it just makes your Timeline take up more space within Flash—the user will never notice the difference. Also, you can change Frame View any time and change it back without changing your file.

FIGURE 7.4

*The stick man anima-
tion is shown with
Frame View set to
Preview. An image of
the onscreen contents
appears in each frame
of the Timeline.*

Using the Onion Skin Tools

Probably the greatest helper for frame-by-frame animations is Flash's Onion Skin tools.
The original onion skin technique was developed for conventional animation. When an
artist draws each frame by hand, he needs a way to judge how much change in the image
is necessary from one frame to the next. He draws a frame on tracing paper (with the
translucency of onion skin) that is placed on top of the previous frame. That way, he can
see through to the previous frame and draw the next image accordingly.

In Flash, the effect is the same, but of course you don't use real onion skin. Flash's
Onion Skin feature allows you to edit one keyframe while viewing as many frames
before or after the current frame as you want.

Open the stick man animation file and click the leftmost Onion Skin button at the bottom
of the Timeline (see Figure 7.5). Select Large by clicking the Frame View pop-up that is
just right of your Timeline's frame numbers. With Onion Skin turned on, you can place
the red current frame marker on any frame you want and edit that frame, and you'll see a
dim view of the other frames in your animation. Which frames appear depends on where
you position the Start Onion Skin and End Onion Skin markers. These markers can be
difficult to grab when you try to move them—I often find myself accidentally grabbing
the current frame marker. It's easier to grab the markers when the Frame View is set to
Large.

FIGURE 7.5

Onion Skin is turned on (the leftmost button), and we can see the contents of adjacent frames.

You would probably turn on Onion Skin while creating an animation (instead of after it's done). To practice, let's try the stick man animation again—this time with the help of Onion Skin.

Task: Using Onion Skin to Help Create an Animation

1. Start a new file and set Frame View to Large.

2. Turn on Onion Skin. Notice that the Start and End Onion Skin markers (Figure 7.6) cannot be moved beyond the beginning or end of your animation (because it's only one frame long at this point).

FIGURE 7.6

The Onion Skin markers indicate how many frames are included in the Onion Skin view.

Start Onion skin   End Onion skin

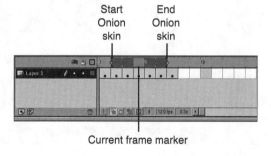

Current frame marker

7

3. Draw a stick man similar to the way we did in the previous exercise (using only lines).

4. In frame 2, select Insert, Keyframe (F6). This copies what was in the previous frame and pastes it into the new keyframe.

5. While editing frame 2 (the red current frame marker should be in frame 2), drag the end of one leg to move it to a different angle. This time, the position of the leg from frame 1 is visible (though dimly) even though we can only edit the contents of frame 2.

6. In frame 3, insert another keyframe. When you move the leg, you can judge how much based on the position of the leg in frame 2.

7. Continue to insert keyframes one at a time. Make an edit to each new frame, then select Insert Keyframe again.

8. When you have several frames, you can experiment with changing both the Start and End Onion Skin markers. By default, the markers are set to Onion 2, meaning you can see two frames ahead and two behind. I rarely use the End Onion Skin marker at all—I just position it at the current frame marker. I'd rather see where I've been than where I'm headed. You can move the markers to several preset positions from the Modify Onion Markers pop-up (the right most Onion Skin button—pictured in Figure 7.7).

Modify Onion markers drop down menu

FIGURE 7.7

The Modify Onion Markers pop-up has several preset options.

Modify Onion Markers has several preset options:

- **Always Show Markers** will leave a faint version of the markers visible in the Timeline even after you turn off Onion Skin.
- **Anchor Onion** locks the two markers where they are (no matter where your red current frame marker is).
- **Onion 2** sets the markers to 2 frames ahead and 2 frames behind.
- **Onion 5** sets the markers to 5 frames ahead and 5 frames behind.
- **Onion All** will move the Start Onion Skin Marker to frame 1 and the End Onion Skin Marker to your last frame.

Before we finish with Onion Skin, let's look at two remaining features: Onion Skin Outlines and theEdit Multiple Frames option. You can choose either Onion Skin or Onion Skin Outlines, but not both. Onion Skin Outlines displays the other frames within the Onion markers as outlines instead of as dim images. Outlines can be helpful if you have a particularly slow computer or if the dim view makes images difficult to distinguish.

Finally, Edit Multiple Frames is quite interesting. In the previous task, we used onion skinning to see the contents of surrounding keyframes, but we were editing only one frame at a time—the current frame. We could move the stick man's leg close to the faded image in the previous frame without affecting the previous frame. Edit Multiple Frames lets you edit the contents of all the frames within the Start Onion Skin and End Onion Skin markers. Generally, Edit Multiple Frames is useful for editing a finished animation rather than creating an animation because you'd never know which you're editing. However, when you want to return to an animation and move the contents of every frame, Edit Multiple Frames is invaluable. In this situation, just turn on Edit Multiple Frames, select Onion All from the Modify Onion Markers menu, select everything onstage (Ctrl+A), and move it anywhere you want.

Enhancing Your Frame-by-Frame Animation

Frame-by-frame animation can be a ton of work. Even with helpers like Onion Skin, it still requires that you draw each frame by hand. Just because it *can* be a lot of work doesn't mean it has to. For animation that has the same look as a feature animated movie, frame-by-frame animation is required, and it involves skill and patience. However, with a few tricks, you can pull off the same effects with a fraction of the work.

In this section, we'll look at a few tricks especially suited to frame-by-frame animation. You'll see more in Hour 21, "Advanced Animation Techniques."

7

Incorporating Pauses

There's no rule that says you must put a keyframe in every frame. If your frame rate is left at the default 12fps (frames per second) and every frame is a keyframe, then the image changes 12 times per second. This may be unnecessary, and it becomes a lot of work when you consider the total number of frames you must draw. What if you don't want the images to change every 1/12 of a second? Incorporating pauses is the answer—and it's very easy.

In the previous examples we inserted a keyframe in every frame, one after another. A keyframe is where you tell Flash that something new is appearing onstage. In addition, you're saying "this image should appear now and it should remain until a new keyframe comes." To incorporate a pause, you just follow a keyframe with a non-keyframe frame. If you want a 1-second pause (and you're running at 12fps), just follow your keyframe with 12 frames.

There are two ways to create pauses, either as you're making an animation or after you've made one. To incorporate a pause while creating an animation, insert a keyframe farther down the Timeline than the next frame. In Figure 7.8 you'll see five keyframes in a row, but then a pause was created by first clicking the cell in frame 11 and selecting Insert, Keyframe. The approach is slightly different when you want to edit an animation you've already created. To insert a pause (or increase one that already exists), click the keyframe you want to pause and select Insert, Frame. This effectively pushes out everything that appears later in the Timeline.

FIGURE 7.8

This frame-by-frame animation pauses after frame 5 because there isn't a keyframe until frame 11—therefore nothing changes onstage between frames 5 and 11.

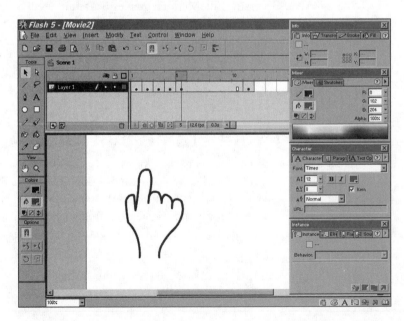

In a practical sense, pauses can enhance your animation. A pause can become a visual element of your animation. Suppose your stick man walks all the way across the stage; then you want him to walk back. You may want to include a pause when he's about to turn around. In Hour 21, we'll see how pauses can cause the audience to anticipate that a change is about to happen, which makes them pay closer attention.

Implying Motion

Two frames is all you really need for an animation. Suppose that Mr. Stick Man begins on the left side of the stage in frame 1. The next frame is a keyframe, and he's all the way over on the right side. Show this "animation" to enough people, and you'll find some who swear they actually saw him move across the screen. In the real world there's no way to get from one place to another without traveling through all points between, but in animation, you don't have to draw every step.

To prove the two-frame theory, just make a simple animation of our stick man kicking a soccer ball. Draw a stick man in frame 1 with a ball near his foot. In frame 10, insert a keyframe and move the ball off to the right. Extend his leg so that it looks like he just kicked the ball. It's pretty amazing, but it looks convincing. If you add just one more keyframe at frame 4 and move his leg back a tad (as if he's about to kick), the animation looks great! Stick man stands (pause), he winds up (pause), and he kicks. Imagine how much more work it would have taken to draw all 10 frames.

FIGURE 7.9

With just three keyframes, we can make an effective animation that implies more motion than is actually occurring.

Creating implied motion is a great skill. In a way, we're trying to fool the audience, but it's more than that. Unnecessary animation is more work and can actually detract from your core message. It's hard enough to tell a story with animation—the last thing you need is a distracting animation that's superfluous.

The Flicker Effect

How do you make something blink? You just need one keyframe with an image in it, followed by another keyframe with *nothing* in it, followed by another keyframe with the original image in it. There are several ways to do this, one of which is demonstrated in the following Task.

Task: Making a Sun Flicker

1. In frame 1 of a new file, draw a sun with radiating rays (as in Figure 7.10).

FIGURE 7.10

The sun image that we're going to make blink.

2. Save the sun into the library. Select the entire image and then select Insert, Convert to Symbol. Name it sun, leave it in the default Movie Clip behavior, and click OK.

3. Click in the Timeline on frame 10 and drag to the left. This will select all the frames from 1 to 10. Notice that we went from 10 to 1. You can't click and drag from 1 to 10 unless you first hold down the Ctrl key. If you position your mouse over the keyframe in frame 1, it appears as a hand, indicating that you can pick up and move the keyframe (don't). When you hold Ctrl, the hand turns to a regular arrow, and you can click and drag to select.

4. Select Modify, Frames, Convert to Key Frames, which should place a keyframe containing the contents of frame 1 into each frame.

5. Click the keyframe in frame 2. The red current frame marker moves to frame 2, and the contents of this frame are selected.

6. Select Edit, Clear (or better yet, click your Delete button). You've just created a keyframe with no onscreen image—also known as a blank keyframe. This is shown as an enclosed white box for the cell in the Timeline, as seen in Figure 7.11.

7. Continue to click the even-numbered keyframes and delete the on-stage contents of each. Although you're deleting, it is the on-stage contents that are being removed, not the keyframe itself. The blank keyframes are the same as normal keyframes, except there's nothing on the screen. You can prove this by drawing something onstage for an even-number frame. You'll see it turn back into a regular keyframe, with the solid dot and all.

FIGURE 7.11

After we insert an identical keyframe in every frame, we delete the contents in alternating frames (shown here after deleting the contents of frame 2).

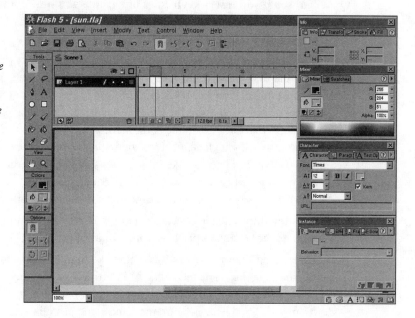

Test your movie to see how this blinking effect looks. How would you lengthen the time the image remains onscreen? What if you want to lengthen the time it's not on screen? Here's where incorporating pauses comes in.

To make the image stay on longer, just click on a keyframe that has contents (those with a solid dot in the Timeline) and select Insert, Frame (or F5). Notice that the "life" of the image in each blink is lengthened. You can continue to insert frames after any keyframe (or blank keyframe), and whatever is in that frame will stay longer.

Summary

This hour we covered frame-by-frame animation—a technique, not a Flash feature. This was more than just an exercise in how to animate the hard way. In later hours, you'll learn better and easier ways; during this hour you had a chance to look at several fundamental concepts. You learned how keyframes can be used to specify when an image is to

7

change and experimented with the Onion Skin animation helpers. Also, you learned how to use pauses and blank frames to imply motion or stop motion. Finally, you made your first animation!

Q&A

Q **When would you insert keyframes one frame at a time rather than insert several by using Modify, Frames, Convert to Key Frames (or Convert to Blank Key Frames) for an entire span?**

A When you want to make a progressive adjustment to each keyframe, it makes sense to draw the first frame, insert a keyframe, then adjust the new frame before inserting a third frame. The process is effective because each time you insert a keyframe, Flash copies the contents of the previous keyframe. Inserting one keyframe at a time assures that each keyframe is the same as the previous one, so that you only need to make a slight change before continuing. When you intend to draw an entirely new image into each keyframe, you should consider inserting blank keyframes (either one at a time or through Modify, Frames, Convert to Blank Key Frames). That way each new keyframe starts with no contents.

Q **What's the difference between inserting a keyframe then deleting the contents onstage rather than simply inserting a blank keyframe?**

A There is no difference; the result is a blank keyframe (shown by an enclosed white cell in the Timeline). The technique of inserting a regular keyframe and deleting the contents is easier to learn because you don't have to think about blank keyframes. All you have is keyframes, and some just don't have any contents.

Q **Is frame-by-frame the best type of animation?**

A No. It's the most appropriate when you want each frame to appear differently than the next, but it takes the most work, too. You'll see that other techniques are often easier and much more efficient.

Workshop

The Workshop consists of quiz questions and answers to help you solidify your understanding of the material covered. Be sure to read the explanations even if you get the answers right.

Quiz

1. If you draw an image onstage in a keyframe, how long does that image remain onstage?

   A. Just the one frame in which you drew the image.

   B. Until another keyframe containing a different image is encountered.

   C. For the entire Timeline.

2. How many frames are necessary to create an animation?

   A. One.

   B. Two or more.

   C. No fewer than three.

3. In what part of this book will we actually get to *animate*?

   A. In the next 2 hours.

   B. In the last 2 hours.

   C. This is it—we've been creating animations all hour!

Quiz Answers

1. B. Think of a keyframe as you telling Flash to put an image onstage now and leave it there until notified otherwise (by another keyframe).

2. B. Although a feature-length movie may have 24 different images each second, you can imply motion very effectively with just 2 frames.

3. C. Frame-by-frame animation *is* animation. The other types of animation we're going to cover are those in which Flash takes care of the frames between keyframes that we create. If nothing else, you should now understand keyframes clearly.

Exercise

Here's a great exercise that will let you experience an entirely different way of creating. Unlike the stick man exercises (where we created each new keyframe based on the previous keyframe), this time we'll draw an entirely new graphic into each keyframe.

Let's draw a bird flying. First select frames 1 to 100 and use Modify, Frames, Convert to Blank Key Frames. Turn on Onion Skin so you can view just the previous two frames. Start on frame 1 and draw the bird (just use the Brush to draw a curved V shape). Press the Next Frame quick key—. (period)—and, using the onion skin as a guide, draw

7

another V that moves across the screen. You can go pretty quickly: next frame, V, next frame, V…. If you want the bird to move fast, increase the space between the current V and the previous one. This is a good exercise to experiment with different types of motion.

Hour **8**

Using Motion Tween to Animate

Creating an animation frame-by-frame (as we did last hour) can be a lot of work, because you have to draw every frame yourself. With *tweening*, Flash will fill in the blank frames *between* two keyframes. Flash has two types: Motion Tweening and Shape Tweening. This hour we'll cover Motion Tweening.

This hour you will

- Create a Motion Tween
- Learn the four basic properties of a Motion Tween
- Experiment with the effects of "ease in" and "ease out"
- Use tricks to make your Motion Tweens look natural and realistic

Creating a Motion Tween

A basic Motion Tween is very easy to produce. Let's do one, and then we can come back to analyze it.

Task: Create a Basic Motion Tween

1. In a new file, draw a circle onstage.

2. Select the entire circle and choose Insert, Convert to Symbol. Name it Circle, leave it set to the default Movie Clip, and click OK.

3. Click in the Timeline on frame 30 and select Insert, Keyframe (or press F6).

4. Click on the keyframe in frame 1; the red current frame marker will move to frame 1. Position the circle where you want it to appear at the beginning—let's move it to the left side of the stage.

5. Click in the last keyframe (frame 30) and notice that the red current frame marker moves to frame 30. Position the circle on the right side of the stage.

6. Try scrubbing. The animation will look pretty abrupt. The circle stays on the left side for 29 frames and then jumps to the right side. To make the movement smoother, Flash will take care of the in-between frames.

7. Tweening is set in the beginning keyframe, in this case the first keyframe (in frame 1). Select the keyframe in frame 1 and open the Frame panel.

8. The Frame panel includes the Tweening drop-down list and a field where you can name the label of the keyframe.

9. Select Motion from the Tweening drop-down list. Leave all the default settings, as seen in Figure 8.1.

FIGURE 8.1

The Frame panel open with our first keyframe selected.

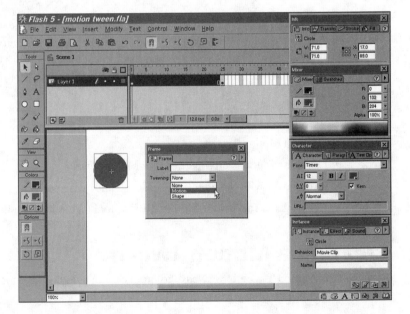

10. That's it! Notice in Figure 8.2 that Flash has drawn an arrow with a blue background to represent the interpolated frames—those between two keyframes. Select Control, Test Movie (Ctrl+Enter) to see what you did.

FIGURE 8.2

Our Timeline includes an arrow on a blue background to indicate that Flash is tweening these frames.

Interpolated frames

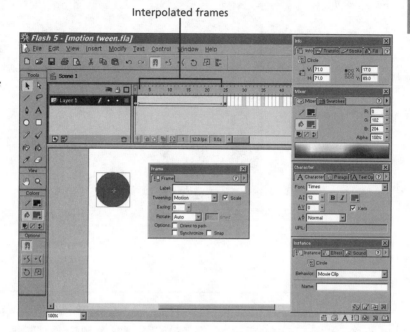

Following the Rules of a Motion Tween

The previous Task worked because the instructions carefully followed the rules of a Motion Tween: You can't have multiple objects in your keyframes, and the one object you do have must be a symbol. Flash is very unforgiving when you don't follow this rule.

The good news is that Flash gives you several hints when you don't follow the rules for a Motion Tween. In the Frame panel for your first keyframe, you'll see an exclamation point button which, when clicked, provides the message "Motion Tweening will not occur on layers with shapes or more than one group or symbol." You don't even have to press a button to know something is wrong—the exclamation point is enough. In addition to this warning, the resulting Timeline will often look different. A dashed line will appear as another indication that you broke the rule. See Figure 8.3.

FIGURE 8.3

If you don't follow the rules for a Motion Tween, Flash warns that something is wrong.

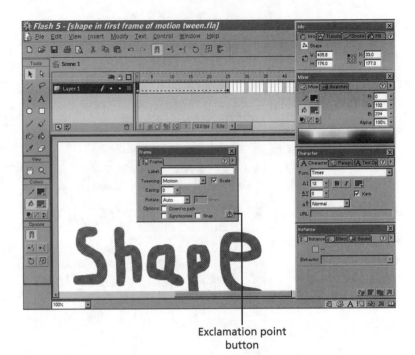

Exclamation point button

You probably noticed when you pressed the Frame panel's exclamation point button that the warning implies that you can Motion Tween either a symbol or a group. Unfortunately, Flash gives you a break here—but I'd still recommend that you follow the rule that you only Motion Tween symbols (and one symbol at a time). If you have a grouped shape in the first keyframe and then you insert a keyframe later in the Timeline, you can use Motion Tween with no apparent harm. However, Flash takes your grouped shape and turns it into a symbol, calls it Tween 1, and pretends nothing happened. It's as if Flash does the thinking for you. Personally, I'd rather be in control and create symbols intentionally when I'm about to do a Motion Tween.

Techniques and Tips

You should feel proud of the circle you moved across the screen. Actually, Flash did the work—you just established the two keyframes. As we're about to see, Flash can tween any two keyframes no matter how different they are. Plus there are some ways to make the process even easier for you.

Tweening More than Position

If you recall in Hour 5, "Using the Library for Productivity," you learned that each instance on stage can be different than all the others, even if you just have one master symbol in the library. Instances can be positioned in different locations, scaled to different sizes, rotated differently, and have their color effects set differently. There are seven ways in which instances can be varied: Position, Scale, Rotation, Skew, Brightness, Tint, and Alpha. Flash will tween changes in these properties as well.

Let's try to tween more than just an instance's position. This is just an exercise to practice tweening—it's not supposed be subtle. We'll get to that in the "Fine-Tuning a Motion Tween" section, later in this hour.

Task: Tween Position, Scale, Rotation, and Color

1. In a new file, use the Text tool to create a text block that contains your name. Don't worry about the exact size, but make it big enough to see clearly.

2. Using the Arrow tool, select the text block (not the text itself). Then select Insert, Convert to Symbol (F8) and name the symbol My Name. Click OK.

3. Now click in the Timeline on frame 30 and insert a keyframe (select Insert, Keyframe or F6).

4. Click on the keyframe in frame 1 (the red current frame marker will move to frame 1) and position your name in the bottom left corner. This is its initial position.

5. Select Motion from the Tweening drop-down list in the Frame panel.

6. Now click on the keyframe in frame 30 so we can edit the end position. With the Scale tool, scale the text large enough to occupy the entire stage. You may need to position it closer to the center.

7. Go ahead and scrub to get an idea of how the tween looks. From this point forward, remember that you'll only be able to edit the Frame panel for the beginning or ending keyframe, not between—that's where Flash is responsible for the tweening.

8. Move the red current frame marker to frame 30, and we'll modify the color effect on the same instance. Select the instance of My Name and open the Effect panel, seen in Figure 8.4. Select the Tint effect from the drop-down list. Pick a bright color. Scrub for a quick preview.

FIGURE 8.4

The Tint effect is applied to the instance in frame 30.

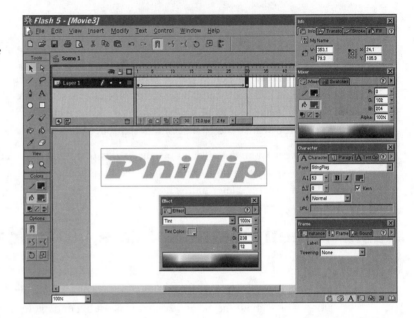

9. Go to frame 1 and with the Scale tool stretch your name really tall. (You may need to adjust the position.)

10. While still in frame 1, use the Rotate tool to rotate your name counterclockwise just a few degrees, as seen in Figure 8.5. Do a little skewing, too. The corner handles rotate and the middle handles skew.

11. Now check out your animation by scrubbing or testing the movie. You created two very different keyframes, and Flash figured out how to animate from one to the other.

Although you can tween the position, scale, rotation, and color effect, it doesn't mean you have to. The Alpha color effect will force your audience's computers to work very hard. The message you're trying to communicate might be overlooked when the user notices everything slowing down to a crawl. I don't want to suggest that you should never tween Alpha, but it's the most processor-intensive effect available, and sometimes you can simulate the same effect in other ways. Consider tweening based on the Brightness color effect. If the background is white anyway, this is visually no different, but it doesn't slow down the computer as much.

FIGURE 8.5

We can change any property of the instance in frame 1, and Flash will tween accordingly.

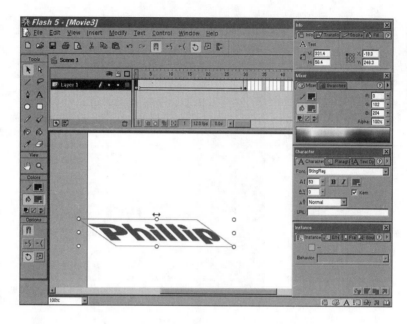

 Since you'll likely use Motion Tweens a lot, there's a great shortcut to know. Just right-click on your starting keyframe (on a Macintosh, click and hold); you'll see the option Create Motion Tween in a pop-up list.

Stay Out of Flash's Territory

You are responsible for establishing keyframes. When you choose to tween, Flash is responsible for the frames between your keyframes. Consider this to be "no-man's-land," although Flash calls these frames *interpolated frames*. If you edit anything you see onstage while the red current frame marker is between two keyframes, you might get some unexpected results.

To illustrate, suppose you have two keyframes and no tweening. Remember that keyframes establish when something should be onstage, where it will remain until another keyframe comes along. If you position the red current frame marker anywhere in the middle and grab the object onscreen, you'll be editing the contents of the previous keyframe and thus influencing every frame from the first keyframe to the next. (You'll see a visual clue of this when you click an object onstage—the span in the Timeline that the first keyframe influences will turn black.)

FIGURE 8.6

The red current frame marker is positioned over the interpolated frames of the Name Tween layer.

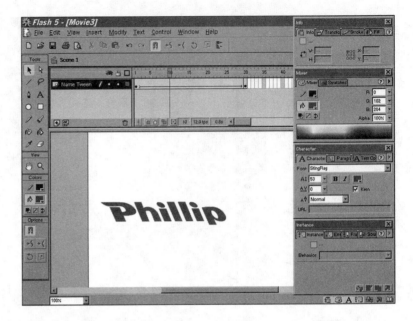

Messing with no-man's-land is much stranger when you have a Motion Tween already established. If you position the red current frame marker in the middle of a Motion Tween (as in Figure 8.6), it won't be apparent that you can even select the symbol onstage. If you click and drag it, you can move it. However, if you move a symbol in the middle of a Motion Tween, you'll add a keyframe. Flash is forfeiting control of that frame to you by giving you a keyframe. Adding a keyframe in the middle of a Motion Tween is sometimes useful, as we'll see later this hour. Just realize that you're taking away Flash's control of a frame when you insert a keyframe (either with Insert Keyframe or by grabbing the symbol and moving it).

Know Where You Are

It's important to pay attention to the red current frame marker as you edit keyframes for a Motion Tween. Consider any of the Tasks we did this hour. If you want the motion to go from the left to the right, your starting keyframe should have the symbol positioned on the left. If you accidentally leave the current frame marker on the end frame and then move the symbol to the left, you're actually editing the end keyframe, and the object will move to the left—not to the right. Always be sure the red current frame marker is in the right place before you edit the contents onstage (see Figure 8.7).

FIGURE 8.7

The red current frame marker indicates the frame in which you are currently editing.

8

Stick to This Pattern

Hopefully you're beginning to see a pattern. To summarize, here's the basic pattern we've used so far. Motion Tween will tween only one object, and that object is a symbol. Make that object a symbol before creating the ending keyframe, or else the new keyframe will contain a shape, not a symbol. After you've created your beginning and ending keyframes, you can adjust the position, scale, rotation, skew, brightness, tint, and alpha of either the beginning or end keyframe (although alpha is not recommended). Keep an eye on the current frame marker in your Timeline to be sure it's located in the keyframe you want to edit. You'll refine your technique over time, but you should follow these basic steps during your entire Flash career.

Fine-Tuning a Motion Tween

Making a Motion Tween is pretty easy once you know how. Making it look good is another matter. There are a few basic techniques to fine-tune your Motion Tween that will make the results more natural and believable. Although we'll see even more techniques later (in Hour 21, "Advanced Animation Techniques"), for now we'll cover concepts that specifically apply to a Motion Tween.

Multiple Keyframes

Every Motion Tween involves just two keyframes. In the first, you tell Flash how to tween to the next keyframe. But suppose you want a symbol to move up then back down. You need three keyframes: one in the initial location, another in the upper location, and a third in the end location. In fact, you'll have only two tweens: one from the first keyframe to the second keyframe, and one from the second keyframe to the third keyframe. It will make the process easier if you can sort things out this simply.

Often, you'll want the end of your Motion Tween to correspond exactly with the beginning (like a yo-yo moving down then back to where it started). Let's try it.

Task: Make an Animation Finish Where It Starts

1. In a new file, draw a circle.

2. Select the circle and convert it to a symbol (select Insert, Convert to Symbol or F8). Call it Yo-Yo, leave the default Movie Clip behavior, and click OK.

3. Position the yo-yo in its starting position, near the top of the screen.

4. Click the Timeline on frame 10 and insert a keyframe (Insert, Keyframe or F6).

5. Before you move anything, click the Timeline on frame 20 and insert another keyframe. At this point you should have three identical keyframes.

6. Now position the red current frame marker on frame 10 and move the yo-yo down to the bottom of the stage. (Clicking the keyframe in frame 10 not only moves the current frame marker but also selects all the onstage contents of this frame.)

7. Now we only need to set Motion Tween for frame 1 (which specifies how to tween to frame 10) and for frame 10 (which specifies how to tween to frame 20). You can use the right-click method if you want. To set tweening for two keyframes (1 and 10) at the same time, click the keyframe in frame 1, hold Shift, then click the keyframe in frame 10. Access the Frame panel and you can set tweening for both keyframes (see Figure 8.8). Select Motion.

8. Select Control, Test Movie (or press Ctrl+Enter). Save the animation; we'll add to it in a minute.

FIGURE 8.8

The Frame panel affects every keyframe selected.

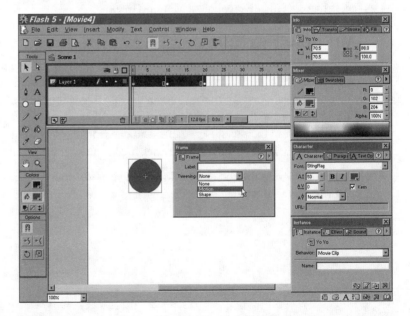

8

Let's step back and consider what we did. We made sure the first and last keyframes were identical before editing the middle keyframe. It's very common in animation to establish the ending keyframes first before editing the initial frames. We did it here so that the first and last keyframes contained Yo-Yo in the same position; in Hour 21 there's a whole section dedicated to this technique.

Ease In and Ease Out

The only problem with letting the computer (or Flash) do our tweening is that the result looks like a computer did it—it's almost too perfect. In the case of our yo-yo, it moves down at the same rate as it moves up, and the entire animation plays at the same rate.

Flash has a way to address the fact that some kinds of motion accelerate while others decelerate. It's called Ease In and Ease Out. Since every tween is between only two keyframes, you only have to think of two keyframes at a time. Ease In means that the motion starts off slowly and picks up at the end. Ease Out is the opposite—the object decelerates at the end of its motion.

You can see the effects of Easing by opening the Yo-Yo animation we just created. Click on the first keyframe and open the Frame panel. Set the Easing slider to -40 (by moving the slider down). Notice that the word "In" appears to the right of the slider. This will cause it to start off slowly and then accelerate at the end (Figure 8.9 shows how the frame panel looks). When you Test Movie, the trip down should look pretty good.

FIGURE 8.9

The Easing setting in the Frame panel of a keyframe can affect acceleration or deceleration.

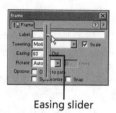

Easing slider

For the second tween (between frames 10 and 20), select the keyframe in frame 10 and open the Frame panel. Set Easing to 80 (move the slider up). Test Movie again. The result is that the yo-yo slows down before it stops at the top, making it look more natural. You'll find other ways to make your animation believable, and this quick experiment should spark some ideas.

What if you want one smooth tween to both Ease In (at the beginning) and Ease Out (at the end)? We know that you can have only one Ease effect per tween. It *is* possible—you just can't do it with only two keyframes. The solution involves three keyframes: one at the start, where you set the tweening to Ease In, one in the middle, with tweening set to

Ease Out, and one at the end. To let Flash help us, we first create a tween between the first and last frames and insert a keyframe in the middle.

Task: Make an Animation Ease In and Ease Out

1. In a new file, draw any shape and make it a symbol. Place the symbol somewhere on the left side of the stage.

2. Click in the Timeline at frame 50 and insert a keyframe (Insert, Keyframe or F6).

3. While the red current frame marker is in frame 50, move the instance of your symbol to the right side of the stage.

4. Go back to the keyframe in frame 1 and create a Motion Tween (right-click and select Create Motion Tween).

5. Test the movie (Control, Test Movie) and remember how it looks.

6. Place the red current frame marker in the middle (frame 25).

7. If you insert a keyframe in frame 25 (where there's already a Motion Tween), not only will Flash copy the contents of the previous keyframe, it will position the contents of the new keyframe in the appropriate midstream location. Go ahead and insert a keyframe in frame 25; you'll notice that nothing moves. Just the keyframe appears, and your symbol is already in its tweened location. Test the movie again; it should be unchanged.

8. Now we can set Easing. In frame 1, set the Frame Properties Tweening setting to Ease In (-100 to make it obvious). In frame 25, set Easing to Ease Out (100).

There were two interesting tricks used in this exercise. First, we needed three keyframes (or two tweened spans) to have two different Easing settings. Second, we squeezed a keyframe into the middle of an existing tween. That way, the newly created keyframe was in the appropriate location—halfway between the two existing keyframes. This will happen to any property that is being tweened. If the symbol in frame 1 was tinted blue and the symbol in frame 50 was tinted red, the newly inserted keyframe would include an instance of the symbol with a tint somewhere between. We just happen to be tweening only position.

This Task was approached differently than the Yo-Yo. In the Yo-Yo we made identical keyframes at the beginning and the end, then repositioned the contents of the middle keyframe manually. In comparison, our last exercise involved establishing keyframes at the beginning and end (in different locations), letting Flash do a tween, and then adding a mid keyframe based on Flash's tween. The fundamental result (three keyframes, two tweens) was the same, but the approach taken was different.

8

Rotating in a Motion Tween

If you manually rotate a symbol in one keyframe, Flash will tween the rotation appropriately. Additionally, in a Motion Tween you can tell Flash to rotate your symbol a specific number of rotations. In the Frame panel for a keyframe set to Motion Tween, set the Rotate drop-down to CW (for clockwise) or CCW (for counterclockwise) and remember to specify a number in the Times field (otherwise it will default to 0 as in Figure 8.10). One rotation is usually plenty; any more will just cause the increments of rotation between frames to be greater. Also, notice that the default setting for Rotate is Automatic, meaning it will tween rotation if you manually rotate the symbol. The None setting will leave a manually rotated symbol in its rotated position during the entire tween. Perfectly round symbols are not usually very interesting to rotate. If you want to try rotating your Yo-Yo, consider drawing a graphic off-center in the master version of the Yo-Yo symbol.

FIGURE 8.10

In the Frame panel of a keyframe with Motion Tweening, you can make Flash rotate an exact number of turns, either clockwise or counterclockwise.

There *is* such a thing as too much of a good thing, and gratuitous animation is a fine example. There's no harm in playing with all the bells and whistles available in Flash—I'd encourage it while you learn. Just realize that to effectively communicate an idea or tell a story (which, after all, is what animation really is for), you want to refrain from superfluous animation, which can ultimately detract from your message. For every effect you want to add, ask yourself: "does this help clarify my message or not?"

Summary

Congratulations! You've covered the fundamental skills of Motion Tweening. It's fun making Flash do all the work, especially after last hour's frame-by-frame animation. If you look back at what you learned, it is pretty simple: Just set two keyframes, specify how you want Flash to tween, and you have a Motion Tween! Although it was simple, when you add Easing, Rotating, multiple keyframes, and all the ways you can modify a symbol instance (scale, rotation, position, and color effect), you have numerous possibilities.

Just because our exercises were fairly simple doesn't mean the Motion Tween is for simple effects. Actually, you should always consider Motion Tween before you choose Shape Tween (covered next hour in "Using Shape Tween to Morph"). Motion Tween is more efficient than Shape Tween, and—when used creatively—can be very effective and natural looking.

Q&A

Q **When I insert a keyframe, Flash automatically creates a Motion Tween from the previous keyframe to my newly inserted one. Why is this happening?**

A When you insert a keyframe, Flash copies the previous keyframe (the contents and the frame settings). If the previous keyframe already has been set to tween, the new keyframe will have this setting.

Q **Why can't I Motion Tween more than one symbol?**

A You can have multiple shapes inside the symbol you're tweening. But the rule says only one symbol per layer. You'll see in Hour 11, "Using Layers in Your Animation," that you need to separate each tweening symbol into its own layer.

Q **When I use the Rotation setting in my keyframe, my symbol rotates but it's very lopsided. Why?**

A The symbol rotates around its center point. You should edit the master symbol and position the graphic in the center. For more about this, review Hour 5.

Q **Why doesn't my Motion Tween follow a smooth path?**

A Motion Tween can tween more than just position. When tweening position, Flash moves directly from one keyframe to the next, finding the shortest path between two points. Wouldn't it be cool if you could draw a curve and tell Flash to follow the path you drew? You can. It's called a Motion Guide layer, and we'll cover it in Hour 11.

Q **My Motion Tween playback is very jumpy—not smooth at all, why?**

A First, if the symbol you're tweening has a changing Alpha color effect, consider a different effect, such as Brightness (Alpha causes the computer to work hard and results in slow playback). If Alpha tween isn't your problem, analyze the frame rate and the total frames in your Timeline. Revisit Hour 6, "Understanding Animation," for a review of these concepts. If your tween spans more frames, each step will be smaller.

Workshop

The Workshop consists of quiz questions and answers to help you solidify your understanding of the material covered. Try to answer the questions before checking the answers.

8

Quiz

1. According to the suggested process of creating a Motion Tween, what should you always do before inserting keyframes?

    A. Save the file because Flash is likely to crash.

    B. Assure the object in the first keyframe is a symbol.

    C. Set the instance properties of the symbol in the first keyframe to Tint.

2. When you want to edit the position of a symbol instance in a particular keyframe, what must you first assure?

    A. That the red current frame marker is in the frame you want to edit.

    B. You concentrate on the frame number you intend to edit then move the instance.

    C. That the symbol isn't red.

3. A Motion Tween requires two keyframes. When establishing that you want a tween between those two keyframes, exactly where do you make your tween settings?

    A. In the Effects panel of the symbol in keyframe 1.

    B. In the second keyframe's Frame panel.

    C. In the first keyframe's Frame panel.

Quiz Answers

1. B. Saving is always a good idea, but not really necessary. You want to make sure the first keyframe contains a symbol, because it will be copied into the new keyframe and you need symbols for a Motion Tween.

2. A. As surprising as it sounds, people often try option B (the E.S.P. method). This issue falls under a general suggestion I call "know where you are." If you want to edit frame 1, you want to make sure the red current frame marker is in frame 1.

3. C. You always establish how Flash is to tween from one keyframe to the next in the *first* keyframe's Frame panel.

Exercises

Most of the Motion Tweens we did tweened only position. Try these exercises that use Motion Tween on other properties such as Scale and Color Effect.

1. Create a bouncing ball that squashes a little before bouncing back when it hits the ground. You'll need 5 keyframes: In addition to the first keyframe with the ball up high, you'll need a keyframe for when the ball reaches the ground and another keyframe for when the ball's in a squashed position. Use Onion Skin to line up the bottom of the squashed ball with the bottom of the unsquashed ball. You need a keyframe in the down position but not squashed, and you need a keyframe at the end that corresponds to the initial position. Try using Easing where you think it helps.

2. Make a simple tween in which text tweens from entirely transparent to its normal opaque (non-Alpha) state. Consider other ways to achieve this without using the Alpha effect. Be sure to make a symbol out of your text before adding keyframes.

Hour 9

Using Shape Tween to Morph

There are several ways to keep your Flash movie small and running swiftly. Recycling symbols from the library and using Motion Tween are two of the best ways. Unfortunately, the Shape Tween we're about to learn is one of the least efficient features in Flash—your file size will grow. However, Shape Tween is pretty cool looking! There's no other way to get the "morph" effect in Flash.

In this hour you will

- Make Shape Tweens
- See alternatives to Shape Tween
- Apply Shape Hints for more control

NEW TERM A *morph* is a kind of animation that naturally changes one shape to another. It's a general term, but it's the closest common term to how Flash's Shape Tween works.

Making a Shape Tween

Shape tweens are fun because they look really cool and they're easy to create. Basically, all you do is draw a shape or shapes in two keyframes and set the tweening in the first keyframe to Shape. Let's do one now and then we can analyze it.

Task: Make a Simple Shape Tween

1. In a new file, draw a circle onstage. (Don't group anything and don't convert anything to a symbol.)

2. Insert a keyframe in frame 30 (click in the Timeline at frame 30 and select F6 or Insert, Keyframe). This will be the end of our tween, and it will match the beginning.

3. Insert a keyframe in frame 15. While the red current frame marker is on frame 15, put a little dimple into the circle: Use your pointer to first deselect the circle (click off the circle), then bring the pointer close to the edge until the cursor changes to a curved-tail pointer. Click and drag toward the center of the circle, as seen in Figure 9.1.

4. Now we just need to set Shape Tweening for the two spans. Click frame 1, hold Shift, and then click frame 15. Open the Frame panel and select Shape from the Tweening drop-down.

5. Test Movie.

FIGURE 9.1

Bending the edge of the circle in one of our keyframes; Flash will do the tweening to get here.

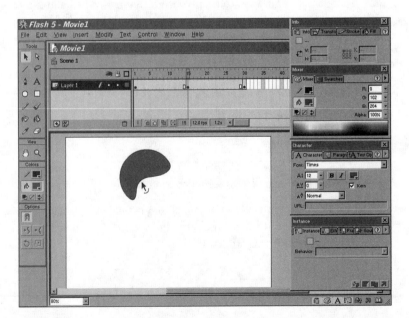

Following the Rules of a Shape Tween

Flash is unforgiving when you don't follow its rules. Luckily, the rules for a Shape Tween are very simple: no groups and no symbols. That's it! Remember this and Shape Tweens will be easy.

If you recall from Hour 2, "Drawing and Painting Original Art in Flash," text acts as if it is grouped from the beginning. This means that you can't use text in a Shape Tween unless you first break it apart (select Modify, Break Apart). Remember, too, that once text is broken apart, it's no longer editable!

9

Although there's no way around the no group, no symbol rule, you can still take advantage of some of the benefits of groups and symbols. For example, groups are often necessary to isolate parts of your drawing. You can use groups all you want while creating a Shape Tween. You just have to remember, as a last step before tweening, to ungroup everything. The same is true with symbols from your library. If you have an image in the library you'd like to use in a Shape Tween, you can—you just have to remember to break it apart before the Shape Tween will work. You can't really get around the rules, but you can break the rules temporarily while working.

Techniques and Tips

Just because the rules for a Shape Tween are simple doesn't mean it's easy to create a good-looking Shape Tween. There are several techniques to make the process easier and the results better.

Keep It Simple

If you ignore all other tips, keeping it simple is one you really should heed. It's almost as though there are no rules for a Shape Tween—as long as you don't group anything or use symbols, it will work. However, when you have a million different shapes tweening to a million other shapes, the results will look random. The two symptoms that you aren't keeping it simple are unexpected results and the "checkerboard" effect we're about to see.

Consider these unexpected results. Maybe you imagined your name morphing gradually into a circle shape, but despite breaking apart the text you got a garbled mess. Or you got the checkerboard effect in the tweened areas (as in Figure 9.2). These are likely symptoms that you're creating something too complicated for Flash. Actually, Flash is interpolating the in-between frames very accurately, but it can be very difficult to go from one extreme such as your name to something as simple as a circle. Flash will get you from here to there, but the trip might look pretty messy.

FIGURE 9.2

The checkerboard effect is the common result of a Shape Tween that's overly complex.

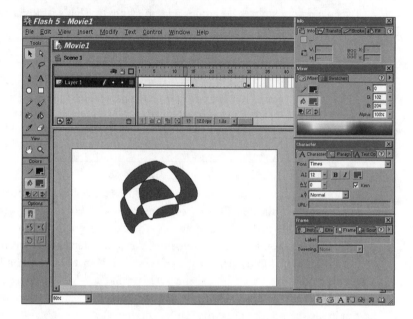

The solution is to keep it simple. Do just one thing at a time. For example, try to tween just one letter of your name into a circle. In Hour 11, "Using Layers in Your Animation," we'll see that it's easy to do several tweens simultaneously (in separate layers). We'll also see later this hour that you can help Flash by using a feature called Hints. However, the simpler the animation is, the better. You'll find that a simple animation will be easier to create and more like what you expect, and it will result in a smaller file that plays better.

Don't Mix Lines and Fills

It's best to avoid tweening between shapes that don't have the same combination of fills and lines, because the results are unpredictable. Tweening a straight line into a bent line usually works fine. But if you try to tween from a line to a filled shape, you may get unpredictable results. For an analogy, consider bending a wire. You could also start with clay and re-shape it. But if you had to turn a wire into a shape of clay it would be difficult or impossible. The analogy is similar to Flash tweening lines and fills. Flash can tween lines; Flash can tween fills; it can even tween a fill with a line. Flash has difficulty, however, when one keyframe has a line and the other has a fill (or when one keyframe has both line and fill and the other only has one). Flash does what it can to interpolate the in-between frames when you mix them, but eventually something has to give; Flash can't perform miracles.

To avoid these issues, convert the lines to fills using Modify, Curves, Lines to Fills. Better yet, keep things simple by drawing in both keyframes just lines, just fills, or both.

Stay Out of Flash's Territory

When Flash is tweening a span of frames, it colors the tweened frames in the Timeline either blue (for Motion Tween) or green (for Shape Tween). These *interpolated* frames (as Flash calls them) are what I call Flash's territory (see Figure 9.3). Generally, you should stay out of this area. For one thing, you can only draw into keyframes, so you can't draw into this territory. Also, in Shape Tweens, you can't even select objects when the red current frame marker is in this territory. (However, we saw in Hour 8, "Using Motion Tween to Animate," that with Motion Tweens you can actually grab and move symbols in interpolated frames, which adds keyframes.)

FIGURE 9.3

The interpolated frames (where Flash is responsible for doing the tweening) will be green for a Shape Tween and blue for a Motion Tween.

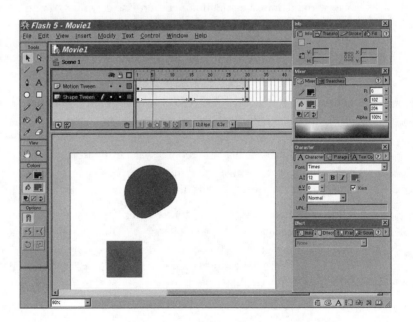

9

You can't do any harm to interpolated frames of Shape Tweens, but it can be very frustrating if you try to edit them. You can't draw into them, and you can't select objects. The best way to think of these frames is that they are Flash's territory—not yours. You are responsible for the keyframes, and Flash is responsible for the tweening.

Know When a Motion Tween Will Suffice

It's easy to fall in love with the Shape Tween. There's nothing like it. Feel free to use it when necessary. However, since Shape Tweens are inherently less efficient than Motion Tweens (the file sizes are larger and play slower), you should always choose Motion Tween when you can. If you can get the same effect with either, you should always opt for Motion Tween.

Let's say you have a shape you want to tween from a blue circle to a red square. Only a Shape Tween will suffice, because the actual shape is changing. However, if you just want to tween a blue circle into a red circle, you're much better off doing it as a Motion Tween. Draw a circle, convert it to a symbol, insert a keyframe later in the Timeline, use the Effect panel to set the tint of the circle instance in the second keyframe, and set Motion Tween in the first keyframe's Frame panel. To do the same animation as a Shape Tween, you'd draw a circle (don't convert it to a symbol), insert a keyframe later in the Timeline, then fill the circle in the second keyframe with a new color and set Shape Tweening in the first keyframe. The result is the same, but the Motion Tween method is better because you have only one master version of the circle and therefore a smaller file size.

Sometimes it's obvious which type of tween is more appropriate. If something's just moving or changing color, a Motion Tween is appropriate, while significant changes to a shape require the Shape Tween. Sometimes, however, it's not so obvious. For example, you can drastically change a symbol's shape using Rotate, Scale, and especially Skew. Notice in Figure 9.4 how several instances of the same symbol can be distorted significantly; a Motion Tween would suffice if you tweened any two of these symbols.

While you should definitely opt for a Motion Tween when you can, don't forget the keyframe techniques we learned in Hour 7, "Animation the Old-Fashioned Way." A few strategically designed keyframes can often be more effective than a drawn-out tween. We'll learn even more ways to trick the user in Hour 21, "Advanced Animation Techniques." It's what the user thinks he sees that matters—not what he actually sees.

FIGURE 9.4

Multiple instances of the same box can be drastically distorted and still used in a Motion Tween. Notice the original box in the library.

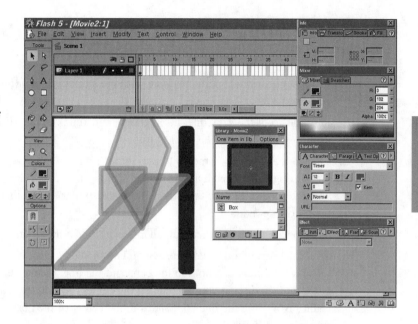

9

Refining and Fine-Tuning Your Shape Tween

Shape tweens don't always come out the way you expect. The tips we just covered are really more like rules and cautions. Even if you heed all the warnings, you still may have Shape Tween results that are anything but what you expect. Flash has a feature especially for Shape Tweening that helps you tell Flash what you really want. It's called a Shape Hint, and it can make the difference between a Shape Tween that looks like a mess and one that looks like what you had in mind.

Using Shape Hints

A Shape Hint gives you a way to tell Flash exactly how to map one point in a shape to another point during the Shape Tween. You'll want to use Shape Hints when Flash doesn't create a Shape Tween that matches what you had in mind. Let's step through how you use Shape Hints.

NEW TERM   Points inside an image are *mapped* during any tween. The term *map* refers to how one point in the starting shape corresponds to a specific point in the ending shape. Consider how every point on a printed map corresponds to a real location. A point on the map can be mapped to a real location. When Flash Motion Tweens a box from small to large, one corner of the small box is mapped to the same corner in the large box. Every point is mapped. Mapping points in a Shape Tween is more complex, so there's a feature called Shapes Hints that lets you control how Flash maps individual points.

Task: Use Shape Hints for a Better Shape Tween

1. In a new file, draw a perfect square with the Rectangle tool (just hold Shift while you drag).

2. In frame 25 of the Timeline, insert a keyframe (click in the Timeline at frame 25 then press F6 or select Insert, Keyframe).

3. Change the shape in frame 25 to a triangle. There are many ways to do this, including starting from scratch and using the Onion Skin to help line up your triangle with the square. I'd like the triangle to be as similar as possible to the square so try the following method.

4. In frame 25, draw a vertical line that doesn't touch the square.

5. Select the Arrow tool (make sure Snap is turned on), click once on the line to select it, and click and hold in the center of the line. (Make sure you have the solid circle, indicating that you've grabbed the center—if not, try grabbing the line again.) Now drag the line so it snaps in the center of the horizontal top of the square (as in Figure 9.5).

FIGURE 9.5

Dragging a vertical line while Snap is turned on lets us position the line at the center of the square perfectly.

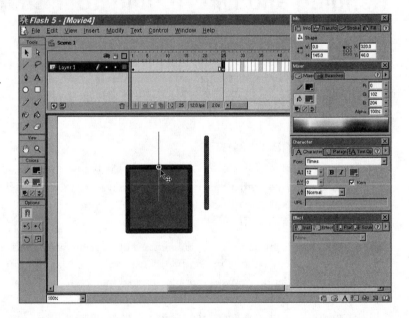

6. Click off the line and grab the top-left corner of your square. Drag it until it snaps to this bisecting line. Do the same for the top-right corner of the square.

7. Select and delete the excess portions of the vertical line.

8. Try setting the first keyframe's tweening properties to Shape, then scrub and you'll see the results. The results are probably not what you expected. Now's our chance to use Shape Hints.

9. Place the red current frame marker in frame 1 and select Modify, Transform, Add Shape Hint (or Ctrl+Shift+H).

10. Notice a little red circle with the letter *a* (a Shape Hint). Temporarily move the red current frame marker to frame 25 and notice there's also an *a* Shape Hint in this frame.

11. Make sure you're back in frame 1 and that Snap is turned on (View, Snap to Objects). Drag the Shape Hint so it snaps to the top-left corner of your square. (Notice in Figure 9.6 that it's still red, indicating you haven't really mapped this point to an endpoint yet.)

FIGURE 9.6

Although we've added a Shape Hint in our first keyframe and even attached it to our shape, it's still colored red because we haven't done so for the ending keyframe.

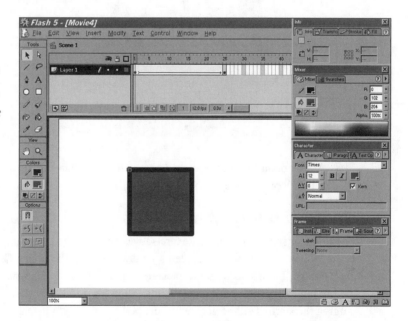

12. Go to frame 25 and position Shape Hint *a* so that it snaps to the middle of the left side of the triangle. Notice that the Shape Hint turns green, indicating that it's been mapped. Also, when you return to frame 1, the Shape Hint is colored yellow to indicate it's been mapped.

13. Scrub to see the results so far—if it looks good, you don't need to add any more Shape Hints. (It will likely look worse for this exercise.)

14. In frame 1, add a Shape Hint (Ctrl+Shift+H), which is automatically given the name *b*, and position it in the top-right corner of the square.

15. In frame 25, map this second Shape Hint *b* to snap to the middle of the right side of the triangle (similar to how *a* was mapped). See Figure 9.7.

FIGURE 9.7

Our second Shape Hint (b) is snapped to the middle of the right side of the triangle in the second keyframe.

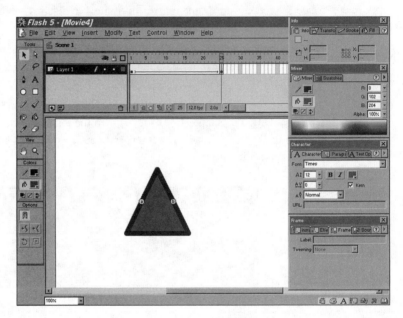

16. At this point the results should be much better than before we added any hints. Do a Test Movie to see.

Understanding Shape Hints

The time-consuming part of the exercise was creating the triangle to match the square perfectly (and this should have been a review). Adding the Shape Hints was fairly simple. Granted, I told you where to place the hints. However, it's usually pretty easy to figure out logical positions for Shape Hints. Think of it this way: You're telling Flash "this point in the starting shape goes with that point in the ending shape."

You should notice that after adding one Shape Hint you can see how the point under the hint in first keyframe hurries to the corresponding point (under the hint) in the end keyframe. Carefully watch the points while you slowly scrub.

Don't use more Shape Hints than necessary. Don't add 10 Shape Hints to the first frame and then map them all. Rather, add one Shape Hint and map it, then evaluate the results—one might be enough. Feel free to continue adding Shape Hints all day long, but realize that sometimes less work is necessary. There's no reason to add more hints than you really need.

9

There are a few more details about Shape Hints that are worth understanding:

- You can't add Shape Hints unless you are currently in the first keyframe of a span with Shape Tweening already set. In other words, you have to have a Shape Tween already and be in the first frame.

- You can use the menu selection View, Show Shape Hints to make the Shape Hints you have invisible (but they will still be used).

- Shape Hints are recognized only after they've been mapped—snapped to a point on the shape in both the first keyframe and the last keyframe. They'll change color after they've been mapped.

- You can remove one hint at a time by right-clicking. Additionally, you can remove them through the menu Modify, Transform, Remove All Hints.

- Shape Hints can be used only with a pair of keyframes! Just as tweening occurs between only two keyframes at a time, Shape Hints work between only two keyframes at a time. However, Shape Hints can't be used from one keyframe to a second then to a third. In the previous exercise, we might want to add a third keyframe where it turns into a square again. If you want Shape Hints from one keyframe to another then a third, you must have four keyframes. Use a Shape Hint from the first to the second, then from the third to the fourth. See Figure 9.8.

Reasons to Avoid Shape Tweens

I suppose the best reason to avoid Shape Tweens is that sometimes you don't need one. Shape tweens inherently create larger files (which means longer download times for your users). Consider what happens when you insert a keyframe. The content of the previous keyframe is copied into the inserted keyframe. If you have a square shape in the first keyframe and inserted a second keyframe, the result is two copies of the square. Even if you modify the second square by distorting it, you have two shapes.

Compare this to what happens in a Motion Tween if you have a symbol of a square in the first keyframe and insert a keyframe (copying the contents of the first keyframe). You have two copies of that symbol, but since it's in the library, the Flash file really contains only one master version of the square. Before you even specify the type of tweening, the two keyframes (with shapes) for the Shape Tween have created a larger file. Add to this all the subtleties that are necessary for a complicated Shape Tween, and the result is that Shape Tweens are larger than Motion Tweens (often twice as large).

FIGURE 9.8

A Shape Hint requires you have only two keyframes. To continue from one tween to the next, put two identical keyframes right next to each other. You're left with two pairs of keyframes—now you can use Shape Hints on the second pair.

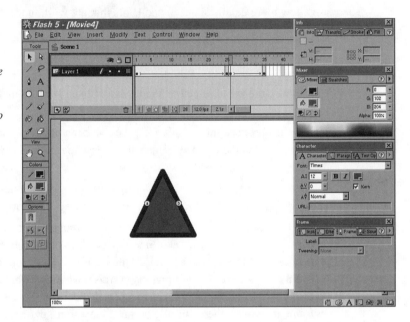

Shape Tweens are also harder for the designer to maintain. If you have a bunch of Shape Hints, it's even harder. Since Motion Tweens use the library extensively, you benefit from all the productivity features of the library (which were covered in Hour 5, "Using the Library for Productivity"). Don't use Shape Tweens unless you must.

Summary

Now that you understand Shape Tweens, you know both ways Flash can do the tweening for you (shape and motion). We learned how a Shape Tween is fundamentally unique in that it allows you to morph shapes. The only rules are that you can't have grouped shapes, and you can't have symbols. This makes Shape Tweens easy to create, but some techniques are necessary to assure the results come out as expected.

Use Shape Hints to help Flash figure out what you have in mind. Adding Shape Hints is a little touchy, but you just need to be very specific.

This is the last hour we'll spend on basic animation. It's about time to move on to fun things such as sound and interactivity. I have two parting tips as you create more and more animations on your own:

1. Although Shape and Motion Tweens can help you create an animation, sometimes the most effective animation is the most subtle. That means sometimes the best solution is frame-by-frame animation, such as we did in Hour 7.

2. Don't be satisfied with serendipitous results. Sometimes mistakes are cool looking, but try to persist in making Flash do exactly what you have in mind. Resist the temptation to accept something that's only *close* to what you want. If you take the time, you can create anything.

Q&A

Q **What causes the dotted line to appear in the green interpolated frames of my Shape Tween?**

A You either did something that contradicts the rule of a Shape Tween that you have no groups and no symbols or you don't have two keyframes. Remember that a tween is between two keyframes. You should check to make sure you have two keyframes and in each you have no groups and no symbols.

Q **My animation is acting funny. Shapes appear only in my keyframes, never in the interpolated frames. I know I did everything according to the rules because I'm not getting the dotted line. What's wrong?**

A Just because the dotted line isn't present doesn't mean you're doing everything correctly. For example, if you have some shapes in the start and the end of your tween, all will appear fine. However, if in either keyframe you have a group, text (which is like a group until it's broken apart), or a symbol, all these objects will disappear during the tween. The only time you see the dotted line is when *all* the objects on screen are groups or symbols.

Q **When I click in the green interpolated frames (Flash's territory), I can set the Frame panel Tweening setting. I thought this area was under Flash's control. Why am I given access to it?**

A You're actually accessing the previous keyframe's Frame panel. Remember that a keyframe with no tweening specifies what will be onstage at that keyframe and will remain onstage until the next keyframe. Any non-key frames after a keyframe are under the influence of the first keyframe. With tweening, it's the same: Interpolated frames get drawn by Flash, but the previous keyframe controls exactly how the tweening will act. One keyframe controls its frame and all subsequent frames until the next keyframe. The good news is that you can access frame properties of keyframes without being really careful where you click. Just be aware of which keyframe you're accessing.

Workshop

The Workshop consists of quiz questions and answers to help you solidify your understanding of the material covered. Be sure to read the explanations even if you get the answer right.

Quiz

1. What is the ideal number of Shape Hints to use for a good Shape Tween?

    A. 10.

    B. No more than 5.

    C. No more than necessary.

2. Which type of tween will result in a smaller file: Shape or Motion?

    A. Shape.

    B. Motion.

    C. It depends on how many colors are used in the file.

3. How can you use text in a Shape Tween?

    A. Text cannot be used in a Shape Tween.

    B. Make sure the text is broken apart.

    C. Make sure the text isn't grouped or in the library.

Quiz Answers

1. C. There's just no reason to use more Shape Hints than absolutely necessary. Each time you add a Shape Hint, check to see if the results are satisfactory.

2. B. It's safe to say Motion Tweens, by definition, will result in smaller files. This is important because some effects can be achieved by either a Shape Tween or a Motion Tween, but you should always opt for Motion Tweens when you can.

3. B. Text acts as if it's grouped from the start. All you have to do is use Modify, Break Apart.

Exercise

You can spend a lot of time playing with Shape Tweens. Here is an exercise that will sharpen your skills.

Create a Shape Tween from one letter to a similar shape, such as from the letter *A* to a triangle or the letter *C* to a circle. Remember that you'll have to break apart the text. Use Shape Hints to make it look the way you want. Tip: Don't try your whole name, just one letter for now.

9

HOUR 10

Including Sound in Your Animation

Sound really makes a movie come alive, but the power of audio is subtle. People often won't even notice or remember the sounds you use. But create a movie without sound (or with bad sounds), and the audience will notice right away. The effect of audio is often subconscious, and that's what makes it so powerful.

Regardless of why sound is useful, it's very important to use audio effectively because it's invariably the largest portion of your exported movie's file size. There's no reason to allow the audio to add more size than it has to. Unfortunately, there's no "Make the Audio Come out Good" button. The choice between good audio and a small file size is more of a battle than a balancing act. It's simply a matter of understanding the technology, and that's the goal of this hour.

In this hour you will:

- Import and use sounds in keyframes
- Learn audio concepts like sample rate, frequency, and compression
- Apply tricks to minimize sound's effect on file size

Importing Sounds

Flash has great support for audio but no internal way to record or create sounds. You'll either need to find an existing sound, have one provided for you, or use sound software to record or create your own. This simply means that, in Flash, you can import sounds but you just can't create them.

Two basic steps are involved in getting audio into your Flash movie. First, you need to import the sound. Then, you need to decide where and how to use it. This is similar to importing raster graphics (like you did in Hour 3, "Importing Graphics into Flash"). When you import a sound, it's stored in the Library like an imported bitmap. But a sound is not quite a symbol. Rather, the item in the Library contains all the individual properties of the particular sound (just like bitmap properties).

There are many sources for existing audio, such as clip media CDs and even Flash's Sounds Common Library (from the Window, Common Libraries, Sounds menu). You may find, however, that rather than searching existing sources, it's often easier to hire a professional musician or narrator who can provide exactly what you need. This is also true for customized graphics or photographs versus clip art. Although in the short term this may mean a much bigger investment, sometimes it's worth it. Consider that you're likely to get the perfect match for your message compared to something you find that's just "close enough" (but not quite right either). Also, you have direct contact with the artist, so you can resolve copyright issues at the start. Finally, by customizing your audio or graphics (and purchasing exclusive rights to its use), you won't risk another company using your art. Several potential problems arise when multiple parties use the same image or sound. Some other company's product or message could reflect poorly on yours, its Web site could be more popular than yours (making you look like a follower), or an image could become overused, making everyone's use look unoriginal and cliché.

Supported Formats

Flash can import digital audio in the following file formats:

- MP3
- WAV
- AIF (also called AIFF)

The only catch is that unless you have QuickTime 4 installed, when running Windows you can't import AIF, and on the Macintosh you can't import WAV. Just download and install the free QuickTime software from www.apple.com and you'll be able to import audio in any of these three formats.

People often want to know which format is best. In general, it doesn't matter. You should simply start with the best quality sound possible. Between AIF and WAV there's no inherent quality difference. A high-quality AIF file is the same as a high-quality WAV file. However, MP3 files always have some compression, so ultimately these files are not best. There are two valid reasons to use MP3s:

- Your only source is an MP3 file.
- The MP3 file you have has already been compressed (as far as you know) optimally.

MP3s won't get any worse after you bring them into Flash, but they certainly won't get any better. What's more, some MP3s aren't very good to begin with. I'd recommend avoiding MP3s as source files unless they're all you have or you're totally satisfied with their current quality.

You'll learn more about digital audio later this hour in the section titled "Digital Audio Fundamentals." For now, it's enough to know that just three sound formats can be imported into Flash. What about songs on audio CDs? CD Audio tracks aren't in WAV, AIF, or MP3 format, so you can't use them directly. Luckily, most sound-editing software provides the ability to extract music from a CD and save it in WAV or AIF format. Of course, you should realize that significant copyright concerns arise when using audio from a published CD.

Task: Import a Sound

The actual process of importing sounds into Flash is very simple. Follow these steps:

1. In a new file, select the File, Import... and then select an audio file to import. (In Windows, you'll likely find a few WAV files in the folder C:\Windows\Media; Macintosh users can run a Find for Files of Type: Sound.) You can filter the files shown in the Import dialog box by setting the Files of Type drop-down list to All Sound Formats, as shown in Figure 10.1).

2. After selecting an audio file and clicking OK in the Import dialog box, you probably won't see (or hear) anything different. However, the sound has been imported and now resides in the Library. Just open the Library window (Ctrl+L) to see it. Now that your movie contains the sound file, you can use the sound.

FIGURE 10.1

When importing audio (or any media type for that matter), you can filter the types of files listed to include just sound formats.

3. Although we're not covering how to "use" sounds in depth until the next section, it's very easy. Let's do it now. There are two basic ways to use the sound in a keyframe. One way is to drag the sound from the Library window onto the stage. However, this method requires an available editable frame (both an unlocked layer marked as editable with pencil, and the current frame marker in a non-tweened frame). The other method requires you to select a keyframe (just click under "1" in your timeline) and then open the Sound panel and select the sound you imported from the drop-down list (as shown in Figure 10.2). This list will display all the sounds previously imported into your movie.

FIGURE 10.2

The imported sound appears in both the Library and in the sound panel.

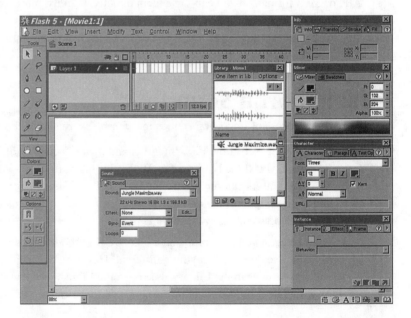

4. Test the movie, and you should hear the sound. (Of course, your computer speakers and sound card must be functioning.)

Importing Sounds from Another Library

I'm sure you'll agree that importing a sound is simple. There is, however, another way to import sounds. You can drag a sound directly from another Flash movie's Library. Either drag the sound item from one Library to the other or drag the sound onto the stage (when the current frame and current layer are open for editing). You can try this by opening the Sounds Library that ships with Flash. Make sure your Library is opened; then select Window, Common Libraries, Sounds. Position both Library windows so you can drag sounds from the Sounds Library to your file's current Library. You may notice that if you try the second method (that is, dragging from the Sounds Library to your stage), each sound will also be added to your file's library. Although a few of the sounds included in the Sounds Library are fun, this method will likely be more helpful when you want to take sounds from older Flash files you've made.

10

Using Sounds

Now that we've imported the sounds into our movie we can explore how to make them play at the correct times. There's really only one place you can use sounds in Flash: in keyframes. (One exception is adding sounds dynamically with the advanced ActionScripting method for sound objects called attachSound.) If you want a sound to play whenever the user places his or her cursor over a button, you still need to place the sound in a keyframe—it's just a keyframe in the button. Attaching sounds to a button is a little more complex and we'll cover that in depth in Hour 13, "Making Buttons for Your User to Click."

Now that we know sounds go in keyframes, we need a way to put them there. The Sound panel provides a way to control what sounds play and when they play. Flash provides other clues for you to "see" where sounds have been placed. For example, if your Timeline is long enough, you'll see a waveform for the sounds being used (as shown in Figure 10.3).

The Sound panel, however, is your best way to see which sounds have been added to which keyframe. But just like any other panel, the Sound panel displays only the sound used in the *selected* keyframe. It's very easy to misread this panel because it's easy to deselect keyframes. Figure 10.4 looks almost identical to Figure 10.3. However, in Figure 10.4, the Sound panel shows that no sound is being used., When you look closely at the Timeline there's a waveform displayed but no keyframe selected. Therefore, it's necessary to look at the Sound panel *after* you've selected a particular keyframe.

The waveform (the picture of the sound) is displayed in the Timeline. This will be helpful when you're trying to synchronize images with specific parts of your sound.

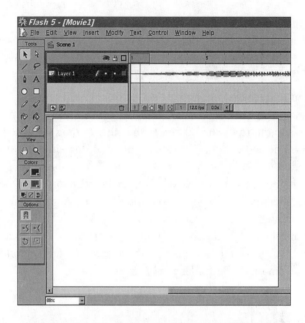

The Sound panel can be confusing. It only displays (or lets you specify) sounds when a keyframe is currently selected. Here, the keyframe isn't currently selected, so the Sound Panel displays nothing.

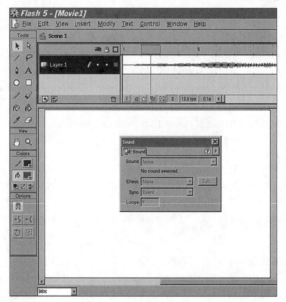

Sync Settings

Once we have the Sound panel reflecting sound for the intended keyframe, we can decide exactly how the sound should play. The most fundamental choice you need to make for each use of a sound is its Sync settings. These control exactly how a particular instance of your sound will play—or more specifically, the priority of the sound compared to the visual elements in your animation. Before you try them out, see the following list and Figure 10.5 for an explanation of each:

- *Event* is the default setting and, generally, the best performance choice, especially for sound effects and other "incidental" sounds. When Event is chosen, sounds will start to play when the keyframe is reached and keep playing until they're done. Event sounds might not coincide with visual elements the same way on everyone's machine. Sounds won't play slower or faster (that would make them sound funny), but a machine with slower graphics performance may take longer to display visual elements. Suppose you have a one-second Event sound and your framerate is 12fps. You'd expect that during the sound, 12 frames would be displayed, but a slow machine might only display six frames a second, in which case the sound would finish in one second, as you'd expect, but after only six frames have been displayed.

- *Start* is almost the same as Event, except multiple instances of the same sound are prevented. With Event, a sound can be layered on top of itself, similar to singing a "round." Think of Start as playing a sound if it's not already playing.

- *Stop* is similar to the concept of "Stop All Sounds," except it will only stop a specified sound. For example, if you import a sound called "background music" and by whatever means have it playing, when a keyframe is encountered with the same sound (background music) set to Stop, just that sound will stop. Any other sounds already playing will continue. This is a bit strange because you use the Sound panel to specify the sound (just like when you want the sound to play), but you're specifying it as the particular sound you want to stop.

- *Stream* will cause the sound to remain perfectly synchronized with the timeline. Because, again, you can't have sounds playing slowly if the user's machine can't draw frames quickly enough, Flash will skip frames to keep up. Stream sounds start playing when the first frame is reached and continue to play as long as there is space in the timeline. In other words, if your sound is three seconds long and you're playing at 12fps, the timeline has to be at least 36 frames; otherwise, part of the sound will never be reached. The benefit of this setting is that synchronization will always be the same. If you place a graphic in frame 12, it will coincide perfectly with the first second of your sound. Just remember that when you're using Stream, you have to ensure there are enough frames in the Timeline to accommodate the length of the sound. Finally, Stream sounds are previewed as you "scrub," thus making the process of lip synching possible.

10

FIGURE 10.5

For each instance of a sound you must select a Sync setting (via the Sound panel).

The decision as to which Sync setting to use isn't terribly difficult. Event should be used for any short incidental sounds—such as *rollover sounds*. Actually, I'd suggest Event for all sounds that don't require critical synchronization. Background music that just plays and loops won't need to be synchronized. Therefore, you should use Event. Start is a perfectly good alternative to Event and will simply prevent the layering of the same sound. For example, suppose you have a row of five buttons. If each button has the same rollover sound and the user quickly moves across all five, an Event sound will play once for each button. If the sounds are short enough, this is probably appropriate. However, if the sounds are quite long, they would become discordant. If you use the Start sync setting, only one instance of the sound would play at a time, regardless of how fast the user moves his or her mouse. So, basically, Start and Event are good for the majority of sounds you'll play.

NEW TERM   *Rollover sound* is a sound effect that plays any time a user places his or her cursor over a button. You'll learn about this later in Hour 13.

The Stop sync setting is very powerful. It gives you a way to stop specific sounds. It can be a little tricky to use because this method will only stop one sound per keyframe. When you learn about Actions (as you will in Hour 14, "Using Actions to Create Nonlinear Movies") you can insert the "Stop All Sounds" Action to stop all sounds at once. Depending on the situation, this may be appropriate. If you're giving the user the ability to get several sounds going at once, you'll want to learn Stop All Sounds. However, suppose you have one sound playing in the background, and when a tween starts you want a special sound effect to play (and keep playing) until the tween ends. You can put the background sound in an early keyframe and then, in the first keyframe of the tween, place the sound effect and set its sync to Event or Start. In the last frame of the tween, you can put the same sound effect but set the sync settings to Stop. This way, the sound effect will stop at the end of the tween, but the background sound will continue.

Finally, Stream is good for one thing: synchronizing graphics with sound. This is especially useful for character animation where you want a character's lips to synchronize with its voice. When trying to synchronize sounds with images, use the "scrub" technique mentioned earlier, but now with Stream sounds you'll hear the sound as you scrub. Because Stream sounds effectively lock themselves to the timeline, you probably don't want to change the movie's framerate. For example, a three-second sound will take

36 frames at 12fps. If you do some work and then change the framerate to 24fps, the same three-second sound spans 72 frames! Flash automatically spreads the Stream sound out so that it takes three seconds when you change the framerate, but Flash won't change your graphics, which will now play in 1.5 seconds. See Figure 10.6 for a before-and-after example of changing the framerate after an animation is built.

FIGURE 10.6

The same animation and sound with framerates of 12fps (top) and 6fps (bottom). Notice that keyframes and tweening are not affected, but the sound needs to take more room when the timeline is only advancing six frames per second (the audio can't expand or contract because that would sound funny).

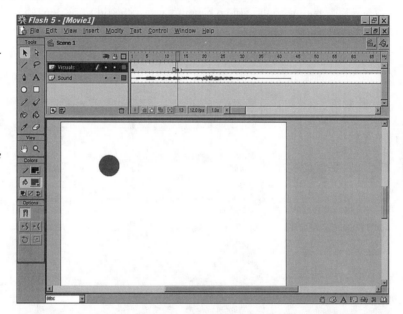

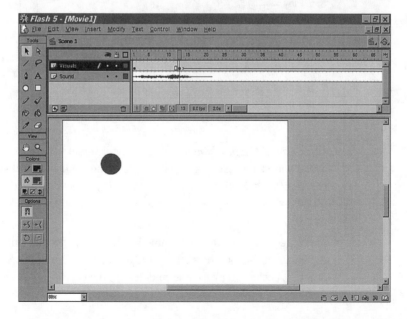

10

Effect Settings

The Sound panel provides some pretty fancy effects you can apply to a selected sound. In the drop-down list next to Effect, you'll find effects such as Fade In and Fade Out as well as Fade from Left to Right and Fade from Right to Left. In order to understand and customize these settings further, you can either select Custom from the list or click the Edit... button on the Sound panel to access the Edit Envelope dialog box, as shown in Figure 10.7.

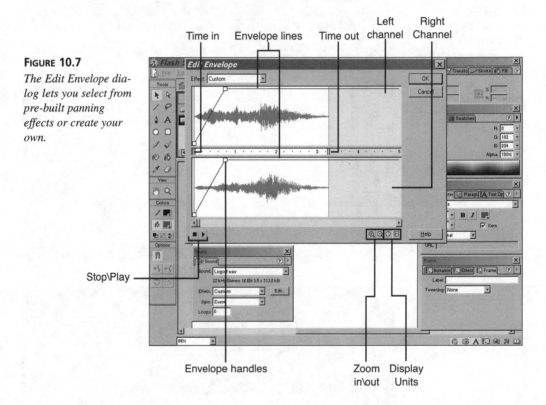

FIGURE 10.7
The Edit Envelope dialog lets you select from pre-built panning effects or create your own.

• *Left Channel/Right Channel* will display different wave forms if your original sound was stereo. Even if you only use mono sounds, you'll get the left and right channels so that you can still create *panning* effects. In the case of mono, the same sounds will come out of each speaker—you'll just be able to modify the volume of each.

• *Envelope lines* indicate the volume level at any particular time in the sound. When the line is at the top, the sound plays at full 100% volume. (Some audio tools are different because they use the middle to indicate 100% and anything higher to indicate amplified or boosted sound, but this is not the case in Flash.) If the envelope line is getting higher as you move to the right, the volume will increase.

- *Envelope handles* are like keyframes within the sound. If you want the envelope lines (indicating volume) to change direction, you'll need to insert a handle, which acts like a "pivot point." All you need to do is click anywhere on a line and a handle will be inserted. No matter which channel you click, a matching handle is placed in the other channel. A handle in one channel must match the moment in time (left to right) of the handle in the other channel. However, the volume (height) can vary between the two.

- *Time In* lets you establish the starting point of a sound. You're effectively trimming the extra sound (or silence) at the beginning of the sound file. You're not telling the sound to start any later, but the sound you hear will begin wherever the Time In marker is placed.

- *Time Out* lets you trim extra sound off the end of a sound file. Often you'll see a moment of silence at the end of a sound file, and even if you don't hear anything, it still adds to the file size! You can get rid of it by moving the Time Out marker to the left. You won't actually destroy the source sound in your Library, but when you export the movie, the unused portions of the sound won't be used (so your file stays small).

- *Stop/Play* lets you preview all the settings you've made. This is important because although the waveform can let you "see" a sound, you ultimately want to judge the effect with your ears.

- *Zoom In/Out* lets you zoom out so the entire sound fits in the current window or zoom in for a close up to control precisely how you place the Time In/Out markers or envelope handles.

- *Display Units (Time or Frames)* simply changes the units displayed (in the center portion) from time units (seconds) to frame units. Time is not as useful when you want to match your sound to a particular frame (where something visual occurs). If the display shows a peak in the music at 1 second you have to use framerate to calculate exactly which frame that translates to. With the display set to Frames, Flash will do the calculations for you.

NEW TERM   *Panning* is an effect that makes sound seem to move from left to right or right to left. It's simply a trick in which the volume for one channel (left or right) is increased while the volume for the other channel is decreased. When combined with a graphic moving in the same direction, this technique can be very effective. Imagine, for example, a car moving across the screen at the same time the audio pans in the same direction.

10

Despite all the details in the Edit Envelope dialog box, you really only have two basic ways to use it: You can either use a preset effect or make your own. Actually, you can start with a preset (such as Fade In) and then make modifications to it, essentially making a custom effect based on a preset. Use the effects in any way you think appropriate. Listen to the effect after each change by clicking the play button. Nothing you do here will affect the master sound in your library. You can actually use the same sound several times throughout your movie, with different effects in each instance.

One of the most important things to remember is that the Time In and Time Out markers can save file size. Only the sounds and portions of sounds actually used will be exported when you publish your movie. Unused sounds in the Library and portions trimmed from the beginning or end of a sound will not be exported. Trimming a few seconds off the end of a sound can mean many seconds (even minutes) saved in download time for your users. Also, changing the volume of a sound has no impact on file size, so it makes no sense to set the envelope lines to the lowest level.

Loop Settings

Finally, note the Sound panel has a field where you specify the number of loops a particular sound should play. This simply makes the sound repeat the specified number of times without any pauses. This is great for sounds that loop well.

Some sounds loop better than others. Basically, a sound that loops well ends the same way it starts. There's an art to making sounds loop. Although it's possible to import a large song and use the Time In and Time Out markers to establish a nice looping sound, it won't be easy. More likely, you'll have to find a sound already prepared by an audio engineer. A professionally prepared sound can loop so seamlessly that you can listen to it and not even notice it's looping; it will just sound like it's endless.

Also, if you have a sound that you want to loop "forever" (and you're satisfied with its loop quality), the standard and recommend practice in Flash is to just put a very large number into the Loop field. Although it seems strange, that's how you do it. If you type **99999999999**, Flash changes this entry to 2147483647 (the Max Integer). I suppose a *very* patient viewer could outlast the total number of loops, but consider that a one-second sound repeated 2,147,483,647 times takes 68 years to finish!

Task: Add Sounds and Sound Effects to an Animation

In this task we add sounds to a sample movie.

1. Select the sample file Help, Samples, Keyframing. Also, open the Sounds common library from Window, Common Libraries, Sounds.

2. Open the Library for Keyframing by selecting Window, Library (Ctrl+L). Position the two open libraries so they appear side by side as in Figure 10.8.

FIGURE 10.8

Position the Sounds common library next to the library for the Keyframing sample file so we can transfer sounds.

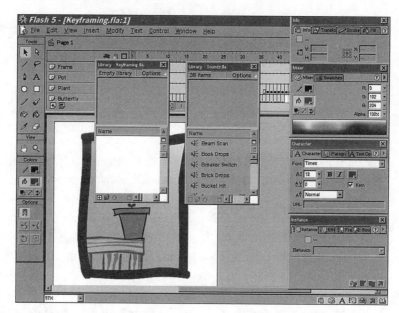

3. Drag the following sound items from the Sounds library to the Keyframing file's library: Book Drops, Smack, Visor Hum Loop.

4. Now these sounds will be available to your file but we need to put them into keyframes. Let's first make a new layer just for the sounds. Insert, Layer (don't worry if it puts the layer under all others—it doesn't really matter where it appears). Name this layer "Background Music".

5. Select the first frame of Background Music, open the Sound panel. From the Sound drop down, select Visor Hum Loop. To make it loop continuously type a bunch of nines (**99999999999**) into the Loops field. Figure 10.9.

FIGURE 10.9

When you type a high number into the Loops field the sound will play continuously.

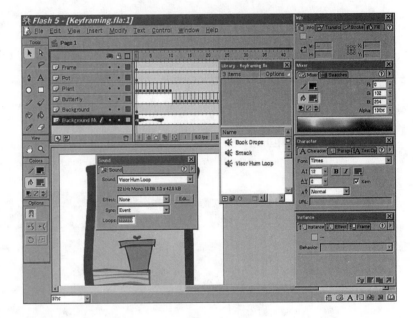

6. Select Control, Test Movie. The sound loops nicely, and it adds a bit of drama to our movie. Let's add some incidental sound effects.

7. Insert, Layer and name it "Sound Effects". We're going to insert a sound effect right when the flower catches the butterfly, which happens at about frame 40 is appropriate. In frame 40 of Sound Effects Insert, Keyframe (F6).

8. Select the keyframe you just inserted and open the Sound panel. Select Smack from the Sound drop-down. Just leave the default settings as we don't want this sound to loop.

9. Select Control, Test Movie. The Smack effect is good, but the hum keeps humming, even though the butterfly is gone.

10. To stop the hum, select 43 of Sound Effects and Insert, Keyframe (F6). Make sure you're selecting just this keyframe then use the Sound panel to insert the Visor Hum Loop again, but this time select Sync Stop to cause any instances of this sound to stop.

11. Finally, let's add a sound effect for when the butterfly is swallowed. At frame 63 of Sound Effects select Insert, Keyframe (F6), select just this keyframe then insert the Book Drops sound. Test Movie and it should be measurably better than the silent version. By the way, these sounds only add about 3K to the total filesize!

Controlling Quality and File Size

Now that you know how to incorporate sound in your movie, it's time to talk about optimizing it for export. A direct relationship exists between quality and file size. If you want the best quality sound, the file size will grow. Conversely, small file size means lower sound quality. This is just a fact. You ultimately need to make a decision as to how you balance this tradeoff. Is a high-quality sound important enough to make your audience sit through an extended download time? Is a speedy download enough to make your audience ignore a low-quality sound? You should be very deliberate in your decision-making process to end up with the best compromise possible.

While exploring this topic further, we'll first cover some digital audio fundamentals and then you'll learn how to apply this knowledge to Flash's compression settings.

Digital Audio Fundamentals

Digital sounds on the computer are not continuous. Similar to how a fluorescent light or your computer monitor flickers, digital audio is a series of discrete bursts called samples. The frequency that these samples occur is so fast that you think you're hearing a continuous sound.

Exactly how fast the samples are occurring is called the *frequency rate* (also sometimes called *sampling rate*). Naturally, a higher frequency rate (many bursts per second) sounds better than a low rate. The frequency rate of all audio CDs, for example, is 44,100 hertz, commonly referred as 44 kilohertz (KHz). Sound editing software can convert an a song to a lower rate but it won't sound as good. Why not always use the highest frequency rate possible? Simple. Each sample takes up disk space and adds to the file size. A sound with a frequency rate of 22,500Hz, for example, is *half* the size of one at 44,100Hz and may still sound good.

In addition to frequency rate, another important factor is *bit depth*. Similar to how each pixel on your computer monitor can be one of 256 colors (when the color depth is 8 bit) or one of 16.7 million colors (when the color depth is 24 bit), each sample in an audio track can be one of many sound levels (think of these sound levels as "shades of sound"). A sound with an 8-bit depth means that for every sample, the sound can be one of 256 different levels. A 16-bit sound has the potential of being one of 65,536 different levels. The higher the bit depth, the better the sound quality. (By the way, audio CDs have 16-bit depth.)

Frequency rate and bit depth are independent. One sound could have a high frequency rate (such as 44,100) but a low bit depth (maybe 8 bit). When you increase either factor (to improve quality), file size grows. To make matters worse, a stereo sound is always

10

twice as large as the same sound in mono (because it contains information in two channels). Finally, the length of the sound affects file size directly—a longer sound is larger.

There are ways to calculate the exact size impact of frequency rate and bit depth. The bottom line, however, is audio takes up a lot of disk space. One minute of CD quality sound, for example, takes about 9 megabytes! The fact that pure CD-quality sound takes up so much space is why you want to find a better way.

One solution is compression. MP3 compression, for example, analyzes the sound file and finds ways to reduce the filesize with minimal sacrifice to quality. Using MP3 compression, that same 9 megabytes of CD quality sound might get reduced to about 1 megabyte! Just like how JPG compression reduces the file size by removing parts of the image you don't notice, MP3 uses a technique to remove the parts of a sound that you're not likely to miss. Exactly how it does this, I don't know. It's magic, I guess. However, Flash can perform MP3 compression based on the level to which you'd like your sounds brought down (namely, the bit rate). The best quality MP3 that Flash 5 supports is 160Kbps. A lower number means lower quality (but also means the amount of data per second is lower). One last note: When MP3 reaches 160Kbps (or whatever level you specify), it makes its own decisions regarding the balance between frequency rate and bit depth.

Export Settings

All this theory is interesting, but how do you apply it to your sounds? You have two places in Flash where you can specify quality settings: the Sound Properties dialog box, unique to each imported sound, and the Flash tab of the Publish Settings dialog box.

Global Publish Settings

To set the default sound format for every sound in a Flash movie, select File, Publish Settings.... Make sure under the Formats tab that you've checked Flash (.swf) and then click the Flash tab (see Figure 10.10). You'll see two different sound settings in this dialog box: Audio Stream and Audio Event. Audio Stream affects sound instances using the Stream sync setting, whereas Audio Event affects sounds using the Event sync setting (it also affects sounds set to Start, although it doesn't say so). If you click the Set button, you can see all the options available, as shown in Figure 10.11. The following list provides a description of each option:

FIGURE 10.10

The Flash tab of the Publish Settings dialog box provides you with a way to set the default sound settings globally for the entire file.

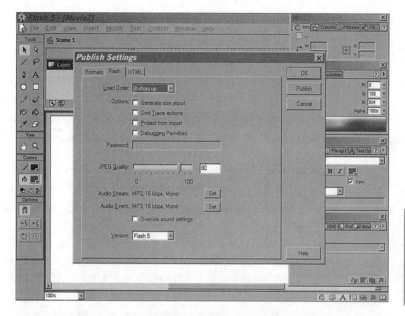

FIGURE 10.11

You can set the type of compression for all sounds in your movie from Publish Settings.

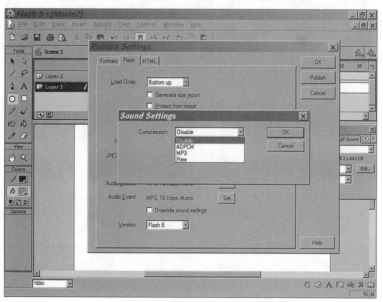

There's a Set button next to both Stream and Event so you can set the compression for sounds used each way separately. There are four choices for sound compression. With the exception of "Raw" (which is really no compression), you'll need to specify additional options for the compression you choose. For example, you can't just say "compress using MP3"—you have to specify how much MP3 compression. As each option has its own unique character, let's look at each in detail.

- *Disable* is pretty simple: It tells Flash not to export any sounds. When you select Disable from the drop-down list, there are no other options to set.

- *ADPCM* is almost the same as Raw (below), except it performs a little bit of compression. The options for Sample Rate and Convert Stereo to Mono have the same effects as discussed earlier, but the ADPCM bits specifies the level of compression. A higher number means better quality but not as small a file. Pretty much the only reason to use this option rather than MP3 is when you have to deliver your movie to the Flash 3 player (which more people have).

- *MP3* provides great compression. When exporting, always use the Quality setting "Best" because it won't affect the file size but will improve quality. However, while working, you might consider temporarily changing this to "Fast," because every time you test a movie (using Test Movie), it will go quicker. The bit rate is simply how much data per second you're letting the MP3 file take. The higher the number, the better. In theory, a bit rate of 56Kbps will be maintainable on a 56K modem, although reality is sometimes different than theory because other factors can slow the download performance. We'll explore more issues related to downloading in Hour 20, "Optimizing Your Flash Site." You really just have to test this out and keep lowering the bit rate until just before the sound becomes unacceptable. You can judge the result by testing the movie or (as you'll see later in "Individual Export Settings") you can test each sound individually.

- *Raw* leaves your sounds intact, although you do need to specify a sample rate (frequency rate). Also, if you select Convert Stereo to Mono, any stereo sounds will become half their original size.

Now you've learned how you can set the default sound settings for both Stream and Event sounds from the Publish Settings dialog box. Also note the Override Sound Settings check box. This will cause the settings you apply here to be imposed on *all* sounds in your movie, regardless of their individual export settings. You're about to see how to specify sound settings individually per sound. Override can be useful when you want to publish a single copy for a special purpose. Say you want a copy to demonstrate from your hard drive—download time isn't an issue, so you could make all the sounds play at their highest quality (Raw).

Individual Export Settings

In addition to a movie's globally specified sound settings, each sound item in the Library can have its own individual settings, which apply to every instance of that sound. Just double-click a sound in the Library (or from the Options menu, select Properties...), and you'll see the Sound Properties dialog box, as shown in Figure 10.12.

FIGURE 10.12

The Sound Properties dialog box provides individual control of exactly how a sound will be exported (regardless of the default publish settings).

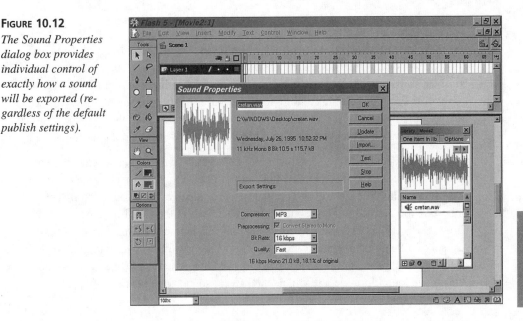

This dialog box is similar to the Bitmap Properties dialog box you studied in Hour 3. Just like how individual imported bitmaps can have their own set of compression settings, so, too, can imported audio. The choice of settings is practically identical to the settings under Publish Settings. However, in this dialog box, for each change you make, you're given details of the effect on file size and quality. Down at the bottom you'll see how much the file compresses for each change. If you click the Test button, not only will Flash perform the compression you specified, but the sound starts playing and you can hear how it sounds (similar to the Test button for bitmaps, although with bitmaps you judge the visual effect). This gives you all the information you need to decide what settings to use. You can listen to the sound while assessing the effect on file size.

The Sound Properties dialog box has a couple other items you should note. The option Default will use whatever settings you specify in the Publish Settings. Also, you have the same ability to replace sounds as you do for replacing bitmaps. For instance, if you've edited a sound in a sound editor and you want to import the replacement sound, just click the Update button (if the file has moved, you'll be asked to point to the new location). Additionally, if you want to replace a sound (without taking the trouble of reassigning every keyframe where you've already used the sound), just click Import and select the new file when prompted.

Tricks for Efficiency

Obviously the best way to reduce file size (in respect to audio) is to avoid using audio. Although this may sound facetious, it's worth consideration. You should force yourself to consider each sound you use, and if it's not adding something to your file, it's most certainly distracting because it's adding to the file size. Gratuitous sound effects are worse than gratuitous visual effects because sounds add significantly to the file size. Just be extra critical when asking yourself whether a particular sound is really necessary.

Once you've decided that a sound is, indeed, necessary, you still have ways to reduce the sound's impact on the file size. The best way is to trim any "silence" at the beginning or end of the audio. Silence still adds to the file size. Ideally, you should do this before importing the audio into Flash, but you can also do it in the Edit Envelope dialog box shown earlier. Another great way to reduce file size is to use a short looping sound instead of a long linear sound. Of course, there's a possibility of selecting a loop that can become monotonous, but you might be surprised how much "mileage" you can get from one simple loop. Sprinkle a few incidental Event sounds independent of the loop, and it can often sound very interesting.

Probably the most subjective question is "Which level of compression is appropriate?" First of all, it makes the most sense to always start with the best quality sound possible and then selectively reduce the file size and quality as appropriate. (The only exception is an MP3 file that you believe already has the best possible compression—in which case you wouldn't want to recompress it.) If you start with a bad sound, it's never going to get any better. You always want to start with top-quality sounds. Determining which level of compression is appropriate is really a subjective decision, but that doesn't mean I can't make a few suggestions. First of all, there's a common misconception that audio containing voice can withstand the most compression, whereas music can't. This is just plain false! A better generalization would be to say sounds of natural items (acoustic instruments and voices, for example) are best kept at a high quality, whereas sounds of synthetic items (such as a distorted electric guitar and synthesized keyboards) will likely be perfectly acceptable at a lower quality. This is true because any sound on the computer is fake—you're trying to make the user believe the sound is one thing or another when, in fact, it's just electronic data. When you attempt to simulate something natural, such as a voice or acoustic instrument, your audience has a good recollection of what that sound is supposed to sound like, and they'll notice if it doesn't sound right. On the other hand, sounds from an electric guitar, for example, can be distorted and still sound perfect. Ultimately, you'll still need to test each compression setting to hear how it sounds, but just remember it's easier to notice that something's wrong when a natural sound gets distorted.

One other fact: If everything else is kept equal, a mono sound will appear "cleaner" than a stereo sound. This doesn't mean that you shouldn't use stereo. Instead, simply realize that in order to maintain quality in a stereo sound, you usually can't compress as much (and add to this the fact that stereo sounds are twice as big as mono sounds). Therefore, just be absolutely sure you *need* stereo sound (and remember you can still pan the left and right channels without a stereo sound).

Summary

Flash supports audio elegantly. Including audio in your movie is a simple process of importing the sound and then deciding in which keyframe you want the audio to play. Many options are available on *how* the audio plays—for example, whether it plays and finishes naturally (Event) or whether you want it to lock itself to the timeline so images remain synchronized no matter what (Stream). You're also given sophisticated envelope controls for each instance of a sound used.

Because the effect on file size is the biggest "cost" of using audio, Flash provides a variety of compression technologies and settings to individually or globally specify the kind of compression you want to use. I'm sure you'll find MP3 the best quality, when considering file size, for almost any sound you want to use, but other alternatives do exist. If nothing else, I hope this hour has made you more deliberate and restrained when adding audio to your movies. Don't get me wrong—the power of audio is great. Just try not to abuse this power when you're given it. (Your slow-connection users will thank you.)

Q&A

Q I placed a long-running sound in the first frame of my movie. However, when I test the movie, it only plays for the first few seconds and then stops. Why?

A Probably you've set the sync (on the Sound panel) to Stream and haven't extended the timeline long enough. If your sound is 10 seconds long and you're playing at 12fps with Stream is selected, you're going to want to make sure there are 120 frames available in the layer of the timeline in which you placed the sound. An Event sound doesn't have this restriction (although it also won't have the same synchronization behavior).

Q I put a sound in the first frame of my movie, but when I click Play, I don't hear anything. I verified that my speakers were plugged in and that my computer sound level was cranked. What else could it be?

A I wish I could say that you must use Test Movie because otherwise the sound won't work. Of course, Test Movie is a better option for visualizing exactly what your users will see. However, even Play should let you preview the sound. You might check two things: First, menu Control, Mute Sounds menu should be unchecked, and the envelope settings for the sound instance should not be two horizontal lines at the lowest sound level. Second, you might check the original sound that you imported to make sure it's not just silence.

Q **With the Sound panel open, I keep trying to select my sound from the drop-down list, but it doesn't appear. I know I imported it because I can see it in the Library. What am I doing wrong?**

A The Sound panel will let you add sounds only when you have a keyframe (in an available layer) selected. (Of course if you have selected a frame after a keyframe, you've effectively selected the previous keyframe.) If no keyframe is selected, the Sound panel doesn't list any sounds. Personally, I wish the Sound panel just turned gray or something, but this is just the way it works. First, select the keyframe and then apply your audio via the Sound panel.

Q **I imported an MP3 file that was only 61KB, but when I export the movie, it becomes 900KB. I'm sure my graphics aren't that big because when I remove the sound, the file goes down to 5KB. What could possibly be wrong?**

A Most likely you're resampling the sound (as Raw) and Flash is converting the sound into the size it would have been as an uncompressed sound. Check the publish settings for Flash and confirm that you don't have Override Sound Settings selected. Then inspect the Sound Properties dialog box for the Library item of your imported sound and confirm that the MP3 settings match the original attributes of your file (shown near where the date and file location are displayed).

Workshop

The Workshop consists of quiz questions and answers to help you solidify your understanding of the material covered. Try to answer the questions before checking the answers.

Quiz

1. Which is a better quality audio format to use for your original files? AIF or WAV?

   A. AIF, because it was developed for the Macintosh.

   B. WAV, because it was developed more recently.

   C. Neither, because they both can be the same quality.

2. Where do you place sounds in order to hear them in the final movie?

   A. In the Library, in symbols, or in keyframes.

   B. In keyframes (no matter where they are).

   C. In the sound layer.

3. How do you make a sound loop forever?

   A. You can't, but you can type a really high number in the Loop field of the Sound panel, and that's close enough.

   B. Type **infinity** into the Loop field.

   C. Make sure the sound file has "loop" in the filename.

Quiz Answers

1. C. There's nothing inherently better about AIF or WAV—either can be high quality or low quality.

2. B. Sounds are placed into keyframes, either via the Sound panel (when a keyframe is selected) or by dragging the sound right onto the stage from the Library.

3. A. Although all these options seem equally goofy, the first option is the one that works. By the way, you can only type integers into the loop field, so something such as "1.5" won't work either.

Hour 11

Using Layers in Your Animation

The most interesting thing about layers in Flash is the fact that most people think they're for visual layering. It's understandable because almost every graphics editing tool has "layers" for just this purpose: to layer graphics on top of or below other graphics. Despite the fact that layers in Flash have a similar effect, that's not their real value. Rather, each layer is a concurrent Timeline. This hour you'll learn how layers primarily help you animate and, to a lesser degree, let you control visual layering. Specifically, this hour you will

- Control animation with layers
- Change layer properties for sophisticated effects
- Incorporate Guides, Motion Guides, and Mask layers

How Layers Work

If you're familiar with Photoshop, Fireworks, or almost any other graphic editing tool, you are already familiar with using layers as a visual tool to control stacking order. In Flash, layers provide the same visual effect. But we already learned graphics can be stacked if they are first grouped or turned into symbols—so why do we need layers?

The True Purpose of Layers

In Flash, multiple layers are really multiple Timelines—and that's their value. The images contained in layers are stacked above or below other layers, but their primary purpose is to provide you with separate Timelines in which you can control animations independently.

You might recall from Hour 8, "Using Motion Tween to Animate," that the rule for Motion Tweens is that you can animate only one thing per layer (and that *thing* has to be an instance of a symbol). Suppose you want two circles to approach each other. It's simple; just use two layers. Let's try something simple to get started with layers.

Task: Use Two Layers to Animate Two Circles

In this Task we'll make two circles move across the screen. One will appear to move more quickly than the other.

1. In a new file, draw a circle, select it, and convert it to a symbol (F8). Name it Circle, leave the default Movie Clip behavior, and click OK.

2. With the instance of Circle onstage, we can do a Motion Tween. To keep things from getting too complicated, name this layer Fast (indicating that the circle in this layer will move fast). To name a layer, click once in the Timeline so that it has the focus, then double-click on just the name of the layer (currently Layer 1) and type a new name.

NEW TERM   *Focus* applies to all kinds of computer buttons and fields generally. In an online form, only one field has focus at a time. That is, if you start typing, you'll be typing into whichever field currently has focus. When you tab through a form, the focus moves from one field to the next.

In Flash, several buttons and fields also reflect focus. Even the stage can have focus (indicated by a dark line around the outside of the window). If you click into the Timeline, it will have focus (indicated by a dark line). Quite often, it might not be entirely clear which window, panel, or button has the focus, but you want to be conscious of which option has focus.

3. Because our Timeline only has one frame so far, position the instance of Circle on the left side of the stage. Then click the cell in frame 31 of the Fast layer. Select Insert, Keyframe (F6).

4. Make sure that the red current frame marker is on frame 31 and move the circle all the way to the right side of the stage.

5. To make a Motion Tween, either right-click on the first keyframe and select Create Motion Tween or access the first keyframe's Frame panel and select Motion from the Tweening drop-down. Most of this is a review of Hour 8.

6. Let's create a new layer. Either select Insert, Layer from the menu or click the Insert Layer button at the bottom left of the Timeline (see Figure 11.1). Before we forget, let's name this new layer Slow, the same way we named the other layer Fast (in step 2).

FIGURE 11.1

The Insert Layer button at the bottom left of the Timeline is a quick way to insert a new layer (just like using the Insert, Layer menu options).

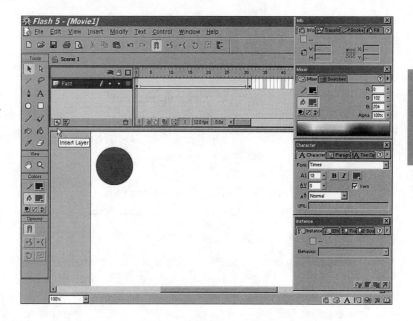

11

7. From this point forward, you want to be conscious of the layer in which you are currently editing (that is, know where you are). You can only be in one layer at a time, which is indicated by the pencil icon in the layer (see Figure 11.2).

8. Now we're going to copy an instance of Circle from the Fast layer and paste it in the Slow layer. Click an instance of Circle (to select it) and copy (Ctrl+C). By clicking an object onstage from the Fast layer, you cause that layer to become active. Before you paste, make sure you make Slow the active layer by clicking the word Slow, then paste. Position the copy of Circle you just pasted on the left side of the stage, but not right on top of the other one.

FIGURE 11.2

The pencil icon indicates which layer is currently active (in this case, Slow).

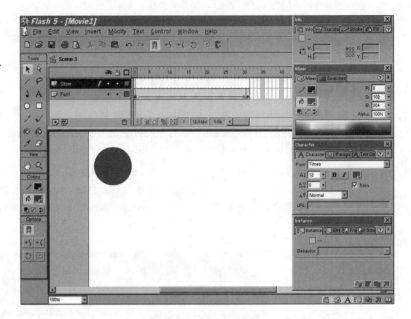

9. To keep things straight, tint the instance of Circle in the Slow layer. Select it and, from the Effect panel, select Tint and then select a color different from the other circle.

10. In frame 31 of the Slow layer, select Insert, Keyframe. Move the instance of Circle in frame 31 over to the right side of the stage (but not as far to the right as you moved the circle in the Fast layer).

11. You can now set a Motion Tween for the first frame of the Slow layer. Test the movie, and you see two circles moving across the screen—two things animating at once!

12. Leave this file open for the next task.

The earlier discussion shouldn't suggest that layers are to be avoided. Just the opposite—feel free to use as many layers as you need, if only for visual layering. Although a Flash file with hundreds of layers might take a long time to open when editing, all those layers are combined upon export (not unlike Photoshop's Flatten Image command). Although layers are useful for organization and stacking purposes, they're absolutely *necessary* for animation effects.

Layer Properties That Help You Edit

We've already seen how the pencil icon indicates which layer is currently being edited. Other icons in the Timeline will indicate layer properties that can be modified. Check out Figure 11.3 for a quick overview of these properties, and then we can discuss each in detail.

FIGURE 11.3

Layer properties that can be modified.

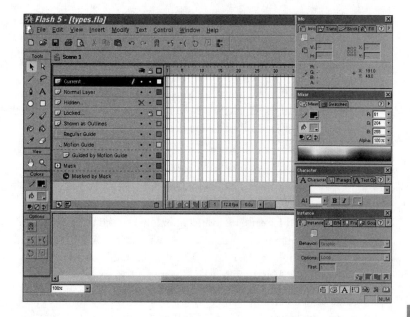

Figure 11.3 shows almost every variation of layer property. Here's a quick introduction to each one:

- **Layer Name** lets you name any layer whatever you like. You'll stay organized better if you take advantage of this feature and name layers logically.

- **Show/Hide Layer** allows you to hide the contents of any individual layer temporarily by clicking on the dot beneath the eye. If you click the Eye button on top, you'll hide or show all layers. Remember that this affects only what is seen while editing, because exporting a `.swf` turns all the Layers to Show.

- **Lock/Unlock Layer** lets you individually lock or unlock layers selectively (or all at once) .

- **Show Layer as Outlines** lets you view the contents of a layer as outlines, almost like making it invisible but not as extreme. Similar to Show/Hide, this setting affects only how the layer appears to you (the author). The outline color can be changed through the Layer Properties dialog (available if you double-click the Layer Outlines button or the Layer Type icon, such as the Page Curl on the far left).

- **Normal Layer** is the plain page curl. This is the default type of layer.

- **Regular Guide Layer** is a special layer into which you can draw anything you want (usually shapes to help align graphics or notes to other team members). Everything contained in a Guide layer is excluded from export when you create a `.swf`, so it won't show up in your final file, nor will it add to file size.

- **Motion Guide Layer** acts like a Regular Guide (they're both guides, after all); however, a Motion Guide layer contains a line to which you associate a Motion Tween, which is in a Guided layer (see below). This is how you make a Motion Tween follow a path.

- **Guided Layers** are available only if the adjacent layer above it is set to Motion Guide. In the Guided layer, you can create a Motion Tween that follows the path drawn in the Motion Guide layer.

- **Mask Layers** let you place any shape or non–Movie Clip symbol that will define the visible (and nonvisible) portion of the layer below it, which is set to Masked. Just like a mask you put on your face, in a Mask layer you draw where you want "holes" in the mask.

- **Masked Layers** are available only when the layer directly above is set to Mask. The contents of a Masked layer will be invisible except in areas where objects are placed in the Mask layer. You won't see this effect until you test the movie or lock both the Mask and Masked layers.

Some of the icons indicating layer properties (in Figure 11.3) are easy to access, whereas others involve several steps. We'll look at guides and masking layer properties later this hour. For now, let's look at the easy ones: Show/Hide, Lock/Unlock, and Show as Outlines.

Task: Experiment with Hiding and Outlining Layers

1. Open the file created in the previous Task and scrub a little to recall how it plays.

2. How do you know which circle is in which layer? If they intersect the same area, you'll see one in front of the other. Move the current frame marker to frame 1. By just looking, you can't really tell which one is which. You could read the layer name that you wrote—but Fast and Slow aren't very clear and, besides, you could have made a mistake. Because the layers contain the same symbol, it's even more difficult to tell. To figure it out, we can temporarily change the Show/Hide option for one layer at a time. Try clicking the eye at the top of the Timeline. Notice that this hides every layer. Click the eye again, and they'll all be shown again. To hide just one layer, click the dot under the eye in the layer of your choice. Click the dot in the Fast layer. Not only do you see a red X over the dot (when it's hidden), but everything onstage from that layer is hidden (just temporarily). By process of elimination, we can figure out which layer is which by making one invisible.

3. Make all the layers visible again, and we can determine which Circle is which another way, using outlines. Click the square button on the top of the Timeline (see Figure 11.4) to Show All Layers as Outlines. This should make the contents onstage appear in outline form. Hopefully, they appear in different colors so that you can tell them apart.

FIGURE 11.4

The contents of layers can be viewed in outline form.

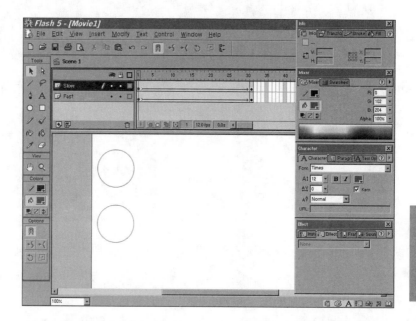

4. If both layers are showing up in the same color, just double-click the Show Layer as Outlines box for one layer. If you click the button once, it toggles between the Outline and Normal views. When you double-click, you're taken to the Layer Properties dialog, similar to that shown in Figure 11.5. Alternatively, you can single-click a layer (to make it active) then select Modify, Layer. We'll cover this dialog more later, but for now, select a different color from the Outline Color swatch and then click OK. The outlines in that layer should have a different color now.

So far this hour, you've learned two things about layers. First, extra layers let you animate more than one thing at a time. Motion tween in particular can animate only one instance per layer. If you want two items to use Motion Tween at once, you must put each animation in a separate layer.

Second, you learned how several layer properties allow us to distinguish and change layers individually. Using Show/Hide, Lock/Unlock, and Outlines, it's quick and easy to change them. Remember, though, that the layer properties we've explored so far (including Name) have no visual impact on what the user sees—changes to these properties are only for you, the author. Even a hidden layer will be visible to the user. There are more properties, which we're about to study, but the ones so far can be considered temporary.

FIGURE 11.5

All layer settings are shown in the Layer Properties dialog (accessible from Modify, Layer or by double-clicking the Page Curl icon or the Show Outlines icon).

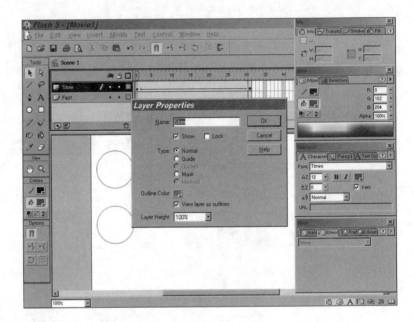

Layer Properties for Visual Effect

The three remaining layer properties (Guides, Motion Guides, and Masks) are very powerful. Unlike the layer properties covered so far this hour, these will have a lasting visual impact on your user. Using these layer properties is more involved than simply clicking an icon in the Timeline. However, when you see what they can do, you'll understand why it's worth the additional effort.

Guide Layers

Guide layers become invisible when you export the movie. I said we'd be covering layer properties with lasting effects, and the first one we look at is something that becomes invisible. However, guides are very useful and, if you use them correctly, they can have a huge impact on what your audience sees, even though they won't be exported with the movie.

Why would you want something you draw to be excluded from export? There are two primary reasons. One reason to use Guides is for *registration* purposes. Into a Guide layer, you can draw lines or shapes to which other objects can snap for consistent positioning. Maybe you want a title to appear in several sections of your movie—if you draw a horizontal line into a Guide layer, all the titles can be snapped to this line. But when the movie is exported, no one will see that line.

Another reason for Guide layers is that you might have lots of visual content that you keep onstage for personal reference or notes to others in your group. If it's all in a Guide layer, you'll see it only while authoring. Similarly, you could have a layer of an animation that—at the last minute—you decide to remove. Instead of actually removing the entire layer, just change it to a Guide layer. It will still be there if you change you mind later, but otherwise no one will see it.

NEW TERM *Registration* refers to alignment. In commercial printing, registration is critical because each color is printed separately. Registration marks are used to line up all the plates precisely. In multimedia, it serves much the same purpose. For example, if you're looking at several pages of text, if they're all registered the same, you won't see text jumping all over the screen between pages.

11

Task: Use a Guide Layer to Define the Off-Limits Area

1. Suppose we're building a presentation that includes onscreen text and a graphic frame that provides borders. We'd like to position the text onscreen without overlapping the borders. A shape in a Guide layer can serve to define the areas safe for text.

2. In a new file, first draw a filled box the size of the stage. Then use the Pencil tool (with the Pencil Mode set to Smooth) to draw an enclosed irregular box within the box you just drew. Select the center shape with the Arrow tool and delete, as seen in Figure 11.6. Select the entire shape and convert to symbol (call it Frame Shape). Name this layer Registration. This will become our Guide layer.

3. Select Insert, Layer and name the new layer Interface. On this layer, a copy of the Frame Shape will tween into place late in the Timeline (which will better demonstrate the need for Guide layers). First select the instance of Frame Shape on the Registration layer and copy. Then go to frame 30 of the Interface layer and select Insert, Keyframe (F6). Verify that the current layer is Interface (if not, click the layer name) then Edit, Paste In Place (Ctrl+Shift+V) on frame 30.

FIGURE 11.6

*This will become our
Guide layer.*

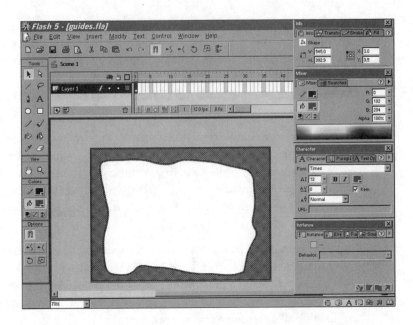

4. Click frame 40 of the Interface layer and select Insert, Keyframe (F6). Now move
the current frame marker to frame 30 and scale the instance of Frame Shape much
larger so that you can't actually see the borders onscreen (as in Figure 11.7).
Finally, set Motion Tween in the Frame panel for frame 30. (Scrub to see that the
Frame Shape won't appear until frame 30, when it tweens from outside the stage.)

FIGURE 11.7

*The first place Frame
Shape appears is in
frame 30. Here we
scale it larger than the
stage so it will appear
to tween from outside.*

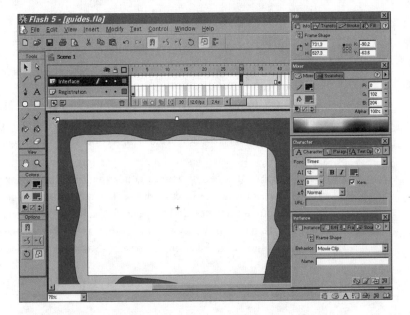

5. Click in frame 40 of the Registration layer. Select Insert, Frame (F5) to make this layer last as long as the other layer. Now click the Layer Outline button for Registration (so that only this layer shows as an outline). Scrub from the beginning of the movie to the end. Notice that the outlined Registration layer gives a clear idea where the Frame Shape will eventually appear, so that we can avoid placing text in that area. However, if you select Control, Test Movie, you'll see that the Registration layer is visible the entire time. Until we change this layer to a Guide layer, it will export with the rest of the movie.

6. To make the Registration layer a Guide layer, just access the Layer Properties dialog by either double-clicking the Page Curl icon to the left of the layer name or (with the layer selected) selecting Modify, Layer from the menu. In the Layer Properties dialog (shown in Figure 11.5 earlier), select the radial button for Guide, the check box for Lock, and the check box for Show Layer as Outlines; then click OK.

7. Insert a new layer (select Insert, Layer) and name this layer Text. Verify that all your layers are normal except Registration, which is a Guide. (If they're not, access each layer's properties individually and set them appropriately.)

8. In frame 1 of the Text layer, create a block of text with a moderately large font size, such as 40. Type as much text as you can, being careful not to exceed the borders shown in the outline in the Registration layer. (See Figure 11.8.)

9. Test the movie. You may want to turn off Loop from the Control menu while it's playing.

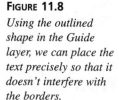

FIGURE 11.8

Using the outlined shape in the Guide layer, we can place the text precisely so that it doesn't interfere with the borders.

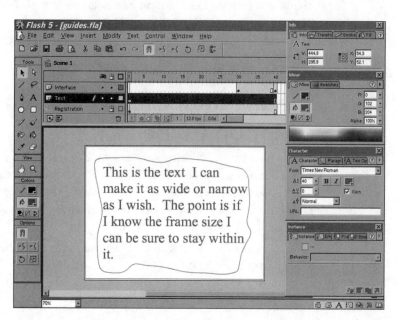

In the previous Task, we created a Guide that defined a safe area on screen for the Frame Shape that hadn't arrived onscreen yet. You may have other shapes that don't appear unless certain conditions are met. For example, if you have buttons that in their Over state expand with large graphics or include a drop-down effect, you may not want other elements onstage to be placed where they will be covered up by the button. You could copy the shape from the button's Over state and paste it right in the Registration layer. If you want to leave reminder notes to other team members or to yourself, those could be entered into a Guide layer as well. The idea is you can put anything you want into a Guide layer, and it won't export with the movie.

Using a Guide layer for registration, as we just experimented with, is nice because you can use any shape, group, or symbol in the Guide layer. The features of Guides (under the View menu) are confusingly similar: Vertical and horizontal lines are dragged from the rulers on any side of the stage (View, Rulers must be selected from the menu)—as we did in Hour 2, "Drawing and Painting Original Art in Flash." Guides become almost identical to using lines in a Guide layer (provided you've selected View, Guides, Snap to Guides).

Motion Guides

If Guide layers are useful, Motion Guide layers are indispensable! A Motion Guide is actually a regular Guide layer that happens to have an adjacent layer (below it) set to Guided. The exciting part is that a Motion Tween in the Guided layer will follow any path drawn in the Motion Guide layer. That means you can draw an s-shaped line in a Motion Guide, and then the Guided layer can include a Motion Tween that follows the shape. Similar to a regular Guide, a Motion Guide will be invisible to the user. The thing to remember with Motion Guides is that two layers are involved: the Motion Guide layer and the Guided layer.

Task: Create a Bouncing Ball Animation Using a Motion Guide

1. In a new file, draw a bouncing line (using the Pencil or Pen tool). This will become the path our ball will follow (see Figure 11.9). You can draw straight lines and then bend them and snap them together. Just make sure it's one continuous line in the end. You don't have to make it a perfect shape, because this is only going to be a Guide (and thus, invisible).

2. Double-click the Page Curl icon to access the Layer Properties dialog (or select Modify, Layer from the menu).

FIGURE 11.9

A pretty simple drawn line will be used as a Motion Guide (for a tween to follow).

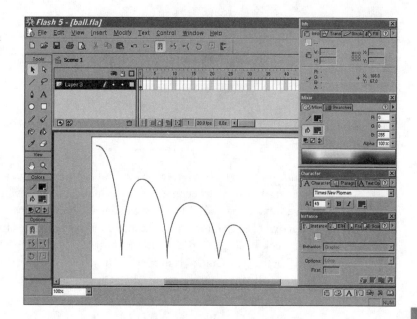

3. Name the Layer Path, lock it (so we don't mess it up), and change its type to Guide. (Notice that there's no Motion Guide option here.)

4. Insert a new layer by clicking the Insert Layer button at the bottom left of the Timeline or by selecting Insert, Layer. Name this new layer Ball.

5. Most likely the inserted Ball layer will appear above the layer Path. We're going to make this new layer Guided (meaning that it can follow the drawing in our Path layer). A Guided layer has two requirements: It must be directly below the layer guiding it, and its Layer Properties Type must be set to Guided. We can change the layer stacking by dragging layers around. Go ahead and drag the Ball layer down (so it's just below Path).

6. Notice that not only did this change the layer order, but it also caused the Ball layer to be Guided. You can see this because Path now has a slightly different icon (the arch), Ball is indented, and a dashed line separates the two, as shown in Figure 11.10. This is what we want, but you might not be so lucky to have everything fall into place like this (depending on exactly how you dragged around the layers). Additionally, when moving layers around, you might not want Flash to change all the layer properties for you. If that's the case, perform an Undo so that you're back to where just the Path layer was a Regular Guide (with the cross icon) and the Ball was above it. We're going to do the same thing again the hard way so that you know how it works.

11

FIGURE 11.10

The Motion Guide layer (Path) has a special icon, and the Guided layer (Ball) is indented. A dashed line separates the two layers, indicating they're related.

7. This time, drag the Path layer above the Ball layer. Nothing changes except the layer order. We can't just change the Path Guide layer to a Motion Guide (which is what we want in the end). Instead, we can make the Ball layer Guided (now that it's directly under a Guide layer). Access the layer properties for the Ball layer (double-click the Page Curl or, with the layer selected, choose Modify, Layer). Notice that the type Guided is available. Only when the layer just above this layer is a Guide will you see this option. Click Guided and then click OK.

8. Now we're going to create the animation and snap it to the guide. Into frame 1 of Ball, draw a circle and make it a symbol (called Picture of Ball). Now, in the Ball layer, click in frame 50 and insert a keyframe (F6). Notice that the Path layer doesn't live this long. In the Path layer, click in frame 50 and insert a frame (not a keyframe) (F5). Go back to frame 1 of the Ball layer and create a Motion Tween (by right-clicking the first keyframe in this layer or selecting Motion from the Tweening drop-down in the Frame panel).

9. One final step will make the ball actually follow the path. You need to snap the instances of Picture of Ball to the path for both keyframes of the Ball layer. Go to frame 1 of the Ball layer (with Snap turned on), grab the center of Picture of Ball, and snap it to the beginning of the path drawn in the Path layer. Go to frame 50 and snap the center of the Picture of Ball instance to the end of the path drawn in the Path layer. Test the movie. The ball should follow the path.

Consider what took all the time in this exercise. It was really just learning about changing layer properties, as well as some mechanics of how they need to be ordered. All you do is draw a path, make it a Guide layer, make a new layer that's Guided, do a Motion Tween, and snap the instance in each keyframe to the drawn path. (Sounds pretty easy when I say it like that but, really, that's all we did.)

Let's quickly explore one other option for Motion Guides. The Frame panel for a Motion Tween includes an option called Orient to Path. The effect of this option is that the instance being tweened will rotate toward the direction it's traveling. You can see the effect of this option best when the symbol isn't perfectly round. We can change Picture of Ball temporarily to see this effect. From the Library window, you can access the master version of Picture of Ball. In the master version, just draw another little circle next to the circle (don't let it touch, because you want to be able to remove it later). Back in your main scene, you can look at the Frame panel for the first keyframe of Ball (make sure that you're in the scene, select the first keyframe, and then bring up the panel for Frame). Select the option Orient to Path and then view the results by clicking Play. Turn off Orient to Path (in the first keyframe) to see the difference.

By following the previous bouncing ball exercise, we purposely stepped in every possible pitfall so that we could learn how to recover. However, it happens to be much easier with the Add Guide Layer button. If you've already drawn your ball, the Add Guide Layer button (see Figure 11.11) will automatically add a new layer, make that layer a Guide, and make the current layer Guided. It attempts to do several steps in one move, but it can be difficult to use. (The exercise we just did avoids this feature in order to learn all the steps involved.)

FIGURE 11.11
The Add Guide Layer button just to the right of the Insert Layer button will do several things with one click.

Masking

If Guides are useful and Motion Guides are indispensable, well, Masking is unbelievable! It's really a different feature entirely. Masking is similar only in that it's a layer property, and you need at least two layers: one for the Mask and one that gets Masked (similar to Guide and Guided). The graphical contents of the Mask layer will determine which parts of the Masked layer will show through. It's as if you're drawing the holes to see through in the Mask layer.

The basic orientation is similar to the Motion Guide/Guided layer arrangement. For Masking, you first specify one layer's Type property as Mask. Then, you'll find the Masked setting available when you access the layer properties for a layer directly below the Mask layer. However, you won't actually see the masking effect unless you test the movie or lock all the layers involved.

Task: Use Masking to Create a Spotlight Effect

1. First let's create the spotlight and its motion. In a new file, draw a filled circle and convert it into a Movie Clip symbol called Spot.

2. Name the layer in which the Spot instance resides Spot Motion.

3. Insert a keyframe in frames 10, 20, and 30. In frame 10, move Spot to a new location and move it again for frame 20. (Leave 30 to match frame 1.)

4. Set up Motion Tweening in frames 1 to 10, 10 to 20, and 20 to 30, either with the right-click method or from the Frame panel.

5. Change the Spot Motion layer's Type property to Mask. Double-click the Page Curl icon for this layer to access Layer Properties.

6. Notice that the Page Curl icon changes to the Mask icon (Figure 11.12). Lock the Spot Motion so that we don't accidentally change this layer.

FIGURE 11.12

Our Mask layer (Spot Motion) no longer has the Page Curl icon—after you change its type to Mask, the icon looks different.

7. Now we can insert a layer below this and change its type to Masked. Press the Add Layer button and the new Layer might appear above the Spot Motion. That's fine, but first name the new layer Buildings.

8. In order for Buildings to be Masked, it must be below the other layer, so click and drag down the Buildings layer. If you get lucky, the Buildings layer will automatically change to Masked (and you'll see an icon like the one shown in Figure 11.13). However, it's easy to do by hand, too. If you must, access Buildings Layer Properties and change the type to Masked (which will be available only if the next layer above it is already set to Mask). The result should resemble Figure 11.13.

FIGURE 11.13

The Masked layer Buildings has a special icon; it's indented, and a dashed line separates it from the Mask layer above.

9. In the Buildings layer, draw lots of boxes (make them different colors and resemble buildings).

10. It should work. However, you'll only see the mask effect if you test the movie or lock all the layers. Change the background color of the movie to black (select Modify, Movie from the menu).

11. As interesting as this looks, there's something missing. It's actually the way a spotlight would look in space where there's no atmosphere. The black background is too dark. Let's make another layer with a dim version of the buildings to make this more believable.

12. First, select all the boxes you drew in Buildings (you'll need to make sure that this layer is unlocked to select it), and convert them into a Movie Clip symbol called Building Graphic.

13. We'll be putting another instance of Building Graphic into a new layer. Create a new layer (click the Add Layer button). Name the new layer Dim Buildings.

14. At this point, you should analyze the Type property of each layer (which is easy to see by its icon). Chances are that the Dim Buildings layer is also Masked. One Mask layer can have several layers that are being masked. We want Dim Buildings to be Normal, but only after you move it down below Buildings. If Buildings is no longer directly under the shadow of Spot Motion, it will also revert to Normal. Drag the Dim Buildings layer down below Buildings, and then set the Type property for Dim Buildings to Normal.

15. Copy the instance of Building Graphic and paste in place (Ctrl+Shift+V) into the Dim Buildings layer. Hide all layers except Dim Buildings (so we're sure which one we're affecting). Then access the Effect tab while Building Graphic is selected. Choose Brightness and set the slider to –40%.

16. Looks great, eh? We didn't need to create this Dim Buildings layer to learn about masking, but it's a nice touch.

There are several things you simply cannot do with masks. Here are a few limits (and some workarounds). You can't have more than one symbol in the Mask layer. When you need multiple objects (like two holes in the mask), be sure to Modify, Break Apart everything in the Mask layer. Also, you can't combine Guides and Masks. Recall that Motion Guides involve a pair: the Guide and the Guided. Similarly, masking involves a Mask layer and a Masked layer. You can't combine them directly to have, for instance, a circle following a Motion Guide and masking the contents of the layer below it. Finally, when you place a Movie Clip symbol in a Mask layer, it actually behaves like a Graphic symbol. We'll see more about what that means exactly in Hour 12, "Animating Using Movie Clip and Graphic Symbols."

11

You can do some sophisticated stuff with masking. For example, you could edit the master version of Spot and maybe cut out part of the fill (using the Lasso tool). The Masked layer will show through only where there's something in the Mask layer. Unfortunately, this is an all-or-nothing situation. That is, your mask is either on or off. You can pull off the effect of a graduated mask by putting the graduation in the Masked layer (because it won't work in the Mask layer).

This exercise was a case of moving the mask. Quite often, however, you'll find situations in which the mask should remain still and the Masked layer is the one moving. Suppose you're building an animation of someone sitting inside an airplane, and you want the effect of clouds passing by the window. If you had a wide picture of clouds, you could easily do a Motion Tween to make it pass by. Without masking, you'd have to cover up the left side and the right side (surrounding the window) with graphics of the inside of the airplane. These carefully sliced covers would need to be in a higher layer (to cover up the picture), and it'd be more work than it needed to be. With masking, all you need is a Mask layer with the exact shape of the window and a Masked layer containing the tween of your wide picture. This is a case of the masked part moving and the mask staying still. Just realize that anytime you want to cut out part of another image, you can do it without really cutting anything. Masking has amazing potential for visual effects.

Summary

We covered a lot of material for something that appears to be a simple interface component—layers. It's hard to say that layers aren't primarily for visual stacking, because that's exactly how they work. Remember that grouping shapes (or, better yet, putting them in the Library) also lets you stack them (within one layer). However, sometimes it's more convenient to create separate layers.

Layers are useful for more than creating the layering effect, however. The number one rule of Motion Tweens requires that only one object (an instance of a symbol) be tweened per layer. If you want more things to animate, just put them in their own layer.

We also discussed layer properties, how entire layers can be hidden or locked at will, and how the Show Layer as Outlines feature gives us a way to view the contents of any layer as an outline. Those properties are accessible right in the Timeline.

The Guide Layer property excludes an entire layer from export but keeps it in the source Flash file for any purpose, including registration. Motion Guides let us pair up the Guide layer with a Motion Tween (in the lower layer) to follow a drawn path. Finally, Mask layers (paired with a Masked layer) give us a way to hide all portions (except those we indicate) of another layer.

Q&A

Q I have one layer set to Mask and another to Masked. When I add a new layer, it automatically became masked. However, if I change the new layer to Normal, it causes my old Masked layer to become Normal too. What gives?

A Masking involves two layers: one Mask and one Masked. They must be directly adjacent, with the Mask layer on top of the Masked layer. If the new layer you added is between the two, changing it to Normal will require the old Masked to be Normal, too. You've got to get that new layer out of the shadow of the mask before changing it to Normal. Often you can't even drag the layer down (it just stays in the shadow of the Mask). You can usually drag it up above the Mask, and it will change to Normal; then you'll likely be able to move it back down (below the Masked layer) with success. However you must maneuver it, just realize that both the Mask/Masked and Motion Guide/Guided features require at least two adjacent layers.

Q Why is the Type setting I want grayed out in the Layer Properties dialog?

A It depends on which setting you want. You can't just make a layer Masked unless the layer right above it is already a Mask layer. Similarly, layers with tweening can't just be turned to Guided unless there's a Guide layer directly above. Sometimes you have to follow a different sequence to satisfy these rules.

Q I made a Guide layer and then I made a 40-frame Motion Tween. I was careful to set the layer's properties so there's a Motion Guide above my Guided layer. However, when I try to attach the contents of frame 40 in the Guided layer to the Guide, the Guide is missing. Why?

A It is likely that the duration of the Guide layer is less than 40 frames (probably just 1 frame). All you need to do is extend that layer by selecting Insert, Frame from the menu. Don't use Insert Keyframe, because that would be necessary only if something is changing visually in that layer—and you probably just want the Guide to remain static.

11

Workshop

The quiz and exercise are designed to test your knowledge of the material covered in this hour.

Quiz

1. If you draw into a Mask layer and the content of the Masked layer is unaffected until you test the movie, what is the problem?

   A. No problem. There's no way to see the effect of masking until you test the movie.

   B. You need to hide the Masked layer.

   C. You need to lock both layers.

2. How many layers can be masked by setting one layer to Mask?

   A. One. If you want two layers to be masked, each must have its own mask.

   B. As many as you want.

   C. None—it's the other way around; one Masked layer can have lots of Mask layers under it.

3. Where is the one place where being efficient (like using the Library) is not especially important?

   A. Nowhere in Flash. You should always be efficient.

   B. In Guide layers, because they don't export with the movie.

   C. In layers you hide, because they're hidden.

Quiz Answers

1. C. Although testing the movie does reflect the actual effect of Mask layers, you need to lock all layers involved to see the effects. (You should still get into the habit of testing the movie, which is always the best way to see your movie as the user will.)

2. B. One Mask can shadow as many Masked layers as you want. It actually appears to happen outside your control sometimes when adding layers. Masked layers have a special icon, and the layer name is indented.

3. B. I suppose you should always be efficient, but Guide layers aren't exported with the movie, so they won't hurt the user in the any way. Also remember that hiding a layer only hides it while you're authoring (just do a Test Movie to see).

Exercises

1. Try this masking exercise. Create a Mask layer containing filled window shapes, and in the Masked layer place a large image (imported or created in Flash) of the sky and some clouds. Motion tween the image to create the effect that the sky is passing by (in the windows). Remember that each window will likely need to be broken apart, since they're in a Mask layer (and there can't be more than one symbol).

2. How can you make a Motion Guide in the shape of a circle? Suppose you want an object to follow a circle during its **Motion Tween**. An enclosed circle for a Motion Guide won't work. However, in the Guide layer you can create an outline of a circle, then cut out a very small segment. Snap the object in the Guided layer to the start of the circle, and in another keyframe snap the object to the other end of the circle. Try this out.

11

HOUR 12

Animating Using Movie Clip and Graphic Symbols

When you see what Movie Clip symbols can do, you'll be blown away. Inside a Movie Clip, you can create an animation and then animate an instance of that clip. This means that, for example, you can create a rotating wheel clip, then animate the rotating wheel so that it not only rotates but moves across the screen as well. Symbols, as a general concept, should not be new to you. We learned quite a bit about them in Hour 5, "Using the Library for Productivity," when we studied the library. Probably the biggest benefit of symbols is that, while you keep one master version in the library, you can use as many instances of the symbol as you like throughout your movie with no significant impact on file size. You should also recall from Hour 8, "Using Motion Tween to Animate," that whatever you tween must be some kind of symbol. I'm sure you've also noticed that, any time you create a symbol, Flash asks if your symbol should have the behavior of a Movie Clip, Button, or Graphic. Next hour we'll learn all about Buttons, but this hour we'll learn as much as we can about animating with Movie Clips and Graphic symbols.

This introduction doesn't try to summarize Movie Clips because there is so much to say it would fail to cover everything. The biggest goal this hour will be to understand Movie Clips and how they compare to plain old Graphic symbols.

Specifically, you will

- Learn how to make and use Movie Clips
- See that a Movie Clip is a symbol with its own independent Timeline
- Learn how Movie Clips are fundamentally different from Graphic symbols
- Discover that Movie Clips are addressable.

Movie Clip Behavior

Some people wrongly think that Graphic symbols are only for when the symbol contains just one frame and Movie Clips are only for when you have multiple frames. You can work this way, but there's more to it. For example, say you make a Graphic symbol of a wheel (a circle with lines for spokes). You can then use an instance of your Wheel symbol inside a Movie Clip called Rotating Wheel—where the Wheel symbol rotates. Then the Movie Clip can be used in the creation of a Car symbol (which is a Graphic symbol because the car itself won't need multiple frames). Finally, the Car symbol can be animated across the screen, and both wheels will rotate the whole time. Don't worry if this is confusing; we'll do an exercise presently to make it clear. Just remember that you don't need to consider Movie Clips only when the symbol is to have multiple frames.

Creating a Movie Clip

Making a Movie Clip is like making any symbol. We're going to first create an animation inside the Movie Clip. Then when we tween an instance of the clip, it will tween as well as animate. Specifically, we'll make a wheel, then use an instance of that wheel to create a rotating wheel. Finally, we'll use two rotating wheels to create a car symbol. We'll animate the car (and see its wheels rotating, too).

Task: Use a Movie Clip to Make a Rotating Wheel

1. Draw a circle with a few lines crossing it. Don't make it perfectly symmetrical—that way we'll be able to see it rotate, like in Figure 12.1. Select the entire shape and select Insert, Convert to Symbol (F8). Name it Wheel, leave it the Movie Clip behavior type, then click OK. We're going to make a Movie Clip of the wheel spinning next, but we need a plain wheel first—remember that we can't Motion Tween anything but symbol instances.

FIGURE 12.1
This Wheel symbol will be easy to notice when it's rotating.

2. Onscreen you should have an instance of the Wheel symbol. Select the onscreen instance and convert it to a symbol. Select Insert, Convert to Symbol (F8), name it Rotating Wheel, make sure you leave Movie Clip as the behavior, then click OK. I know we already had a symbol, but consider what converting to symbol does—it takes what's selected and puts it into the library. In step 1 we put a shape in the library. In this step we took an instance of the Wheel and put it in the Rotating Wheel symbol.

3. Now let's go inside the master version of Rotating Wheel. Simply double-click the instance onscreen. In the address bar you should see Scene 1: Rotating Wheel. If you now single-click to select the instance (inside Rotating Wheel) you should see Wheel in the Instance panel. This just means that Rotating Wheel contains an instance of Wheel.

4. Great, now we can do a simple Motion Tween inside the master version of Rotating Wheel. Click in frame 20 and insert a keyframe (F6). Select the first keyframe and from the Frame Panel select Tweening Motion, Rotate CW 1 time.

5. Go back up to the scene. You should see an instance of Rotating Wheel—though now it has a 20-frame rotation you can't see. Do a test movie and see that it rotates.

12

6. Now create another instance of Rotating Wheel by either copying and pasting this instance or dragging another from the library. Position the two Rotating Wheels side-by-side and then use the Brush tool to draw the car body. Select everything and convert it to a symbol called Car (leave it with Movie Clip behavior).

7. You can now insert a keyframe at frame 30 (in our main Timeline), then in frame 1 set Frame Panel to Tween Using Motion. Move the instance of Car in either frame 1 or frame 30 and you should be able to see the car move when you scrub (just like any other Motion Tween). You'll have to test the movie to see the wheels rotate, however.

If you aren't familiar with nesting symbols, this exercise might be a little confusing. Review Hour 5 if necessary. We worked from the specific to the general. We made a Wheel symbol, and we made a Rotating Wheel symbol that contained Wheel because we needed a symbol *inside* Rotating Wheel to do a Motion Tween. Then we used two instances of Rotating Wheel in the creation of the Car symbol.

Compare Movie Clip Symbols to Graphic Symbols

It makes no difference whether your master symbol is a Graphic or a Movie Clip. This affects only the default behavior for instances dragged straight from the Library. What matters is the behavior of the instance onstage. If you drag a Movie Clip from the library, it will start with the Movie Clip behavior, but you can change it (for a given instance) to Graphic using the Instance panel, as seen in Figure 12.2. It's the instance behavior that matters.

Multiframe instances set to Graphic behavior have a few unique options. The First field in the Instance panel lets you specify which frame (within the symbol) will appear first. Additionally, the Options drop-down provides a choice between Loop, Play Once, and Single Frame. By combining these settings, you can vary exactly how an instance behaving like a Graphic appears.

Suppose you have two instances of a Rotating Wheel that uses 20 frames for one rotation. You could use both instances as Graphics and set both to Loop, but on one, set the first frame to 10—they'd both rotate continuously but they'd be offset by 180 degrees.

FIGURE 12.2

An instance onstage (regardless of the master symbol's default behavior) can have any behavior you select from the Instance panel.

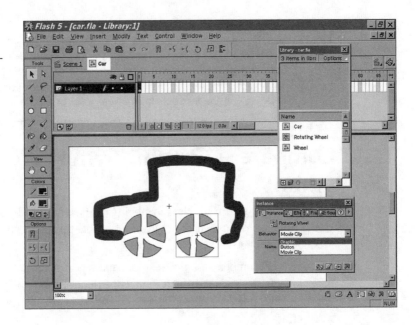

If you compare the options in the Instance panel for a Movie Clip, you'll notice only one seemingly minor field for Name. It really isn't minor at all, as you'll see in the section "Addressable Movie Clip Instances," later in this hour and again in Hour 14, "Using Actions to Create Non-Linear Movies." For now, just realize that you can name instances individually in the Instance panel.

If the only difference was a few settings in the Instance panel, we could do exercises with Loop, Play Once, and Single Frame, and that would be the end of it. However, Graphic symbols differ in another major way. Multiframe Graphic symbols (even when set to Loop) become locked to the Timeline in which you place them. For example, a 10-frame Graphic symbol placed in frame 1 of a Timeline will display frame 1 in frame 1, frame 2 in frame 2, and so on. If you use this Graphic symbol in a Timeline that's only 5 frames long, the instance of the symbol will display frame 5 when it gets to frame 5 but go no further. It's locked to the Timeline.

Instances behaving as Movie Clips are independent. They always play all their frames and loop. Think of a Movie Clip as marching to the beat of its own drummer. A 10-frame Movie Clip doesn't care if it has 10 frames to live, 100 frames, or just 1 frame. It'll play all its frames when it can, like the Rotating Wheel used in creating the Car in our first exercise.

12

Just because a Movie Clip has an independent Timeline doesn't mean you can change the framerate. "Marching to the beat of its own drummer" doesn't mean you can have independent framerates. You get one framerate for an entire movie. There are some advanced tricks to simulate framerate changes, but the fact remains that there's only one framerate per movie.

Task: Compare a Graphic Symbol to a Movie Clip Symbol

1. In a new file, select Insert, New Symbol (Ctrl+F8), name it Numbers, select Movie Clip for the behavior, then click OK. (Notice that this takes you inside the master version of Numbers.)

2. In frame 1 of Numbers, use the Text tool and type 1 near the center of the screen. Insert a keyframe in frame 2 and change the onscreen number to 2. Continue inserting keyframes and changing the contents to match the frame number all the way to frame 10.

3. Get back to the main scene (make sure you're not still in Numbers) and drag an instance of Numbers onto the stage from the Library. Select Control, Test Movie (Ctrl+Enter) (remember, Test Movie is the only way to see Movie Clip animation). All 10 numbers appear in sequence, even though we used only 1 frame of the main Timeline.

4. Back in the scene, insert a frame (not a keyframe) in frame 5 (click frame 5 then select Insert, Frame or F5), which really just extends the life of this Timeline. Test movie again and you should see no change.

5. Drag another instance of the Numbers Movie Clip onto the stage. For just this instance, change the behavior to Graphic. That is done by selecting the Instance panel while the instance onstage is selected. With the instance still selected, make sure the Options field is set to Loop. Now test the movie again.

6. If it's playing too fast, try a lower framerate. The result is that only frames 1 through 5 of the Graphic instance are displayed, while the Movie Clip continues to run. Back in the Timeline, try scrubbing back and forth in the main scene. Although the Graphic symbol shows only the first 5 frames (it has only 5 frames to live), it also gives you a good preview while scrubbing.

7. One last thing to try while you're testing the movie is to select Control, Stop. That stops the red current frame marker from advancing, but notice that the Movie Clip keeps right on playing. The Graphic is locked to the Timeline into which it's placed, while the Movie Clip plays independently.

There are a few additional points to notice. First, Movie Clips always loop. (There's no Play Once option.) In Hour 14 we'll learn how to create an ActionScript that says "stop at the last frame." But because of this, Movie Clips are sometimes extra work. Also, it may seem like a drag that only Graphic symbols are previewed when you scrub, but there's good reason for this. Graphics are previewed because they're locked to the Timeline, and therefore Flash knows exactly how they'll play. Movie Clips play at their own rate (and can be started or stopped any time through scripting). Therefore, Flash has no idea exactly how they'll play and can't give you a preview. If nothing else, just remember to always Test Movie if you want to see what the user will see.

When to Use Movie Clips

Generally, use Movie Clips for everything you can, even if it's just a static (single-frame) graphic. We'll see later that Movie Clips contribute less to the file size than Graphic symbols, so using them is almost a no-brainer. However, there are some reasons to use Graphic symbols instead.

Multiframe Graphic symbols are appropriate any time you really need to preview while you're working. The fact that Movie Clips don't preview when scrubbing can be a real hassle. For example, if you're synchronizing lip movements in a character, you probably want to use multiframe Graphic symbols. Also, a Movie Clip's automatic looping means more work putting a script to make it stop into the last frame if you don't want it to loop. Also, it's so easy to specify a First frame using multiframe Graphic symbols that it's hard to resist this feature. Using scripting in Movie Clips to do this is more complicated and definitely more work.

While the Graphic symbols lock themselves to the Timeline (making synchronization easier), there are difficulties to overcome as well. A common problem arises when the number of frames in the symbol doesn't match (or divide evenly into) the number of frames where you place it. For instance, if we use Graphic symbols for our Rotating Wheel in the first exercise, we have to make sure the Car symbol has exactly 20 frames for the wheels to fully rotate. If the car has 1 frame, the wheels won't spin. If the car has 10 frames, you'll see half the rotation, and then it will repeat. A Movie Clip, in contrast, will continue to play regardless of how many frames it is given. If your animation has a different number of frames than your Timeline, either use Movie Clips or make sure the Graphic symbols have the appropriate number of frames. It's usually much easier to use Movie Clips, because they're more flexible.

12

This discussion shouldn't distract from the main reason to use either, which is that you want to create a Motion Tween. You can use Motion Tweening only on an instance of a symbol. If the symbol you're tweening happens to have multiple frames, so be it. By nesting clips inside of clips, you can create very complicated effects that would be very difficult to create by hand in one Timeline. So while either a Graphic or a Movie Clip qualifies (as a symbol instance) for Motion Tweening, the difference is that a Movie Clip animates on its own time, and it doesn't matter how much space you provide in the Timeline where it is used.

Subtleties of Movie Clips

We've already discussed the biggest difference between Movie Clips and Graphic symbols—a Movie Clip's Timeline is independent. Obviously there's more. Movie Clips are addressable, in that you can use Actions to direct messages to individual instances of a Movie Clip, such as a Stop Action. Also, Movie Clips are usually smaller than Graphic symbols, in that file size is minimized.

Addressable Movie Clip Instances

Remember that the Instance panel provides a place to name a Movie Clip (see Figure 12.3). What's the point of naming an instance if the symbol already has a name in the library? It provides a way to name each instance onstage with a unique name. Only then can we address individual Movie Clips. Think about how you address a person. You first say his name, then you tell him what you want. If you want him to stop, you say "Joe, stop." This is the concept of addressing, which we'll cover more in Hour 14.

Do you recall how the Movie Clip kept animating even when we stopped the Timeline in the last exercise? Stopping the Timeline is like yelling stop into a crowd. Simply saying *stop* isn't enough. You have to say "Hey, Movie Clip 1, you stop." But you can't talk to an individual instance unless that instance has a name. We'll do much more than tell Movie Clips to stop.

FIGURE 12.3

The Instance panel (when set to Movie Clip) gives you a way to name a particular instance onstage.

Don't confuse the master name for a symbol in the library with the instance name for just one instance onstage. Every item in the library must have a unique name, but symbols in the library exist just once. You can drag as many instances of a symbol as you need to use throughout the movie. Any instance with its Behavior set to Movie Clip can be given its own instance name, regardless of the properties of the master in the library. If the name is unique (different from any other instances), you can address it directly. People often think that since the master in the library has a name, the instance does, too. The truth is that an instance has no default name.

File Size Savings

Movie Clips (especially those that contain nesting of other Movie Clips) are smaller than Graphic symbols. You only need to do a few tests to prove this. Let's say you have a line and you make it a Movie Clip. Use that line to create a square (make the square a Movie Clip). Use four instances of the square clip to make another Movie Clip (called Four Square). Continue this for several more nestings. Export the movie and note the file size. Try it again using plain Graphic symbols (which, by the way, would be perfectly appropriate since there are no multiframe symbols in this case). Compare how much bigger the file is using Graphics! When I conducted the above test between two otherwise identical files, the one using Movie Clips was one tenth the size of the other! This example alone could mean the difference between a site that downloads in 10 seconds and one that takes nearly 2 minutes!

Flash lets you scrub to preview the effects of a Graphic instance, and this is a clue as to why they're bigger. Scrubbing works because Flash knows exactly how a Graphic instance will behave. With Movie Clips, Flash doesn't know exactly because Movie Clips can be addressed dynamically. We haven't seen this yet, but Movie Clips can start and stop (and more) during runtime. Flash waits until it's playing the movie to decide how the Movie Clip will perform.

12

When you export the movie, Flash calculates exactly how the Graphic symbol will act. This is known as *prerendering* the Graphic symbol, and it takes a bit more disk space to contain that information. Prerendering means that the file plays a bit more swiftly. But when you have symbols inside of symbols inside of symbols, all that nested prerendering starts to take up file space. As a result, Graphic symbols are bigger.

The lesson here is that you should almost always opt for Movie Clips unless you're taking advantage of one of the benefits of Graphics.

NEW TERM *Runtime* refers to the point at which the user is watching your movie (as well as when you're testing the movie). You can do almost anything while authoring but, once you export the movie, you're limited to what's possible at runtime. A lot of things get locked down—for example, you can't change the framerate at runtime.

The way I'm using *render* refers to the work that the computer must do to draw everything onscreen. Some text and graphics are rendered ahead of time. Prerendering may take a long time but, by doing the work ahead of time, playback speed is quicker. Most digital video is prerendered. In Flash, some graphics get prerendered and others are rendered on-the-fly during runtime. Generally, rendering on-the-fly takes more processor power (though it's seldom enough to overwhelm the user's machine).

Summary

This hour didn't contain a lot of new material. You already knew two big concepts: how nesting symbols works and how symbols can be used for both Motion Tweens and efficiency. When doing Motion Tweens, maybe you tried to make the symbol a multiframe symbol. Now you should understand that you can do that and that there are options as to whether the multiframe symbol you're tweening is behaving like a Movie Clip or a Graphic.

You can't scrub when using Movie Clips, or at least you won't see them animate until you run Test Movie. This is another reason to avoid Movie Clips when you really need the capability to scrub—such as for lip synching. Also, after you do a couple of file size tests, you'll remember that Movie Clips are fundamentally smaller. Finally, the fact that only Movie Clips can be given an instance name will prove, in the long run, to be the most significant attribute of Movie Clips.

Q&A

Q I did the Car with Rotating Wheels exercise, but when I first made the Rotating Wheel symbol I forgot to specify the default behavior as Movie Clip. I went back to the library to rectify this error, but it still doesn't work (the wheels don't rotate). Why not?

A Changing the properties of the item in the library affects only any new instances you drag from the library, which will have the properties of the master in the library.) However, instances already in your movie will have the same behavior they started with. Your instances of the rotating wheels are behaving like Graphics. Go to where they're used (inside the Car symbol) and, with the Instance panel visible, select each wheel. Then change the Behavior setting to Movie Clip.

Q I can't find the Loop Once option on the Instance panel for a Movie Clip I have onstage. I swear I've seen it before. Where is it?

A You could have seen Loop Once in the Instance panel, but not when a Movie Clip was selected. Only instances behaving as Graphics have this option—which is a good reason to use Graphic symbols. Of course, when you become accomplished in ActionScripting, you'll find ways to achieve the same effect when using a Movie Clip—though it still may take more work than simply using the option available to instances of Graphics.

Q I keep reading (in this book) the phrase "instances behaving as Graphics." Why don't you just say "Graphic symbols"?

A There's a difference. The master symbol has one default behavior, which you can change by clicking the library's Option menu and selecting Properties. However, each instance onstage can be changed to something different from the master that spawned it. An instance always starts the same as its master. But not only can each instance be changed (to behave like any type), changing the master has no affect on instances already onstage.

Workshop

The Workshop consists of quiz questions and answers to help you solidify your understanding of the material covered. Try to answer the questions before checking the answers.

Quiz

1. How many frames can you use inside a Graphic symbol? How many inside a Movie Clip?

    A. One frame for a Graphic symbol, as many as you want for a Movie Clip.

    B. As many as you want for either.

    C. It doesn't matter how many frames you use in the master symbol, only whether the instance behaves like a Graphic, which can have one frame, or a Movie Clip, which can have as many as you wish.

2. What happens if you name two symbols in the library the same? What about naming two Movie Clip instances the same?

    A. You can't do either.

    B. You can't name two symbols the same, but there's no problem naming two instances the same.

    C. You can name two symbols or two instances the same, but it's a bad idea because Flash might lose one.

12

3. Since Movie Clips use much less file space, is there any reason to use Graphic symbols?

   A. No. You should avoid them always.

   B. Yes. Graphic symbols enable you to synchronize Graphics to the Timeline and sometimes even make the file play faster.

   C. Yes. Graphic symbols are easier on the eyes because they're prerendered (and antialiased).

Quiz Answers

1. B. You can use as many frames as you want in the creation of Movie Clips or Graphics. Depending on where you use Graphics, though, you may need to concern yourself with the number of frames the instances are given to live.

2. B. Though there's no problem naming multiple instances the same, it may become a problem when you try addressing just one, such as when George Foreman addresses one of his many sons named George, Jr. But there's certainly no rule against it.

3. B. Some people actually agree with A (Graphic instances should be avoided), but for truly varied applications, using Movie Clips to simulate Graphic symbols can be problematic. Plus, who cares how big the file becomes if you're not delivering to the Web? Finally, if something saves you a *ton* of time in production, it could be worth the cost (in larger file sizes)—especially if the cost doesn't turn out to be terribly significant.

Exercises

1. Despite all the negative talk about Graphic symbols, here's an activity that practically requires them.

   Create an animation of a steam engine train. First, make a Graphic symbol of just the stack. Animate the smoke stack, possibly by using a shape that starts out normal, Shape Tweens to frame 5 where it's bulging, frame 6 where it's extra tall and expels smoke, and frames 7 through 10, where it's normal again.

   Use the stack symbol in the creation of the train itself (be sure to give the train exactly the same number of frames as the stack). Bring the train into the main Timeline and Motion Tween it across the screen. By scrubbing, you'll be able to judge where the clouds of smoke appear.

   In another layer, add symbol instances of clouds, which will appear and stay in the same location as they Motion Tween to 0% alpha. Try this by using Graphic symbols for everything.

2. Create an animation of a Ferris wheel.

   First, make the passenger car a Movie Clip so that you can animate it. Inside the One Rotation Graphic symbol, use a circular motion guide to Motion Tween the passenger car one full rotation in about 28 frames.

   Now place 10 instances of One Rotation inside a 36-frame Movie Clip named Ferris Wheel. For each instance of One Rotation, access the Instance panel and specify the First frame for each. Start one on frame 1, the next on frame 4, the third on frame 7, and so on. In the end, you'll have 10 cars rotating in the same manner but starting at different locations.

12

PART III

Adding Interactivity and Advanced Animation

Hour

HOUR 13

Making Buttons for Your User to Click

Now that you've learned how to create basic drawings and simple animations in Flash, we can move on to what's possibly the most compelling attribute of Flash—interactivity. A plain linear animation can be quite powerful on its own. When you add interactivity, though, the user is engaged. They become part of the movie. In this hour and the next, you'll learn how to add interactivity to your movies.

The most straightforward way to add interactivity is by adding buttons. This way, your users can click a button when they feel like interacting—maybe they want to stop and start an animation at will. Or maybe you'd like them to be able to skip ahead past an introduction animation.

Flash makes it easy to create very sophisticated buttons using any shape. Additionally, it's easy to add visual enhancements, Animation and sound effects! This hour you'll learn how to create the visual elements of buttons. Then, in Hour 14, "Using Actions to Create Non-Linear Movies," we start making the buttons do things.

There's plenty to do with buttons. In this hour, you will

- Create a simple button
- Create multi-state buttons, which include a *down state* and an *over state*
- Create buttons with advanced features such as animated states and sound effects
- Control exactly what area on a button is clickable, or how to create invisible buttons

NEW TERM Button *states* are simply the different visual versions of a button as a user interacts. For example, all the dialogs that appear in Flash contain an OK button. That button has a *down state*—what it looks like when a user clicks on it—which is slightly different (visually) from the normal up state for the button. The buttons you create in Flash can also have a down state. Actually, you can easily create an over state too (which is the visual look of the button while the user puts his cursor over it). For example, all the tools in Flash have an over state that looks like a raised box. You'll learn to create this kind of effect too.

Making a Button

Any time you create a new symbol, you must specify the Behavior as a Graphic, Button, or Movie Clip. So far we've only chosen Graphic or Movie Clip. To create a button, it's actually no more difficult than selecting button—but, of course, we'll look at it in more detail.

Task: Make a Super Simple Button

1. In a new file, draw an oval or rectangle that will become your button.
2. Choose the Arrow tool and select the entire shape.
3. Convert this shape to a symbol by selecting the Insert, Convert to Symbol menu option(or by pressing F8).
4. Name your symbol **MyButton** and make sure that you select the Button option for Behavior and then click OK.
5. Test your movie (by using the Control, Test Movie menu option or Ctrl+Enter) and notice the way your mouse cursor changes when you place it over the button (as shown in Figure 13.1). You can close the movie that's being tested, but leave open the source file as we'll add to it in the next task.

FIGURE 13.1

Any shape can be used as a button. The user's cursor changes to a hand when they're over it.

This looks easy, doesn't it? Even though we did make a button, it probably falls short of your expectations in two general ways: It doesn't look like a button (with various states), and it doesn't act like a button. (Currently nothing happens if you click your button while testing the movie.) We'll address the issue of making the button *do* something in Hour 14. For now, though, let's make our simple button look better by adding an over state and a down state.

Task: Add Multiple States to Your Simple Button

1. In the file containing your super simple button (created previously), double-click the instance of the button to be taken into the master version of this symbol. By the way, if you're having trouble clicking the button because you keep getting the hand cursor every time you go over the button, select the menu Control, and make sure that the menu item Enable Simple Buttons does not have a check mark next to it.

2. Now that we're in the master version of the MyButton symbol, you should notice that this symbol has only four frames—and instead of being numbered, they're named Up, Over, Down, and Hit (see Figure 13.2). You can call these frames by their numbers (1–4) or by their given state names. Into each frame, we'll draw how we want the button to appear for various states. The Up state already contains how the button looks normally.

FIGURE 13.2

Inside a button symbol, you'll see four named frames.

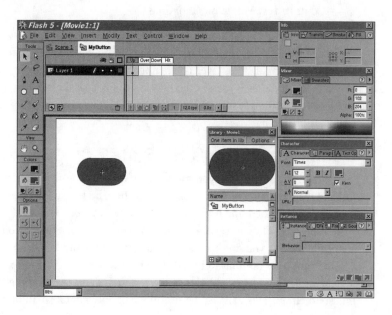

13

> Up state contains the visual look of the button in its normal state. Over contains the look for when the user hovers his cursor over the button. Down is when they click. Hit is a special state in which you place a visual representation of what portion of the button you intend to be clickable. This is what the user must "hit" in order to see the Over and Down states.

3. In the Over state, we want to draw how the button will look when the user's cursor hovers over it. To create an Over state, insert a keyframe into the second frame of the button. (Click in the Timeline under Over and press F6 or select Insert, Keyframe from the menu.) Select the Paint Bucket tool and a color similar but slightly lighter than the color currently filling the rectangle shape. Fill the shape in the Over state with the lighter color.

4. Insert a keyframe in the Down state frame. (Click in the Timeline under Down and press F6 or select Insert, Keyframe from the menu.)

5. Select the entire contents of the Down frame and—using the arrow keys on your keyboard—nudge the shape down and to the right three pixels (click three times with the right arrow, and three times with the down arrow).

6. We're done editing the master button, so let's get back into the main scene (either click Scene 1 at the top left of the Timeline or select Scene 1 from the Edit Scene clapper at the top right of the Timeline) and test the movie (by selecting the Control, Test Movie menu options).

This task proves you can create a pretty advanced button with very little effort. The various states contain the graphics for how the button will look in different situations: Up is the button's normal state, Over is when the user passes his cursor over the button, and Down is when the user presses the button. In this task the states only changed the color and location of the graphic, but you can put anything you want in each state (and you will later this hour).

Defining a Button's Hit State

While editing your button, you might have noticed that there are four states. In addition to Up, Over, and Down, there's one called Hit. The Hit state is never visibly seen by the user. It defines where the user must position her cursor to show a button's Over state, or where she must click to see the button's Down state. Imagine if you had a doughnut shaped button. If you don't set a Hit state, the user wouldn't be allowed to click anywhere in the hole (similar to Figure 13.3). However, if you inserted a keyframe and drew a solid circle (no doughnut hole) in the Hit frame, the user could click anywhere within this solid circle. This can also be useful when you want a small button, but you don't want to frustrate the user by requiring her to have the precision of a surgeon. I say, "give them a break," and make the Hit state big enough to easily click.

FIGURE 13.3

Changing the shape contents of a button's Hit state affects what portion is clickable.

This button's Hit state matches the visual shape.   This button's Hit state includes the center area.

The first four frames of a button are used regardless of whether you place keyframes (or even frames) into all four frames. Compare this to a normal Timeline where you only insert 2 frames. By the time the playback head reached frame 3 or beyond, you won't see anything onstage. However, buttons break this fundamental concept by effectively inserting frames (not keyframes) in all four frames—at least that's a good way to think about it. Therefore, if you draw only into frame 1, that image will remain as the visual element for all four frames (Up, Over, Down, and Hit).

Task: Make a Button with an Extra Large Hit State

1. In a new file, use the Text Tool to draw the word Home.

2. Using the Arrow tool, select the text block you just created and convert it into a symbol (by pressing F8 or selecting Insert, Convert to Symbol from the menu). Name it **Home button**, make sure that you select Button Behavior, and then click OK.

3. Go ahead and test the movie (select the Control, Test Movie menu options) and notice how the button is sensitive to where you move your cursor. You'll only see the Hand cursor when you're exactly on top of the text.

4. Back in our file, we can fix this by creating a larger Hit state for the button. Double-click the button (so we can edit the master button).

5. Now that we are inside our button, insert a keyframe in the Hit frame (click in the Hit frame, press F6 or select Insert, Keyframe). Realize that the Home text in the Hit frame is just a copy of text in the Up frame (inserting a keyframe copies the contents of the other frame). After we draw the Hit state, we can delete this text as the user never actually sees anything in the Hit frame.

13

6. While in the Hit frame, use your Oval tool to draw a filled oval that's slightly larger than the text (turn off Snap temporarily if you wish). When you've got your oval, you can delete the text (from only the Hit frame).

7. If you test your movie now (select Control, Test Movie or press Ctrl+Enter), you'll see the button Gives the User a Break because it's much easier to click.

The button you just created used a Hit state to create a larger area for the user to click. Often you can forgo creating a Hit state and the button's solid areas will define the click-able (or "hot") area. Just remember that without a Hit state, the closest keyframe to the left of the Hit frame will define what's hot—that is the graphics in the Down state.

Minimizing a Button's Impact on Filesize

Regardless of how fast everyone's Internet connections are getting, there's no excuse for a file that's bigger than it has to be. And just because we're creating buttons doesn't mean that we can ignore filesize considerations. For example, in the previous task, I instructed you to insert three keyframes and Paint Bucket the shape in each differently. I didn't want to diverge from the main task, but hopefully you were thinking, "Hey, if all we're doing is changing the color, we should be using symbols instead of a new shapes in each keyframe."

Using Symbols Inside Buttons

Although most people understand why symbols are useful and important, many don't use symbols as much as possible. If a multi-state button, for example, has three identical keyframes, the contents of each keyframe is duplicated. This isn't a problem if you use instances of a symbol on each frame. People often mistakenly think that because a button is a symbol, editing its contents will take full advantage of symbols. You need to consider using symbols while inside symbols. *Anytime* you copy and paste (which happens when you insert a keyframe), you should consider using symbols, even if you happen to be editing a symbol's contents.

Let's try that multi-state button again, this time using the symbols in each state instead of new shapes.

Task: Remake a Multi-State Button Using Symbols in Each State

1. We'll do this exercise from scratch, so in a new file, draw an oval (which will become your button).

2. Select the Arrow tool, select the oval you just drew, and covert it to a symbol (using the Insert, Convert to Symbol menu options). Name it **MyButton**, make sure that the behavior is Button, and then click OK.

3. Now, let's edit the master version of the button we just created. Double-click the instance of the button and you'll be taken inside the master version.

4. Now that we're inside the master button, you should see the oval shape you drew. Notice that it's not a symbol—it's a shape. After all, you just told Flash to convert the shape into a symbol, so inside the symbol we have a shape. This will be an issue if we start adding keyframes inside the button.

5. To be totally efficient, let's convert the oval shape itself to a symbol. Select the entire shape, select the menu options Insert, Convert to Symbol, name it **Oval**, leave the default Movie Clip Behavior, and then click OK.

6. Now that our first keyframe contains a symbol, insert a keyframe in the Over frame. Tint the instance of the Oval symbol (in the Effect panel, choose tint, pick a hue and leave the amount set to 100%). If you want, you can even scale the instance of Oval and make it slightly larger.

7. Insert a keyframe in the Down frame. (Flash copies the contents of the previous frame.) The tinted instance of Oval in the Over frame can now be nudged down and to the right. (With the Oval symbol selected, click your down arrow twice and your right arrow twice.)

8. Go back to the main scene and test your movie. It should look like Figure 13.4, plus the file size will remain small because you did it all with just one shape.

FIGURE 13.4
A visual change occurs in the three states of the button: tinting for the Over state, and change of position for the Down state.

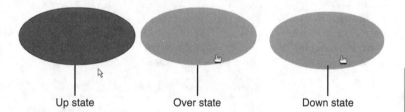

Up state   Over state   Down state

13

Instances of Buttons

Hopefully, you're beginning to get excited about the power you have to create buttons. Even the "quick and dirty" buttons we're making in these exercises are looking pretty good. Although we're *still* going to wait until next hour to make the buttons do anything, it's worth taking a quick peek ahead so that you understand where we're headed.

Similar to any other symbol, you can have as many instances onstage and it won't significantly affect filesize. Each instance can have a different position, size, color effect, and even rotation. It is on each instance of a button that we will have the opportunity to attach an *Action*. It might seem premature to even mention this, but it's important to understand how Actions are placed in individual instances of a button—not in the master version of the button in the Library. The only thing we put into the frames (states) of a master button are visuals (and audio, as we'll see in a minute). A common mistake is to try to place an Action inside the button itself—but that doesn't work. I suppose it makes sense if you want an Action to occur when the user's cursor is over the button: It's logical to think you could put the action in the Over state of the button. Regardless of how logical that sounds, it doesn't work that way.

NEW TERM   *Actions* are your way to tell Flash to do things such as stop, play, or jump to another Web site. Actions and how they're used is covered next hour. The concept needs to be mentioned now—as we discuss buttons—because one of the places you put Actions is on instances of buttons. (The other places are in keyframes and on clip instances.)

You put Actions on instances of buttons. Let's take a quick peek—but nothing more. Select an instance of a button in your scene and right-click (Ctrl+click on the Macintosh) for the context sensitive menu, and then select Actions. Press the Plus (+) button and select Basic Actions, On Mouse Event. Notice at the bottom of the Actions panel, you see several *Events* listed as in Figure 13.5. Next hour we'll select from these available options to specify exactly when is to react to the user. As you can see, there are many different Events which can execute the Action. Remember, putting Actions on instances of buttons is the only way buttons work in Flash.

FIGURE 13.5

Actions on button instances specify what Event will cause the Action to execute.

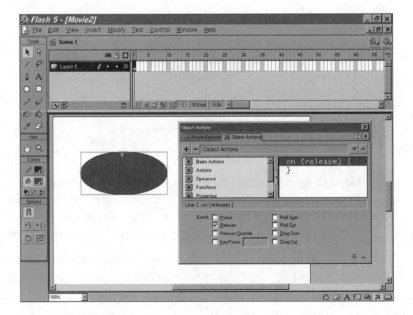

NEW TERM *Events*, generally, are things that happen. In multimedia, Events either happen when a user interacts (for example, he starts to drag something or click a button), or events happen automatically (for example, the movie starting could be an event). With buttons, the only Events with which to concern yourself are Mouse Events; that is, different ways the user interacts when he presses a button—that's an Event, or when he lets go—that's another Event. Events could be happening all the time. The interesting concept is that you can specify that an Action is acted upon if a particular Event occurs. That is, you can be waiting for an Event to occur and be ready with a response. Actually, you have to be very specific as to which Mouse Event you want to respond. For example, we can't just say "Stop when the user clicks the button," you have to specify exactly which Event (On Press or On Release—two possible events from which to select). Most of your animation is not event driven, rather it's controlled by the frames in your Timeline (frame based). Interactive portions are event driven.

That's as far into the future as we're going to go right now—don't worry, we'll get there soon enough. Besides, there's plenty of interesting things to do in Advanced buttons coming up. For now, remember that it is under the instances of buttons that we specify what should happen when they're clicked. Inside the button itself, we specify only how the button will change visually.

Advanced Buttons

If you think the buttons we've been making are exciting, just wait. We're about to make some very sophisticated buttons. It's going to be a chance to apply both your new knowledge of basic buttons plus a little of what you've learned about animation from previous hours.

Animated Buttons

Creating an animated button in Flash is easier than you might imagine. Do you want a button that is animating at all times? Or, one that just animates when the cursor passes over? How about both? You can do anything you want—just put an animated Movie Clip in the appropriate states of the button. That's it.

Task: Create an Animated Button

1. In a new file, use the Text tool to type the word **Home** onstage (make it fairly large). Select the text with the Arrow tool, convert this to a symbol (select Insert, Convert to Symbol), name it **Plain Text**, leave the default Movie Clip Behavior, and then click OK. This symbol will be used extensively.

13

2. Now, the text on screen is an instance of the "Plain Text" symbol. Let's create a Movie Clip symbol that animates the "Plain Text" symbol onstage. With it selected, select Insert, Convert to Symbol, name it **Animating Text**, and leave the default Movie Clip Behavior, and then click OK.

3. Now, let's edit the Animating Text symbol. We can access the contents of this symbol by double clicking. Just make sure you're in the Animating Text symbol before continuing (look at the address bar to make sure).

4. Inside the master Animating Text symbol, insert a keyframe at frame 30 and one at frame 15. (Create 30 before changing the instance at frame 15—so it ends in the same location as where it starts.) Scale the Plain Text symbol instance in frame 15 so that it's a little larger. Go back and set tweening in frame 1 and frame 15 to Motion (right-click on each keyframe, individually, and select Create Motion Tween). Scrub the Timeline to get a feel for our animation.

5. Go back to our main scene (click Scene 1 at the top left of the Timeline). Delete everything onstage (select Edit, Select All, and then select Edit, Clear—or better yet, press Ctrl+A and then click Delete). You're not deleting any symbols; they're both safe in the Library. Open the Library (select Window, Library or press Ctrl+L). Drag an instance of the Plain Text onstage.

6. Now we're ready to create our button. Once again, select the Plain Text symbol onstage and convert it to a symbol (select Insert, Convert to Symbol), name it **Animating Button**, make sure that you click Button Behavior, and then click OK. By converting the existing Plain Text symbol into the Button symbol, we're using an instance of a symbol to create the button.

7. Now let's edit our button and make it animate. Double-click the instance onstage (the Animating Button symbol) and you're taken inside the button—which you can confirm already has an instance of Plain Text in frame 1.

8. Now we're going to place an instance of the Animating Text Movie Clip in the button's Over state (frame 2). You could drag it from the Library and align it to the Plain Text instance in the Up state. However, we're going to do it another way that won't require any manual alignment. Insert a keyframe into the Over state. This will copy everything from the Up frame (an instance of the Plain Text symbol).

9. In the Over frame of the button, access the Instance panel and select the Plain Text instance onstage). Press the Swap Symbol at the bottom of the Instance panel shown in Figure 13.6.

FIGURE 13.6

The symbol to which an instance is linked can be swapped without changing any other properties (like position) of the instance.

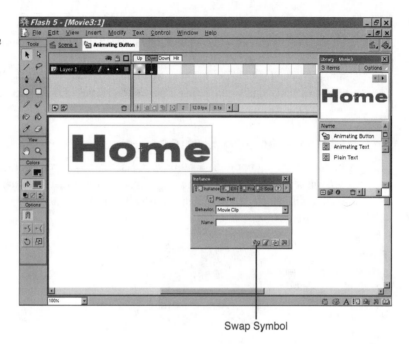

Swap Symbol

10. From the Swap Symbol dialog you'll see all the symbols in your Library and a dot next to the one the current instance is linked to (see Figure 13.7). Click on Animating Text and then click OK. You've now swapped the instance (previously Plain Text). You'll also notice the name of the current symbol at the top of the Instance panel has changed.

FIGURE 13.7

Through the Swap Symbol dialog you can select a different symbol.

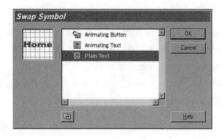

13

11. The button is lacking a nice large Hit state. It has a Hit state, but it's kind of a "moving target" and difficult to access. In the master version of the button's Hit frame, insert a keyframe and draw an oval that is at least as big as the word "Home." After you draw the oval, you can delete the instance of "Animating Text" that was automatically placed in the Hit frame when we inserted the keyframe as it's not necessary.

We created a button that uses a Movie Clip in its Over state. However, instead of creating from the "top down" (that is making the button, and then putting a Movie Clip in the button) we did it from the "specific to the general" (or from "inside out"). First we created a symbol with text (Plain Text). Then, we animated Plain Text in the Movie Clip we called Animating Text. Finally, we created the button and used the Plain Text symbol in the Up frame and the Animating Text in the Over frame.

Button Tracking Options

A button's tracking option is a subtle attribute that gives you additional control over exactly how a button acts. In Figure 13.8 you'll notice that from the Instance panel while any button is selected there's a choice between Track as Button (the default) and Track as Menu Item.

FIGURE 13.8

The Instance panel lets you specify whether a button will "Track" as a button or menu item.

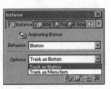

The easiest way to understand tracking is to have more than one button and with Over states that are visually different from their Up states. (You could have two instances of the same button.) If you leave them both in the default Track as Button, when testing the movie, you can click and hold one of the buttons and you won't be able to access any other button while you keep the mouse down. Many Flash buttons work this way. For example, click a button and keep the mouse pressed while you roll over other buttons—only the one that you clicked initially will be affected. This is Track as Button.

Now, if you set two buttons to Track as Menu Item and test again, you'll see that even if you've started to click on one button, if you hold your mouse down and roll over the other button, it will react (and it will register if you let go). This is similar to regular menus: When you click and hold, and then move up and down, able to let go on any item in the menu.

While the difference between these options is very subtle, realize they're available. The Track as Menu Item option be appropriate when you have many buttons on screen. Often the default Track as Button is fine.

Sounds in Buttons

There are several ways to include sounds in your buttons. In simplest form, a sound can be placed in any keyframe. For a sound to occur when the user's cursor goes over the button, just put a sound in the Over state. Fancier effects can get more complicated. For example, to make a sound loop *while* the user's cursor is over the button takes a few more steps. Ultimately, however, to create complicated sounds and effects, you'll need to learn about targeting movie clips, which is covered next hour and expanded upon in Hour 15, "ActionScripting Applications for Advanced Interactivity." For now we'll cover two basic forms of sounds in buttons: simple sound effects in the Over state, and looping sounds within a button.

Task: Create a Button with a Roll Over Sound Effect

1. In a new file, draw a rectangle shape, convert it into a symbol (select Insert, Convert to Symbol), name it **Audio Button**, and make sure that you click Button Behavior before clicking OK.

2. Let's go edit the button. Double-click the instance so we can edit the master button.

3. Now that we're inside the master version of the button, we can concern ourselves with the Over state (where we'll include a sound). Of course we'll need a new keyframe in the Over state as sounds are only placed in keyframes. However, before we insert a keyframe (which, if inserted now, would copy the shape from the Up frame), let's convert the shape in the Up frame to a symbol (select it all, select Insert, Convert to Symbol, name it **Shape of Button**, and click OK).

4. Insert a keyframe in the Over frame. (You can tint Shape of Button or scale it if you want a visual effect when the user rolls over the button.) We'll also place a sound in this frame. With the Over frame selected, access the Sound panel. Notice that you won't find any sounds listed from the drop-down list in the Sound panel because we haven't imported any (see Hour 10, "Including Sound in Your Animation").

5. Instead of importing a sound from file, let's use one that comes with Flash. From Window, Common Libraries, select Sounds. Open your file's Library (Window, Library or Ctrl+L) and drag the Beaker Switch sound item into your Library. Now select the Over frame and use the Sound panel to select Beaker Switch (since it's been imported into your file) as shown in Figure 13.9.

13

FIGURE **13.9**

On the Over state of our button we specify a Sound to play.

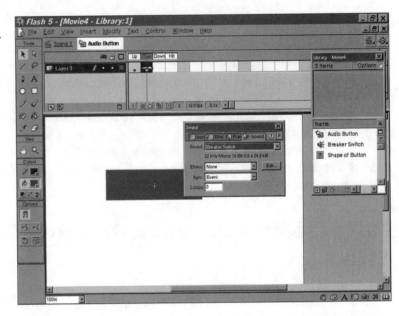

6. It should work. Of course you'll need to test the movie to see (and hear) it work. (Save this file as we'll use it in our next task.)

That wasn't so bad. Just put a sound in the keyframe of the Over state of a button! I suggested the Breaker Switch sound in particular for two reasons. First, it saved you the hassle of finding a sound. Also, I wanted a short sound. Had you chosen a longer sound such as Beam Scan, you might have noticed that there's enough time to roll over the button, roll off, roll back on quickly, and the result will be a layering effect on the sound—which is not exactly pleasant. This can be fixed by changing the Sound panel's Sync setting to Start (as we did in Hour 10).

We'll see how a long sound (or worse, one that loops forever) requires such addition consideration in our next task. Generally, I'd suggest that incidental sound effects—such as rollover sounds—should be very short so that they don't become tiresome for our users. A gratuitous sound effect that's cute the first time can become really annoying when it repeats.

Task: Create a Button with Looping Sound

1. Edit the master button we created in the previous Task. If you aren't already inside the master button, double-click the instance of the button.

2. Select the keyframe in the Over state. In the Sound panel, type a very large number such as **999999999999999** into the Loops field to get to the Max Integer. (See Hour 10 for more information on this.)

3. Test the movie now. There are some problems. The sound Breaker Switch doesn't loop well. However, that's the least of the problems—and one that could easily be rectified with an alternative sound. The serious problems that we'll address are (1) the sound will layer on top of itself every time you roll off and then roll back on the button, and (2) when the sound starts, it never stops.

4. You might recall from Hour 10 that three other Sync settings exist besides the default Event. We want the sound in our Over state to only start playing if it isn't already playing. In the master Button symbol, set the Sync setting for the sound in the Over frame of the button to Start (in the Sound panel, select Start from the Sync drop-down list). Test the movie again, and you'll see that we fixed the issue of the sound starting again after it has already started.

5. But the sound still never stops once started. The opportune time to stop the sound is when the user rolls off the button—the Up state. There happens to be an Action called Stop All Sounds; however, recall that we don't put Actions inside of buttons—besides, what if we want other sounds to continue playing? We only need the particular sound that's looping to stop. In the Up state's keyframe, we add the same sound. But this time, select Sync Stop, which will cause only that particular sound to stop. To do this, select the first keyframe (in the Up state), from the Sound panel, select the same sound we're using in the Over state ("Breaker Switch") from the drop-down list of sounds available, set the Sync to Stop. Test the movie and it should work.

Invisible Buttons

Invisible buttons are very useful. They're easy to make too, as you'll see in the next Task. Flash will let you (the author) see the invisible button as semi-transparent blue. The user won't see anything.

It might seem useless to make a button the user can't see, but it's actually quite useful. The only trick is you'll probably want to place the invisible button on top of something visual. For example, what if you had a map on which you wanted the user to be able to click specific areas (maybe cities) and learn more about the one she clicked? All you'd need is one big picture of the map and lots of invisible buttons placed in key locations. This would be more practical than cutting the map into little pieces and making buttons out of each piece.

13

Task: Make an Invisible Button

1. Select Insert, New Symbol from the menu, name it **Invisible**, click Button Behavior, and then click OK. This takes us to the master version of the symbol we're creating. Flash expects us to draw something here in the master version of the Invisible button symbol.

2. Leave all the frames of this button blank, but in the Hit frame insert a keyframe. (Because the previous keyframe is blank, this is the same as inserting a blank keyframe.)

3. Draw a circle around the center (the plus) in the Hit frame (to center it, you can draw a circle and then cut and paste or use the Info panel to set the center to 0, 0). Your button's Timeline should resemble Figure 13.10.

FIGURE 13.10

An invisible button looks like this—nothing in any frame except the Hit frame.

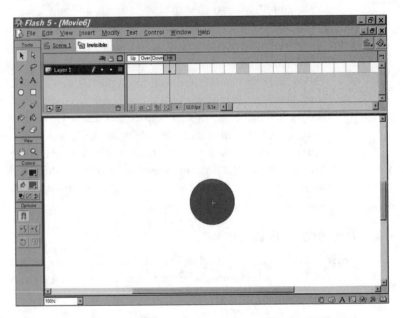

4. We're done here; just go back to your main scene and drag an instance of this Invisible button from the Library to the Stage. Check it out; it's blue. Now, test the movie, and you'll see nothing (except your cursor change when it reaches the button's location).

5. In the main scene, draw a large box and then a few circles in different locations on the box (as shown in Figure 13.11). Imagine that this box is a large map and each circle indicates a city. Then drag an invisible button from the Library for each circle you drew. Line up the buttons and scale them appropriately to cover each circle.

FIGURE 13.11

Invisible buttons can be placed on top of any drawing.

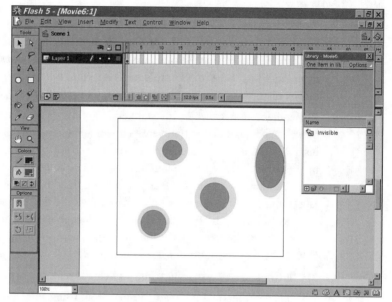

For something you can't even see, invisible buttons are actually quite powerful. It's safe to say I've never done a project without them. The main advantage is they keep the visual elements separate from the button's functionality. You can place invisible buttons on top of anything to effectively create a button the user can see and click. In Hour 22, "Working on Large Projects and in Team Environments," you'll learn how such code-data separation can make you more efficient. For now, just realize invisible buttons (or any buttons for that matter) won't do anything until you attach Actions to them.

Summary

Now you should understand how to create buttons from any shape in Flash. You also learned how to make the button change visually when the user's cursor rolls over or clicks it. You learned how to control exactly what part of the button is clickable (the Hit state) as well as how to make an animated button. Not only visual stuff, you learned how to put sounds in buttons and even how to make invisible buttons.

Now you should be able to apply many of your animation skills to make compelling buttons. Alas, we've only done the first half (how to make the buttons *look* cool), we're about to embark on making the buttons function—making them *do* things by attaching Actions.

13

Q&A

Q **I accidentally dragged a Movie Clip to the Stage, and used the Instance panel to change it to Button Behavior. Now my Movie Clip doesn't play, and it kind of works like a button. (There's an Over state and hand cursor when the user moves his mouse over the button.) What's up with that?**

A Remember that because the master version of a symbol is a Movie Clip (or any other behavior), it doesn't prevent you from changing the behavior of individual instances onstage. If you change an instance of a Movie Clip to Button Behavior, the first frame of the Movie Clip acts as the Up state, the second frame is the Over state, the third is the Down state, and the fourth is the Hit state. You won't see the labels in the master version of a symbol unless the default properties of that symbol was Button in the first place (or if you change the properties of the master symbol by way of the library's Options menu). (There's more information about this in Hour 5, "Using the Library for Productivity.")

Q **My buttons aren't working when I click Play. Why?**

A If you haven't learned it already, forget about using Play to really see what the user will see. Use Control, Test Movie from the menu. Alternatively, you can turn on Enable Buttons from the Control menu—it's a pain because you must turn that option off before you can click to edit a button instance. (With the option on, the button will act like a button, not like an instance on which you can click.)

Workshop

The Workshop consists of quiz questions and answers to help you solidify your understanding of the material covered. Try to answer the questions before checking the answers.

Quiz

1. How many frames can appear to animate when you roll over a button?

    A. It depends on how many keyframes you have in your button.

    B. No more than four frames.

    C. As many as you want because you'll use a Movie Clip.

2. Can I have a different sound in two different instances of one button?

    A. No.

    B. Yes.

    C. It depends on whether the sound loops—for looping sound, yes; for non-looping sound, no.

3. What happens if your button has no graphics in any state except the Hit state?

    A. It won't work.

    B. You'll have an invisible button.

    C. Flash will crash.

Quiz Answers

1. C. Although, in the master button itself you only have the space of one frame for each state, in each frame you can place a multi-frame Movie Clip (of any length) and, like all Movie Clips, it will play on its own.

2. A. If you put a sound in the master version of a button, that sound will be heard in each instance of the original button. However, if all the visual contents of your buttons are instances of other symbols, you can have two master buttons without affecting filesize negatively. That way you can have a different sound in each master button. (Of course, with two different sounds, you'll add to filesize.)

3. B. That's how you make invisible buttons.

13

HOUR **14**

Using Actions to Create Non-Linear Movies

Flash's programming language is called ActionScript. Like any programming language, ActionScript lets you write instructions that your movie will follow. Without ActionScript, your movie will play the same way every time. If you want the user to be able to stop and start the movie, for example, you need ActionScript. Individual elements of ActionScript are called Actions. It isn't necessary for you to learn ActionScript to add Actions to your Flash movie. Using the Actions panel, you can select preprogrammed Actions and put them in any order. Last hour you learned how to create buttons. This hour you'll learn how to attach Actions (like "Stop" and "Play") to those buttons.

Specifically, you will:

- Learn the three places you can put Actions
- Edit Actions to make them do exactly what you want
- Direct Actions so they affect only part of your movie
- Discover some basic approaches to combining Actions for specific effects

Depending on how you count them, there are more than 50 Actions available in Flash. We won't cover all of them this hour. Rather, we'll cover the basic concept of their use and the general approach you should take. This way, you'll build a good foundation on which to grow at your own pace.

Using Actions

Use Actions like building blocks. Select any Actions you want, put them in any order and, if it all makes sense, the results will be interesting. However, that freedom also means you can create illogical combinations or even contradictions—like Play Stop. Just select the Actions you need, put them in the right place and in the right order, and fine-tune them for your purpose.

All Actions are inserted via the Actions panel. Open the Actions panel and follow along as we explore. Click the Show Object Actions button, shown in Figure 14.1. You can also select Actions from the Window menu or select Ctrl+Alt+A. (Of course, if the Actions panel is already open, these maneuvers will close it.) Take a quick look at Figure 14.2 and then we can cover a few more details before doing a few exercises.

FIGURE 14.1

At the bottom right of your movie's window are several buttons to launch panels. The arrow button will Show Object Actions—that is, the Actions panel.

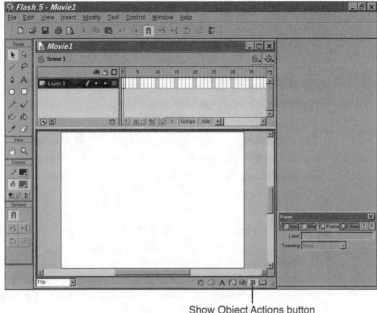

Show Object Actions button

Add/Delete Statement

Toolbox list

FIGURE 14.2

The Object Actions panel has several components.

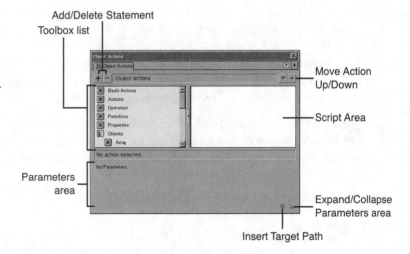

Move Action Up/Down

Script Area

Parameters area

Expand/Collapse Parameters area

Insert Target Path

- The Toolbox list provides access to all available Actions. Organized like folders (notice the Objects category is open and Array is inside).

- In the Script Area, your Actions will appear in order of execution.

- The Move Selected Action Up/Down buttons will move any Action in the Script Area up or down one line at a time. However, you can also select lines and drag them to create another order.

14

- The Add Statement button will pop up a menu that provides the same Actions as found in the Toolbox List. The menu will also show the key combination for each Action (see note, below).

- The Delete Statement button will remove a selected Action in the Script Area.

- Use the Expand/Collapse Parameters area to minimize the size of the Actions panel. Leave this expanded all the time.

- Assuming the Expand/Collapse Parameters Area button has expanded the Parameters Area, you'll be able to see and set parameters for Actions that have been added to the Script Area. Some Actions have no parameters (because they're so simple) but the ones that do are accessible here.

Action Key Combinations

In the Actions panel under the add statement "+" you'll find key combinations such as "Esc+go". This means the Action can be inserted by simply clicking the following keys in sequence (not at the same time): Esc, g, o. If you find yourself inserting the same Action repeadedly you might use this method instead as it's quicker.

While you're learning, it's best to stay in Normal mode. The options arrow at the top right of the Actions panel provides a list of options, including the choice between Normal mode and Expert mode. Normal mode assures that the *syntax* of your Actions is correct. If this option is in Expert mode, Flash will not correct the syntax of your ActionScript, so it requires knowledge of the ActionScript language.

NEW TERM   *Syntax* is unique to each programming language. Every Action has a very spe-
cific form that must be followed, for instance every email address has to have the form "name@domain.com" or it won't work. When using the Action panel's Normal mode Flash will make sure your syntax will always be correct. That's not to say it will work the way you had in mind—only that you won't have any syntax errors which would prevent Flash from following any instructions.

The easiest way to add Actions is to first select one from the Toolbox List on the left. Either double-click the desired Action or drag it to the right side of the Actions panel (the Script Area). Each Action you add occupies one line on the right. Rarely is an Action just one word; more often an Action is complex enough to require a whole sentence, or statement. A statement is a code sentence that uses only words from the ActionScript language. The entire assembly of statements is a *script*.

Once you add an Action, there are two ways to modify it. As you add Actions, each appears as a complete statement in the order that you add them, and they'll occur in that order. You can change the order of any statement either by clicking its line in the Script Area and dragging it to another position or by selecting it in the Script Area and clicking the Up or Down arrow at the top right.

The other way you'll likely need to modify an Action is to specify *parameters*. For example, an Action called gotoAndPlay makes the playback head jump to a different frame. However, you need to specify the frame to which you want to go. In this case, the frame number is a parameter. To view the Parameters Area of the Actions panel, make sure the Expand/Collapse arrow is pointing up so that the parameters are exposed. Some Actions don't need parameters.

You can resize the Actions panel, and there's an option for Font Size (under the options arrow). In the same menu you'll find an option for Colored Syntax. This is a great way to learn, especially when you venture into Expert mode, because it will color the text as you type. Each component of ActionScript has a unique color (properties are green, keywords are blue, and so on). It's not critical to understand what each color means right away, but colored text helps you identify when you've typed something that is from the ActionScript language. (The other options under this menu are for basic editing procedures, such as Find and Replace.)

Specifying Actions with Parameters

Now is a chance for you to try out Actions and parameters. You'll see that some Actions are quite simple. However, most Actions are more complicated. Let's walk through a quick exercise that uses Actions and parameters, then step back to analyze what we did.

Task: Make an Action That Loops Part of Your Movie

1. In a new file, use the Text tool to create a text block containing the word Welcome. Select the block and convert to symbol. Make it a Movie Clip and name it Welcome Text.

2. Position the text in the center of the screen, and insert keyframes at frame 20 and frame 30.

3. Move the current frame marker to frame 1 and move Welcome Text all the way off stage to the left. Set Motion Tweening for both frame 1 and frame 20. In frame 20, use the Frame panel to make the tween rotate one time clockwise (CW) on its way to frame 30. Look in Hour 8, "Using Motion Tween to Animate," for a

14

review of this. Test the movie. Notice that the whole movie loops over and over. Instead we're going to make the rotation part (from frame 20 to frame 30) loop forever.

4. Select frame 30 and access the Actions panel (you can click the Show Actions quick launch button as in Figure 14.3 or use the Window, Actions menu). Make sure frame 30 remains selected when you edit the Actions panel. We're going to set an Action to execute when the playback head reaches frame 30.

FIGURE 14.3

The Actions panel is opened right after frame 30 is selected so that we can set an Action to execute when the playback head reaches that frame.

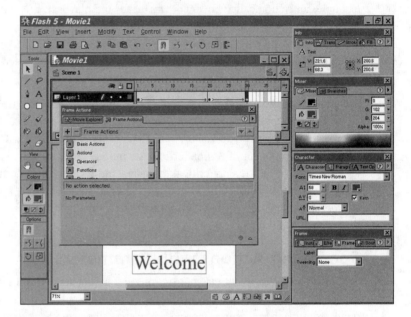

5. In the Toolbox List on the left of the Frame Action panel, first scroll up and expand the Basic Actions folder and then find the Go To Action. Double-click Go To and you should see a Go To Action added to your script in the Script Area on the right (see Figure 14.4). The parameters default to what's shown, but we'll edit these. Notice that in the Timeline, a small *a* appears in the keyframe where you added the Action.

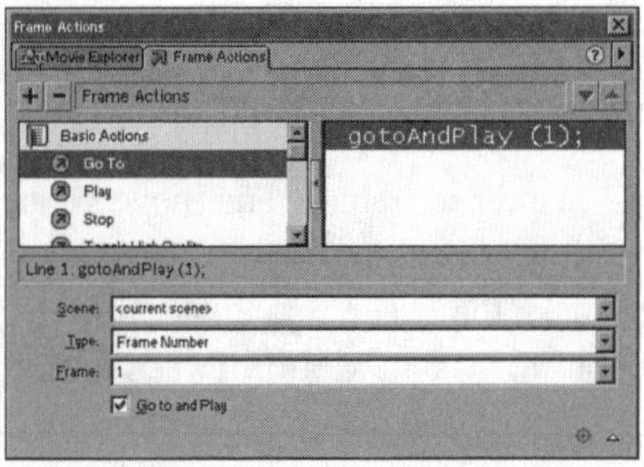

FIGURE 14.4

The Actions panel immediately after inserting a Go To Action.

6. If your Parameters Area is not revealed, click the little arrow button at the bottom-right of the Actions window.

7. The Parameters Area is where you specify all the details for the selected Action (Go To, in this case). For this exercise, leave most of the defaults but enter 20 in the Frame field. The final Action in the script area should read `gotoAndPlay(20)` (as seen in Figure 14.5).

FIGURE 14.5

The finished form of the Action attached to frame 30. Every time the playback head reaches frame 30, it goes back to frame 20 and plays.

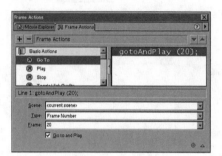

8. Test the movie. It plays once, then every time it gets to frame 30 it goes back to frame 20 and plays again.

As easy as that exercise was, there is one thing in particular that could make it better. Consider the amount of work involved if you changed the location of the keyframes. For example, what if the second keyframe (from frame 20) had to move to frame 25? Of course, the initial tween would take longer to play, and the rotation would be quicker, but the loop would also stop working properly. To fix it, you'd need to remember to edit the Action in frame 30 so that it read `gotoAndPlay(25);`. You'd have to repeat this fix every time you changed the location of the keyframe where the rotation starts.

Naturally, there's a better way. Instead of making the destination of our Go To an explicit frame number, we can change the parameters to make the destination a named frame label, which will be the same for the frame no matter where it is located in the Timeline.

Task: Use a Frame Label as the Destination of a Go To

1. In the file created above, access the Frame panel for frame 20 (or whatever frame the rotation starts in). Label this frame Loop Start (see Figure 14.6).

14

FIGURE 14.6

If we label frame 20 (via the Frame panel), the destination of our Go To can change from an explicit number (20) to a label name (Loop Start).

2. Go back to frame 30 and open the Actions panel.

3. We're going to modify the gotoAndPlay line in the Frame Actions panel. Of course there's only one line, but to access the parameters for this line, we need to select it. Now, change the Type drop-down to Frame Label. Then, select the Frame drop-down and you should see all the labels available in the current Timeline. We've added only Loop Start, so that's all that's available—but you'd see more if you had more. Select Loop Start from the drop-down list; this is more dependable than typing it and possibly adding a typo (see Figure 14.7). If you don't see the drop-down arrows to the right of your panel, resize the panel expanding outward until you do.

FIGURE 14.7

This new version of our Go To is better because the destination is a frame label.

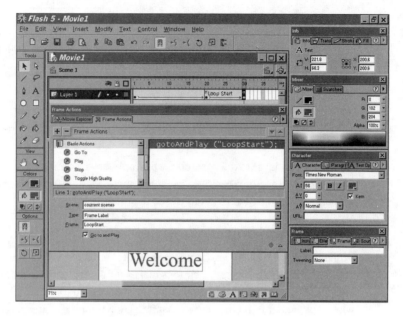

4. Test the movie; it doesn't look any different to the user. Now go back to the Timeline and click and drag the Loop Start keyframe to frame 10.

5. Test the movie again. The animation now loops back to frame 10, where you moved the Loop Start keyframe. The power of using a label as the destination of your Go To is that you can now go back and move the location of the Loop Start keyframe to any frame you want and it still works!

Frame Actions

We just saw how placing one Action in a keyframe and changing its parameters makes the playback head jump to a different frame. But let's step back a second and consider what else we learned. Actions are instructions that we want Flash to follow. Actions do things. Actions can be modified by changing their parameters. All good information, however, if Actions are instructions, exactly when does Flash *follow* those instructions?

The answer depends on where you put the Action. There are three places you can put Actions: in keyframes, on Button instances, and on Movie Clip instances. Our last exercise placed the Action in a keyframe. In that case, the Action was followed when the playback head reached that frame. If we put an Action in frame 10, it will not be followed until the playback head reaches frame 10.

14

With an Action in a keyframe, the user doesn't do anything but wait for the playback head to reach that frame to see the Action happen. Although this isn't exactly "interactivity," it's quite powerful. For example, often it's useful to place a Stop Action in the first frame so that your movie won't play until a Play Action is encountered (usually when the user clicks a button). Another example might be when you want to stop in the middle of an animation. All you need is a keyframe and a Stop Action. There are many more types of keyframe Actions, which are good for when you want something to happen at a certain moment in the animation—not just when a user clicks.

Notice that in our previous exercise we simply used frame Actions. The Actions were executed when the playback head reached that frame. This is just one of the three places we can put Actions; we're about to see the other two.

Button Actions

While putting Actions in keyframes causes the Action to execute when that frame is reached, putting Actions in instances of buttons makes the Action execute when the user clicks a button. The decision to put an Action in a keyframe or a button is simple. If you want an Action when a particular frame is reached, put it in a keyframe. If you want the Action when the user acts (for example, he clicks a button), put the Action in an instance of the button.

Keyframe Actions are pretty straightforward: You just assign them to the keyframe. Buttons, however, require that you specify to which *mouse event* you want to respond. Do you want to respond when the user presses the button or releases the button? Maybe you want the Action to execute when the user rolls over the button. This level of detail gives you the power to make the Action perform exactly as you wish.

New Term   *Mouse Events* are specific situations that refer to exactly how the user is interacting with a button. For example, one mouse event is "press" another is "release". When you specify to which mouse event you want the Action to respond you are specifying exactly when the Action is to execute. Only in Actions attached to buttons do you need this extra level of specificity as Actions in keyframes simply execute when the keyframe is reached.

The best way to see this is to try it out. We'll add buttons to our last exercise that let the user stop and continue the animation while it plays.

Task: Add Buttons to Your Animation to Stop and Continue Playback

1. Either use the file created in the previous exercises or make a new file with a Motion Tween over several frames (make sure you can see something moving while the animation plays).

2. Insert a new layer for the buttons. We don't want to place buttons in the layer with an animation; that will affect the tween. Name this layer Buttons.

3. Into the new Buttons layer, draw a rectangle that will become our button. Select it, and then convert to symbol (F8). Name it MyButton and make sure the behavior is set to Button.

4. We're going to need two buttons, so either copy and paste the instance already onstage or drag another instance of the MyButton symbol from the Library onto the Stage in the Buttons layer. Apply a Tint effect to each instance—one red (for Stop) and one green (for Play). As you recall, this is done by selecting the Button instance onstage and opening the Effect panel, selecting Tint, then selecting a color.

5. Now we need to attach an Action to each button individually. Select the red button and access the Actions panel. From the list of Actions in the Toolbox List on the left, double-click Stop to add an Action statement to the Script Area on the right. (You'll find Stop under both Basic Actions and Actions.) Notice that even though you tried to add just one Action (Stop), you were given three lines. That's because you can't simply put Actions in Button instances—you have to put them inside mouse events. The default event is Release, meaning the Action will execute when the user clicks and releases the button. We'll look at others later, but if you want to explore other events, select the first line in the Script Area and notice the check boxes in the Parameters Area of the Actions window (see Figure 14.8).

FIGURE 14.8

The Stop Action (attached to the button) can't go anywhere except within a mouse event.

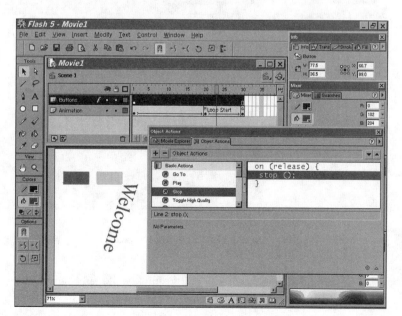

14

6. Now select the green-tinted Button instance and assign the Play Action, found under Basic Actions. Test the movie.

That Actions on Button instances must be contained within a mouse event makes sense because you have to specify precisely when the Action is to be executed, but it's still a bit disconcerting when extra lines are added to your script. You can take another approach that may make more sense and might feel like you're more in control.

In the last exercise, we first determined what Action (Stop or Play) we wanted and then noticed a default mouse event was selected and we just accepted it. Of course, we could have gone back and made adjustments, but we picked the result first and then noticed the event that would cause that result.

The approach that may help you is to first specify the mouse event (the cause), then specify the resulting Action. Instead of first adding an Action (like Stop or Play), you can add the mouse event first. onMouseEvent is listed under the Basic Actions section of the Toolbox List. Insert this first and specify the parameters (that specify which mouse event will cause the nested Action). Then insert the Action you want to happen after this event. The resulting Action or Actions have to be placed between the curly brackets ({}) (see Figure 14.9).

FIGURE 14.9

After a mouse event is specified, an open bracket ({) precedes the Actions that execute when that mouse event occurs. A closing bracket (}) goes after the last Action.

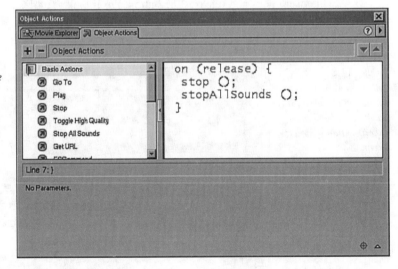

Following this approach may make more sense because you're assembling the script in a chronological order.

So far our Actions have been pretty simple, but there's great power in mouse events. You can have several Actions attached to one button. One mouse event could trigger several Actions to execute. Plus, you can have different Actions (or series of Actions) execute for different events. For example, one button could have a Stop Action associated with the Press mouse event and a Play Action associated with the Release mouse event. In this case the movie will pause only while the user holds the button.

A few issues are worth discussing before we conclude with the basics of attaching Actions to Button instances. First, it's important to remember to put Actions on Button instances, not any of the keyframes in the master button. It might seem convenient to include Actions as part of the master symbol so that those Actions will be included automatically. It might be nice and people often try. It simply won't work. However, you can attach an Action to a Button instance and then convert that instance to a Movie Clip (basically a clip with an instance of a button in it already). We'll see many other such techniques later in this hour and the next. For now, just remember that Actions don't go inside the master symbol of a button.

Movie Clip Actions

We've seen how to place Actions in keyframes and on Button instances. Most of the Actions you'll encounter probably will fall into one of those two cases. However, there's a third place where you can attach Actions: instances of Movie Clips. It's a little confusing because, unlike buttons, you can put Actions inside a master Movie Clip in the Library. However, you can only put Actions in keyframes and Button instances inside the clip. We've already discussed putting Actions on buttons and in keyframes—and those techniques will work inside master Movie Clips. But now we're going to see how Actions can be placed *on* instances of Movie Clips.

Actions on Movie Clips are powerful. It would get complicated to fully explore this feature now, but we can do an exercise that gives you a taste. Advanced topics such as this are more fully explored in Hour 15, "ActionScripting Applications for Advanced Interactivity," and in Appendix B, "Programming with ActionScript."

Task: Place Actions on a Movie Clip Instance

1. Create a Movie Clip with several frames and some kind of animation (so we can see if it's playing).

2. Place this Movie Clip onstage and test the movie (to verify it's animating).

3. Back in Flash, select the instance of the Movie Clip onstage and open the Actions panel. Notice that almost all the Actions in the Toolbox List are available (that is, they're not grayed out).

4. Under the Basic Actions category, insert Stop (by either double-clicking or dragging it over to the right). Notice that Actions in Movie Clip instances have to be wrapped inside a clip event. The default clip event is load, so you should see something like Figure 14.10.

14

FIGURE 14.10

A Stop Action attached to a Movie Clip is automatically surrounded by a clip *event.*

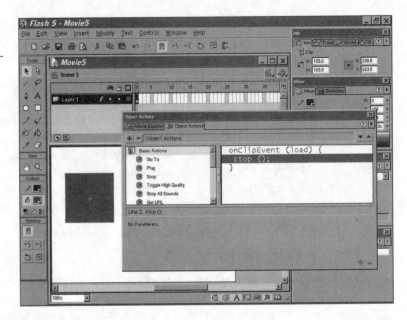

5. Test the movie now and, when the Movie Clip loads (that is, when it first appears onstage), it stops. Another way to create the same effect is to put a Stop Action on the first keyframe inside the master Movie Clip. There's nothing wrong with that technique, but a Stop inside the master Movie Clip means every instance will exhibit this behavior. Placing the Action on one instance—as we did—affects just that one.

6. We will add two more Actions that respond to the mouse down and mouse up events. When the user clicks (mouse down), the Movie Clip should start to play. When he stops clicking (mouse up), the Movie Clip should stop. If the line currently selected in your script is within the curly brackets, you won't be able to double-click onClipEvent in the Actions section of the Toolbox List, because you can't put an event inside an event. Remember: Double-clicking to insert an Action will try to put the Action right below the line currently selected in your script. However, you can drag the onClipEvent script below the ending curly bracket. Alternatively, you can select the last line and double-click onClipEvent.

7. To add more clip events, drag a Play Action below the last line in your script. It will automatically be wrapped inside an onClipEvent load script. Then, drag a Stop Action below the last line in the script.

8. It doesn't make too much sense the way it is now because you have three versions of onClipEvent (load). Leave the first you created alone. Click the first line of the second event (the one with Play inside). With this line selected, you can change the parameters of the clip event to respond to mouse down instead of load. The last

event should start with a clip event of mouse up. When you're done making edits to this script, it should look like that seen in Figure 14.11.

FIGURE 14.11

The complete set of Actions for this Movie Clip.

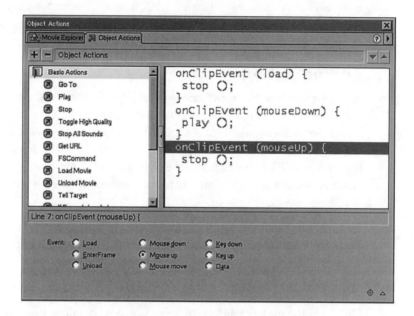

9. Test the movie. It's actually pretty sophisticated, despite the simplicity of the script. Go back and re-read the script (in the Script Area of the Actions panel) attached to our Movie Clip instance.

There are a few important things to note about this exercise. First, the clip events mouse down and mouse up respond to any mouse click—not just clicks on the clip itself. If you want something that responds to clicks right on a graphic, you probably want to use a regular button.

Also, the Actions you attach to a clip instance apply only to that instance. You can prove this to yourself several ways. First create a new layer and drag another instance of your Movie Clip from the Library (and don't attach any Actions to this instance). When you test the movie, the Stop and Play Actions apply only to the clip with the Actions attached. Now, try this: In the layer with the first Movie Clip instance (the one with the Actions), insert a keyframe at frame 20 (F6). Drag the instance in frame 20 to a new location onstage, then set a Motion Tween on the first frame. (You can add frames to extend the life of the other layer if you want.) Now when you test the movie, the Stop and Play Actions have no effect on anything except the Movie Clip to which they're attached. The rest of the movie keeps on playing but the Movie Clip stops whenever the user does a mouse up.

14

You can go really far with this technique. The basic things to remember are that just like buttons, Actions on clip instances are wrapped inside an events. Buttons respond to the onMouseEvent event (also called on) while Movie Clips respond to the onClipEvent. Finally, Actions attached to clip instances affect only the particular instance to which they're attached.

Editing Actions

We've learned how to attach Actions to keyframes, Button instances, and Movie Clip instances. We've already made slight modifications to the Actions after they've been added. For example, when we did a Go To, the parameter specifying which frame number to go to needed to be typed into the Frame field in the Parameter Area. This was editing an Action. So we've already done some editing of Actions (it's kind of difficult to do anything without editing them). There are a few more details worth discussing as applied to editing Actions.

First, become familiar with all the features in the Actions panel. For example, the Parameters Area should always be expanded (so you can see the appropriate parameters when you select an Action). Also, notice the + button (adds a new item to the script), which contains the same Actions available from the Toolbox List. This button also lets you see all the key combinations to insert Actions into your script. For example, if you click your Escape key followed by st, a Stop Action will be inserted. It pays to learn the ones that you use often, because searching is not very efficient. Also, you can drag Actions from the Toolbox List to the Script Area, and you can click and drag statements around (to change their order) once they've been placed. Finally, the - button (delete the selected action) works the same as simply clicking an Action and then pressing your Delete key. There are some basic but useful functions in this panel that are worth learning.

You can only do a few things with the Actions panel: insert Actions, edit Actions, and delete Actions. Like any panel, the Actions displayed at any one time apply only to the selected keyframe, button, or clip instance. If it appears that you can't even create a script, this is usually the result of not first selecting a frame, button, or clip. It's also easy to think you've lost a script only to find that you deselected the item to which the script is attached. This isn't anything new (all panels work similarly), but when working in the Actions panel it's important to work deliberately.

Finally, although we're not going to explore the Expert mode, I'd like to mention a few things now. The Actions panel mode is specific to the particular script; if you have a script attached to a frame and change it to Expert mode, other scripts in your movie will remain in Normal mode. Also, you can change the default setting (Normal or Expert) from Edit, Preferences (General tab). Basic Actions are not listed in the Toolbox when in

Expert mode because the Basic Actions are just copies of Actions found in other categories. Finally, when you're ready to venture into Expert mode, a good way to ease into it is to create your script in Normal mode and then change to Expert mode. Remember, though, that you won't be able to change this script back to Normal if the syntax isn't perfect!

So just remember to be deliberate. If you want to add an Action—do it. But do it with a reason. You can create a mess pretty fast if you randomly try adding different Actions. Do one at a time, and each time take a moment to analyze the parameters you've set. We'll get into some more sophisticated tasks soon, but just take it slow.

Types of Actions

Now that we know how and where to place Actions, we can take a tour of some of the Actions available. While we can't cover each one in detail, we can cover some of the more common ones.

Navigation

Although there's no category of Actions called Navigation, there are basically two Actions that let your users navigate. Let's look at these.

Go To

Go To (as we've explored) jumps the playback head to a specific frame number, a frame label, or a different scene. The first exercise we did this hour used the Go To to jump back to a previous frame. Of course, we could have put this Action in a Button instance—perhaps gotoAndPlay(1), which would jump back to frame 1 and play, to let the user restart an animation. Whether the Action executes when the user clicks a button or when he happens to reach a keyframe, the Go To Action navigates.

NEW TERM   *Scenes* are a way of breaking up your Timeline for organization—almost like pages in a book. Playing a movie automatically plays one scene's Timeline after another as though it was one long Timeline. Use the Scene panel to insert, reorder, rename, and delete scenes.

Notice that Go To (when in Normal mode) has the default option checkbox Go To and Play (see Figure 14.12). Because of this, you don't need to add an extra Play Action at the keyframe you're going to, nor do you need one right after the Go To Action. Similarly, if you want to go to a frame but not play when you get there, just leave this option unchecked.

14

FIGURE 14.12
The Go To Action has a Go To and Play option. When this is unchecked, the Action changes to gotoAndStop.

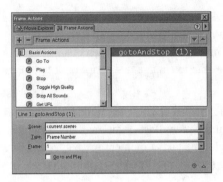

Get URL

While the Go To Action jumps the playback head to another frame, Get URL jumps the user to another Web page. If you're familiar with how a hyperlink works in HTML, Get URL is the same thing. With Go To you need to specify (as a parameter) the frame to which you are navigating. In Get URL, you need to specify to what *URL* you want to navigate.

NEW TERM *URL* stands for Uniform Resource Locator and is the address for any web page. If you want to use the Get URL to jump to my homepage, for example, you need to know the URL (which is http://www.teleport.com/~phillip).

There are a couple other parameters to specify when using the Get URL Action but we'll cover those in Hour 17, "Linking Your Movie to the Web." We can do a quick one right now to see how easy it really is.

Task: Make a Button That Hyperlinks to Another Web Page

1. In a new file, create a Button symbol and place an instance onstage.

2. With the Button instance selected, open the Actions panel.

3. Insert the Get URL Action (from the Basic Actions section of the Toolbox List). With the Get URL Action selected, type **http://www.teleport.com/~phillip** into the URL field (in the parameters area).

4. Test the movie (or, better yet, select File, Publish Preview, Default, F12—so you'll watch this in a browser). Just click the button in the Flash movie and, if you're connected to the Internet, you'll hyperlink to my home page.

Targeting Movie Clips

The navigation Actions we just saw are good for jumping around within a Timeline or throughout the Web. However, you know Movie Clips have their own Timeline. What happens when you want to jump around within a Movie Clip? If you put your Action inside the Movie Clip or if you attach the Action to the clip, it's pretty straightforward. If you have a Stop Action inside the Movie Clip, for example, it will cause the Movie Clip to stop (provided it has multiple frames). So it's easy when you put an Action in the master clip or on a clip instance.

It gets a little more complicated when you want to send an Action to another clip remotely. For example, say you have a Movie Clip and a button onstage (the button is not inside the clip). If you put a Stop Action on the button, it will cause only the main Timeline to stop (the Movie Clip won't stop). To direct an Action to a clip, you first target that particular instance of the Movie Clip (remember, you could have several instances onstage at once). This can be executed in Flash in two ways.

Consider that we have to do two things: address the clip and tell it what to do. Remember from Hour 12, "Animating Using Movie Clip and Graphic Symbols," that instances of Movie Clips can be named (via the Instance panel). If the clip is named, it will be easy to address. Now we just need to learn how to tell it what to do. Although there are more elegant ways to achieve this, the easiest to understand is through an Action called with. This Action is a little tricky because you need to take two steps: one to identify the clip instance you're targeting and two to add the Action or Actions you want it to do. By the way, the old version of the with Action was called Tell Target. Tell Target is only worth considering when publishing your movie to an older version of the Flash player (as you'll see in Hour 24, "Publishing Your Creation"). Tell Target and with can be used interchangeably, but with is suggested as Tell Target is being phased out.

When you select with from Actions in the Toolbox List, the only parameter you must specify is the object you're targeting. You can enter the name of the instance you're targeting as seen in Figure 14.13. Immediately following the with Action (and before the ending curly bracket), you place the Action to send to that Movie Clip.

14

FIGURE 14.13

The with Action requires that you specify the clip instance name you're targeting. You also include the Actions you want this target to perform.

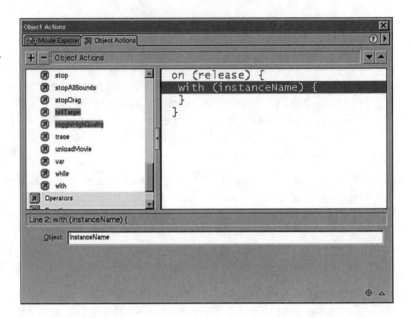

Naturally, it's not always that simple. Suppose you have a clip instance inside a Movie Clip. As long as you name each instance, it's easy to address them individually. Let's try it with a relatively complex Movie Clip containing clip instances.

Task: Use with to Target Nested Instances

In this task we use the with Action to Stop instances of wheels that are inside a clip of a car.

1. We'll need a car with rotating wheels like we made in Hour 12 in the task titled "Use a Movie Clip to Make a Rotating Wheel." If you recall we achieved this by working from the inside out. First we made a clip of a wheel called "Plain Wheel" (a circle with lines that would be noticeable when it rotated). Then we used an instance of the Plain Wheel to create another clip called "Rotating Wheel". Rotating Wheel contained an instance of Plain Wheel in frame 1 and frame 20. A Motion Tween to rotate the wheel was set in the first keyframe of Rotating Wheel. Finally, two instances of Rotating Wheel were used in the creation of the Car. Either revisit the task in Hour 12, or create the Rotating Wheel clip and we'll pick up from there.

2. Drag one instance of Rotating Wheel to the Stage. Test the movie to confirm the wheel is rotating and take note what direction it's rotating.

3. Drag another instance of Rotating Wheel and place it to the left of the other instance. With the Instance panel, name one of the instances "front_wheel" and the other "back_wheel" as in Figure 14.14.

FIGURE 14.14

Using the Instance panel we name each instance of the Wheel so it can be targeted individually.

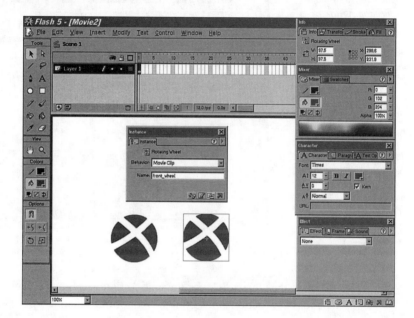

4. Draw a car body around the two wheels (nothing fancy). Select everything and choose Insert, Convert to Symbol (F8). Name this new Movie Clip "Car".

5. Onstage you have an instance of Car, but it has no instance name yet. Use the Instance panel to name this instance "the_car".

6. Finally, insert a keyframe at frame 40 and move "the_car" to another place onstage. In the first keyframe set Motion Tween.

7. In a new layer draw a rectangle to be used as a button. Select it and covert it to a symbol called "myButton" and make sure to set its behavior to Button. Copy and paste this button so we have two instances. Use the Effect panel to tint one green and one red.

8. Select just the red instance of myButton. Open the Actions panel. Insert a Stop Action (and leave it with the default release mouse event).

9. Test Movie and you'll see the stop button stops the car from moving across the screen, but it doesn't stop the wheels from spinning. We need to add additional Actions to stop each wheel.

10. Back in Flash, access the Actions for your button and insert the with Action right after the Stop Action as in Figure 14.15.

14

FIGURE 14.15

Within the release mouse event, we insert the with Action after the stop Action.

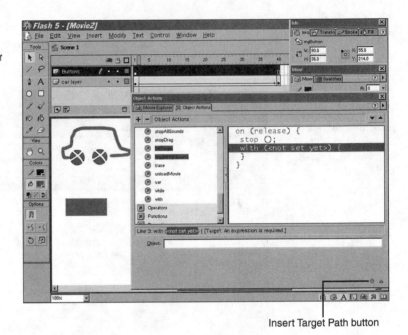

Insert Target Path button

11. Click in the Object field for the with Action's parameters then click the "Insert Target Path" button at the bottom-right of the panel; it looks like cross hairs.

12. The Insert Target Path dialog pops up with a hierarchy of named clips instances in your movie. Next to Car click the plus sign to see the named clip instances inside it. Click front_wheel then click OK. See Figure 14.16. Notice the object field should now read the_car.front_wheel (this follows the form of general to specific).

FIGURE 14.16

Using the Insert Target Path dialog we can target an individual instance.

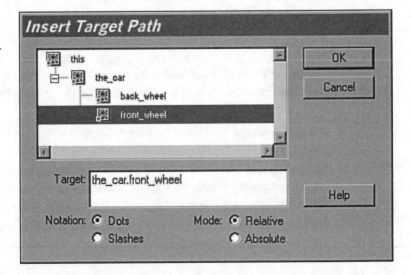

13. Now we have to say what we want to do with the front_wheel instance. Select the line containing with then double click the Stop Action from the Toolbox List to add it after the with Action. The result should look like Figure 14.17.

FIGURE 14.17

Between the two curly brackets of the with Action we insert the stop Action.

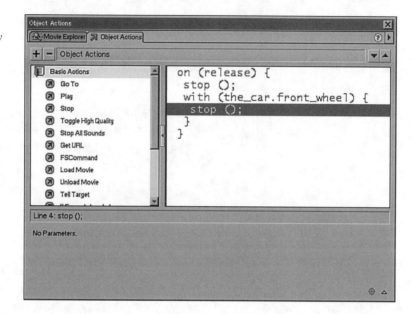

14. Repeat the process to target the back_wheel instance. Make sure when you add another with Action that it gets placed before the last curly bracket of the mouse event, but after the ending curly bracket for the first with Action. The final script should look like Figure 14.18.

15. Test Movie. When you click the red button, the car and both wheels stop. You could repeat this process with the play Action on the green button to allow a user to make the car move again.

14

FIGURE 14.18

The finished script targets the both instances of Rotating Wheel.

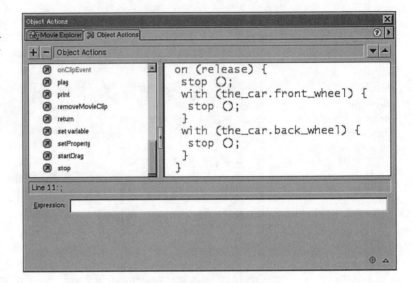

It may seem complex because we had to target three different Timelines just to stop the car! There happens to be a slightly easier way to achieve the task at hand. Notice the tricky part about the with Action is once you target the object, you have to place the stop Action before the ending curly bracket. Using a more direct approach you can simply use the evaluate Action and type: **the_car.back_wheel.stop()**. It's the same thing, but all run together in one line. However, it's more difficult because you have to know the exact syntax of the stop Action (the extra parenthesis are required, for example).

We'll look at this method next hour, but before you try to forget the with Action, notice the difference is you can only direct one Action to a target at a time using this direct method. Using the with Action, you can direct many Actions to a target, as long as they appear before the ending curly bracket. In Figure 14.19, I used the comment Action which doesn't *do* anything—I'm just trying to make the point you could target several Actions at once "with" the target clip.

FIGURE 14.19

The with Action is particularly useful when you want to send more than one Action to a targeted clip.

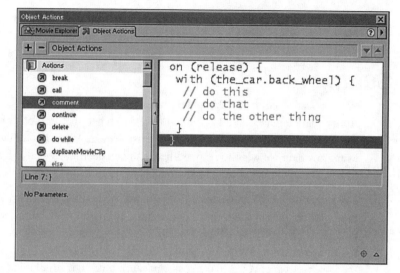

Finally, targeting clips is simple as long as you remember to name your instances. The Insert Target Path dialog is a nice way to learn the syntax to targeting. When you choose the file from the hierarchy, Flash will automatically put it in the correct syntax. Targeting clips goes from the "general to the specific" as in "the_car.back_wheel", but until you know these conventions, it's probably safer to use the Insert Target Path dialog.

Efficiency Tricks

Once you have an idea how to insert Actions, we can work on fine-tuning the technique. Besides the general suggestion to be deliberate and include no more Actions than necessary, there are a few more objective ways to be efficient.

The first technique is to use a separate layer for all frame Actions. You can put an Action in any keyframe, but sometimes you want an Action to execute when the playback head reaches the middle of a tween. Instead of inserting a keyframe (and effectively messing up the tween), use a separate layer to insert new keyframes. Not only will this prevent tweens from breaking, but you'll have only one layer in which to manage your frame Actions. Otherwise, you might be hunting through all your layers looking for Actions.

Another similar technique is to use a separate layer for all frame labels. In the second exercise, we saw the beauty of using labels as destination points for our Go To Actions. Just as you don't want to restrict the design of your tweens to accommodate frame Actions, it's nice to keep all your labels in a layer of their own. There's no reason to be stingy with layers—insert them as needed. Layers don't affect file size, and they can help organize your movie. (Layers affect the .fla file's size but not the exported .swf.)

14

There are many more efficiency tricks, but these are just a few that apply to Actions. We'll learn more throughout the rest of the book.

Summary

We've touched on the fundamental things you can do with Actions. We learned how an Action can be placed in a keyframe to execute when that frame is reached and in instances of buttons to execute when the user clicks. We learned that the exact mouse event to which we want to respond needs to be specified. We also learned how Actions can be placed on instances of Movie Clips.

Not only did we cover where Actions go, but we learned that many Actions require further specification in the form of parameters. If you understand this simple concept, you'll be able to apply that knowledge to almost any Action you encounter, because most require parameters. We just scratched the surface of how to use Actions, but hopefully the concepts we covered make sense, because the same structure and terms apply to all kinds of scripting in Flash.

Q&A

Q I put an Action (`gotoAndPlay (5)`) in the last frame of my movie and I swear it's never reaching the last frame, because I have some text that is supposed to appear briefly onstage. It works only if I put the Action one frame after the graphics—why?

A This is a critical concept: Frame Actions are executed *before* the on-stage graphics of that frame are displayed. If your Action says to go to another frame, it goes to the other frame before drawing the stage.

Q Why does my movie loop (effectively doing a `gotoAndPlay(1)` on the last frame) even though I haven't put any Actions in the movie?

A The option to automatically loop is set by default when you test the movie (and when you publish the movie). While testing, you can uncheck the option to loop from the Control menu (the Control menu of the Flash Player—not the Flash authoring program). If you turn this off, you most certainly won't see the movie loop unless you include an Action. By the way, normally you don't need a Stop Action at the end of your Timeline; if you simply uncheck the Loop option (when you publish), it will automatically stop on the last frame.

Q Which Action do I use to create a game such as I might see in a commercial video game?

A I hope it's obvious that we are taking baby steps first. It's amazing the kind of powerful things we've done this hour. It's going to take a lot more work before you're cranking out video games—though amazing games can be created, it takes a lot of work. We're just laying the foundation.

Workshop

The Workshop consists of quiz questions and answers to help you solidify your understanding of the material covered. Try to answer the questions before checking the answers.

Quiz

1. Where can Actions be inserted in Flash?

   A. Inside Button symbols, on keyframes, and inside Movie Clip symbols.

   B. Any keyframe except frame 1 (plus buttons and Movie Clips).

   C. On keyframes, Button instances, and Movie Clip instances.

2. What is an Action, anyway?

   A. Anything that moves onstage.

   B. A prebuilt Flash component that *does* something.

   C. What programmers call *functions*.

3. How many Actions can you place in one button?

   A. One for each mouse event.

   B. No more than two.

   C. As many as you want.

Quiz Answers

1. C. Remember you don't put Actions inside master Button symbols! Of course, within master Movie Clips you can have Actions in keyframes and buttons, but answer C covers those places.

2. B. It's a pretty generic term, so this is the best definition. You can learn more about functions in Appendix B, but strictly speaking most Actions are actually methods.

3. C. There's really no limit. One event could result in many Actions being executed, and you can have several events within one button.

14

Hour 15

ActionScripting Applications for Advanced Interactivity

You saw last hour how a few strategically placed Actions can control how your movie plays. An Action under a button instance gives the user the power to make that Action execute when he or she clicks the button. Also, you can place Actions in a keyframe to make the movie jump back to another frame—effectively looping. Last hour was fun, but it was just the tip of the iceberg!

This hour continues on the subject of adding interactivity via ActionScript. You won't spend time learning exactly how to place Actions (that was covered last hour); instead, you'll forge ahead into applying the scripts for more complex tasks.

In this hour you will:

- Create drag-and-drop objects
- Learn the fundamentals of programming to track user data and set the visual properties of movie clips (to see them change)

You have a huge task in front of you! Even if you don't see yourself as a "programmer," this hour should give you a sense of Flash's potential. If you're already into programming, this hour may not challenge you, but it will give you the fundamental tools with which you can grow on your own later.

Making Drag-and-Drop Interactions

One of the most effective ways to give your users the power to interact is by letting them drag items around the Stage. It is essential for the creation of most games, and it's also a particularly effective teaching method because some people are "tactile" learners (whereas others might be visual or aural learners). For whatever reason, you may desire to let your users move items around the Stage. This is simple to do in Flash.

There's a slight dilemma, however. In Flash, the simplest way to determine when a user clicks a specific area involves the use of buttons. That's okay, because you'll be able to place a StartDrag Action on a button instance. The problem is that the StartDrag Action requires you to specify (as a parameter) the Movie Clip you want to start dragging, which means that StartDrag only applies to Movie Clips. However, you want to associate the Action with a button. (Although it's possible to use the mouse down clip event instead of a button with a mouse event, remember that the mouse down clip event is triggered when the user clicks anywhere—not just on the clip itself.)

Basic Method

Overcoming the dilemma that while only buttons have mouse events, only movie clips can be dragged is actually pretty easy: You just place a button inside the Movie Clip. The Action on the button will say "Start dragging the Movie Clip I'm inside of" (although not in exactly those words). You'll do just this in the following task, and it should all make sense.

Task: Make a Simple Draggable Movie Clip

In this task you'll create the simplest draggable Movie Clip possible. Here are the steps to follow:

1. In a new file, draw a square, select it, and convert it to a symbol. Call the symbol "Button" and make sure its behavior is Button.

2. Select the instance of the button you just created and convert it to a symbol. (Of course, it's already a symbol, but this will create a new symbol with an instance of a button inside.) Call it "Clip w/Button" and make sure the behavior is Movie Clip.

3. Be sure the instance onstage is the Movie Clip and not the button. Now you're going to go inside the clip and attach an Action to the button that effectively says "drag me." Double-click the Movie Clip instance (so you're editing the master version of the clip, as shown in Figure 15.1). Select the button instance and open the Actions panel. From the Toolbox list in the Actions category, double-click startDrag.

FIGURE 15.1

You want to make sure you're attaching the startDrag Action to the button instance inside the clip "Clip w/Button" (as you can see by the address bar).

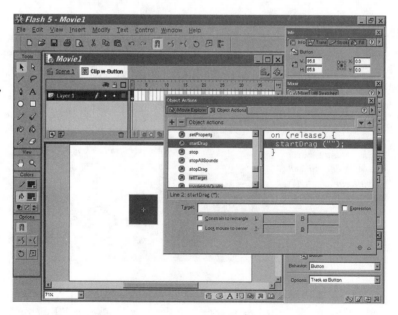

4. Go ahead and test the movie to see what works and what doesn't. If you click and drag, the Movie Clip doesn't move. However, if you click and let go on the square, you'll start dragging—but that's after you let go!

5. To fix this, go back to the button instance inside the Movie Clip and change the mouse event from the default "Release" to "Press," as shown in Figure 15.2. (Because you can have more than one mouse event, you'll have to deselect Release and then check Press.) If you test the Movie Clip now, you'll see that it works fine, except you can't let go of the clip once you start dragging.

FIGURE 15.2

Selecting the first line in the script lets you change the specific mouse event to which you're going to respond.

6. The button instance in the clip needs to respond to two events. For the Press event, it needs to start dragging (which it does), and for the Release event, it needs to stop dragging. Therefore, drag the stopDrag Action from the Toolbox to *below* the bottom of the script in the Script area of the Action panel, as shown in Figure 15.3.

FIGURE 15.3

Dragging the stopDrag Action below the end of the Press mouse event causes a new mouse event to be created (Actions attached to buttons must be inside a mouse event).

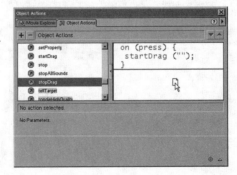

7. The second mouse event (wrapping the stopDrag Action) uses the Release event by default. This is good, but you should also click Release Outside, which will work if the user releases outside this button. Basically, this is a failsafe way to make sure the user can let go of the clip. The result should look like what's shown in Figure 15.4. Take a good look at the result, which should now make sense to you as it currently reads. It should also work when you test it.

FIGURE 15.4

The finished version of a simple draggable Movie Clip script.

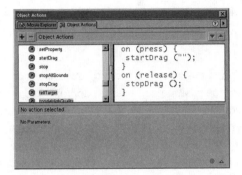

15

The Nitty-Gritty of Draggable Clips

The preceding task took more effort getting the mouse events right than it did figuring out the startDrag and stopDrag Actions. It was a little funky the way you had to put a button inside a Movie Clip to get the task to work. Other than that, it was really simple. However, now a couple of parameters in the startDrag Action need to be discussed.

In Figure 15.5 you can see a parameter named "Lock mouse to center." This parameter makes the clip snap into position so that the mouse is centered on the clip. You can test how this changes the behavior of the draggable clip you just created. This may not seem terribly important, but it makes the clip "feel" different. The user really knows this clip is draggable because as soon as he or she clicks to see it, the clip snaps into place. This is not necessarily what you always want, but it's nice to know this feature is available. When this parameter is checked, notice that the condition 'true' appears in the Script area.

FIGURE 15.5

A startDrag Action with the "Lock mouse to center" option selected causes the clip that's being dragged to snap into position so that the mouse is always centered on the clip.

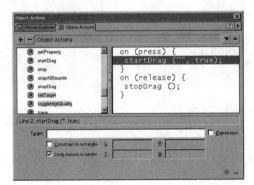

The other parameter is the "Constrain to rectangle" option. This lets you specify a rectangle inside which the clip will be draggable. If you select the Constrain option, you'll have to specify the sides of this imaginary rectangle outside which the user will not be able to drag the clip. You must specify the left (L), top (T), right (R), and bottom (B) sides. If nothing else, this can prevent the user from dragging the clip off the Stage entirely!

To calculate what numbers to use, first go back to your main scene and, by hand, position the clip in each extreme position and note the appropriate coordinate in the Info panel. As shown in Figure 15.6, you should make sure the Info panel's "center point" option shows the pixel positions of the center point, because the startDrag Constrain option uses the center point as a reference. Next, take careful note of the pixel coordinates in the X and Y boxes because that's what you'll need to use in the parameters for Constrain to rectangle. (By the way, you can use the Align panel to quickly position your clip to align with the edges of the Stage if you want.)

FIGURE 15.6

The Info panel can help you determine the X and Y coordinates of objects on the Stage.

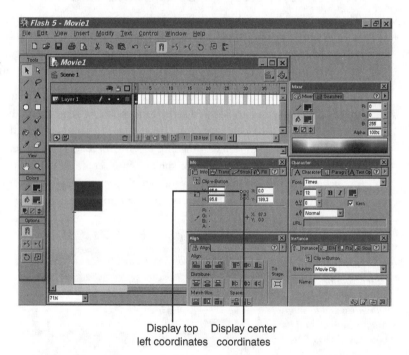

Display top   Display center
left coordinates   coordinates

Finally, the preceding task involved the most common use of draggable clips—making the user click a button to drag a clip. However, you don't necessarily have to put the startDrag Action in a button instance. You can have a startDrag Action in a keyframe. Suppose that in the very first frame of your movie you want to use startDrag so that the user's mouse has a Movie Clip "stuck" (that is, the Movie Clip moves along with the user's cursor). Although this situation may not occur often, it does bring up the last parameter in the startDrag Action—the Target field.

The Target field is where you specify the instance name for the Movie Clip you want to start dragging. In the task, you didn't specify any target, but it worked because when you leave the Target field blank, Flash assumes you're referring to the Movie Clip you're currently in. Sort of like when you address a letter to someone in another state, you don't need to include "USA" in the address. If you omit this, the post office knows you're targeting the country in which the letter is mailed. However, if you send a letter from another country, you should certainly include "USA" in the address. Similarly, in Flash, if you put the startDrag Action inside the clip you want to drag, you don't need to specify a target. However, if you use a keyframe Action to start the dragging, you'll need to specify the instance name of the clip you're targeting. The same dot or slash syntax used in the with Action (mentioned last hour) can be used to target the clip you want to start dragging.

Programming in Flash

It seems like there's a lot to draggable clips. I've included a lot of detail so far because using draggable clips is one of the most advanced features that doesn't require programming. The term *programming* gets tossed around a lot, but as discussed last hour, my definition of programming is using the ActionScript language to make a Flash movie play back differently based on user input, user interaction, timing issues, or data found outside of Flash. If you want your movie to play back the same each time (like a narrative or a cartoon, for example), you don't need to do any programming. Even if you want relatively sophisticated interactivity (buttons, draggable clips, and so on), you can achieve it with basic Actions. However, for a much more dynamic (changing) movie, you're going to need to do some programming. Fortunately, ActionScripting is fairly easy to use. Using Flash's Action panel makes it easy because you just fill in the parameters as needed. When you approach the process of programming in small steps it will be easier than one would imagine after looking at the cryptic code some programmers create. It doesn't have to be difficult.

The rest of this hour introduces you to most of the programming capabilities of Flash. An entire book could be devoted to this topic, so naturally, it can't be fully covered in just this hour. I'm just going to point the way. If you have little interest in programming, it's safe to skip the rest of this hour. You can always come back later if needed. There's plenty more information in later hours, so only jump ahead to Hour 16, "Using Smart Clips." (Don't skip the rest of the book!)

Variables

Variables are a safe (yet temporary) place to store information. Imagine each variable as an individual whiteboard. You can write whatever you want on the whiteboard, erase it, and then write something else in its place. Variables are similar. Variables are useful because you might want to save data while the movie plays.

A key concept with variables is that each one has a name and a value. With a whiteboard, whatever is written on the whiteboard is the current value. If you have several white-boards—maybe one has a phone number, another has an address, and so on—you'd want to name (or label) the whiteboards so you know which one is which. If you name one "phone_number" and the other "address," you could simply find out the value of "phone_number." It would be less complicated than trying to remember which white-board is which. Transferring this analogy to real variables, imagine that you have a vari-able named "phone_number" whose value is whatever number you put into it.

You can do two things with variables:

- Set or change their values
- Ascertain or check their values

Notice, I didn't mention that you can create variables. You don't really create them, they simply exist as soon as you set the value for one.

You can actually view variables right on the Stage. First use the Text tool to place some text on the Stage and then select the block of text (with the Arrow tool). From the Text Options panel and change the type from the default "Static Text" to "Dynamic Text"—which will be updated from the variables you set—or "Input Text" if you want the user to be able to change the variable's value. Next, you need to associate a variable with this (Dynamic or Input) text. The field Variable lets you specify the name for the variable (see Figure 15.7). Once you've done this, the text becomes attached to the variable. In Dynamic Text, if the variable's value changes, the text reflects the change. If it's Input Text and the user changes the text, the variable's value changes. This is pretty useful because you can change (or let the user change) a variable's value at any time—that way, the text onscreen changes.

FIGURE 15.7

The Text Options panel lets you specify the type of text block (in this case Dynamic Text). For Dy-namic and Input Text, you must specify a vari-able name that's associ-ated with this block. The current value of the variable will always be displayed in this text block.

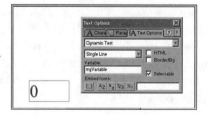

15

In practical terms, common tasks that you'll need variables for might include the following:

- Asking the user for his or her name (so you can use it later)
- Counting how many times the user has been to part of your movie (so you can change the course after he or she has seen something several times)
- Quizzing the user and tracking his or her score
- Displaying text that changes frequently such as a prompt. You can use Dynamic Text to reflect the current value of a variable that you keep changing.

In the following task, you'll learn how to use a variable to get a user's name.

Task: Use a Variable to Get the User's Name

This task involves letting the user input data (his or her name), and it also shows how you can monitor the user's input. Here are the steps:

1. In a new file open the Text Options panel (which normally affects text already created but can also affect text about to be typed). Set the drop-down list to "Input Text" (the default is "Static Text"). Also, check the Border/Bg check box. Select the Text tool and click once to create a block of text. The little square at the bottom right of the text can be used to change the margins of the text box. One thing that's interesting about Input Text (and Dynamic Text) is that you can create a text block with nothing in it.

2. With the text block selected (using either your I-beam cursor in the field or the Arrow tool, select the entire block), set the Variable field in the Text Options panel to read "username" (see Figure 15.8).

FIGURE 15.8

An Input Text block into which the user will type his or her name.

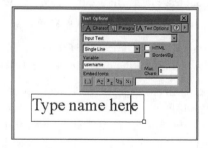

3. Put a "stop" Action in Frame 1.

4. Create a button and put an instance next to the text block you just created. Put a "play" Action on the button instance. The default mouse event, Release, is fine; however, in the event the user clicks Enter on the keyboard this should effectively

press the button too. Therefore, select the first line in the button action and click the check box labeled Key Press (in the parameter area). Make sure the I-beam cursor is blinking in the field next to Key Press and go ahead and press your Enter key (for Macintosh users, press your Return key). Notice that Flash fills in the key press option.

5. At frame 10, insert a blank keyframe (F7) and create another text field. This one should be Dynamic Text (so the user can't edit it) and be associated with the variable "message."

6. Now you're going to put a couple Actions in the keyframe on frame 10. Select the keyframe and then open the Actions panel. The first thing you'll do is to use the Set Variable Action (found under Actions) to *populate* the text field—or more specifically, change the value of that variable. Insert a Set Variable Action while frame 10 is selected. Now you can specify the parameters.

7. The Variable field requires that you input the name of the variable. Type `message` into the Variable field.

8. The Value field is where you specify what goes into the variable. You're going to make it read "Welcome blank," where "blank" is whatever name the user types into the field on frame 1. This is going to require you to build the string dynamically. Select the Expression check box to the right of the Value field, because you want Flash to *evaluate* what is typed. You don't want Flash to use literally what is typed verbatim because you can't possibly know what the user's going to type. With Expression checked, in the Value field, type `"Welcome " + username`. The plus sign concatenates (or *connects*) these two items. The first part is simply the string "Welcome " (notice the extra space). Because it's in quotes, Flash will display it exactly as typed. The second part refers to the variable "username." Because this is not typed between the quotes, Flash will use the *value* of the variable, not its name.

9. Add another Stop Action at frame 10. Using Test Movie, see how it works.

> **NEW TERM** *Populate* is a popular term for the process of filling in data. It can be a manual process that you follow while editing or it can be done at runtime with scripting.

The preceding task lets you experiment with two basic features of variables: controlling variables (by setting values) and showing variables to the user. You let the user directly affect the variable (by typing right into the Input Text). Consider that the user got to see the value of the variable onscreen. Of course, the "message" variable was assembled before you let the user see it. Often, you'll need to use variables but you have no need (or desire) to show them to the user. For instance, maybe you're tracking the total number of questions users have answered correctly. This is not something they need to see.

The next task shows you how to increment a variable. It's very simple: A variable named "count" will increase every time the user clicks a button. Then, just to prove it's working, you'll have another button that reveals the current value of "count." This exercise may seem simplistic, but it's very useful. What's more, incrementing variables is so common that you need to know how to do it.

Task: Increment a Variable

This task demonstrates incrementing a variable and then revealing it to the user. Here are the steps:

1. In a new file create a button and a Dynamic Text block (with a zero in it). Associate the variable "count" with the text. This automatically creates the "count" variable.

2. On the button, insert the "evaluate" Action. This Action lets you type anything you want. Type **count++**. This means to increment the value of the variable "count." (That is, add 1 to it.) (See Figure 15.9.)

FIGURE 15.9

The Action attached to the button will increment the value of "count."

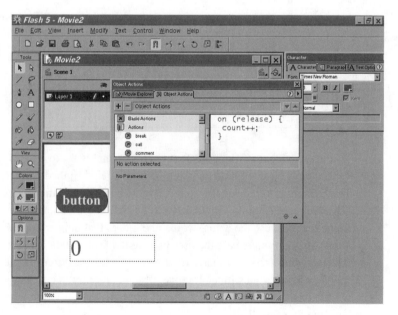

3. Test the movie and you should see the "count" variable increment. Too easy, eh? Okay, change the variable associated with the text field to "message." Test the movie again. Is it working? Just because you don't see the value of the "count" variable doesn't mean it's not changing. (Actually, as you'll see in Hour 23,

"Learning How to Learn Flash," the Debugger can be opened to reveal the value of all your variables.) Leave the "message" variable associated with the Dynamic Text.

4. Drag another instance of your button onto the Stage and insert another evaluate Action. Then type `message="Your total is "+count`.

5. When you test the movie, click the first button seven times. Then when you click the new button, the message text changes onscreen. The point is that your variable can be changing even though you don't see it onstage.

6. Finally, the only bug in this program comes if the user starts clicking the incrementing button after he or she has clicked the new totaling button. It creates the message fine the first time, but then the information becomes old. You should add an evaluate Action to the incrementing button (the first button). Within the same mouse event that's using "count++" (maybe right below it), insert the evaluate Action and type `message=""`. This way, the field will be cleared every time the user presses the increment button.

To Increment the value of the variable "count" you simply used the script count++. You can also decrease a variable's value with the script count-- (that is, use your variable's name followed by two minus signs). Finally, if you want to increment by a larger number than 1 use: count+=5 which will increase the variable count's value by five. To decrease in larger numbers use count-=5. (Replace the 5 with whatever number you want the increments to jump by.)

You may notice that when the Text Options panel is set to either Dynamic Text or Input Text, there's a row of buttons at the bottom labeled Embed Fonts (see Figure 15.10). This is similar to the "device fonts" issue when using Static Text, as explained in Hour 2, "Drawing and Painting Original Art in Flash." These options only apply to Dynamic and Input Text because the actual words and letters that appear may change. Flash needs to know whether you expect the user to have the font installed already. If you use a fancy font that your users don't have (and you leave these buttons deselected), another font will be used as a substitute. The overall look and the spacing may change drastically if you do this. (Of course, it won't be an issue on your machine when you test because you have the font installed.)

If you're not sure your users have the selected font (the safest bet is that they don't), you can opt to "embed" the entire font outline (of your special font) so it will appear properly no matter what the contents of the text block may become. This, naturally, adds to the file size significantly. Alternatively, you can select one or several of the other buttons to selectively include a subset of the whole font—that is, just uppercase characters, just lowercase characters, or just numbers. You could even specify the exact characters you in the field at the bottom right of the Text Options panel. Including the minimum necessary will help maintain a small file size.

FIGURE 15.10

The bottom row of buttons in the Text Options panel (when Dynamic or Input Text is selected) provides options on how to handle fonts.

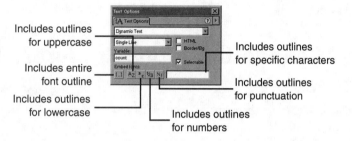

Includes outlines for uppercase

Includes entire font outline

Includes outlines for lowercase

Includes outlines for numbers

Includes outlines for specific characters

Includes outlines for punctuation

You may have noticed that the evaluate Action was used to create a home-made version of the Set Variable Action. However, the result was the same. It's almost as though you went into Expert Mode (found in the menu under the options arrow at the top right of the Actions panel), which allows you to type anything you want. With the evaluate Action, you can type anything you want into the parameters, one line at a time. This is handy if you intend to do something simple (such as increment a variable) and you don't feel like hunting down the appropriate Action. Just realize that this freedom opens the opportunity for you to type something that may not work. Luckily, while in Normal mode, Flash highlights faulty syntax and adds the required semi-colon at the end of each line.

Properties

Every object has properties that can be changed during authoring. You can think of *properties* as visual attributes (although some properties are not visible). For example, every object has two position properties (one for x and one for y). Common built-in properties include _x (X position), _y (Y position), _alpha (current alpha setting), and _rotation (the current rotation of a clip). By the way, all the built-in properties are listed in the Properties category of the Toolbox list in the Actions panel. Movie Clips are a type of object that works differently than other objects in Flash. Not only can you set Movie Clip properties during authoring in Flash, but through ActionScript you can change them dynamically during runtime, too. For instance, you can effectively move a Movie Clip instance by changing its _x and _y properties.

Setting Properties

Although instances of buttons and Graphic symbols can have color effects and other properties changed while authoring, only instances of Movie Clips can change during runtime. To change a property of a clip with ActionScript, you simply target the clip, specify the property, and set it to a new value. The following task shows you just how easy this can be.

Task: Change the Alpha Property of a Clip Instance

This task changes the alpha of a movie clip when the user clicks a button. Here are the steps to follow:

1. In a new file, place a button and a Movie Clip on the Stage. Select the Movie Clip onstage and use the Instance panel to name the instance of the clip "theClip."

2. In the button instance, insert the evaluate Action and type **theClip._alpha=50** into the Expression parameter as shown in Figure 15.11.

FIGURE 15.11

The evaluate Action attached to the button refers to the clip instance named "theClip" to change its alpha.

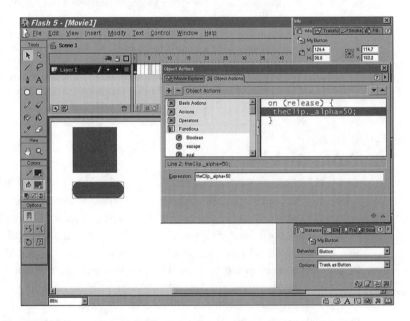

3. Test the movie, and you'll see "theClip" instance change to 50% alpha.

The preceding task required very little scripting. The evaluate Action "theClip._alpha=50" might seem a bit cryptic. Just so you know, there's another way to achieve the same result. You can use the Set Property Action instead. The advantage of Set Property is you'll be stepped through each parameter. You simply specify the property you want changed, the target clip you want to change, and the value you want it changed to as in Figure 15.12. This feature is left over from Flash 4. You may find it easier, although you'll see the technique you used in the preceding task is more versatile.

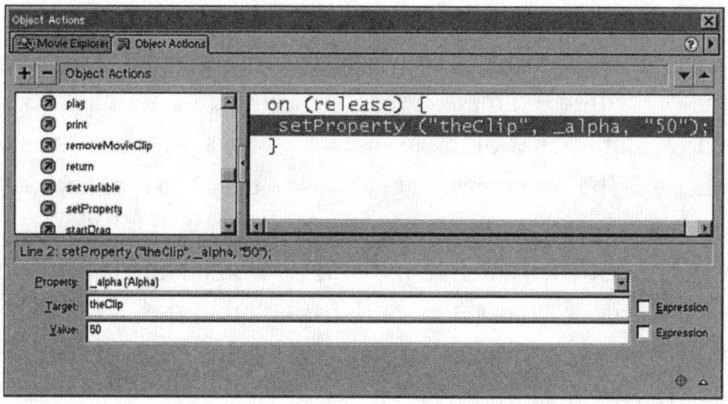

FIGURE 15.12

The Set Property Action is, in some ways, easier because you simply fill in parameters.

The seemingly cryptic line of code you put into the button above is actually pretty simple. It uses *Object Property syntax*. It's a little funky at first, but once you get it, there's no stopping you. It always follows the form "object.property." In this case, you want to change the alpha of an instance called "theClip." The object is the clip instance, and the property you're changing is _alpha. (Notice that all built-in properties are preceded by an underscore.) Translated, this means, "theClip's alpha is assigned the value 50."

The fact you're referring to the clip from outside (that is, from the button, which is not inside the Movie Clip) means you had to target the clip. If there were a clip inside the clip that you wanted to affect, you could have targeted the clip in the form of **theClip.clipInAClip._alpha=50**, where "clipInAClip" is the instance name of the clip inside the Movie Clip. Notice targets and properties are all separated by periods (when speaking you'd say "dot" which is why it's called "dot syntax"). Remember from Hour 14, "Using Actions to Create Non-Linear Movies," you targeted a clip within a clip to make it stop the same way you're targeting clips to change their properties.

It's not always so tricky. You could change the code to read **_alpha=50**. Go ahead and try it. First, draw a circle or something on the Stage (so you'll see more than just the button and Movie Clip). Then change the script inside the button (to **_alpha=50**), test the movie, and notice that everything on the Stage changes! Now go back and cut the button from the main scene and paste it inside the master Movie Clip. Now when the button is pressed, everything inside the clip instance (including the button) changes to alpha 50. Copy and paste the clip so you have multiple instances of the clip (now with the button inside each one). You'll see the button only changes the alpha of the instance in which you clicked. This is kind of cool, considering you don't even have to name any instances or specify the clip you're targeting. In conclusion, you can target specific clip instances by name or (if you omit the target) Flash will automatically target the clip instance where the script is contained.

Getting Properties

Besides setting properties (like how you *set* the alpha of the clip), you can also ascertain—that is, *get*—the current value of any property. To access a property, use the same form as the preceding example (you'll just check it, not change it). For example, maybe you have a Dynamic Text block associated with a variable "message" and an Action that reads `message="The current alpha is "+theClip._alpha +"%"`. Since `theClip._alpha` is not within quote marks Flash will get the current alpha value of the clip and stick it between the two parts of a string. Then the whole (combined) string is placed in the variable "message," and displayed in the dynamic text box. Access to properties follows the same form whether you're setting the property or getting the property. It's always "*object dot property.*"

Getting a property can be combined with setting a property. In the following task, you'll use two buttons that change the alpha of a clip. One button reduces the alpha, and the other increases it. Obviously, this will require more than just setting the alpha. You can't just set the alpha to "10 less." You have to know "10 less than what." Therefore, you'll first get the current alpha and set the alpha to 10 less than that. (This is easier to see when you try it.)

Task: Make Buttons That Increase and Decrease the Alpha Setting of a Clip

This task involves both setting and getting properties of a clip. Here are the steps:

1. On the Stage you'll need two buttons and one clip. Name the clip instance (as before, not the name in the library) "theClip."

2. Attach an evaluate Action to one of the buttons and type `theClip._alpha=theClip._alpha-10` as in Figure 15.13 (This means theClip's alpha should be assigned the value of "theClip's alpha minus 10.")

FIGURE 15.13

This evaluate Action set theClip's alpha to whatever the clip's alpha is currently minus 10.

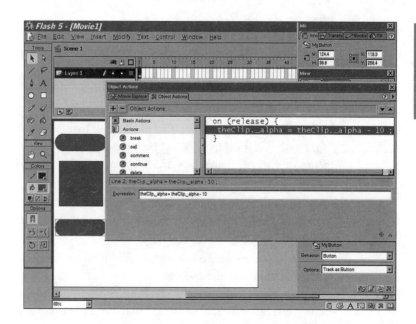

3. The other button should also have an evaluate Action, but with this code:
    `theClip._alpha=theClip._alpha+10`.

4. Test the movie!

Making Homemade Properties

One last concept about properties: It's easiest to think of properties as being visual or physical. Position, alpha, and scale are some of the built-in properties of Movie Clips. Even people have properties that are visual or physical in nature—hair color, height, weight, and so on. However, people can also have invisible properties, such as IQ and creativity. In Flash, there are built-in (visual) properties, but you can make up your own properties, too. These properties, most often, will not be visible—but they're still real. Therefore, clip instances can have homemade properties.

Once you get the concept, it's actually very simple. A variable that's inside a Movie Clip becomes a unique property of each instance created. Just like the built-in property "position" can be unique to every instance of the same clip, if you have a variable inside a clip, the value for that variable will be unique for each instance of the clip. This is how you make homemade properties! To create a variable in a clip instance (which is, effectively, a property), you just start using the variable—just like how you "created" variables before. In the following task, you'll actually see the variable displayed, but that's just so you can watch it working.

Task: Create and Increment a Custom Property in a Movie Clip

In this task you're introduced to using variables that are unique to instances of a clip (that is, homemade properties). Here are the steps:

1. Draw a circle and a Dynamic Text block close together. Associate a variable named "age" with that text block. Select both the circle and the text block and convert them to a symbol. Name the symbol "Aging Clip" and make sure it's a Movie Clip.

2. Step 1 should leave one instance of "Aging Clip" on the Stage, but you'll need one more. Therefore, drag another instance from the Library (or copy/paste the one on the Stage). Name one instance "Clip1" and the other "Clip2" (via the Instance panel).

3. Create a button and make two instances of it on the Stage. In one button, insert the evaluate Action with the code `Clip1.age=Clip1.age+1`. (Notice that homemade properties aren't automatically preceded by an underscore, although you can include one in the variable's name.) In the other button, do the same thing but use the code `Clip2.age=Clip2.age-1`.

4. Check it out! Each click of the button increments the age variable inside the clip as though it was having a birthday. It's really the same master clip, but two different instances. Each has its own unique properties, including the made up "age" property. I should stress that this would have worked just as well even if you didn't have the Dynamic Text inside the master clip—you just wouldn't have seen anything.

Naturally, there's a lot more you can do with scripting. Some of the common programming routines, such as if statements, loops, and functions, haven't even been touched. That's not to say you can't do anything until you study these routines—just the opposite! With Flash, you can do a little bit of scripting, and it works. Then as you build your skills, you can add more sophistication. Your scripts can grow with you.

Summary

Once you get it, programming in Flash is pretty easy. The hard part becomes organizing the task at hand—that is, deciding what you have to do. Once you know what you need to do, it's almost routine to execute it. When you have a good handle on targeting, variables, and properties, you'll be unstoppable.

This hour explored draggable clips extensively. Remember you don't need to specify a target when the script you write is in a clip or attached it to a clip. The only tricky part with draggable clips is determining which mouse event (Press or Release) to respond to.

We covered two significant programming concepts: variables and properties. Variables store data while a movie plays. You can change variables, watch them change (in Dynamic Text blocks), let the user change them (via Input Text blocks), and ascertain their values any time by simply referring to them in a script. You learned how to "set" and "get" properties of clip instances. Setting built-in properties such as _x, _y, and _alpha will have immediate and visual effects on clip instances. You learned the *object* dot *property* syntax for referring to or changing properties of specific clips. Finally, you learned how variables in clips are effectively homemade properties—they can be ascertained or changed just like the built-in properties, although they often don't change anything visually.

Q&A

Q Attached to a clip instance, I've placed a startDrag wrapped in a "mouse down" clip event and a stopDrag inside a "mouse up" event. This seems to work fine. So, why did we bother doing it with a button *inside* the clip?

A It may seem to work, but what you described will actually let the user drag the clip wherever he or she clicks—even if the user doesn't click the clip! The button was used because only buttons allow you to control where the user must click.

Q I put a Dynamic Text block onscreen that's associated with the variable "counter." When I use the code counter=counter+1, I see 1's inserted at the end of the text block (not added). What's up with that?

A You're encountering a few things. First, the "+" symbol both adds numbers and concatenates strings. You could try the code counter++, which effectively does the same thing. However, this won't work if you have a non-number in your text block initially (you'll likely see "NaN," which means "not a number"). The issue is that numbers are different from strings. Flash figures that if something's in a Dynamic Text block, it's probably a string. Suppose someone asks you how many square feet you weigh. This doesn't make sense because the data types are mixed. Similarly, you'll encounter this kind of issue when mixing strings and numbers (two kinds of data). You can fix this particular problem with the Number function (for example, counter=Number(counter)+1).

Q I set the "IQ" property of one Movie Clip to 55 (with theClip.IQ=55) and another one to 120, but they don't look or act any differently.

A If you use one of the built-in properties (such as _x or _alpha), you'll likely see a change, but homemade properties are really just variables inside the clip. You can change them all you want, but if you want to see a change, you need to *use* those properties in conjunction with the built-in ones. For example, you could put a script in a frame or button that reads `theClip._x=theClip.IQ * 10`. This would locate one clip at the x-coordinate 550 and the other at 1200. (The asterisk performs multiplication.)

Workshop

The Workshop consists of quiz questions and answers to help you solidify your understanding of the material covered. Try to answer the questions before checking the answers.

Quiz

1. How does Flash know which clip instance you intend to drag when you use a startDrag Action?

   A. It's obvious because you'll start dragging the clip you clicked.

   B. Flash doesn't know—that's why you always have to specify the clip instance name as a parameter in the Target field.

   C. Flash will either let you start dragging the clip specified in the Target field or (if none is specified) let you start dragging the clip in which the Action is placed.

2. How do you create a new variable?

   A. Wait until the playback head has at least reached frame 2.

   B. Just start using them as you need them, any time you want.

   C. By inserting the Action newVariable.

3. Do you have to use ActionScripting to change the alpha of a clip instance?

   A. Yes, you do it via the _alpha property.

   B. No, you can use the _visibility property.

   C. No, you can do it by hand via the Effect panel.

Quiz Answers

1. C. Either you specify the intended clip by its instance name or, if you leave the Target field blank, Flash figures you mean the current clip. If you leave the Target field blank and you're not in a clip (if you're in the main scene, for example), Flash will start dragging the entire movie!

2. B. Although it's possible to initialize a variable another way, it's not necessary. You can just start using variables as you need them.

3. C. This is, of course, a trick question. There is a _visibility property, but you haven't learned about it yet. When _ visibility is set to 0, the clip disappears. When _visibility is set to 1, the clip is fully visible. I just wanted to point out that you can change properties by hand during authoring (using the Effect panel, for example), although this doesn't enable you to see properties change at runtime.

15

Hour 16

Using Smart Clips

Last hour you studied programming. For some, it was probably more technical than you'd prefer; for others, it wasn't technical enough. This split is natural. Some people like to express their creativity by solving puzzles, whereas others like more artistic endeavors. One of the great things about Flash is it can appeal to both types of people—and a Smart Clip is a great example of this fact.

A *Smart Clip* is a version of a Movie Clip that has programming code encapsulated in it so that a nontechnical person can use it without having to know how it works. Anyone can use a Smart Clip. Depending on the features built into the Smart Clip, it can do some pretty fancy stuff.

In this hour you will:

- Explore how to use a few of the Smart Clips that ship with Flash
- Learn the basics of how to make a Smart Clip
- Practice using Smart Clips in your movies

This hour you'll learn how to create and use Smart Clips—but mainly how to use them. First, though, it's important to get one concept straight: Smart Clips are used while authoring Flash, but someone had to create them. It's not as simple to say *the author* and *the user* anymore because there's another author who created the Smart Clip to begin with. I'll often refer to the *using author*, meaning the person who's using the Smart Clip while authoring their Flash file (not to be confused with the author who created the Smart Clip).

What Is a Smart Clip?

I described Smart Clips as Movie Clips with code in them. However, a Movie Clip with Actions inside (maybe on a button or in a keyframe) doesn't automatically become a Smart Clip. A Smart Clip is different because each instance can have unique parameters. Just as each occurrence of a Go To Action has a unique value for the parameter specifying which frame to go to, Smart Clip instances have clip parameters that can be set uniquely.

You'll learn exactly how you create a Smart Clip later, but first you're going to use one of the Smart Clips that come with Flash 5. Before you do this, I want to stress that these aren't "built-in" Smart Clips. A talented Flash programmer created these with Flash. Macromedia provides a few sample Smart Clips to give you something you might be able to use as well as to show you how they're made. You can make them yourself, too!

In the following task, you'll try one of the Smart Clips that ships with Flash—this way, you can see where you're headed. You'll find several Smart Clips from the Window, Common Libraries menu. Either select Smart Clips or Learning Interactions.

Task: Use the "Menu" Smart Clip

In this task you learn how to insert, modify, and use a Smart Clip that ships with Flash.

1. In a new file, select Window, Common Libraries, Smart Clips (this opens—as a Library—a file found in the Common Libraries folder, next to your installed version of Flash). Drag the Smart Clip named "Menu" into your movie (see Figure 16.1). The Menu Smart Clip lets you create a customized drop-down menu.

FIGURE 16.1

The Menu Smart Clip (found in the Smart Clips Library under Window, Common Libraries) lets you create a customized drop-down menu.

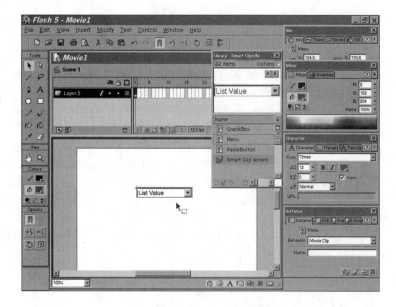

2. Close the Smart Clips Library to avoid any confusion. When you dragged the Menu clip into your movie, it was copied into your file's library, so you don't need the Smart Clips Library any more.

3. Select the instance of Menu on the Stage and open the Clip Parameters panel Either right-click (Control+click for the Macintosh) or find it under Panels in the Window menu (see Figure 16.2).

FIGURE 16.2

The Clip Parameters panel is available whenever an instance of a Smart Clip is selected. This is where you specify unique parameters for this instance.

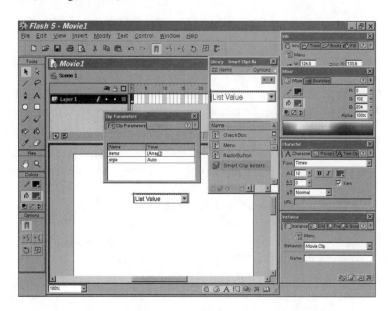

4. The Clip Parameters panel is where you specify unique parameters for this particular instance of the Smart Clip. Each parameter you can set is listed with both its name and current value. When you double-click a value, you can change it. The Items parameter contains the name of each item in the menu you're building. Because the menu will contain several names, it uses an *array* variable. Arrays are populated through the Values dialog box. Go ahead and double-click the value for "items" (it's listed as (Array[])). This will pop up the Values dialog box.

5. For now, just fill in a few names for your menu. From the Values dialog box that pops up when you double-click (Array[]), double-click the first name (DefaultValues1) and change it to "Small." Double-click "DefaultValues2" and change it to "Medium." Finally, change "DefaultValues3" to "Large." You can remove the two extra items by first selecting the line and then clicking the button with the minus sign. You could also add more, if necessary, using the plus sign button (see Figure 16.3).

FIGURE 16.3

Because the parameter that indicates which items go into your menu may contain several items, the parameter's form is "array." Arrays are populated through the Values dialog box.

6. You can test the movie and see how this Smart Clip (which you populated) works. It automatically uses the names of the items you specified, plus it resizes to accommodate how ever many items you've added.

NEW TERM   An *array* is a special kind of variable that contains several items in its value. Remember a variable has a name and a value. If the value for a variable is an array, that means there are actually several values.

Just so you can see the different types of parameters, go back to the instance of the Menu Smart Clip and access Clip Parameters again. Notice the other parameter (style). If you double-click the value (defaulted to Auto), you'll see drop-down list with the choices Mac, Win, and Auto. Go ahead and try Mac (if you're on a Windows machine) and see the effect. It's pretty cool because the menu normally behaves differently based on the user's operating system (this option will override the automatic feature). The type of variable used is "list" (whereas the last one was "array"). The difference is simply that the author using this Smart Clip may only select from a predetermined list (not add or subtract items, as in the case of "array"). The Smart Clip you're going to make will use the plain "Default" variable. When it comes to setting the parameter, you won't get the Values dialog box (as you did with the "items" array) and you won't get a fancy drop-down list (as was the case with "style"). Instead, you'll simply get a text field you can edit within the Clip Parameters panel (see Figure 16.4).

FIGURE 16.4

In the homemade clip you're going to make, the parameters can be typed in by hand. The first task, however, used both "array" and "list" parameter types.

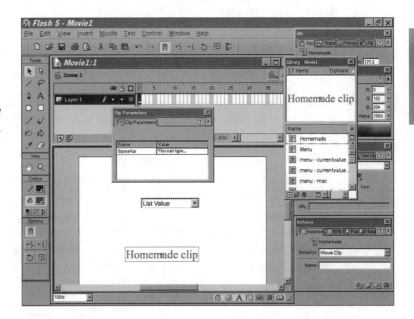

By the way, you could drag another instance of the Menu Smart Clip and set unique parameters for it to make a totally different drop-down menu. That's the idea behind Smart Clips. All the code is deep inside the clip; you (the using author) simply specify how you want your parameters set. The method is always the same—you input the values via the Clip Parameters panel.

Making Smart Clips

Creating your own Smart Clip can be a lot of work. However, as you just saw in the last task, once it's built, a Smart Clip can be very useful. It's often worth the time investment to make a Smart Clip if you think you can use it many times. I'm not going to get into all the details of making a Smart Clip, but I think it will be valuable for you to walk through the process of creating a simple one.

Besides demystifying the process, this section will help you identify the process of designing a good Smart Clip. Even if you never create one yourself, knowing the basic process will help you if you specify (to someone else) what kind of Smart Clip you'd like built. The truth is, once you have a clear idea what you want, building it is just a matter of execution.

Suppose you want a circle to move across the screen. Twelve times a second (or whatever your framerate is), you'd like the circle to move a little to the right. When it goes all the way to the right, you'd like it to start over again. You could simply create a clip and on an instance put the following code:

```
onClipEvent (enterFrame) {
    _x = _x+10;
    if (_x>550) {
        _x = 0;
    }
}
```

As you may recall from the last chapter, _x indicates a property—an object's location along the x-axis. The line _x = _x + 10 uses the "evaluate" Action. The first two lines say to set the _x property to 10 more than it is currently. The second two lines say that if the _x property is greater than 550, then set the _x property to 0.

If you want to reuse this code, you could copy and paste it on several instances of the clip. You could even adjust the first line to _x = _x+20 on one and _x = _x+5 on another, so the particular instance of the clip would jump by bigger or smaller steps and effectively look like it was moving faster or slower. However, suppose you changed your movie properties to a width of 400. You'd have to go back and change the Actions attached to each instance. (Of course, you could have used a variable, say "movieWidth," instead, but I'm just trying to make a point.) One of the problems with placing Actions right onto clip instances is that each clip has a unique copy of the code (so fixing it means fixing each instance).

If you put this code *inside* a clip, making an edit to the master Symbol would affect every instance. The only catch is that the enterFrame clip event (which happens 12 times a second) is only available to clip instances, not to graphic or button instances! The dilemma is more complicated than the solution. All you have to do is put the clip (with its attached script) inside another clip. The following task illustrates this point. Afterward, we'll look at more problems that crop up (which, luckily, can be solved with Smart Clips).

Task: Make the Start of Your First Smart Clip

This task lays the groundwork for the Smart Clip you're going to build. Follow these steps:

1. Draw a circle, covert it to a symbol called "Circle," and make sure it has the Movie Clip behavior. Select the clip you just created and convert it to a symbol. Call it "Clip containing Circle Clip" and make it a Movie Clip, too.

2. On the Stage you should have an instance of "Clip containing Circle Clip." Double-click it and you'll be editing the master symbol. Inside this symbol, you should have an instance of "Circle." Single-click this instance to select it, access the Actions panel, and insert the evaluate Action (Esc, E, V). Type **_x=_x+10**. Notice the first line, `onClipEvent`, is responding to the "load" event. Select this line and change it to `enterFrame` (see Figure 16.5). This means that this Action will be performed every time your Timeline goes to a new frame. If your movie is running at 12fps, this Action will occur 12 times a second.

16

FIGURE 16.5

Changing the clip event to which this code responds will make the "Circle" (inside "Clip containing Circle Clip") move 12 times a second.

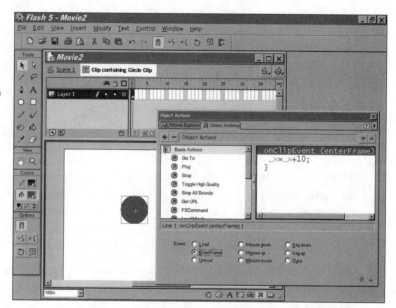

3. Right after the line _x=_x+10, insert an "if" Action (found under the Actions section of the Toolbox). The parameter for "if" is the condition that has to be true in order for the code that follows to execute. In the condition field "of the parameters" type **_x>550**. Next, insert another evaluate Action (just type Esc, E, V) and then type **_x=0**. The result should look like Figure 16.6.

4. Save your file—you'll be building on it later. Test it out!

FIGURE 16.6

The finished version of the script attached to the "Circle" instance.

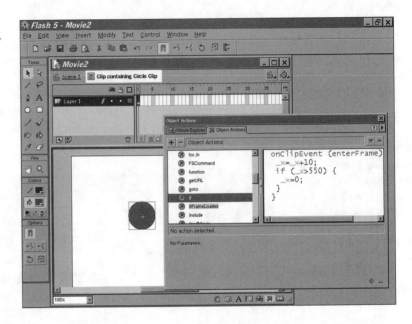

This task fixed the issue of "550" being duplicated in several instances. Go ahead and drag more instances of "Clip containing Circle Clip." They'll all work fine. Plus, if you change the "550" inside the master clip to 100, the change will be reflected in each instance. However, if you want the effective speed to vary (and change _x=_x+10 to _x=_x+20), you'll notice this change is reflected everywhere, too!

So how do you make it possible to change the effective speed of each instance without taking the code out of the master clip? Remember, you can have two instances of the same clip, but must have a unique _x property. You'll create a homemade property called "speed" that can be different in each instance. So where you had been using _x=_x+10, you'll change it to read _x=_x+speed. Then your only job will be to set "speed" differently for each instance. Just realize you're moving one tiny step at a time, but you'll get there.

Task: Add a Homemade Property

In this task you'll create a property that can vary in each instance of the Smart Clip. Here are the steps:

1. Inside "Clip containing Circle Clip," select the clip instance of "Circle" and open the Actions panel. Change the line _x=_x+10 to _x=_x+speed, as shown in Figure 16.7.

FIGURE 16.7

You can change your "hard-wired" 10 to a made-up property that will vary in each instance.

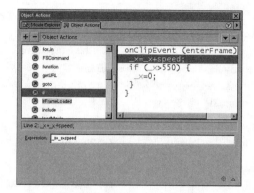

2. While you're inside "Clip containing Circle Clip," create a Dynamic Text block (right next to the clip of "Circle"). Type **0** in it as a placeholder. Associate the variable "speed" through Text Options, as shown in Figure 16.8. Also, make the margin big enough as speed (the contents of this field) will reach the double-digits.

FIGURE 16.8

Creating a Dynamic Text block right in the soon-to-be Smart Clip allows you to monitor the value of the property.

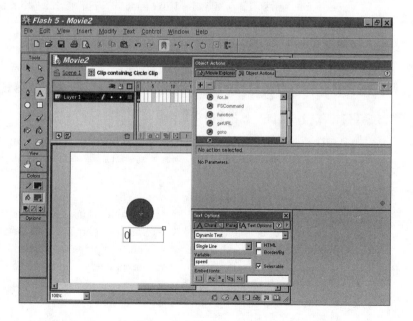

3. You're going to make a Smart Clip that allows the using author to change "speed" for each instance. Before that, though, you'll get it working by hard-coding some numbers.

4. Go back to your main scene and remove all instances of "Clip containing Circle Clip." Then drag one fresh from the Library. Name this instance "oneClip" in the

16

Instance panel. Now, select the first keyframe and open the Actions panel so you can place an Action that will execute right from the start. All you want to do is set the "speed" property for the one instance on the Stage (and see if it works). Therefore, insert an evaluate Action into the keyframe and type `oneClip.speed=10`. (Notice this is the same format as setting any other property—such as alpha—but "speed" is a homemade property.)

5. Test the movie. Although it doesn't move the clip across the screen, you should see the field containing the "speed" variable display the correct value (10).

The reason the clip doesn't move across the screen is that you're setting the "speed" property of the instance of "Clip containing Circle Clip" but the Action that moves the clip is attached to an instance of "Circle" *inside* "Clip containing Circle Clip." The simple solution is to change the Action attached to "Circle" to refer to the "speed" property of the clip in which it's housed. When the Action attached to Circle refers to "speed" without preceding it with a target path, Flash assumes you're talking about the "speed" of the "Circle" clip. You need the Action on "Circle" to say "set my _x property to my _x property plus the speed of the clip I'm inside of." For "Circle" to refer to any property (not just a homemade property) of the clip in which it resides, the property name must be preceded with _parent.

Task: Change the Homemade Property to Refer to the Parent

1. The preceding long explanation comes down to simply changing the Action in the "Circle" instance to `_x=_x+_parent.speed`. Go ahead and do so and then test the movie.

2. Okay! It works. Now, you can use the Smart Clip's Clip Parameters feature to get rid of that funky Action in your first frame. Consider all the work that Action causes. For example, you had to remember to name your instance of "Clip containing Circle Clip" (otherwise, you couldn't change the "speed" property directly). Also, every instance has to be named uniquely, and then every instance has to have its "speed" initialized in the first frame. Instead, you can make it so that the author using this Smart Clip can set each instance's speed via the Clip Parameters.

3. To make a Movie Clip become a Smart Clip, you simply have to specify which parameters (properties) you intend to let the using author change. Just open your Library window, select "Clip containing Circle Clip," and from the Library's Options menu, select Define Clip Parameters. You'll see a dialog box like the one shown in Figure 16.9. After you establish the properties the author may edit, this clip becomes a Smart Clip.

FIGURE 16.9

Selecting a Movie Clip in the Library and choosing Define Clip Parameters from the Options menu displays this dialog box. After you establish the properties the author may edit, this clip becomes a Smart Clip.

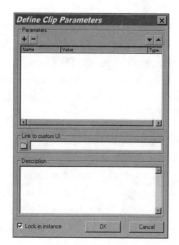

16

4. All you need to do for this task is to make "speed" a parameter the using author may edit. Click the plus button and then double-click "varName" (the default name for the variable you just inserted). Change this to speed. You can change "DefaultValue" to 10. Just remember to click the OK button when you're done.

5. Get rid of the Action in frame 1 (select frame 1, access the Actions panel, and delete the entire script). Drag several instances of "Clip containing Circle Clip" on the Stage. For each one, open the Clip Parameters panel and change each instance's "speed" to a different number. Run the Test Movie command. You've just created a Smart Clip!

Although this may seem like a lot of work, I wanted to walk you through the process involved. If you had just done the minimum steps, you wouldn't have had to work through the solutions. We took a necessary side trip to discuss whose "speed" property is being used—the clip "Circle" or its parent "Clip containing Circle Clip." This information is valuable because you need to understand the process involved so you can apply it to other Smart Clips.

By the way, accessing a clip's properties requires only that you use dot syntax as we did last hour (that is, someClip.speed). If you want to refer to a property of a clip in a clip, you use oneClip.instanceInAClip.speed (where "instanceInAClip" is the instance name of the clip in a clip). Dots are great for "talking down" the hierarchy. In this task, however, you had to "talk up" the hierarchy (when referring to "speed" in the clip one level up). The built-in keyword _parent was used. You may consider reviewing hour 15 to brush up on targeting.

Using an .swf for Clip Parameters

A Smart Clip's code is inside the clip, and the using authors only need to specify parameters from outside—via the Clip Parameters panel. This way, they won't accidentally break the code inside the clip. The Clip Parameters panel is the interface between a using author and the Smart Clip itself. However, you can replace that interface with an interface created in Flash—namely, an .swf.

This .swf (called a *custom UI*, which stands for *user interface*) can do anything a Flash movie can. Just remember its goal, though. Its only real job is to set the parameters that would otherwise be set via the Clip Parameters panel. For example, you might see that the .swf UI has a little animation at the beginning. This may be neat to watch, but it's not necessary. I don't want to discount the power of animation—just don't let it distract you. These custom UIs have one purpose: to serve as a replacement for the Clip Parameters panel.

In this section, you're not going to learn how to make an .swf into a custom UI; however, you will look at the overall structure. First, select Window, Common Libraries, Learning Interactions. Drag the Smart Clip "DragAndDrop" from the Library onto your Stage. With the instance on the Stage selected, access the Clip Parameters panel and notice it isn't the default "name - value" list you saw in other Smart Clips' Parameter panels. You're actually looking at an .swf instead. In this particular case, the process of specifying parameters is more graphical and clearer. You'll look at how to use some of the Smart Clips later this hour. I just wanted you to see what a custom UI looks like first. (By the way, you can resize the Clip Parameters panel, and the .swf inside scales so you can see the options better.)

You can use these (and other) Smart Clips without getting into all the details of how they work, but I do want to point out something that is important to understand—namely, how to specify the location of the .swf file you're using as a custom UI. If you dragged "DragAndDrop" from the Learning Interactions library (do so if you haven't already), then you should have a copy of this Smart Clip in your movie's library. Close the Learning Interactions library and open your file's Library (Ctrl+L). You should notice several symbols were added (all the symbols used by the DragAndDrop Smart Clip). But only one is the Smart Clip (it has a special icon, as you can see in Figure 16.10).

FIGURE 16.10

When a Movie Clip has properties editable through Clip Parameters, it becomes a Smart Clip (and has a special icon).

Smart clip ——

Regular Movie clip ——

If you select this in the Library and access the Define Clip Parameters dialog box from the Library's Options menu, you should see a name and location for an external .swf file specified in the field next to Link to Custom UI. (By the way, if you click the folder icon, you can point to a replacement .swf.) The address the "DragAndDrop" clip uses is `Learning Interactions UIs\IntDD_ui.swf`, meaning there's a folder called "Learning Interactions UIs" and in that folder the custom UI .swf is "IntDD_ui.swf." It's possible to unlink from this (just clear the text in the field). You can always relink by either typing an address for the file or pointing to a file by first clicking the folder button (see Figure 16.11).

FIGURE 16.11

The master version of a Smart Clip in the Library has all its properties defined in the Define Clip Parameters dialog box. In addition, the "Link to custom UI" feature lets you replace the Clip Parameters panel with an .swf.

Using Radio Buttons

Before we delve into radio buttons, I want to make it clear that although these are well designed and very useful, they were created by regular people using Flash. If you see one that looks particularly interesting, feel free to venture inside and try to deconstruct how it works. In Hour 23, "Learning How to Learn Flash," you'll develop some skills that will help you deconstruct others' files. For this section, however, we'll just look at how RadioButton, one of the Smart Clips that ship with Flash 5, can be used and applied to your projects.

With radio buttons (like the old mechanical buttons on car radios), you can only select one button at a time. Selecting which radio station to play requires that you pick one. If you change your mind, that's fine, but you can't play two stations at once. It's important to only use radio buttons for this kind of situation—for instance, when the user selects from mutually exclusive choices, such as male or female. On the other hand, check box buttons allow for multiple selections.

The following tasks involves using the RadioButton Smart Clip.

Task: Use the RadioButton Smart Clip

In this task you'll use a radio button to ask the user to specify his or her skill level (novice, intermediate, or expert). Follow these steps:

1. In a new file, from Window, Common Libraries, open the Smart Clips Library. Drag an instance of "RadioButton" onto the Stage. Close the Smart Clips Library (when you need more instances of RadioButton, you can either copy the instance on the Stage or drag one from your own Library, because the Smart Clip was copied into your file when you took it from the Common Library).

2. Select the Smart Clip instance you put on the Stage and access the Clip Parameters panel, as shown in Figure 16.12. Note that the person creating a Smart Clip can include a description that, in this case, explains how the clip works.

FIGURE 16.12

The RadioButton Smart Clip has several properties you can modify in each instance. Also, a text description was provided by the person who created this Smart Clip.

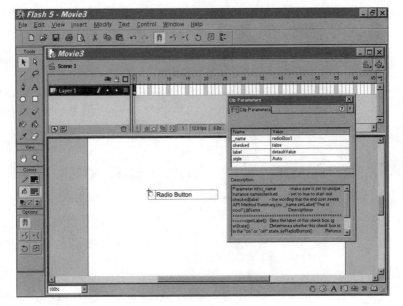

16

3. _name contains a unique identifier because each instance of RadioButton has to have to have a unique name—leave it as "radioBox1" for now. checked contains the default settings for either true or false (which could change when the user selects it). label is important because it contains the words the user sees next to the button. Double-click the value field and type **Novice**. Finally, style is pretty fancy. By default, this Smart Clip will display differently on Macintosh and Windows computers. Using style, you can override the automatic feature by specifying Mac or Win. (I'd suggest leaving it alone for now.)

4. You've just changed label to read "Novice." Now, either copy and paste this instance twice or drag two more copies from the Library. Make sure all three instances have a unique name—use radioBox1, radioBox2, and radioBox3. Also, give the two new instances the labels "Intermediate" and "Expert," respectively.

5. Test the movie. It works great! Either save it or leave it open; you'll be using it again.

The only weird thing about this Smart Clip is that if you want two "groups" of radio buttons (for exclusive choices within a group), you have to know a trick. For example, if you just put two more RadioButton Smart Clips on the Stage (one labeled "Male" and the other "Female"—they'll also need unique names) and then test the movie, you're given a choice of any one of the five buttons on the Stage. But you really want one group of three and another group of two. Putting grouped radio buttons in their own Movie Clip solves the issue. Simply select the three "skill level" instances and convert them to a Movie Clip. Do the same thing with the two "gender" buttons.

That was a pretty easy fix. It also shows how you can adapt the Smart Clips for your own purposes. The following task shows how you can use the first group of radio buttons in an applied way. Return to the main scene (by clicking "Scene 1" in the address bar) and break apart any Movie Clips you just created so only the three radio button Smart Clips you created in the previous task are onstage.

Task: Apply the Radio Buttons

This task tries to make some practical use out of the radio buttons. Here are the steps you should follow:

1. Using the task you just completed, draw a rectangle (which will become a button) and put the text "proceed" on it. Convert it to a button and name it "Proceed."

2. Make sure the button is on the Stage in frame 1 (with the three instances of radio buttons). Go to frame 2 and insert a blank keyframe (F7). On the screen, create a Dynamic Text block and associate it with the variable name "message." Go back to frame 1 and make it so that when the user clicks "proceed," the user's skill level is checked first and then the second frame displays a message.

3. Select the instance of "Proceed" and open the Actions panel. Insert an evaluate Action. Leave the default event "release" intact and type `message = "You didn't select anything."` (which will account for the case that the user didn't select any button). Now insert an "if" Action right after the evaluate Action. In the Condition field, type `radioBox1.getState()`, which means "if radioBox1's (the novice button) state is 'true,' then execute the following line(s) of code." (If your radio buttons are all in a Movie Clip—as described in the text after the previous task—you need to target radioBox1 by preceding it with an instance name of the clip, plus a dot: `clipName.radioBox1.getState()`. Alternatively, just Modify, Break Apart the clip first.) getState was built into this Smart Clip to give you easy access to the current state of the button (to find out whether it is selected). Immediately following the line containing "if," insert another evaluate Action and type `message = "Welcome Novice!"` (see Figure 16.13).

FIGURE 16.13

The Action attached to the "Proceed" button starts with "message" being set to "nothing." Then if radioBox1 is selected, it's set to "Welcome Novice!"

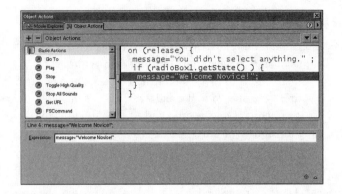

4. You just need to insert two more "if" Actions. However, their placement is important. Each should start where the previous one ends. The first "if" took up three lines—the last line ends with a curly bracket (}). Also, after each "if" (but before the end of the mouse event), you'll want a `gotoAndStop(2)` line, which makes the playback head move forward one frame. Anyway, it might be easiest to look at Figure 16.14 instead of stepping through exactly how you insert two more "if" Actions.

FIGURE 16.14

The finished version of the Action on the "Proceed" button should look like this (notice the Go To Action must leave the "Go to and Play" option unselected).

5. Put a "stop" Action in the first keyframe and then test the movie several times, selecting a different radio button each time.

Making Advanced Smart Clips

Although I can't cover all the details of how to make your own Smart Clips within the course of this hour, I do have some tips for when you're ready. The best way to make your own Smart Clip is to first experiment with using the Smart Clips that ship with Flash. Determine the ones you like and why you like them. Also determine the ones you don't like. It's important to concern yourself with usability, because making a Smart Clip can be a big investment of time. If it's not very usable, you've wasted a lot of time.

Despite the fact that a Smart Clip can take a lot of time to program, the real time investment is in designing it. Clarifying what you want is the tough part. Once you have a clear idea where you're headed, it's rather easy to execute the programming. In addition to designing the Smart Clip to be usable, you should try to make it very useful. That is, make it generic enough that you can use it in many situations. Instead of making one clip that does everything, make several that do unique tasks. This way, you can mix and match them for your purpose. Obviously, this discussion is a bit vague, but the point is that you can always improve on a design. Just spend the time to create a good design upfront.

Finally, here are some suggestions for when you want to attack the programming aspect of creating a Smart Clip. First, try to make a plain-old Movie Clip that works great when you hard-wire properties. Then figure out which properties need to be adjusted by the using author. Only "extract" those properties to become the Clip Parameters. All the properties you want the user to have access to must be properties of the clip itself. That's not to say you can't have variables or properties inside the clip, but the ones the using author can change have to be on the surface of (attached to) the Movie Clip. If you can keep that straight—as well as all the related targeting issues—then the process isn't too bad.

Creating a custom UI to replace the Clip Parameters panel can involve a lot of work. If you're just trying to make the standard dialog more graphic, you're going to invest a lot of time for something of limited value. After all the standard Clip Parameters panel works fine. However, if you want to save the using author the effort of calculating parameters which would—otherwise—be a lot of work for them, then creating a custom UI might be worth the effort.

Additional online resources are mentioned in Appendix C, "Resources." Also, you can see the source code of many of the Smart Clips that ship with Flash 5. Be sure to make good use of the information that's out there.

Summary

The Smart Clip is one of the coolest new features in Flash. Exactly what they're going to mean is anyone's speculation. I think they'll bridge the separation between programmer and nonprogrammer. A real "programmer" can create a sophisticated Smart Clip that can mean the nonprogrammer can use sophisticated features in his or her projects without learning all the ActionScripting necessary. The Smart Clips that ship with Flash are just a taste of what's likely to come from talented programmers all around the world.

To review, you first learned how a Smart Clip is just like any Movie Clip—it just happens to have a bunch of code in it. Through the Clip Parameters panel, the author using a finished Smart Clip can "populate" it with his or her own content or data. When you create a Smart Clip, you make homemade properties for the Smart Clip, and through Define Clip Parameters, you can specify which properties can be modified by the using author. The entire Clip Parameters panel can even be replaced with an .swf created simply as a customized user interface for inputting data. You walked through some very basic examples and then actually used a finished Smart Clip in a practical situation.

You can use Smart Clips or make Smart Clips. Making one is a lot of work, but if you can use the Smart Clip many times, it's often worth the extra work.

16

Q&A

Q I had a file that used one of the Smart Clips that ships with Flash. When I returned to the file, I found that the fancy .swf interface for the Clip Parameters panel was gone and I was left with the old "name value" table. How do I get the .swf interface back?

A If you go to the master version of the Smart Clip in your Library and then access the Define Clip Parameters dialog box (from the Library's Options menu), you can click the folder icon and point to the .swf that's supposed to be used. You may even first notice that the name (and path) to the original UI .swf is listed but that the path is no longer valid (that is, the file is no longer in that location).

Q Do Smart Clips have to be so complicated?

A Of course not. First of all, these examples are relatively basic (that is, they could be much more sophisticated). Take this for a simple Smart Clip example: Suppose you have a text heading that appears in many places throughout your movie. Using the same Smart Clip means that if you ever need to change the font style, you just edit the master version of the clip, not every occurrence of a heading. As for the contents of the headings, that's where a parameter comes in. Just make a Dynamic Text block, associate it with a variable called "message," convert it to a symbol (Movie Clip), define the Clip Parameters on the master, and create a new property called "message." Then in each instance that you drag into your movie, you can specify the value of "message" (in other words, the text of that heading) via the Clip Parameters panel.

Workshop

The Workshop consists of quiz questions and answers to help you solidify your understanding of the material covered. Try to answer the questions before checking the answers.

Quiz

1. Smart Clips are simply Movie Clips that have properties the author can edit via the Clip Parameters panel.

   A. True.

   B. False, you edit the properties via the Effects panel.

   C. False, Smart Clips require an .swf as the parameter interface.

2. Flash only ships with a few Smart Clips, so once you exhaust their possibilities, you'll have to wait for Flash 6 for any new ones.

   A. True, unless an interim release comes out, such as Flash 5.5.

   B. False, Smart Clips can be used to create more Smart Clips (called *Clip Mutation*).

   C. False, you or any other talented programmer can create Smart Clips from scratch.

3. Radio buttons should only be used when providing the user with a selection of audio tracks.

   A. True, why do you think they're called "radio buttons"?

   B. False, radio buttons can be used for any purpose you want.

   C. False, radio buttons should only be used for mutually exclusive choices.

Quiz Answers

1. A. That's a perfect definition. The .swf that can be used as an alternative to the Clip Parameters panel is called a *custom UI*, and it is optional.

2. C. Anyone can make a Smart Clip. You made a Smart Clip this hour. The trick is to make a good one that's really useful.

3. C. Radio buttons should only be used for mutually exclusive choices (such as male/female). Check box–type buttons are for selections where you can have multiple selections (such as pepperoni, olives, and sausage).

PART IV

Putting It All Together for the Web

Hour

HOUR 17

Linking Your Movie to the Web

Now that you've explored all the basics of creating images, animations, buttons, and interactivity, you can move on to "putting it all together for the Web." In this first hour of this section of the book, you'll learn about getting your Flash movies into Web pages and linking them to other pages. The knowledge you've acquired up to this point will make the task at hand easy. It helps, however, if you've seen a few Flash Web sites so that you'll have an idea where you're headed.

A Flash movie can simply be played on your computer (as is the case every time you do a "Test Movie"). The fun part comes when you upload your Flash movie to a Web server so anyone (with a browser and the free Flash player) can see it. Not only can your movie be seen by anyone in the world, but you can include links that give the user a way to jump to other sites. You'll do all that this hour!

In this hour you will:

- Publish your Flash movie with the required HTML document
- Incorporate hyperlinks inside your movie to enable the user jump to other pages or even help them send an email
- See some of the ways Flash and HTML can be combined
- Get a basic introduction to uploading your files to a Web server

NEW TERM   A *hyperlink* is often just a word or static picture in a web page that you can click to navigate to another Web page. In Flash we can put hyperlinks on buttons or even in keyframes. This way the viewer will have a chance to jump out to other parts of the web.

Basic Publishing

Flash's Publish feature makes the process of preparing your movie for the Web a snap. I know I've said that a lot of tasks you perform in Flash are simple, but publishing in Flash is both simple and quick. Basically, you select Publish from the File menu! Publish will not only export a .swf, but it will also create the HTML file that's necessary.

NEW TERM   *HTML* stands for Hyper Text Markup Language. It's a text file that uses special code to describe how a Web page is to be displayed. A user's browser program will first download the HTML and the code included will determine how the web page is displayed. The reason it's important is that every Web page that you visit is really an HTML file that describes what is to be included in the page layout. Therefore, you can't just upload a Flash .swf. You upload an HTML file (with an embedded .swf) and that is what the user visits.

It's interesting to know that when you type in a Web address (www.teleport.com/ ~phillip/, for example), your browser looks for file named *index.html* (it will also look for other similarly named files if it can't find index.html). The index.html file is read in by the browser, which makes sense of its contents. Besides containing the actual text that appears onscreen, the HTML file contains the details about which size and style text to use (such as italic or bold). Because the HTML file doesn't actually have images in it, if the Web page includes photographs, the HTML must specify the name and location of the image file (such as trees.jpg). The browser accumulates all the information specified in the HTML file and shows it to the user as an integrated layout of images and text.

In the case of a page that includes a Flash movie, it works almost the same way. The HTML file specifies where the Flash movie (that is, the .swf file) is located and how to display it onscreen. This is almost the same as how it a specifies static image, such as a .gif or a .jpg. In the case of the .jpg or .gif image, additional information can be included—parameters such as the height and width of the image. Similarly, the HTML referring to a .swf can include parameters such as width, height, whether the movie loops, whether it should be paused at the start, and more. This HTML basically says to put an image here, a Flash movie there, and so on. The actual code is relatively easy to learn, but it's not exactly intuitive. Besides, it's unforgiving if you make mistakes.

Fortunately, Flash's Publish feature will create the HTML file for you, so you don't really have to learn HTML. However, it is a good idea for you to learn some HTML, and one of the best ways to learn is to take a peek at the HTML Flash creates. Regardless, it's a neat feature—you just select the Publish command, and Flash will do all the work.

Publishing in Flash has three aspects. For now, you'll concentrate on Publish and Publish Preview, where your .html and .swf files will be exported (the only difference with Preview is that you'll see the results right away in your browser). An important component of Publishing involves how you can modify every detail via the Publish Settings command (under the File menu). As you'll see in Hour 24, "Publishing Your Creation," the Publish Settings command lets you specify details as well as decide what media types to export (because Flash can export more than just Flash and HTML files). The third aspect of publishing involves using, modifying, or creating templates, which give you extensive control over the HTML created when publishing. (Templates are also covered in Hour 24.)

In the following task, you'll try out the File menu commands Publish and Publish Preview.

Task: Publish a Movie

In this task you'll quickly (and easily) publish a movie for viewing in a browser. Here are the steps to follow:

1. In a new file, create a simple animation. Save the file into a new or empty folder (maybe a folder called *Test* on your Desktop). Call the file *testmovie*.

2. From the File menu, select Publish Settings..., select the Formats tab, and ensure that Flash and HTML are the only options selected (this is the default). Click OK. (See Figure 17.1.)

FIGURE 17.1

Publish Settings lets you specify what kind of files will be created every time you publish. The default simply exports a Flash .swf and the HTML that holds it. You can change these settings any time.

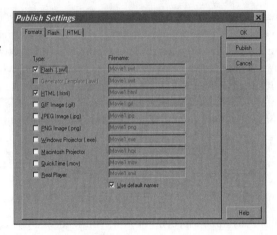

3. Select Publish from the File menu. What happened? Nothing much seems to appear, but if you go look inside your Test folder, you should find (in addition to your source .fla) two files—one .swf and one .html. Both have the same base name as your original .fla file. If you double-click the HTML file, you'll launch your default browser and see your movie play! (For some reason, seeing a movie in a browser is exciting to many people.)

4. If you simply upload the .html and .swf files to a Web server, anyone can see your movie, provided they're given the address and have the Flash player.

When you checked Publish Settings… in the preceding task, I asked you to make sure that both an HTML and Flash (.swf) file would be exported upon publishing. Not only does the Formats tab allow you to specify more file types to exported, but for each format you select, you're given another tab. For example, because you have HTML and Flash selected, you'll see a tab for each. If you look in those tabs, you'll see several parameters you can modify. You'll spend more time on this in Hour 24, but go ahead and check out these tabs now if you like—most of the settings are pretty self-explanatory.

A couple final notes on publishing: First of all, after you selected Publish in the previous task, you found the files Flash exported. Instead, you could have—in one fell swoop— exported the file and launched it in your browser automatically. Use the File, Publish Preview, Default (F12) menu to export the appropriate files and view them in a browser in one step. You'll likely use this method in more ways than the one I've showed you, so it's good to understand exactly what's happening.

Second, you'll notice that the name of both the .html and .swf files match your source .fla file's name. If you want to change the .html file's name to, say, *index.html*, you'll have no problem doing so. However, if you want to change the .swf file's name, you have to be careful. The HTML file "points" to the .swf file. If you open up the HTML file in a text editor (such as Notepad), you'll find two references to the .swf file's name. (To open the file in Notepad, either drag the file onto the Notepad icon or open Notepad and select File, Open, making sure you change "Files of Type" to "All Files," as shown in Figure 17.2, and point to the .html file.

FIGURE 17.2

If you want to view html files through Notepad (to see what Flash created), you just need to specify "All Files" from the dialog box after selecting the File, Open menu.

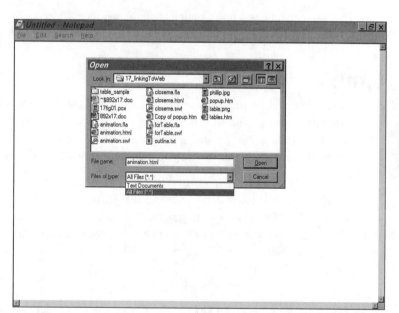

17

The two references to the .swf file's name correspond to the HTML code created for Netscape and Internet Explorer. Although the following code is just part of the HTML file created, you'll find the two parts:

```
src="testmovie.swf"
PARAM NAME=movie VALUE="testmovie.swf"
```

Without explaining the HTML entirely, both lines of code need to point to the correct file. If your Flash file's name is indeed testmovie.swf, this code works. If you change your file's name, you must change these lines in your HTML code to match the new name.

Another thing to keep in mind: You don't have to export both the .html and the .swf file every time. You can select Export Movie from the File menu to just create a new .swf based on the latest edits in your source .fla. Maybe you've already created the HTML, or maybe you've made some edits to it that you don't want overwritten by publishing again.

All you need to do is select Export Movie and then select Flash Player from "Save As Type" in the Export Movie dialog box. When exporting this way, you'll see one more dialog box, which lets you specify details of the Flash movie. This dialog box is identical to the Flash tab in Publish Settings (for now, just accept the defaults). For still another way, you can just do a "Test Movie," which immediately exports a .swf file (same filename as the .fla file, but with the .swf extension—and located in the same folder).

This may sound like a lot of options, but the main decision is whether you want to export just the .swf (as in Export Movie) or both the .swf and the .html (when you Publish).

Simple Hyperlink

So you've seen how to take your movies and publish them to the browser. But what good is a Flash movie in a browser if it doesn't do "Web stuff." There's nothing wrong with making a Flash movie that simply entertains. But if your users are already on the Web, you might as well give them a way to hyperlink to other Web pages.

There's only one Action you really have to learn to create a hyperlink: Get URL. (If you already know how to create a hyperlink in HTML, this Action is the same as an A HREF.) Specifically, when Flash encounters the Get URL Action, it will take the user to a new Web page, either within your site or to another Website altogether. That's the simple explanation. Naturally, there are more details. You'll use this Action to see how it works in the following task.

Task: Use Get URL to Create a Hyperlink

In this task you'll create a button that, when clicked, takes the user to another Web site. Here are the steps to follow:

1. Create a new file and save it in an empty folder. (This step isn't absolutely necessary, but it is useful when you're creating complex Web sites because all the files and folders can get out of hand; therefore, I like to start with a nice clean folder.)

2. Draw a rectangle, which will become a button. Convert it to a symbol and name it "MyButton." Make sure it's a button and click OK.

3. Now you'll attach the Get URL Action to the button. Select the instance of the button on the Stage, open the Actions panel, and then find the Get URL Action from the Basic Actions section of the Toolbox list. Insert the Get URL Action by double-clicking or dragging it over to the script area on the right.

4. You need to specify the parameters for this Action. Basically, you need to indicate the Web address to where you want to navigate. In the URL field, type `http://www.mcp.com/sams/`, as shown in Figure 17.3. You'll learn about the other parameters later, so leave them alone for now.

FIGURE 17.3

Attaching a hyperlink Action (Get URL) to a button is simple. Just specify a URL, and the rest of the parameters can be left at their default settings.

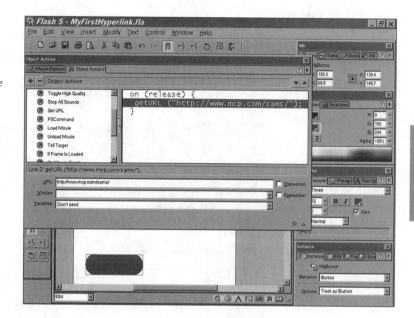

17

5. From the File menu, select Publish Preview, Default. You can watch the Flash movie and when you click you'll be taken to the Sams Publishing Website. Naturally, you could spice things up by animating the button or giving it an Over state.

You can see how this feature can be used in your Web pages. Realize that because Get URL is an Action, you can put it anywhere you can put any other Actions (button instances, clip instances, and keyframes). In the preceding task, you put the Action on a button. However, maybe at the end of an animation you'll want to automatically jump to another Web page. In this case, just put Get URL in a keyframe at the end of your Timeline. It's just like a "Go To" Action, except Get URL "goes to" a Web page.

There are two other ways you can create hyperlinks inside Flash. First, any text block can have a URL associated with it automatically. You'll learn about this method in the following task.

Task: Create a Hyperlink Using the Character Panel

In this task you'll use an automatic feature to associate a hyperlink with a block of text. Here are the steps:

1. Create a block of text using any font you like—just make it big enough to read.

2. With the text block selected, access the Character panel and type a legitimate URL into the URL field. In Figure 17.4, `http://www.teleport.com/~phillip` is used. The text becomes *hypertext*, or *hyperlinked text*.

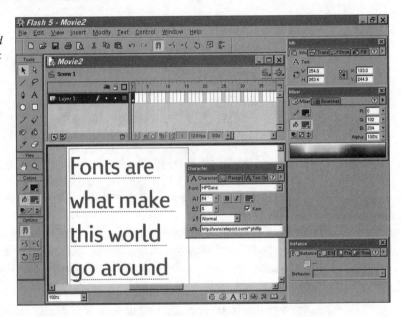

3. Now select Publish Preview. One thing to notice about the behavior of this hyperlink text is it opens a new browser window. As you'll see in the "Targeting Windows" section, later this hour, the target window in this case is effectively what is called "_blank."

Now you'll learn the third way you can create hyperlinks: using Dynamic Text. This feature, like the previous one, only applies to text. Dynamic Text also has an option for HTML. This allows you to populate your text block (through setting the associated variable) with actual HTML code. You'll see how this is done in the following task.

Task: Use Dynamic Text to Create a Hyperlink

In this task you'll create HTML within a Flash text block. Follow these steps:

1. Use the Text tool to create a long block of text (it doesn't matter what you type because the text will be replaced).

2. From the Text Options panel, select Dynamic Text and associate a variable called "myText" with this block. Also, make sure you select the HTML check box (see Figure 17.5).

FIGURE 17.5

Selecting Dynamic Text and the HTML option on the Text Options panel will allow you to create HTML in Flash.

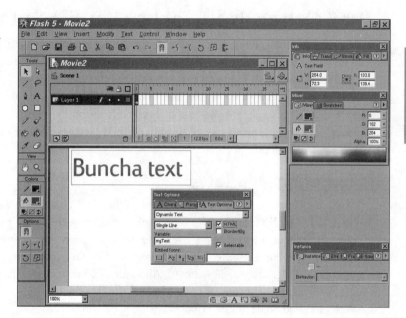

17

3. In the first keyframe, you're going to set the "myText" variable. Therefore, select the first frame and access the Actions panel. Insert the Set Variable Action. In the Variable parameter, type **myText**. In the Value parameter, type **This is <A HREF="http://www.yahoo.com">Hot</A>**.

4. If you understand the HTML, great. Otherwise, just accept it for now. It will make sense later. Select Publish Preview.

Normally, I'd suggest using the evaluate Action to set a variable and just use something like myText="whatever". However, because the contents of myText included quotation marks, it gets tricky, as Flash needs to know which quotation marks are meant to be taken literally (within the string)

and which quotes begin and end a string. In other words, `myText="I said "No""` won't work because Flash will think the quotation mark right before `No` is the ending quotation mark for the string started before `I`. If you want a quotation mark to be part of the string you're creating, you must precede it with a backslash character (\). This just makes the task harder to follow and easier to make mistakes. When you use the Set Variable Action, Flash adds the slashes where they're needed. This is a great way for you to learn.

What Other Web Tasks Can Flash Do?

For the rest of this hour, you'll learn some useful and powerful ways to combine Flash with standard HTML. If you already know HTML, you should be able to take this information and run with it. If you're not familiar with HTML, the rest of this hour should still be useful because you'll see some examples of what's possible. In addition, you'll be given some code snippets that you can probably use in the future. If you'd like to learn more, all the concepts discussed this hour would be covered in any good HTML resource.

Targeting Windows

You probably noticed that when you clicked the button created in the second task this hour "Use Get URL to Create a Hyperlink," not only were you hyperlinked to another page, but the page you were viewing (the one with your Flash movie) was actually replaced with the new page. This is the default behavior for any hyperlink (as is the case with the HTML equivalent, A HREF). Alternatively, you can specify the "window" parameter to change the behavior from "replace this page with another" to "jump to a new Web page and put it in new window."

NEW TERM In HTML, *window* refers to the rectangular frame into which the user views a Web page. Some pages just have one big window while others are made up of an arrangement of several windows. Windows can be given names so that you can specify into which window particular content should go. There are also some generic window names. Compare this to how you can refer to houses in your neighborhood specifically using addresses or you use generic terms like "next door" or "across the street."

In the Action panel, Get URL's "window" parameter is the same as what is referred to as a *target window* in HTML. Don't get this mixed up with Flash's targets (in Flash, a *target* is usually a clip instance—something different all together). Here, the window you specify as a target is the window in which the specified URL will load. If this parameter is left blank (as in the previous task), the hyperlink loads the new Web page directly inside the same browser window. If you specify a window name (which generally applies only to frames), the new Web page is loaded into that window. If no such window exists, a new browser window (of that name) is created. For example, suppose your Flash movie has several buttons—each one causing a different window to change it contents. As you click the buttons, the Flash movie stays in its own window, while other windows are opened as necessary.

NEW TERM One way to arrange several windows in HTML is through framesets. One frameset can have as many *Frames* as you wish. Each Frame can be designed to have specific dimensions and features such a menu bar or title bar.

Additionally, there are four reserved "generic" target window names. If you click the drop-down list next to the Window field, as shown in Figure 17.6, you'll see _self, _blank, _parent, _top. Most of these names apply to frames, which you can learn about in an HTML reference, but one name comes in handy when frames aren't being used. The name _blank causes the selected URL to load into a new browser window, and it leaves the current window open. To see this in action, simply change the Window parameter in the previous task to _blank. You should notice that when the button is clicked, a whole new browser window is created. (You won't notice any effects when using the other generic target window options unless your HTML includes frames.)

17

FIGURE 17.6

The Get URL Action provides the generic target window options from a drop-down list in the Window field.

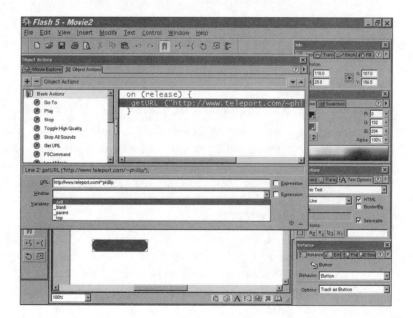

Sending Email: The `mailto:` Command

Although you'll have to use more advanced techniques to actually *send* email from a Web page, here's a quick-and-dirty way to do something close. The HTML command `mailto:` can be used in conjunction with Get URL to automatically open a user's email program with a preaddressed email. The user just needs to type a message and then send the email.

It's really simple. Instead of specifying a Web address in the URL field of a Get URL Action, simply type something like this:

`mailto:flash5@teleport.com`

Here, `flash5@teleport.com` is the email address. If you select the Publish Preview command, you should see (when the Action is encountered) that a new email is created that's already addressed. As the user, you only need to type the message and click Send. The only catch is that the user must have a default email program identified on his or her computer (most people do).

If you want the email to pop up with the subject and body content already created, you can change the simple `mailto` string to something like this:

```
mailto:flash5@teleport.com?subject=Subject goes here&body=Body goes here
```

Simply replace `flash5@teleport.com` with the address you want the email sent to, replace `Subject goes here` with whatever subject line you want, and replace `Body goes here` with whatever message you want in the body of the email.

Using Flash Inside a Larger Website

Although you can create a Website entirely in Flash, sometimes it's not necessary or even desirable. Often you'll just want to use Flash to supplement a more conventional Website. In this section, you'll learn several ways to use Flash within a larger Website. This should help spark some ideas that you can use in your own site.

Pop-up Windows

You can supplement your plain HTML Website by simply including a link to a Flash Web page. Imagine a Web page, complete with text, images, a simple hyperlink (in HTML, A HREF) that points to a page you created with Flash's Publish command. This is the basic hyperlink you've seen a million times on the Web. Somewhere in your HTML file you include this:

```
<A HREF="published.html">Click for Flash sample</A>
```

This creates a line of hypertext on your Website that, when clicked, opens up the HTML file that contains your published Flash movie. You can even make this link cause the Flash site (published.html) open up in a new (blank) window:

```
<A HREF="published.html" target="_blank">Click for Flash sample</A>
```

If you're creating your Web page using Macromedia Dreamweaver, you'd simply use the Properties window to specify the Link and Target settings, as in shown in Figure 17.7. The Link and Target fields are equivalent to the URL and Window fields, respectively, in the Get URL parameters of Flash.

FIGURE 17.7

Using Dreamweaver, you can turn text into hypertext via the Properties window.

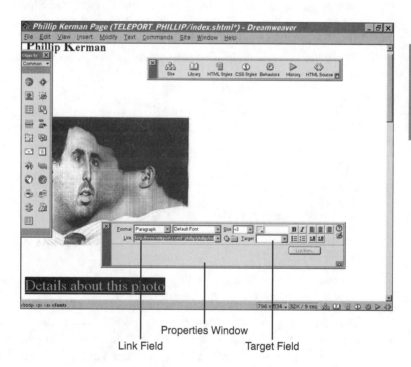

Properties Window

Link Field   Target Field

Okay, so that's easy enough. However, you can add some sophistication to this link from a regular site. The preceding methods will simply cause the browser to hyperlink to another page (perhaps in a new, blank window). However, one technique that may be appropriate is to pop up a new browser window with specific features. That is, the pop-up window can be sized to your specifications (instead of being the same size as the current browser window). You can specify other features to remove or disable certain browser attributes (such as resizing, viewing the buttons, and so on). This involves a little JavaScript (which I won't explain in detail but will provide here) attached to a line of hypertext. Here's an example:

```
<A HREF="#"
script language="JavaScript"
```

```
onMouseDown="window.open('animation.html', 'thename', 'width=300,height=335');">
click here!</a>
```

The key portion is `window.open()`. The first parameter is the filename you want to open (in this case, animation.html). The second parameter is the arbitrary name you're giving this window, and the third parameter is a string full of the features you're including. In this case, only the width and height are specified (in pixels). You can find more features that can be included here in a good JavaScript reference.

If you want to let the user close the window that has popped up (besides using the browser's close button), you can provide some simple JavaScript to perform the task. In this example, I first made a Flash animation file (called *animation.fla*), with the movie size set to 300×300, and then published it to .swf and .html files. Then I opened the HTML file I created (animation.html) using a text editor (Notepad). At the very end of the file, I found these lines:

```
</OBJECT>
</BODY>
</HTML>
```

I simply inserted some JavaScript (to close the window) between `</OBJECT>` and `</BODY>`. Here's the result:

```
</OBJECT>
<A HREF="#"
script language="JavaScript"
onMouseDown="window.close();">Close</a>
</BODY>
</HTML>
```

Note that although the movie is 300×300, the `window.open` code creates a window that's 300×335 to make room for the hypertext (Close).

This shows how a little JavaScript in your HTML file can close a window, but what does it have to do with Flash? Not much, except that it's an effect you may want to try. However, let me now show you a technique that lets you execute JavaScript from inside Flash. For example, what if you want a button created in Flash that executes the `window.close()` code? You can simply use the Get URL Action and, in the field for the URL parameter, type **javascript:window.close();** (see Figure 17.8). All you do is start with `javascript:` and follow with the actual JavaScript code! This technique works pretty well. If your JavaScript code is more involved, you can use another method, involving the FSCommand Action, which not only is more advanced, but it will work on very old browsers (whereas the JavaScript technique shown here won't work). For more information about FSCommand you can check out an article I wrote on the subject plus an annotated presentation on the topic at: `http://www.teleport.com/~phillip/flashforward2000/presentation/`

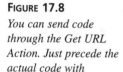

FIGURE 17.8

You can send code through the Get URL Action. Just precede the actual code with `javascript:`.

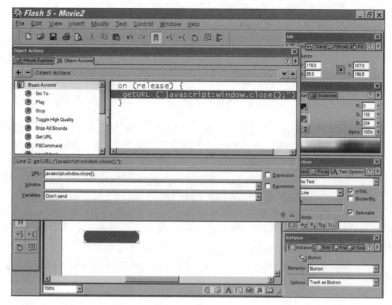

One last detail related to pop-up windows: The HTML that the Publish feature creates is solid and works great. However, it's not necessarily what you'll want to use in every case. You'll learn in Hour 24 how to change the exact behavior of Publish. However, there's one tiny adjustment I make almost every time—and it's especially applicable to the animation.html used in the example. I would probably change the top part of the HTML file (`<BODY bgcolor="#FFFFFF">`) to this:

```
<BODY bgcolor="#FFFFFF"
leftmargin="0" topmargin="0" marginwidth="0" marginheight="0">
```

This edit simply positions the Flash movie with no margins. Without this adjustment, the 300×300 Flash movie would get cut off in a 300×300 window. (In Hour 24 you'll learn how this can be incorporated as the default so you don't have to make this edit by hand every time.)

Including Flash Within HTML

You first learned how to publish a Flash movie (which created the .html and .swf files). Then you learned how to make links that let the user jump out of Flash. Finally, you learned how to make links from a plain page to a Flash page (including popping up a sized window). So far, it might appear that the conventional HTML pages have been kept separate from the Flash page. Actually, the "all-Flash" page you published was really an HTML page with nothing but Flash on it (no text or images). It's easy to combine regular HTML with Flash: You can insert Flash almost the same as you insert text and images into a regular HTML page.

Here are the three basic approaches:

- Let the Publish feature create an HTML file and then add to that file in a text editor.
- Copy a portion of the published HTML file and paste it inside an HTML file created elsewhere.
- Insert a Flash file into a Web page using a Web layout tool such as Dreamweaver.

To add regular HTML to the file Flash's Publish feature created, first open the .html file with a text editor such as Notepad or Simple Text. Then you need to decide whether you want the content you're adding to go above or below the Flash animation. If you want to put content above the Flash file, simply add it after the `<BODY bgcolor="#FFFFFF">` tag and before the `<OBJECT classid=...>` tag. To add content under the Flash file, insert your content after the `</OBJECT>` tag but before the `</BODY>` tag. What you must remember is that everything between the first and second `</OBJECT>` tags specifies details about the Flash file—don't edit this. Later, when you learn to extract a portion of this file, you'll be taking everything between `<OBJECT` and `</OBJECT>`, inclusively. See Figure 17.9 for an example of an .html file opened in Notepad.

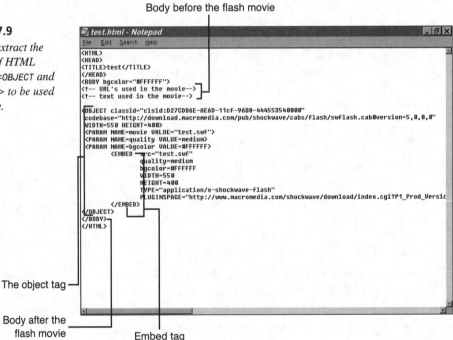

FIGURE 17.9

You can extract the portion of HTML between <OBJECT and </OBJECT> to be used elsewhere.

If you're using Dreamweaver, this entire process is extremely simple. All you do is decide where you want to insert the Flash movie, open the Objects window's Common section, and click the Insert Flash button. The Properties window lets you specify parameters (almost identical to the Flash tab in the Publish Settings dialog box). If you use this method, you don't need to publish the HTML code from inside Flash, because this creates the same HTML code that Publish would have otherwise (but it does so inside the file currently open in Dreamweaver). See Figure 17.10 for an example.

The insert flash button

FIGURE 17.10

When you use Dreamweaver to insert Flash you'll find parameters like those found in Flash's Publish.

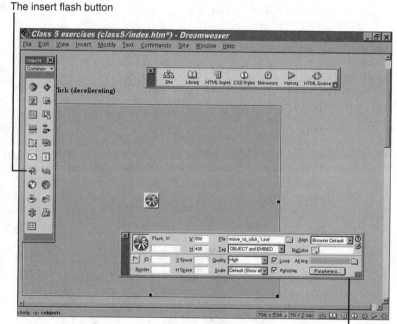

The parameters for the flash movie

Therefore, just like you can insert images in HTML, you can also insert Flash movies. What's more, the HTML that Publish creates has room for you to make edits and add HTML content (such as text and images). All in all, you can combine HTML and Flash quite seamlessly.

Including Flash in Tables and Frames

Although you can insert Flash anywhere in an HTML file, there are two layout techniques worth knowing because they'll help you position any element (images, text, and Flash movies) in specific locations. These techniques involve tables and frames.

An HTML table is just like a table in a word processor—into each cell you can put text, images, or even Flash. Tables can scale to fill a percentage of the browser window or display at a size that you specify. The contents of each cell can be automatically centered or justified to the left or right. For each cell, you're given a great deal of control. Check out Figure 17.11 for an idea of how tables work.

FIGURE 17.11
An HTML table lets you put discrete information in specific cells.

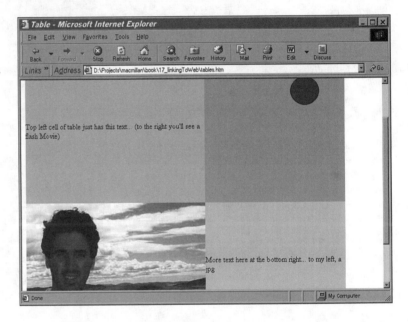

Using Macromedia Fireworks, you can take one large image and "slice it up" based on where you draw boxes (see Figure 17.12). Not only will Macromedia Fireworks export separate image files for each slice, but it will write the HTML that creates a table to reassemble everything in a browser. Although Fireworks doesn't directly import Flash elements, you can include Flash inside a Fireworks table (or any table for that matter) with a little bit of hand-coding in a text editor.

FIGURE 17.12

A complex table can be created in Fireworks by simply drawing boxes.

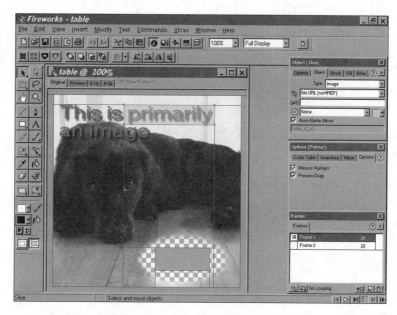

For example, in Figure 17.12, I created a sliced table by using some of the features in Fireworks. But in one section, I placed a dark rectangle, with plans to replace that section with a Flash movie. I let Fireworks do all the work, slicing and creating an HTML table. Then I snooped through the separate files created by Fireworks and determined the filename for that dark rectangle (table_r4_c3.jpg). I then found the reference to that filename inside Firework's HTML table. (This is the part that needs to be replaced.) I made my Flash movie (in the same dimensions as my rectangle) and published both the .swf and the .html files. Then I opened the HTML created by the Publish feature, copied the necessary portion (everything from <OBJECT to </OBJECT>), then pasted that code in the Fireworks .html file where table_r4_c3.jpg was referred. The result was a table with one cell containing a Flash animation, as shown in Figure 17.13.

FIGURE 17.13

The finished table with a Flash movie in place of one of the cells.

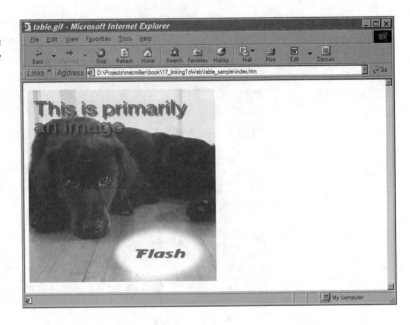

You don't have to use Fireworks to create a table. You can actually do it by hand. You may even be working in a team environment where someone else is working on the HTML. Basically, all you have to do is determine what portion will be occupied by Flash. Into that part of the HTML, you simply paste the critical portion of a Flash-published HTML file (the part between <OBJECT and </OBJECT>, inclusively).

Frames provide another way to modularize the portions of a Web page. Basically, a page that uses frames has one main .html file (say, index.html). Inside this file is specified the dimensions of the framesets (similar to tables) and the contents of each frame. The contents of each frame actually comprises another complete .html file. The main difference between cells in a table and frames in a frameset is that a table is defined entirely in one .html file, whereas a frameset consists of several frames, and inside each frame an entire .html document is displayed. Check out Figure 17.14 to see how this works. The image on the left shows the HTML for the page, index.html, and the output of two other HTML documents, buttons.html and main.html. On the right, you can see how both of these documents are displayed when a user requests the document index.html.

FIGURE 17.14

The result on the right was created by the code on the left that combines two HTML files.

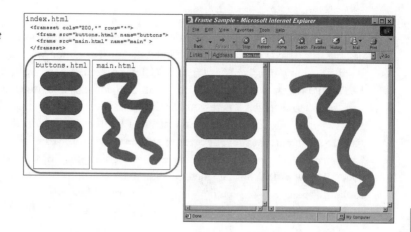

The main reason I mention frames is that with Flash's Get URL Action, you can target frames by window name. For the user, frames offer a nice experience. The entire browser doesn't have to reload every time—just one frame at a time can change. On the other hand, there are disadvantages to having only one frame change each time. However, these disadvantages are unrelated to Flash, so just realize that you can use Flash inside frames.

Uploading

Probably the most critical step in this entire hour involves actually uploading all the necessary files to a Web server. Although you can test your files on your computer, other people won't be able to see your creation unless you put it on a Web server.

NEW TERM A *Web server* is a computer connected to the Internet that is configured to let others view files through common Internet means (like a browser). Your computer is likely connected to the Internet, but unless you're running server software (and have the right kind of connection) other people won't be able to browse the Web pages on your hard drive. Many service providers, however, provide space on their Web servers for subscribers to upload files.

The process of uploading may be simple if you have a Web server connected to your computer. Maybe you work at a company, where the process is as simple as copying files to another computer's hard drive. In the simplest of cases, you just copy the .swf and .html files to the hard drive, making sure you put them both in the same location.

If you have an Internet Service Provider (ISP) that gives you a certain amount of disk space on its Web server, you can simply copy the files to this location. Your ISP should be able to give you more information, but the most common way of uploading files involves using a File Transfer Protocol (FTP) program. There are several popular (and free) FTP programs that let you specify an FTP address, a login name, and a password to gain access to a server, where you can copy and move files. A simple (although not ideal) way to upload files is to use a new version of Internet Explorer and type into the address bar `ftp://login:password@ftp.server.com/`, where `login` is your login name, `password` is your password, and `ftp.server.com` is your ISP's server name. Again, check with your ISP, but this method should allow you to copy files from your hard drive to the ISP's server—all you do is drag files into the Internet Explorer window, as shown in Figure 17.15.

FIGURE 17.15

Although this isn't the best method, you can use Internet Explorer to upload files to a server.

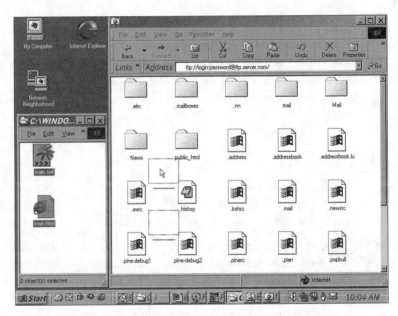

Because many Web servers use UNIX file-naming conventions, and UNIX *is* case sensitive, your best bet is to (from the start) keep all your filenames lowercase. That is, if your .fla is called myMovie.fla and you publish it, Flash will create files named myMovie.html and myMovie.swf. This is asking for trouble, because if you change the .swf to *mymovie.swf*, the HTML file may not find it. The rule of thumb is simple: Keep all files entirely lowercase.

Summary

You've learned a lot this hour—and not everything you learned involved Flash! That's okay, because the emphasis of this hour was what to do with your Flash movies when you're ready to distribute them to the world. Although you can certainly create amazing Flash movies that never go up on the Web, it doesn't take much effort to get them onto the Web when you're ready.

Although some of Publish's details won't be discussed until Hour 24, you did see how it exports the necessary .swf and .html files through Publish or Publish Preview. Displaying your Flash content on a Web page *can* be as simple as clicking a button. However, we learned how to use the Get URL Action to include hyperlinks to other Web pages. The Get URL Action can also be used to send JavaScript commands straight from Flash.

Besides JavaScript, you also explored several aspects of HTML, including the A HREF tag (the equivalent of Flash's Get URL Action), tables, and frames. Hopefully, this overview has inspired you to learn a little more about HTML and try using it with your Flash projects. Regardless, the tricky part isn't figuring out how to get something done—it's figuring out and deciding what you want to attempt. Like many things in life, once it's clear where you're headed, it's usually easy to get your task done.

17

Q&A

Q When I use Publish Preview, everything looks great, but when I put the files on my Web server, they don't work. Why?

A Well, the reason could be due to one of a million things. Here's a rundown of a few of common problems. Did you use any uppercase characters in any of the file-names? If so, you should try using all lowercase because your server might be case sensitive, and some FTP programs automatically rename files to all lowercase. Did you copy all the correct files to the server? Did you put all the files in the right location (such as the .swf file in the same folder as the .html file)? Is your server properly configured for Flash's MIME setting? (If you want to learn more about this setting, check out Macromedia's Technote 04151—just type **04151** into the search field at www.macromedia.com.)

Q Can I have more than one Flash movie on a Web page?

A Of course. You can have as many as you can track. For example, it makes sense, maybe in a table, to have a Flash movie in two different cells. You could also design a frameset where one Flash movie is contained in a frame that never reloads (and contains background music) and a bunch of other Flash movies load into frames that change. Whatever you want, it can probably be done.

Workshop

The Workshop consists of quiz questions and answers to help you solidify your understanding of the material covered. Try to answer the questions before checking the answers.

Quiz

1. If you select the Publish command and nothing seems to happen, is there something wrong?

   A. Yes. Publish has a bug and doesn't actually work.

   B. Possibly. You need to be connected to the Internet for this command to work.

   C. No. Publish simply exports the files selected in Publish Settings. If you want to see the results, try Publish Preview (or find the exported files).

2. Is it necessary to use the Get URL Action only on buttons?

   A. Yes. Otherwise, you wouldn't know exactly when the user wanted to navigate to a new Web page.

   B. No. You could also put the Action on a keyframe or a clip instance (like any Action).

   C. No. You can put Get URL on keyframes but not inside a clip instance.

3. True or false? If you read all the material in this hour, you should now have a good grounding in HTML.

   A. True. It was concise, yet comprehensive.

   B. False. If you didn't know HTML before this hour, you probably still don't—but at least you know some of the potential.

   C. False. Only when you finish this book will you become an HTML pro.

4. Is the Get URL Action the only way to create a hyperlink?

   A. Yes. Except if you do it in HTML.

   B. No. There is an entire section of Actions in the Toolbox list to create hyperlinks.

   C. No. There are also some automatic ways to create hyperlinks with text.

Quiz Answers

1. C. Publish creates files but you won't see anything unless you first find the files created. Publish Preview, creates files and immediately previews them in your browser.

2. B. Get URL is an Action and, therefore, you can put it anywhere Actions go (keyframes, clip instances, and button instances).

3. B. The idea wasn't to teach HTML but rather to point those with some HTML experience in the right direction and give others an idea of what's possible.

4. C. Static Text, through the Character panel, has a field in which you can specify an URL to jump to. Also, Dynamic and Input Text can have "HTML" style, effectively letting you write HTML in Flash.

17

HOUR 18

Designing Your Website to Be Modular

It's possible to create a huge Website entirely with one giant Flash file. However, separating the site into modular segments has distinct advantages. Just to name a few, you can load portions of the site as needed (instead of making every visitor download everything), several team members can be working on the same site simultaneously, you can update portions of the site as they change instead of having to reedit one master file, and you can create different versions of the site for different languages by just swapping out portions with language-specific content. There are other reasons why modularity is good, but it comes down to efficiency, your productivity, and the user experience.

This hour covers several ways a Flash site can be modularized as well as some of the issues you'll need to consider in deciding when and where to modularize.

In this hour you will:

- Learn how the Load Movie Action lets you play one movie inside another
- Learn the benefits of and how to use Shared Libraries
- See how scripts can be stored outside the Flash file using the Action #include

Although the technical issues covered this hour are not particularly difficult, the Flash features discussed are strict and unforgiving. Once you get the features covered this hour to work, it's fine. The difficulty comes in deciding the appropriate use of such features. That is, it's easy to learn *how* these features work, but it's more difficult to decide *when* to use them and *where* to use them. For each feature, you'll first learn how it works and then look at practical uses.

Load Movie

Load Movie is an Action that lets one Flash movie play another. Effectively, the second movie plays on top of the first. It's easier to understand, though, if you think of one movie as the *host* and the other movie (the one that's load on top of the host) as the *submovie*. Think of a big entertainment system—a wall of stereo and TV equipment. The movie you put into your VCR can only play on the TV screen. If you think of the TV as the host Flash movie, then video you put into your VCR is loaded on top of it.

One reason to do this is because you may have several submovies that only play one at a time. You may want to give the user the choice as to which submovie to play. If you use Load Movie, when the user clicks a button an Action tells Flash to load this movie now. It's sort of like a jukebox, where each record is a separate submovie. The reason Load Movie is beneficial is that only the submovies the user requests have to download.

It's time to look at some of the technical issues with Load Movie; then you can try it out. First, Load Movie can only load .swfs into .swfs. Therefore, not only will you have to "Test Movie" to see the results, but the movie (or movies) that are loaded must have already been exported as .swfs. Second, when you use Load Movie, one of the parameters is Location, where you specify into which location you want to load the movie. Movies are loaded into one of two basic locations: a clip instance or a level number. If you load a movie into a clip, the clip is replaced with the movie that's loaded. If you load a movie into a level, anything that happens to be in that level currently is replaced by the movie.

NEW TERM   *Levels* are the numbering system Flash uses to describe the stacking order of loaded movies. Your host movie is always in level 0 (referred to as `_level0`). If you load one movie into `_level1` and another into `_level2`, the `_level2` movie will appear on top of everything.

Finally, remember when I said when you load a movie, it gets loaded "on top"? That's not entirely true. When you load a movie into a clip, the loaded movie is in the same layer as the clip. That is, if the clip was in front of something or behind something, the loaded movie will be too. In the case of loading a movie into a level, the loaded movie will be in front of everything else that happens to be assigned lower-level numbers and behind items assigned higher-level numbers. The _root Stage is always _level0. Therefore, if you load a movie into _level1, it will be on top. However, if you load another movie into _level2, it will be on top of everything—the first loaded movie (_level1)will be sandwiched between the Stage and the new loaded movie. By the way, it's bad style to load movies into _level0 because this effectively wipes out your main host movie.

Task: Use Load Movie

In this task you use the Load Movie Action to selectively let the user download just the segments he or she is interested in. Here are the steps to follow:

1. The name of the game for this task is organization. Remember, haste makes waste. Start with a new empty folder into which you'll save and export all your movies.

2. Create a new file and set the movie's width and height both to 300. Use Modify, Movie (or Ctrl+M) to do this and make sure that Ruler Units is set to Pixels.

3. Create a simple tween of your choice, but make the tweening object entirely red. Save the movie as red.fla in your folder created in step 1. Do a Test Movie, which will export a movie called red.swf in the same folder as your red.fla file.

4. Do a Save As, name the file green.fla, and change the color of the tweening object to green. (You may need to change the color in each keyframe.) Remember to save and then Test Movie to create the .swf.

5. Repeat step 4 but create a file with everything blue.

6. You should have three .flas and three .swfs (red, green, and blue for both). Close all the Flash files. Then create a new Flash file and save it as main.fla in the same folder. Set this movie's size to 500×500.

7. This "main" file will load movies into a clip. Draw a square exactly 300×300 (draw any rectangle and then use the Info panel to change its dimensions to 300×300). Make sure there's a line around the box and then delete the fill. Select the entire box and convert to it a symbol (make it a Movie Clip and name it "box"). Name the instance on the Stage "theClip" in the Instance panel while the box is selected.

18

8. Now draw a rectangle in the main scene (to become a button). Convert it to a symbol (button) and then access the Actions panel for this button instance. Insert a Load Movie Action (from the Actions section of the Toolbox list). For the URL parameter, just type **red.swf** for the Location setting, select Target (which really should be thought of as "clip"), and then in the field to the right of Target type **theClip**, because this is the name of the clip into which you want to load the movie (see Figure 18.1).

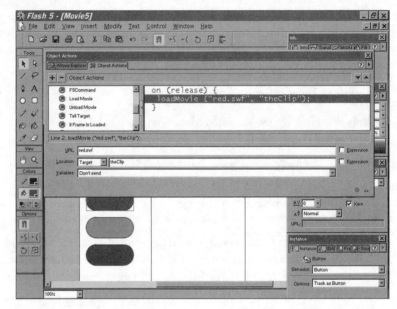

9. Test the movie. It should work, except the movie loads into its box too far down and to the right. Although the movie that gets loaded is the same size as the box, it gets positioned with its top-left corner registered to the center of the clip into which it is loading.

10. The way to fix this is to go inside the master version of the "box" clip and move the contents (the box you drew) so that the top-left corner lines up with the "center" plus sign inside the Movie Clip (see Figure 18.2). You can use the Info panel while inside the Movie Clip to set the top left corner of the selected shape to position 0,0. When you return to the scene, your clip appears to have moved, but really you've just repositioned where the contents load. Move the box to a location toward the center of the screen (basically, wherever you want it).

11. You can now make two more buttons and use the same basic Load Movie Action, except change the URL to point to green.swf and blue.swf.

Figure 18.2

Editing the relative center point of the master version of the clip in which you're loading movies will affect the positioning of the loaded movie. That is, the loaded movie's top-left corner corresponds to the clip's center point.

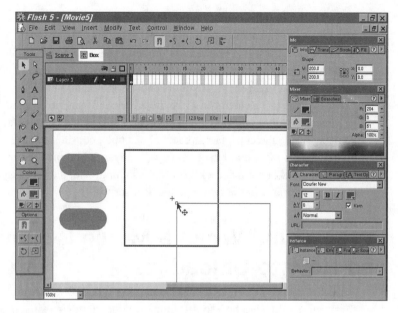

Targeting Levels or Clips

In addition to learning how to use Load Movie, one lesson you learned in this task was that the top-left corner of loaded movies lines up with the center of the clip into which they are loaded. In the preceding task, you loaded movies into a clip. However, you can also load them into levels. Simply change the Target parameter to Level and type a level number into the field on the right (see Figure 18.3). Personally, I don't prefer loading into levels for two reasons. First, the positioning is *always* based on putting the top-left corner of the loaded movie in the top-left corner of the main movie which makes registration difficult. Second, you have to keep track of level numbers (as opposed to clip instance names). It's not as though there's never a need to load movies into level numbers, but for the registration issues mentioned, I don't think doing so is as easy.

Figure 18.3

Load Movie can also load a movie into a level number. You just have to specify "Level" from the Location parameter, and you must specify a number in the field on the right.

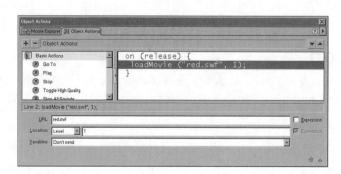

One of the cool things you can do with movies once they're loaded is address them the same way you can address clip instances. More specifically, you can set any property of a loaded movie just like you set any property of a clip. For example, you could stop the loaded movie by adding a button. In this new button, you would insert an evaluate Action and type `theClip.stop()`. (If you loaded the movie into level 1, you'd just type `_level1.stop()`.) Remember, there are a bunch of generic properties (such as _x, _y, _alpha, and so on), plus any homemade properties (that is, any variables you happen to be using inside the clip). For a practical example, consider the M3 snowboard site I programmed (it's located at `http://www.m-three.com` and pictured in Hour 3). Here, I've loaded movies of various tricks. From the main movie, the user can start, stop, and even jump to any frame in the movie as the user scrubs.

Determining When a Movie Is Fully Loaded and How to Unload It

Now that you know how to load a movie, it's a good idea to learn how to unload it. But, first, you should learn how to determine whether a movie that's loading has completed loading! This will be important if the movie that's loading is large. It's nice to let the user see that a movie is indeed downloading. You might actually want to *make* the user wait for it to fully load. All these things require you to determine whether a loading movie has downloaded.

To determine whether a movie has loaded, you use two built-in properties: _framesloaded and _totalframes. If their values are the same, then you know the movie has downloaded. If you're loading into a clip and you want to know how many frames have loaded, you can use `theClip._framesloaded` (where "theClip" is the instance name of the clip). Of course, if you write this script *inside* or *attached to* the clip itself, you don't need to precede the property with the instance name (Flash knows you must be inquiring about the _framesloaded property of that clip).

Task: Determine Whether a Movie Is Fully Loaded

In this task you'll check the _framesloaded property against the _totalframes property to determine when a loaded movie is totally loaded. Here are the steps to follow:

1. First create the submovie that will be loaded. Set the movie properties (Ctrl+M) to 300×300. Then create a linear animation that starts in frame 2. That is, click frame 2, select Insert Keyframe (F6), and then build the animation that plays through many more frames (maybe out to frame 60). If you have a series of bitmaps (like still frames of a video), this would be ideal because you want something that takes a little while to download.

2. In the first frame of this submovie, put a stop Action followed by an evaluate Action (Esc, E, V). Type in the Expression field **waiting=true**, as shown in Figure 18.4. (You'll use this in the main movie to make the host movie wait for the submovie to load.)

FIGURE 18.4

The variable "waiting" is set to "true" because the host movie is going to wait until this movie is entirely downloaded.

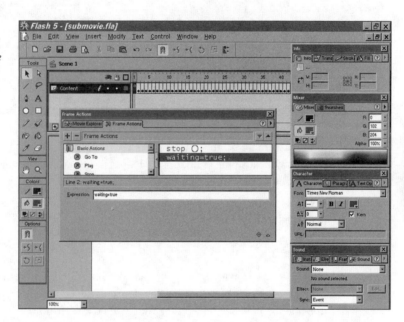

3. In frame 1 on the Stage, put the Static Text "Loading…" and then create a Dynamic Text block with "0" in it, but be sure to associate a variable called "percent" with the Dynamic Text (see Figure 18.5). This will show the user the status of the download.

FIGURE **18.5**

While the movie's stuck on frame 1, the user will see a message that includes a Dynamic Text block containing a variable (which you'll be changing) called "percent."

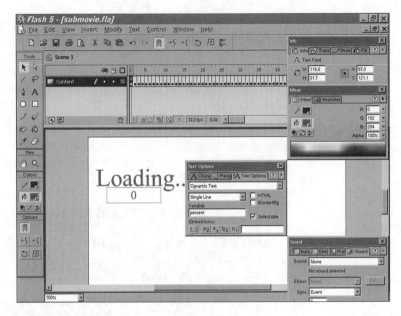

4. In the last frame of this movie place GoTo Action and set the frame parameter to 2. This will cause the animation to loop, but not all the way back to frame 1 (where the loading screen appears).

5. In a new folder, save this movie as submovie.fla and then do a Test Movie (Ctrl+Enter) to create an .swf called submovie.swf. (When you Test Movie, the movie just sits on frame 1—you'll control this issue from the movie into which it loads.)

6. Now in a new movie, draw a box that's exactly 300×300 (remove the fill), select Convert to Symbol (F8), call it "holder," and make sure it's a Movie Clip. Be sure to name the instance now on the Stage "theClip" (from the Instance panel). Now, edit the master version of this clip (just double-click it). Select View, Grid, Snap to Grid. Now select the entire square and then grab the top-left corner and snap it to the center of the clip (the little plus sign in the center of the screen).

7. Back in the main scene of this movie, create a button and make a total of three instances of it. In the first instance, insert a Load Movie Action with URL specified as **submovie.swf**, Location set to "Target," and **theClip** specified in the field next to "Target."

8. The other two buttons should each use a simple evaluate function using theClip.play() for one and theClip.stop() for the other.

9. Now it's time to create the script attached to the instance of the "holder" symbol (instance name, "theClip"). Select theClip and open the Actions panel. First, insert

an "onClipEvent" from the Actions section of the Toolbox list. Change the parameter for which clip event to "EnterFrame" (the first line of the script). Then insert an evaluate Action (Esc, E, V) and type the following in the Expression parameter: `percent=_framesloaded/_totalframes`. This tells the Dynamic Text onscreen to display the results of dividing the number of frames completely loaded by the number of total frames (in this case, the number of frames in your submovie). This isn't complete, but let's think about it. The variable you're calling "percent" will be .5 when half the total frames load. When they're all loaded, it will equal 1. If you simply multiply this number by 100, you'll get the kind of percentages you expect. Therefore, using `percent=_framesloaded/_totalframes*100` is better. Finally, just so you don't have to come back and fix this later, you can eliminate decimal values if you change the expression to an integer (a number with no decimals). The final version should look like this: `percent=int(_framesloaded/ _totalframes*100)`. Notice that "int" is inserted right after the equal sign and you need parenthesis around the rest of the code on the right.

10. You're not out of the woods yet. This only tells you what percent has loaded. You want to do two things when the movie is totally loaded: tell the loaded movie to start playing and to stop checking whether it's totally loaded. You know you should still be checking when "waiting" is true, and you know the movie will be finished loading when "percent" is 100. Therefore, insert an "if" Action from the Actions list with `waiting & percent==100` in the "Condition" field. This code looks for the condition where "waiting" is true and "percent" happens to equal 100. Notice the double equal sign. This is different from the normal equal sign, which performs an assignment (that is, `percent=100` will make "percent" equal 100). The double equal sign is a comparison—more like "Does percent happen to equal 100?" Finally, add a simple play Action (that is, if the condition is true, it's time to play the movie). Also, you should turn "waiting" to false so that checking can stop. To do this, add a simple evaluate Action with `waiting=false`. Figure 18.6 shows the finished version of this code.

FIGURE 18.6

The finished code attached to the clip into which the movie loads.

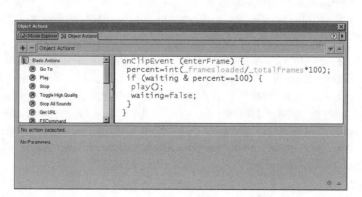

11. Test it out. The movie should work great. If you really want to test it, put it up on a Web server and try it from a slow connection. Note that if you test it twice, it might appear to download instantly the second time. That's because the loaded movie has already downloaded to your browser's cache. Basically, you either have to clear the cache or delete the .swfs from the folder full of downloaded files (for example, Internet Explorer uses C:\WINDOWS\Temporary Internet Files).

Now that you know how to load movies and check to see whether they've totally loaded, it's important to learn how to unload them. There are two basic methods. One, you simply load something else into the movie's place (effectively removing one and replacing it with another). It may not seem very clean to blast one loaded movie away by loading another in its place, but it's good to know you can. Otherwise, you might find yourself unloading one movie, only to immediately load another movie right away. Two, you can use the Action Unload Movie. The only trick with the Unload Movie Action is that you have to remember the location where you loaded the movie (that is, a target clip or a level number) so that you can unload it from the same location. Other than that, unloading is quite simple.

Flash's Unload Action will display an erroneous error when testing your movie in the Flash player (that is, when you Test Movie). It works fine when you play your movie in a browser (or use Publish Preview).

Shared Libraries

Shared Libraries are a productivity enhancement in Flash 5. Consider a regular Library. All the instances of a symbol used throughout your movie will reflect any changes you make to the master in the Library. Now consider being able to have one Library that's shared among several Flash movies (maybe even shared by other members on your team). If a change is made to an item in this Shared Library, you'll see that change reflected in every instance of every movie that uses the Shared Library!

This can save a ton of time. Imagine if you had 100 movies on your site that all shared the same Library. You could make an edit to any item in this Shared Library. Then when you save, export, and upload the Shared Library, all those 100 movies would reflect the change automatically. With a little bit of planning, you could create design templates that could be updated for every season (maybe change background and button colors once every few months). You could also create several different language sites with the same core programming—just make a different Shared Library for each language. Just a bit of planning is required.

Not to discount the power of Shared Libraries, but at their core they're just an automatic version of Load Movie. One important enhancement, however, is the fact that you can store fonts in a Shared Library. Therefore, in addition to the productivity value of Shared Libraries, you also have download time benefits. If the same font is used in several files the additional download time required can add up, but if the font is in a Shared Library, it only downloads once!

How to Use Shared Libraries

Using a Shared Library involves two basic steps. First, you need to create the Library that will be shared. Then, in each file that will use the assets in the Shared Library, you need to establish a link to the Shared Library. To limit the confusion during this discussion of the different files, I'll call the Library *shared* and the various files that use the library *user files*. In the following task, you'll create a Shared Library.

Task: Create a Shared Library

In this task you'll create a Shared Library so it can share its assets with other user files. Follow these steps:

1. Create a new file and immediately save it as shared.fla in a folder called LibraryTest. Import one bitmapped image (.jpg, .bmp, .pct, for example). Delete the bitmap onstage (don't worry, it's still safe in the Library). Also, import one sound file. Finally, create a rectangle and convert it to a symbol (F8). Then make it a Movie Clip, name it "box," and click OK.

2. You should now have a Library with three items. Any file's Library can act like a Shared Library if you just export an .swf first. However, normally when you export an .swf, all unused library items are excluded; therefore, they don't contribute to the file size. The problem is that this time you want all the items in the Library to export with the file! Sure, this will add to file size, but you want these assets to be available to many user files. To ensure that each item is included in the .swf export process, you'll define the linkage for each item.

3. To define the linkage for the sound you imported, find it in the Library, select it, then select Linkage… from the Options menu (or right-click). The default for Symbol Linkage Properties is No Linkage. Change this to Export This Symbol, which will force this item to be exported. Finally, you need to give this symbol a unique identifier because if you replace it, you can use the same identifier in the replacement. Unique identifiers are discussed later. For now, just type **sound_1** (see Figure 18.7).

18

FIGURE 18.7

When you select Linkage... for a Library item, you can specify that it will definitely export (even if it isn't used on the Stage). This way, files sharing this Library will have access to it. You give it a unique identifier because if you replace it, you can use the same identifier in the replacement.

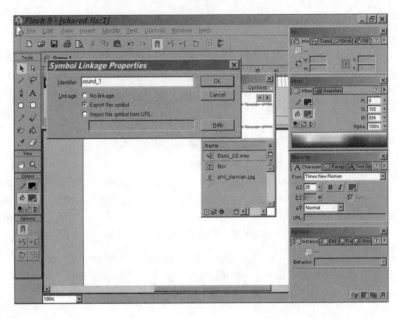

4. Go ahead and define the linkage for the bitmap (type **bitmap_1** into the Identifier field) in the Library as well as in the "box" Movie Clip (use "clip_1" for its identifier). Just make sure each one has a unique name in the Identifier field.

5. Now, save (Ctrl+S) and then export this file. You can just do a "Test Movie" (Ctrl+Enter) because it's already saved in the right folder.

6. The Shared Library is now finished (unless you want to edit or add to it).

Now that you've created a Shared Library, you can use its assets in any other file. The other files just have to identify shared.fla as their Shared Library, and then its items can be used just like any other Library. In the following task, you'll start *using* the Shared Library, and then it should start to make sense.

Task: Start Using a Shared Library

In this task you'll create a user file that can access the contents of the Shared Library you created in the previous task. Here are the steps:

1. Create a new file (Ctrl+N) and save it as user1.fla in the LibraryTest folder (from the previous task). Select File, Open as Shared Library... and then from the Open As Library dialog box select the file shared.fla. You'll see the Library from

shared.fla, but notice it's darkened a bit to represent that it's from another file. You can now use instances from this Shared Library without adding to the file size of the user1.fla file.

2. You can either drag items from the (now open) Shared Library to the Stage of user1.fla or to its Library. Either way, you'll see what looks like a duplicate in user1's Library. Drag the bitmap onto the Stage. Then open the Library for user1.fla (Ctrl+L) and notice that the bitmap looks like it was copied into the Library. Now, try dragging the sound from the Shared Library to user1's Library. Finally, drag the "box" onto the Stage. File user1.fla now seems to have three items added to its Library (see Figure 18.8). However, these are really just instances pointing to the master version in the file shared.fla.

FIGURE 18.8

After you bring assets from a Shared Library into a user file, they appear to be included in the user file's Library.

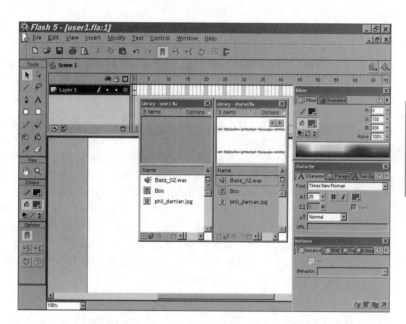

18

3. Go ahead and double-click the "box" clip in your user1.fla movie. You'll see a dialog box like the one shown in Figure 18.9. Click No. The point is that you can only make edits to the master when you open shared.fla. By the way, you can drag instances from user1's Library onto the Stage, and you're still using instances of the masters saved in "shared."

FIGURE **18.9**

Trying to edit the clip (which you took from the Shared Library) will cause this dialog box to appear. It basically says that if you want to edit the clip here, it won't be linked any more. Editing the original is done through the source of the Shared Library itself.

4. Do a Test Movie and then look at the file sizes. The shared.swf file should be rather large (it has a bitmap, sound, and Movie Clip). The user1.swf file should be tiny, because it only points to the shared.swf file. By the way, if you move or change the name of shared.swf, the file user1.swf won't work!

What's the big deal? You have two files, and one's bigger than the other. So what? First of all, you can repeat the last task, but this time you can name the file *user2.fla*. You can use instances of the same symbols (maybe in different ways), and user2.swf will be tiny, too! Visitors to your site will download shared.swf only once, regardless of whether they view user1.swf or user2.swf, or both. Additionally, you can change the contents of shared.fla—maybe change the bitmap or the "box" symbol. After making a change and exporting shared.swf again will enable all your user files (user1.swf, for example) to reflect the change. This is just like how you can change a master symbol and every instance reflects that change. You'll now give it a try. (If you want to first repeat the preceding task first, but name your file user2.fla, you may.)

Task: Update Shared Assets in a Library

In this task, you'll learn how to update the contents of a Shared Library. Follow these steps:

1. Open the source of your Shared Library (shared.fla). Take note of what the identifier is for the bitmap (select it and select Linkage... from the Library's Options menu). Delete this bitmap from the Library and import another bitmap that will serve as a replacement.

2. Access the newly imported bitmap's Symbol Linkage Properties via Linkage... on the Options menu and then set them to Export This Symbol and specify the same identifier as the old bitmap (probably bitmap_1).

3. Save the movie and export an .swf (Ctrl+Enter).

4. Now double-click any user files you've made (user1.swf, for example). They should now reflect the change.

That was almost too easy. You simply created a new library item in the master shared Library file (shared.fla), made sure it would export, and gave it an identifier name that matched the old one. Then, as soon as you exported the .swf, it worked. Basically, each user file doesn't care what's inside the master Shared Library; it simply looks for items that match identifier names. For example, if you have a Movie Clip containing English language text and swap it with one containing Spanish, as long as the identifier is the same, it will work fine (it would just appear in a different language).

Although you can probably start to see how Shared Libraries can enhance productivity, remember that their other benefit is file size savings. The shared.swf file only downloads once. It makes sense, then, to use Shared Libraries for larger items (especially when those items can be used by various movies). Sounds and bitmaps generally have the biggest file sizes. However, fonts can actually add to your movie's size significantly. For example, if you use a special font to create a single letter, that simple use causes font information to be added to your file. (This is why it's actually sometimes better to "break apart" (Ctrl+B) text that's used in this way.) Of course, if you use the same font throughout your movie, this is not necessary. However, if you use the same font throughout several movies, it makes sense to store the font inside a Shared Library. You'll do just that in the next task.

18

Task: Share a Font

In this task you'll put a font into a Shared Library that can be used by as many user files as you want. Here are the steps:

1. In a new file (or your shared.fla Shared Library source), open the Library window. From the Options menu, select New Font....

2. You'll see the Font Symbol Properties dialog box, which requires you to specify both a new name for your font and which font you want to copy. Suppose you own a font called *Blur*, and you want that font in the Library. You need to find and select Blur from the Font drop-down list and then give it a new name. Anything will work (except a name used already). However, let me suggest that you use the original font name plus "_IMPORTED." This way, when you're in the user file, you can find the font alphabetically, but there will be no question which one is imported. Notice in Figure 18.10 that I've given the Blur font the name *Blur_IMPORTED*.

FIGURE **18.10**

*When creating a new
font, you must specify
the font and the name
you want to give it.
Adding "_IMPORTED"
to the end of the origi-
nal name makes it clear
which font is the
"imported" one.*

3. Now you need to make sure Flash exports the font when you export the movie. So, after you're done making a new font, you should notice the "font" item in your Library. Select it and access the Linkage properties (right-click or select the Options menu). Choose Export This Symbol and give it the unique identifier "myBlur" (it just has to be a unique name).

4. Save this movie as shared.fla, export it (Ctrl+Enter), and then close it. Create a new file and save it as user_of_fonts.fla in the same location as the shared.fla.

5. Select File, Open As Shared Library… and point to the file you just created (shared.fla). Type Ctrl+L to open the Library of user_of_fonts and then drag the font Blur_IMPORTED (or whatever you named the font) from the Shared Library to your file's Library. Now, finally, we can use this font in the user file. Simply create some text and use the Character panel to select Blur_IMPORTED from the list of fonts! (See how the name you chose made it easy? Flash also puts an asterisk after any imported font names.)

One last note on this subject: Using fonts in Shared Libraries isn't just for file size savings. You can use them like "styles" in a word processor. For example, you can go back to the shared.fla file and edit the font (just double-click the font item in the Library and choose a different font from the Font Symbol Properties). If you then re-export (to replace) shared.swf, you'll see the new font being used in each user file. Notice that in this case, since you're just editing a symbol (the font) you don't have to worry about the linkage settings. If, on the other hand, you actually replaced an entire Library item, you would need to set the linkage and provide the same unique identifier used earlier.

Basically, all the upfront work in Shared Libraries can be very useful, provided you use the same styles and assets throughout many files. It also means that everyone on the team could be given a copy of the latest version of shared.swf to use on their computers. In the end, when everything's published, the latest version of shared.swf will be used by everyone. All it takes is a little planning.

Linked Scripts

I'd like to mention the topic of linked scripts here because it fits very well with the other topics mentioned this hour. Remember all the ActionScripting you did in the Actions panel? Anything you can type in that panel can be stored as text in a text file. Let me just show you how it works.

The options arrow in the Actions panel allows you to "Export as File…" any code you've created in Flash. You can also copy and paste from Flash's Actions panel into a text editor. Flash happens to be a convenient place to create ActionScript—it colors your text and has easy to use parameter drop down menus for example. But since Flash is almost identical to JavaScript you may likely find a third party text editor will do almost as well. You can create a text file full of ActionScript by simply typing by hand into a text editor. It isn't terribly important how you get your ActionScript into a text file, but that's the first step to using linked scripts.

Once you've created your text file full of ActionScript you can return to Flash. Use the Actions panel to select the Action "include" and specify, as its parameter, a named text file. For example, if in a keyframe you open the Actions panel and place the script `#include "scripts.txt"`, Flash will use the contents of the file scripts.txt as if it were inside this keyframe. Presumably, the content of scripts.txt is a legitimate ActionScript. This is great because you can change the script without ever opening Flash. Just remember if you change the script file, you'll need to export the .swf again (as this is when the code is copied into Flash). This is a great feature.

One note: Macromedia suggests that you use ".as" as a file extension (instead of ".txt") so that everyone knows the file contains ActionScript (Get it? The .as extension stands for *ActionScript*.)

Just like Load Movie and Shared Libraries, external scripts let you modularize your projects for easy updates. The key is that you must plan for likely updates.

Summary

This hour you saw several ways to cut your movies up into little pieces. Such modularization can have performance advantages as well as productivity value. The perceived download time is reduced if users only need to download segments, as needed. You and your team's productivity is increased by breaking a site into smaller files—not only can several people work simultaneously but you can impose consistent styles with Shared Libraries. You also learned the steps necessary to modularize. However, the challenging and creative part comes as you decide when and where to modularize.

18

The first feature discussed was the Load Movie Action. This allows you to (at runtime) play another .swf on a level number or in a clip instance. You also learned about Shared Libraries, where an .swf can act as a Library shared between several files or among several team members. A lot of upfront work is involved to get a Shared Library built, but this time investment will be paid back in the form of greater productivity. You can share any kind of Library item, including a font. Finally, I pointed out that there's a way to store your scripts outside the Flash file (as a text file) so that you can share one script and make edits to it without returning to Flash.

Q&A

Q **I've created the submovies that I intend to load into my main movie via Load Movie. I've saved them all in the correct folder, but when I test the main movie I get the error** Error opening URL "c:\windows\desktop\somefolder\ submovie.swf" **in the output window (and my movies don't load). What's going on?**

A Most likely, when you made your various submovies, you saved them correctly, but you need to take the extra step of exporting them as an .swf (simply do a Test Movie). Only .swfs can be loaded using Load Movie.

Q **My Website is getting pretty messy with all the little submovies in the main folder. Is there a way I can keep the movies that load in a separate folder to keep everything straight?**

A Yes. When you specify (in the URL field of Load Movie's parameters) the movie you want to load, if you simply type mymovie.swf, Flash will look for mymovie.swf in the same folder. If you want to store mymovie.swf in a subfolder called "movies," you would change the URL field to read movies/mymovie.swf. (By the way, you can use all the standard HTML relative references as well, such as "../" to mean "up one folder.")

Q **If I know I'm going to use a Shared Library for a project, but I don't actually have the master media elements (such as the bitmaps I want to share). Is there anyway I can start now?**

A Sure. Just import any bitmap into the file that will become the Shared Library. Hopefully, you can find a bitmap that's the right size. Just set the export settings for the bitmap and come up with a unique identifier name. Go ahead and use this shared item as you would if it were the final version. When you get the final bitmap, import it into the Shared Library. Remove the old version, but when you're defining the export settings for the replacement, use the same identifier name. Everything will update as soon as you export the Shared Library again (that is, create an .swf). By the way, if you're concerned about the positioning, in the Shared

Library you could create a Movie Clip symbol from the bitmap and use *that* as your shared item. When you go to replace it, if every instance in your "user" movies gets shifted, you can go back to the master and move the contents of the master symbol to offset the shift.

Workshop

The Workshop consists of quiz questions and answers to help you solidify your understanding of the material covered. Try to answer the questions before checking the answers.

Quiz

1. How many movies can you load into _level3?

    A. None, this level is reserved for sounds.

    B. As many as you want.

    C. One.

2. If you want to rotate (that is, set the _rotatation property of) a movie that gets loaded, into what location must you load it?

    A. A Target clip.

    B. A _level number.

    C. Either Target or Level.

3. How many people can simultaneously edit the master version of a Shared Library?

    A. One.

    B. As many people as you want.

    C. A number equal to how many user files you have.

Quiz Answers

1. C. Into any level number (or into any clip instance, for that matter) you can only load one movie at a time. If you try loading another movie into an occupied level or clip, the new movie just replaces the current occupant.

2. C. Although it seem easiest to change the properties (including _rotation) of a clip instance (because you just have to use `clipInstanceName._rotation=180`), you can also set a property of any level number—for example, `_level1._rotation=180`. I think it makes more sense to load movies into named clips, but you don't have to.

18

3. A. Only one person can actually edit the master version of the Shared Library. Once it's turned into an .swf, you can share it throughout a network—or just redistribute copies to everyone involved. Keep in mind that in order to drag an item from a file opened as a Shared Library, you're actually using the source .fla file.

HOUR 19

Creating an Interface to Match Your Message

If you like to flex your creative muscles, this hour might be the most fun in the entire book. We're going to study creating an interface, starting with nothing and ending with a design that dictates how you'll build an entire site. Making a good interface is challenging and rewarding. It's not easy, but I hope you agree it's fun.

You have a user, and you have content. Between the two is your Flash interface. The goal of an interface isn't to be cute or fancy—it is to be transparent. Your user should be able to access the content effortlessly. He shouldn't have to fight with the interface. He should also find the content he wants without becoming confused. It sounds easy enough, but it's quite a challenge to do it well.

This hour you will

- Learn some proven, effective designs and how to use them for your purposes
- See common pitfalls and learn how to avoid them
- Learn how to quickly prototype your ideas before going too far to change them

Whole books have been written on the topic of interface design. It's possible to discuss theory without any practical application to Flash, but this hour will focus on and apply what we learn in Flash. The skills you learn in this hour will be useful in every future project. The learning shouldn't stop here, though: You can always improve your interface-design skills.

Good Interface Design

Sometimes the best way to learn good interface design is to study bad interface design, either your own failed attempts or those of others. You can probably think of a Web site or a particular piece of software that you had difficulty figuring out. It doesn't even have to be software. For example, how many times have you filled in the cells of a form only to find (on the last line) that you had been putting information on the lines right above the labels when you were supposed to be filling in the cells below the labels? In Figure 19.1, do you put your name above First name or below it? Don't blame yourself if you can't figure something out—it is bad design. Learning from good examples is more difficult, because if an interface does its job well, you won't remember it.

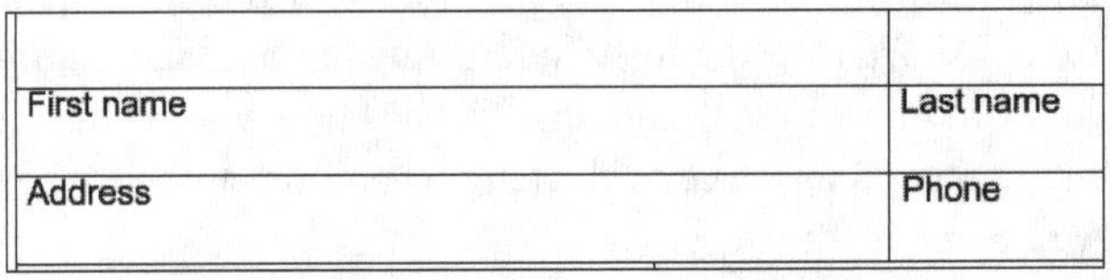

FIGURE 19.1

If you've ever filled in a form and wondered into which cell the information should be written, you've experienced a bad interface.

| First name | Last name |
| Address | Phone |

Elements That Make a Good Interface

Having said that it's easier to learn from a bad interface design than a good one, there are certain elements that define a good interface. Some of this is subjective. So remember that the ultimate gauge is not whether an interface follows the rules listed here. Rather, judge an interface on its success or failure. For example, watch someone else test your initial Flash site. If you find several people making the same mistake, don't expect that you can simply tell them the correct way. Take it as a sign that you have a problem to address. Just remember that "The user is always right."

Make Buttons Look Different from Other Elements

I was going to call this section "Make Buttons Look Like Buttons," but I don't want to suggest that all buttons should look generic. Go ahead and make your buttons as crazy looking as you want. However, make sure they don't look identical to other interface elements. For example, the interface in Figure 19.2 includes a series of buttons on the left side. The buttons are rounded-corner rectangles. But there are also interface elements that use similar rounded-corner rectangles. It's nearly impossible to tell the difference between a design element and a button.

This interface example uses the same shape for buttons as for interface decoration.

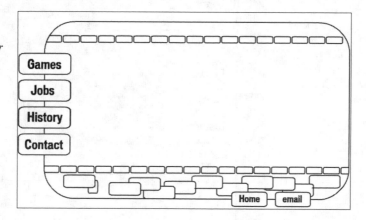

Buttons Should Give Immediate and Clear Feedback

When a user clicks a button, he should know that his click counted, that the interface detected his click, and that his request is being processed. There are two common reasons a user may not know his click registered. Sometimes the click is requesting something that takes a long time to load. For example, a Load Movie may have started but, because of the time required for the movie to download, the user is sitting there without a clue that he's supposed to wait. A simple "Loading" message, like the one we created last hour, could be enough.

The other reason this happens often is that the result of the click may have occurred but there's no indication of the result—visual or otherwise. For example, if you have a button that turns off the audio and the user clicks when there's a break in the audio, you need a visual clue (like the button changes) to tell the user his click counted.

For example, in Flash 5 (which is generally a great interface) dock the Mixer panel and the Swatches panel (in their default layout) as in Figure 19.3. In the Mixer panel, pick any color from the color bar. Now, with the Mixer panel's options arrow, choose Add Swatch (see Figure 19.4). Did anything happen?

19

FIGURE 19.3

The Mixer and Swatches panels (in their default arrangement) contain a subtle interface problem.

FIGURE 19.4

Select a color in the Mixer panel, and you can access Add Swatch, which adds a custom color to the Swatches panel—which is hidden. The user doesn't know if Add Swatch worked.

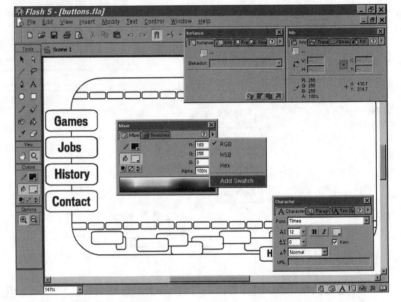

In fact, you added a swatch, but you were given no feedback to that effect. Undock the Swatches panel and scroll all the way down. You'll see that the last color is the one you just added. Keep both panels visible separately, and try adding another swatch (by way of the Mixer panel). If you watch the Swatches panel while you select Add Swatch in the Mixer panel, you'll see a color added—but this isn't much feedback because it appears in another part of the screen.

Create Selected States for Buttons

After you select a button that results in an onscreen change, it's important to give the user a visible clue which button (and therefore, which content) is currently selected. If the user clicks a button labeled Red Square and then a red square appears onscreen, he will remember the last button he clicked. However, it's not usually this clear. Repeating the button label and changing the button graphically can make a world of difference to clear things up for the user. In the slightly redesigned screen (see Figure 19.5), when the user clicks Games, the large blank area fills with game content. However, it may not be clear that the user is looking at game content. It would be better if there were additional clues to make it more apparent.

FIGURE 19.5

It's not entirely clear that the current section is Games. A selected state for the Games button would solve this problem.

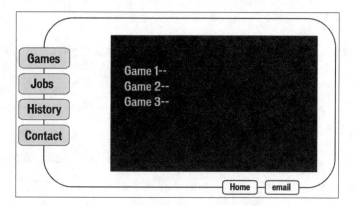

We made some sophisticated buttons in Hour 13, "Making Buttons for Your User to Click." You could create Over states and Down states very simply. Unfortunately, buttons you create in Flash don't have an automatic selected state. That's okay. We can achieve the same effect with just a little work. This will be a good opportunity to start to build something more complete than most of the exercises we've been doing.

Task: Create Selected States for a Set of Buttons

In this Task we'll create a set of buttons, each of which will have a selected state so that the user knows at any time what section he is in.

1. Create a generic button (no text on it) that has a rollover state. Draw a rectangle, with rounded corners if you want. Make sure it has both a Line component and a Fill component. Select just the fill and convert to a symbol (F8). Call it Button Shape and make sure it's a Movie Clip. Now select everything onstage (the Button Shape instance and the outline shape). Convert these to a symbol (F8) called Generic Button and make sure it's a Button. Click OK.

2. Now, double-click the Generic Button instance so we can edit the master button. Rename the layer with everything in it Outline. Insert a new layer (Insert, Layer) and call the new layer Fill. Click to select the instance of Button Shape. Cut this, then click the Fill layer and select Paste in Place (Ctrl+Shift+V). Reorder the layers

19

so that Outline is on top. In the Outline layer, click the fourth frame (under Hit) and Insert Frame (F5). Do the same for the Fill layer. In frame 2 of Fill, insert a keyframe (F6) and select the instance of Button Shape onstage. Access the Effect panel and change this instance color to something obviously different (I made mine bright yellow). See Figure 19.6 for an idea of how the button's Timeline should look.

FIGURE 19.6

The button uses two instances of the Button Shape clip to make the Over state but just one instance of the outline, so we use two layers.

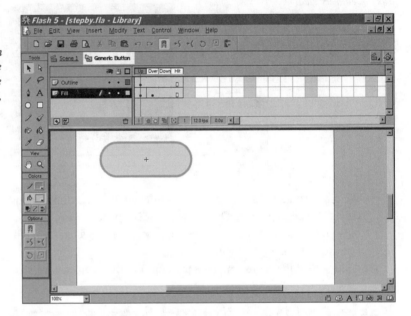

3. Test the movie. This should be a review from Hour 13, but notice that all we got was an outline that doesn't change color. It's worth it.

4. In the main scene, copy and paste two more buttons and space all three buttons evenly. Create three blocks of text that serve as labels for these buttons—for example: This, That, and Other. I made them a medium blue color.

5. Select the three text blocks and convert to symbol (F8). Call it Button Labels and save it as a Movie Clip. Now, select the instance of Button Labels we just made and convert it to a symbol. Call it Labels and Highlights and save it as a Movie Clip. Double-click on the instance of Labels and Highlights you just made (to edit the master version), and you should find an instance of Button Labels inside.

6. While inside the master version of Labels and Highlights, rename layer 1 Plain Labels. Insert a layer and name it Highlights. Copy the instance in the Plain Labels layer, and then click to select the Highlights layer and Paste in Place (Ctrl+Shift+V). Since there's a clip instance in the Highlights layer, we can set Effect to Tint in another color. Access the Effect panel when you select the instance

in Highlights. Tint the three labels (all one symbol) a different color—this will be the selected color.

7. The basic design will have the plain text on all the time, but the Highlights layer will be masked to reveal just one highlight at a time. All the layers will last at least 4 frames, to match the length of the Button symbol. Therefore, you should click in frame 4 of each layer and Insert, Frame (F5).

8. With the Highlights layer active, Insert, Layer and call this layer Mask. In frame 2 of Mask, draw a rectangle that covers the first button's text. Make it extra wide in case the button names change, but don't make it too tall because it shouldn't cover the other buttons' text. Convert this rectangle into a symbol (called Box) to save on file size. In frame 3 of Mask, Insert, Keyframe (F6) and move the new instance of Box to cover the second button's label. In frame 4, Insert, Keyframe (F6) and move Box to cover the third button's label.

9. We don't need the Highlight layer to show anything until frame 2. Carefully click once to select just the keyframe in frame 1 of Highlight. Then click and drag to move the keyframe to frame 2. (See Figure 19.7.)

FIGURE 19.7

The Highlights layer doesn't need to appear in the first frame, so we move the first keyframe to frame 2.

19

10. Finally, set the layer properties for the Mask layer (Modify, Layer) to Mask. Then set the layer properties for Highlights to Masked. Lock all layers and scrub to see how this will work. Before we finish inside the Labels and Highlights clip, put a Stop Action in the first frame of any layer. We will make this clip jump to the right frame, but we don't want it to loop through all the layers from the start.

11. We're in the home stretch. Go back to the main scene and give the instance of Labels and Highlights an instance name (via the Instance panel) of Labels.

12. Select the first button and open the Actions panel. For the first button's Action insert Evaluate (esc ev) and into the Expression parameter type `Labels.gotoAndStop(2)`. (Be sure to follow the capitalization shown for gotoAndStop.) When the user clicks and releases the button, this tells Flash to go to frame 2 of the instance named Labels and stop there.

13. For the second button, insert an Evaluate with `Labels.gotoAndStop(3)`; for the third button, `Labels.gotoAndStop(4)`. You can copy and paste the actual contents in the Script area of the Actions panel, then modify the part that changes—in this case, the number between the parentheses.

14. That was a lot, but it was worth it. Check it out by testing the movie.

15. Finally, it's simple to add content that appears when the user clicks. Double-click the instance of Labels and Highlights and click the top layer (Mask). Then insert a layer. Call it Content. In frame 2 of Content, insert a keyframe and put in all the content for the section This. I just drew the word This freehand onscreen (see Figure 19.8), but you could import a bitmap, insert another Movie Clip, or add whatever content you want. However, repeating the labels from the button (in this case, This) makes it even more clear to the user what section he is viewing. To finish with the Content layer, you can insert a blank keyframe in frame 3 and create the content for That, and then in frame 4 insert a blank keyframe and create content for Other.

FIGURE 19.8

We can add content to the clip (originally designed for high-lights). We just added a Content layer and graphics in the appropriate frames.

This was a big Task. The button didn't really need that extra outline, but it looks better. Also, the shape in the button was first created (as a symbol) primarily for efficiency. While there are other ways to do what we did, this approach eliminated redundant shapes. For example, the text labels occur only once, in Button Labels. If you need to change the words, they only have to change in one place. Everything will be updated.

Finally, it was simple to create a selected state for the buttons. Our treatment was to highlight the text. This could have been done other ways, such as with a big circle around the button. It's especially important to consider other solutions when you're only highlighting one of two buttons. Consider two buttons labeled True and False. If you're trying to highlight one and you simply change the color of the text to green, the user will only know that one is green and the other isn't. He won't know that the green one is selected. You have to come up with a graphic treatment that makes it clear which button is selected. See Figure 19.9.

FIGURE 19.9

The example on the left clearly shows that the True button and False button are different, but you don't know which one is selected.

If It's Not Adding Anything, It's Probably Distracting

Everything in an interface should have a purpose. You have precious little screen space with which to work. Consider a user with his monitor set to display 800×600 pixels. Even if his browser is maximized, all the buttons and interface components of the browser leave only about 750×400 pixels to display your page (see Figure 19.10). If you add a simple 10-pixel line around the outside of your interface, that uses almost 10% of the total screen space. Since you have only so much space, you shouldn't waste it on superfluous interface decorations.

19

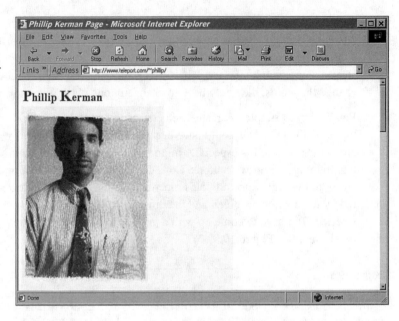

This same rule can be applied to other elements, such as sound. It's doubly important not to burden users with sounds they don't really need, because sound means longer download times. A cute sound effect every time a user enters a section of your Web site might be fun the first time, but it can become distracting. Ask yourself if an element adds anything to the message. If so, fine—figure a way to use it. But if it doesn't add to your message, take it out.

Graphic designers hate this rule. They use whitespace as a design element. Those who are experienced in creating graphics for print have a particularly difficult time with this problem. I don't want to squash people's creative talents—I'm actually doing them a favor. The amount of information you can fit on a computer screen is very limited. First and foremost, your message should be heard. Realizing that screen space is limited can encourage graphic design that is appropriate for the medium. If you're used to creating feature-length films, you might have trouble adapting to 30-second TV commercials. Similarly, adjustments are necessary for communicating through the Internet.

Restraining the Urge

You can do some amazing stuff with Flash. That doesn't mean you should. By adding too much to an interface, you can make it complicated to use, slow to download, and less likely to achieve its purpose. It's good to know what's available, but it's also good to know when to refrain from using it all. Let's discuss some of the common urges that must be restrained to stay on track.

Leverage Off Standard Designs

The history of computer software is long enough that you can learn from the designs of others, and there are standards that are important to follow. For example, a radio button (discussed in Hour 16, "Using Smart Clips") behaves in a particular way. When the need for this kind of button arises, your users probably expect something that *looks* like a radio button. This is just one type of standard after which you can model your program.

First try to learn the accepted standards. There are countless books on the topic of "human computer interface design." It isn't essential that you follow every standard explicitly. Rather, once you understand the standards you can make an educated decision based on each situation. Respect the standards but feel free to make exceptions where appropriate. Whatever you do, you should never contradict a standard. For example, you're free to use buttons that look like standard checkboxes; however, don't create checkboxes that behave like radio buttons.

Don't Be a Slave to Consistency

A consistent interface is a good thing. For example, if most buttons in your site have a yellow Over state and respond to the Press mouse event, they all should. However, developers sometimes get hung up on consistency, and it can actually work against you. Sometimes it's okay to break your own rules.

For example, suppose that when the user selects background info from a main menu, the main selections (on the main menu) disappear and the background information content fills the screen. You'd probably include something like a Main Menu button somewhere on every content screen, and it would be labeled the same on every page. The Main Menu button should be consistent and labeled properly. For example, don't label the button Home if the title at the main menu reads "Main Menu". Also, the Main Menu button should appear in the same location—pick a location where it won't get in the way so you don't have to move it.

However, you could take the rule for consistency too far and say, "The main menu is always only reached by clicking the main menu button." The goal is to be consistent, but who said there could be only one route to the main menu? For example, if one of your content pages has page forward and page back buttons, it would make sense that pressing the page back button on the first page or the page forward on the last should navigate the user to the main menu. Multiple routes to the same destination are okay. Look at how many ways you can save in your word processor program. A rule of consistency taken out of context or to an extreme can work against you.

19

Zeroing In on What Works

In the process of designing the perfect interface, you should continually prove a design works by testing it on real live humans. Ideally you have a group of representative users at your disposal. Whether that's a reality or not, I have some suggestions on how to test your designs. Take it as a warning (and a blessing) any time you find yourself misinterpreting any part of your interface. For example, if you click a button to take you one place and it takes you somewhere else, there's a problem that needs to be addressed. Maybe the button should do what you expected, rather than what it currently does. Don't discount your own mistakes by thinking, for example, that the user will figure it out because the button is labeled. How many users read everything? Besides, if you keep making the same mistake, you can be sure users will, too.

Another way to zero in on a good interface design is to make drastic changes while testing. Although subtlety in design is a good thing, if you're trying to see if a design change is worthwhile, make it obvious. Consider the way you adjust the water temperature for a shower. You don't just nudge it a little hotter. You push it farther than you think you need to, and then back off more than you need to, until you settle on the perfect temperature. When testing a change to your interface, make the change drastic. If you go too far, just back off. It's easier to judge the effectiveness of a change when it is clear.

Finally, if and when you test the usability of a design with a user, be sure only to observe. Don't sit right behind him and correct his mistakes. It's difficult to resist, but it's essential if you are to gather accurate data.

Summary

An interface should enable the user to access the content without drawing attention to itself. I provided several tips which should be considered—not followed blindly. When you embark on a large project, the tips in this hour might prevent you from going too far in the wrong direction.

If you find yourself with a really bad interface, try to let go and start over. This might not always be practical, but what good is the information on your Web site if users can't get to it easily? Starting over is sometimes the best tack.

Q&A

Q Where can I learn more about this subject?

A Several authors have written on the subject of human-computer interface design, but don't limit yourself to books on that specific topic. You may have a difficult time finding books specific to Web sites. You can learn a lot from traditional information design. Two notable authors that have influenced me include Edward R. Tufte and Donald Norman.

Q In the exercise this hour we put practically everything inside a Movie Clip. Does this kind of encapsulation make a site easier to manage?

A There are a lot of ways to make a site manageable (see Hours 18 and 22 in particular). However, for complex interactions, the less you do in the main Timeline, the better. For example, if navigation between sections occurred in the main Timeline, we'd need to use four frames (or however many) for the four buttons. Everything else in the movie would be dependent on the four frames in the main Timeline. Putting everything in a Movie Clip makes the buttons more portable. For example, to take 10 frames to tween the buttons onstage before stopping, we could simply tween the entire Movie Clip in the main Timeline. In using your main Timeline, you become locked to its duration.

Q That exercise seemed like a lot of work. Is there a way to make a button that behaves in the same fashion using ActionScript?

A Sure. It would be more work up front (probably), but you could use it over and over. For a great example, check out the Radio Button clip that ships in Flash's Smart Clips Common Library (under the Window menu).

Q How do I convince an artist that usability is important?

A It's difficult to trash a design that works well. Go back to the original concept that you're just trying to make content accessible. All the pretty graphics in the world can't justify an interface that doesn't work. Everyone involved should be able to explain the purpose of anything they add. Use the "If it isn't adding anything, then it's distracting" argument to remove superfluous decoration.

19

Workshop

The Workshop consists of quiz questions and answers to help you solidify your understanding of the material covered. Try to answer the questions before checking the answers.

Quiz

1. What's an "interface"?

   A. The graphics onscreen.

   B. An imaginary pane between user and content.

   C. The buttons onscreen.

2. What's the maximum number of buttons you should use in an interface?

    A. Five, plus or minus 2.

    B. Fewer than 10.

    C. As many as are needed.

3. If you give a user clear and immediate feedback that he clicked a button, is there still any reason to make a selected state for a button?

    A. No. The feedback is enough.

    B. Yes. You want the user to be able to look away then look back at the screen and always know which button he clicked last.

    C. Yes—Phillip says so. See the section "Create Selected States for Buttons," earlier in this hour.

Quiz Answers

1. B. Technically, A and C are part of the answer, but I want to stress that the interface is what's between your user and the content. It's the visuals onscreen, but it's also how those things work.

2. C. I've heard answer A thrown around, and I believe it's based on a study of how many items a user can remember. However, a user can "scan" many items. For example, can you find your favorite cereal in a supermarket's cereal aisle? Of course. Depending on the situation, you can have as many buttons as seem to be needed.

3. B. I suppose if you have a title on screen that matches the label on the button, that's effectively a selected state. Answer C was thrown in (as a wrong answer) because these tips should not be considered rules that you must follow. They're only tips.

HOUR 20

Optimizing Your Flash Site

By now, you can draw, animate, and design a site that's both interesting to look at and easy to use. Of course, you always run either Test Movie or Publish Preview to get an accurate idea of how your movie will play. However, there can still be a marked difference between how the movie plays on your computer's hard drive and how it plays when viewed by your Web audience. Not only do connection speeds vary, but each user's computer may perform differently. The result might be a movie that, although it instantly plays smoothly on your computer, takes a long time to download and then stutters as it plays on someone else's computer.

Optimization involves two unrelated issues: reducing a movie's file size to speed download times, and improving playback to ensure that the movie plays equally well on different computers, regardless of processor speed. This hour investigates both issues in an attempt to ensure that your movie downloads quickly and plays well on all your users' machines.

In this hour you will:

- Reduce the file size of your movie without affecting quality
- Remove unnecessary special effects to improve performance
- Find appropriate alternatives to Flash

File Size Considerations

The fastest way to lose your audience is make it wait a long time for a movie to download. In a minute, you'll see how to calculate how long a movie takes to download. The simple formula, however, is this: The faster the movie downloads, the better. Even as Internet connections are speeding up (with technologies such as DSL and cable modems, for example), the reality is that the majority of your potential audience is still connected via dial-up connections (56KBps modems or slower). Even if you decide to target only those people with fast connections, there's no reason to create movies that are larger than absolutely necessary. The natural tendency is to push the technology to the limit and then push it a little further. If you fill a storage closet to capacity and then you are given a larger closet, most likely you'd just fill the new closet and think you need even more room—this is natural. Just because you can make large Flash files doesn't mean you should.

Calculating Download Times

It doesn't take any fancy math to estimate how long a file takes to download. You just need to know how big the file is and the rate at which it downloads. This is similar to estimating how long it takes to travel in a car; you just need to know the total distance and the speed of the car. For example, if the total distance is 30 miles and your rate of speed is 60 miles an hour, your trip should take one-half hour. Total distance in miles divided by miles per hour equals time in hours (distance / rate = time).

Applying this formula to download times is similar: file size / rate = time. A file size that's 10 units downloading at 5 units a second will download in 2 seconds. That was easy! We didn't even have to talk about bits, bytes, and kilobytes. All these terms refer to different units—like inches and feet or dollars and pennies. The formula works the same as long as the units for file size and rate are the same. A car traveling 100 kilometers per hour will travel 50 kilometers in one-half hour. We'll eventually discuss bits and bytes, but for now, just keep the size/rate=time formula in mind.

In reality, you can only estimate (not calculate) how long it takes to travel somewhere by car because your speed will vary slightly. The same is true with Flash movies because download speeds vary. Just because you have a 28.8 modem (which, in theory, downloads 2.88 kilobytes a second), doesn't mean a 100 kilobyte (KB) file downloads in 34 seconds (that is, 100KB / 2.88KBps = 34 seconds). Depending on several factors, including Internet congestion and the performance of the Web server, the file may take longer to download. If the actual rate of download is only 2.3KBps, for example, that 100KB file will download in 43 seconds. When it comes to calculating download times, realize it's always just an estimate.

What's Big? What's Small?

The formula to estimate download speed can be summed up as this: the bigger the file, the longer the download time. Therefore, a goal to reduce download time is really a goal to reduce file size. In this section, you'll learn which Flash features tend to create larger files—or more importantly, you'll learn alternative techniques to achieve the same effect with less impact on file size. Although a few Flash features should certainly be avoided at all costs (such as Modify, Shape, and Soften Fill Edges, for example), you don't need to avoid features that increase file size—you just need to use them only when they're needed.

Lines Take Up Less File Space Than Fills

When you draw either a fill or a line, Flash stores the math required to display your drawing. In the case of fills (drawn with the Brush tool, for example), information is stored for all sides of the shape. You can change just one side of a fill, as shown in Figure 20.1. Lines, however, don't really have sides—they have two endpoints, but no thickness. Suppose you draw a green line and give it a stroke of 10. Flash stores just the line, the stroke, and the color. Flash doesn't really store the thickness—only that the line needs a stroke applied to it. The same shape drawn with a brush would require Flash to store information about all sides of the shape—in this case, think of a simple line as a four-sided shape. Check out Figure 20.2, where I drew two lines, turned one into a fill (via Modify, Shape, Convert Lines to Fills), and then selected everything with the Subselect tool. You'll see there are many more anchor points in the fill, meaning it will result in a larger file.

20

FIGURE 20.1

Fills take up more file space because Flash must store information about all sides of the shape (whereas lines have no thickness).

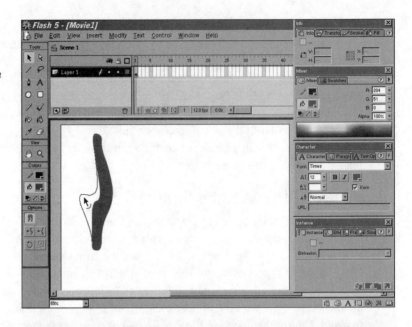

FIGURE 20.2

The line on the right was converted to a fill. The Subselect tool can be used to see the additional complexity of the fill.

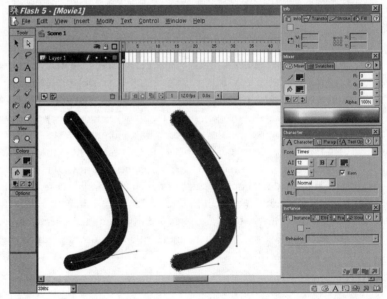

Breaking Apart Text

When you select a block of text and choose Modify, Break Apart, the text turns into a shape. Besides the fact you won't be able to edit the text once it's broken apart, your file size usually increases because Flash stores all the curves in every character of the text. Actually, leaving the text alone also requires the font outlines are stored as well—but that's handled by the font itself, which tends to be very efficient. For example, the letter i might appear twice in the text `Phillip` but it's only stored once in the font. If it were broken apart, it would store it each time. Generally, broken-apart text will almost always add more file space than regular Static Text.

Suppose you have a paragraph of text. Likely, breaking it apart will make your file bigger because Flash must save the shape information for all the characters. However, suppose you have one special font you use for a single character. If you break apart just that letter, you may find your file is actually smaller! That's because when you use just one character (in Static Text), the necessary information Flash stores for that font might be more than the shape information had the character been broken apart. The upshot is that if you are using the same font in several places in your movie or if you have a lot of text (with the same font), you shouldn't break it apart. If it's just one character, you'll probably want to break it apart. (Later this hour, you'll learn ways to measure the difference so that you can just compare the effect of one method over the other.) Of course, the decision between broken-apart text and regular Static Text needs to include other considerations (such as whether you're absolutely sure you'll never need to edit the text again).

Dynamic and Input Text with Embedded Fonts Can Be Large

There are times when you don't have a choice between using broken-apart text and Static Text. If you're using Dynamic or Input Text, there isn't an option to break it apart (otherwise, the text wouldn't be changeable anymore). However, when you use Dynamic or Input Text, you have options as to which font outlines to include (if any). Figure 20.3 shows where you can choose to include font outlines. More information on how to use these settings appears in Hour 15, "ActionScripting Applications for Advanced Interactivity," but it's worth mentioning that you shouldn't embed more font outlines than absolutely necessary because this adds significantly to the file size.

20

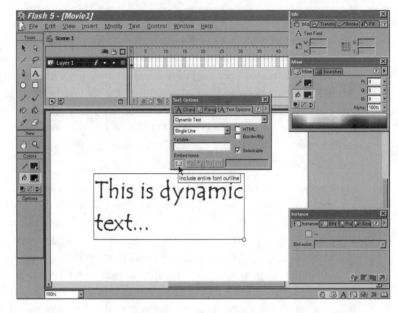

FIGURE 20.3

Including all font out-lines is necessary when you want a dynamic field to display custom fonts—but this adds significantly to the file size.

Nested Movie Clips Are Smaller Than Nested Graphic Symbols

This topic is discussed in great detail in Hour 12, "Animating Using Movie Clips and Graphic Symbols," but it's worth mentioning here. Simply put, Graphic symbols are great if you need to preview their changes in the Timeline. However, Movie Clips (which are nested inside other Movie Clips) will result in a smaller file size.

Shape Tween, Motion Tween, and Keyframes

Ignore, for a moment, the visual and functional differences between the types of tweens and using keyframes for animation. Generally, Shape tweens add to file size most significantly. The difference between using Motion tweens and multiple keyframes is not so cut and dried. Basically, you want the fewest keyframes as possible. A Motion tween, however, requires Flash to create in-between keyframes (even though you won't see them). In reality, if you use a Motion tween to move a circle across the screen with a keyframe on frame 1 and another on frame 10, the effect would be the same as 10 individual keyframes. (Of course, in either case you'd be using an instance of the Circle symbol, so there won't be multiple copies of the shape.) Basically, frame-by-frame animation and Motion tweens are about the same. However, using frame-by-frame animation, you may find that you can pull off the same effect with fewer frames! Not only can this make the movement look more believable and fluid, but fewer frames are used, which results in a smaller file size. To sum this up, avoid Shape tweens and look for ways to use fewer frames.

Take Optimization with a Grain of Salt

Although these preceding tips (and more follow this hour) may seem like rules to live by, it's worth remembering that the file size–creating features of Flash do have useful purposes! For example, there's nothing like a Shape tween to get a "morph" effect. Just because Shape tweens tend to add to your file size doesn't mean you can never use them. Look for alternatives where appropriate, but feel free to use Shape tweens when you have to. When you know which features tend to affect file size, you can make more educated decisions. These tips provide a good starting point. Later this hour you'll see how you can calculate the file size impact of each feature.

Sounds and Bitmaps

In the previous section, there was no mention of sounds and raster graphics (such as .jpg and .bmp files). They have such a huge impact on file size that this entire section is devoted to studying them. The file size savings you gain from other tips (such as using lines instead of fills and Movie Clips instead of Graphic symbols) pale in comparison to the significance of managing sounds and bitmaps. That's not to say text and vector graphics don't matter, but sounds and bitmaps are more significant. Anything you can do to reduce their size will result in a major savings in the file size of your movie.

Sounds

Flash has several ways to compress audio and bitmaps. You've already seen where these compression settings are specified individually for each imported bitmap or sound in Hour 3, "Importing Graphics into Flash," and Hour 10, "Including Sound in Your Animation," (namely, via the Library item properties). You'll also see in Hour 24, "Publishing Your Creation," how you can set compression settings for all imported bitmaps and sounds at once via Publish Settings. Although you know where to set the compression settings, you may not fully understand how this affects your movies.

Different types of compression exist. For audio, you should always use MP3. Although Flash supports ADPCM, only use this if you are publishing your movie as Flash 3 or lower. (That is, you want the audio in your movie to work for people who have only the Flash 3 player.) If you happen to be delivering your movie to run only on your hard drive (maybe you're creating an enhanced slide presentation that you're not distributing via the Web), you can specify no compression (use Raw). Barring those two situations, MP3 is the best choice.

A simple relationship exists between quality and file size. You learned how to set the compression settings individually for just one sound in Hour 10. Basically, you try one setting and listen to how it sounds. As you try different levels of compression, you'll both hear the difference and see the file size change. It's just a matter of balancing these two priorities (good quality and small file size).

20

There are a couple additional ways to optimize sounds. The easiest one to remember is that stereo sounds are twice as big as mono sounds. Therefore, let Flash always convert stereo to mono, unless you truly *need* stereo. Keep in mind you can still use stereo panning effects on sounds that are mono. Through the Sound panel's Edit Envelope feature, you can use preset effects (such as Fade Right to Left) or make your own to give a mono sound stereo-like effects (see Figure 20.4).

FIGURE 20.4

The Edit Envelope feature (accessed from the Sound panel) lets you create panning effects using mono sounds.

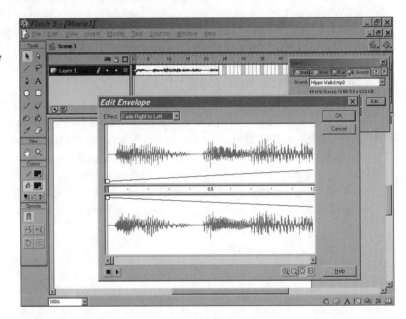

Another great way to reduce the impact of sounds on file size is to trim excessive silence from the beginning and ending of every sound. It's customary for audio engineers to pad every sound file with a little silence. However, sounds take up the same file space for every second they're played, regardless of whether they're audible. Ideally, sounds should be trimmed before they are imported, but you can trim them inside Flash through the Sound panel's Edit Envelope feature. You can review this technique in Hour 10, but for now remember that it means smaller file sizes. For example, by trimming excessive silence in the Beam Scan sample sound (found in Window, Common Libraries, Sounds), I cut the sound by 10 percent. That may not seem like a lot, but because sounds can be very large, 10 percent of a large file can be significant. What's more, because I just trimmed out the silence, I didn't lose anything.

Bitmaps

You can reduce the file size impact of bitmaps in several ways. First of all, consider not using bitmaps at all. Although this may seem like a flippant tip, it's worth thinking about. Of course, you should avoid any unnecessary raster graphics (`.jpg`, `.gif`, `.bmp`, and so on) because each pixel's color is saved in the file, unlike vector graphics, which store only the math necessary to redraw the shapes. However, there are certain types of images (such as photographs) that only work as bitmaps. Therefore, it's not simply a matter of choice.

One warning though: The Modify, Trace Bitmap feature explored in Hour 3 does convert a bitmap into all-vector shapes. However, you should use this feature only when the bitmap contains clear and bold sections. If you find it necessary to set the Trace Bitmap dialog box to draw lots of tiny vector shapes instead of large bold areas, as shown in Figure 20.5, you'll probably end up creating a vector version that's larger than the original bitmap. People tend to think that vector graphics are small and bitmaps are large, but taken to an extreme, vectors can be quite large, too. Therefore, use Trace Bitmap only when the content of your image file is better served as a vector—that is, it contains bold geometric shapes. (Of course if you're trying to achieve a particular special effect, Trace Bitmap can be used—just realize the potential file size impact.)

FIGURE 20.5

Using Trace Bitmap on a photograph would require such small values for Threshold and Minimum Area that the image would increase in size.

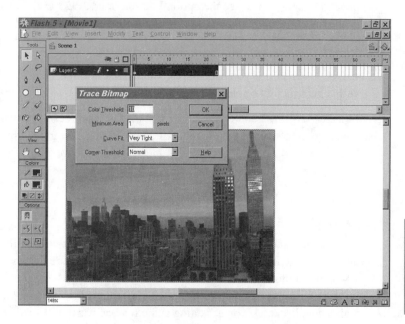

As a bit of a review, I think it's worth mentioning the difference between the bitmap export options.

Importing High-Quality Media and Then Compressing It

Although it may seem counterintuitive, it's best to start by importing the highest-quality sound and bitmapped graphics possible. This will certainly add to the file size of your source `.fla`. However, you can let Flash do the compression before publishing your movie. Either through the properties for individual sounds and bitmaps in the Library or through Publish Settings, you can control how much Flash compresses your media. For example, instead of converting an image into a compressed `.jpg` before importing it into Flash, try to start with the best-quality uncompressed `.bmp` or `.png` file. Once it's imported, you can specify how Flash is to compress it upon export. This way, you can always decide to compress more or less. If you start with something that's already compressed (and therefore lower quality), you can't make it any better inside Flash. High-quality sounds should start as `.wav` or `.aif` format (MP3s are already compressed). Raster graphics should be `.bmp`, `.png`, or `.pct` format. (Note that `.jpg` files are always compressed and `.gif` files can only have 256 colors.)

However, if you have a sound or image that's already compressed (such as an `.mp3` or `.jpg` file) and either you don't have access to a better-quality original or you're confident the current compression is ideal, there's no need to first covert it to another format. Just import it as it is, but make sure that Flash doesn't recompress it. For imported compressed images, you'll see the option Use Imported JPEG Data in the Library item's properties. This will prevent Flash from recompressing the file. The only time to recompress an image that's already compressed is when you have no access to the original. Compressing a compressed image will indeed bring the file size down, but the quality will be lower than if you had simply compressed it to the same level once by starting with a high-quality original.

In the case of MP3 audio, make sure that the file size doesn't increase when you choose a compression setting! For example, if after clicking Test in the Sound Properties dialog box you see `145% of original`, that means you made the file bigger. Attempting to recompress the file this way will only increase the file size (and it still won't improve the quality).

Using the Bandwidth Profiler

So now that you understand how to manage file size by compressing audio and bitmaps and using certain drawing techniques, you need to measure the impact of each. Even if you know audio adds to file size, you still may want to use it. Your decision, however, needs to be based on how much file size the audio adds. If it means the user will simply wait a couple extra seconds, adding audio may be worth it. However, if adding a piece of music means the user waits 10 minutes, you probably shouldn't use the music. In order to decide whether a particular media element is worthwhile, you need to know how much it affects file size. The Bandwidth Profiler helps you assess exactly how much each media element adds to your file size. Basically, you try out a file size–reduction technique (such as compression) and then use the Bandwidth Profiler to judge how much the change helped. If you make another change, use the Bandwidth Profiler again to measure the improvement. The previous section taught you how to identify ways file sizes grow; this section will teach you how to measure the impact.

Turning on the Bandwidth Profiler is easy, but deciphering the data it provides is a bit tricky. The following task introduces you to the basic features of the Bandwidth Profiler.

Task: Use the Bandwidth Profiler to Judge Download Times

In this task you are introduced to how the Bandwidth Profiler can help you assess how a movie might play over the Internet. Here are the steps to follow:

1. Open the Keyframing sample file from Help, Samples. Do a Test Movie (Ctrl+Enter).

2. As the exported .swf plays, select Control, View Bandwidth Profiler (Ctrl+B). Notice that this is an option in the Flash Player, not the authoring tool. Therefore, you'll only see it while you're testing.

3. The Bandwidth Profiler provides information while your the movie plays, as shown in Figure 20.6. You see data on the left and a graph on the right.

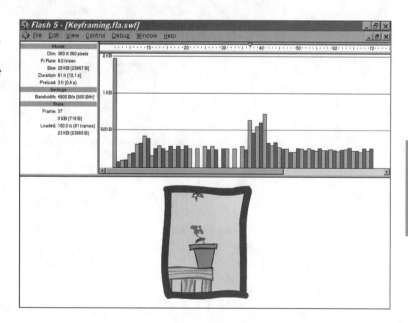

20

4. Now you'll look at the first section of data, called *Movie*. Most of this information is simply a recap of the settings you can change in your source movie (such as dimensions and frame rate). In addition, you'll see two settings whose numbers will vary: Size (or file size) and Preload. When I tested this movie, I got a file size of 23KB (or exactly 23,667 bytes). Later, when you attempt to optimize this file, you'll see whether the size is reduced. Preload displays how many frames must "preload" (and how long that takes) before the movie will start playing. Of course, this depends on your user's Internet connection. The Bandwidth Profiler can make estimates such as preload time based on the modem settings (found under the Debug menu).

5. Go ahead and select the Debug menu. Notice that one of the modem types has a check mark (56K, by default). Change this to 14.4 (for 14.4KBps modems), and you'll see the Preload setting change from less than 1 second to 11 seconds!

6. From the Debug menu, select Customize..., which opens the Custom Modem Settings dialog box, as shown in Figure 20.7. Here, you can modify the presets or create your own. Add an option for the common DSL bit rate of 256KBps. In the fourth field, change User Setting 4 to 256K (DSL) and the number in the bit rate column to 32000. Click OK.

FIGURE 20.7

The Custom Modem Settings dialog box lets you simulate any Internet connection speed.

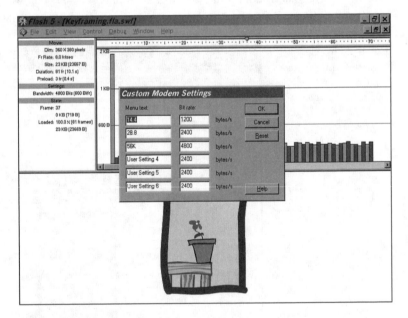

7. Select your new setting from the Debug menu. You should see the preload time reduce to nearly nothing.

8. The Bandwidth Profiler lets you simulate exactly how long a movie takes to download at the bit rate selected from Debug. Select View, Show Streaming. The movie will start over, and you'll see a green progress bar move across the top of the graph. Change the bit rate to 14.4 (from the Debug menu) and try Show Streaming again. Even with this relatively basic movie, the current frame marker in the graph (an arrow) catches up to the green progress bar and must occasionally wait for the content to download. This isn't desirable, but it's an accurate representation of how this movie will look on a slow connection. (You'll learn ways to address this in the next task, "Improve a File with the Bandwidth Profiler's Help," but for now you're just learning how to identify problems.)

9. There's one other feature you should investigate. Confirm the View menu has Frame by Frame Graph selected (or press Ctrl+F). The graph shows a vertical bar for the file size of each frame's contents. A tall bar means a frame has more data. The red horizontal line represents the sustained data transfer rate the current bit rate can maintain. In other words, if a frame's bar is higher than the red line, Flash may need to pause at that frame while it downloads. For example, in the Keyframing sample file, you'll notice a few relatively high bars starting at frame 36. This makes sense. Close the test movie and look at the source file. Right at frame 36, there's a series of keyframes containing new content in two layers. All this new data means more data to download (see Figure 20.8).

FIGURE 20.8

Frame 36 is the first frame where two layers of keyframes appear. This requires more data to download (as shown in the Bandwidth Profiler).

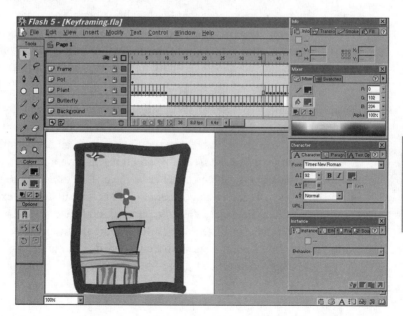

20

In the preceding task, you specified 32,000 bytes per second for a 256K modem. This was calculated based on modem speeds listed as "kilobits per second" (or 256,000 bits per second). Computer file sizes are often displayed in kilobytes or megabytes (not bits). Because one bit is one-eighth of the size of a byte, you can convert bits to bytes by dividing by 8. Therefore, 256,000 bits per second is the same as 32,000 bytes per second. A 64-kilobyte image will download in 2 seconds on a 256K modem (256Kbps / 8 = 32KBps; therefore, a 64KB file will download in 2 seconds at that rate). Another issue, however, is the fact an Internet connection may not download at a consistent rate. Note that the presets in the Debug menu for 28.8 modem and 56K modem are lower than what you'd expect (2400 and 4700 instead of 3600 and 7000). That's because the Flash presets are padded to more accurately represent an actual modem download speed. Generally, you don't have to do a lot of math. In this case, however, doing the math might be interesting.

Use the Bandwidth Profiler's Show Streaming option to watch how the movie will play. Analyze the movie frame by frame by scrubbing to view which frames are exceeding the red streaming limit. By the way, just because a vertical line is above the red line doesn't necessarily mean playback will pause at that frame. When possible, Flash will start to download frames before they are encountered. For example, several frames might not involve any onscreen changes, but Flash will maintain a constant speed of download. While displaying these frames, Flash can start to download frames from later in the movie. Frames that have no visual changes don't take long to download; therefore, Flash can concentrate on downloading future frames. This behavior is a form of streaming.

The Bandwidth Profiler has an option to show such streaming in a graph similar to the Frame by Frame graph. Select View, Streaming Graph, and you'll still see each frame's vertical box. Basically, each frame is shown as alternating light and dark gray boxes. The red horizontal line represents the maximum data that can be transmitted in the time one frame takes to play (that is, 1/12 of a second if you have a frame rate of 12fps). If the first frame (dark gray) can download in less than 1/12 of a second, you'll see frame 2's bar in dark gray stacked on top of frame 1's light gray bar. As an example, open the Keyframing file again, select View, Streaming Graph, and select Debug, 56K. In the time it takes to play frame 2, Flash can download more than four frames (see Figure 20.9). As a result, the entire 81-frame movie is downloaded in the time it takes 40 frames to display. (Select View, Show Streaming for a view of this effect in real time.)

FIGURE 20.9

The Streaming Graph view (not Frame by Frame Graph view) displays how quickly Flash will preload upcoming frames.

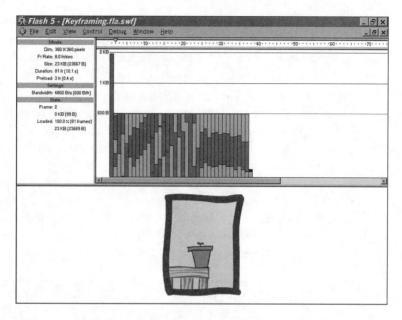

The Bandwidth Profiler is very useful. However, it doesn't fix problems; it only helps you discover problem areas. Ideally, you should simply avoid making your file too large in the first place. The Bandwidth Profiler is still worth learning, but just remember it's only for identifying problems that could have been avoided. The following task steps you through a scenario of using the Bandwidth Profiler to help identify a problem and solve it.

Task: Improve a File with the Bandwidth Profiler's Help

In this task you walk through a situation where the Bandwidth Profiler can help improve a file. Follow these steps:

1. Select Help, Samples, Keyframing. Immediately determine the total size of the exported movie. All you need to do is run Test Movie and look at the data at the top-left area of the Bandwidth Profiler (press Ctrl+B if it's not up). For example, I get 23,667 bytes for the total size. Write down whatever number you get as a reference for later.

2. Close the movie that's testing. Select File, Publish Settings... and then select the tab for Flash. Notice the slider for JPEG Quality. Move that all the way to the left (the lowest quality) and click OK.

20

3. Test the movie again to see the change made by using compression. You shouldn't see any change because JPEG compression is applied only to raster graphics, and this file has none. (If this file had raster graphics, you'd likely see that this change made the file smaller but lowered its quality.)

4. The change you'll make in this step will cause a difference—you're going to optimize the curves in every drawn shape. Unlock all the layers (by clicking the padlock icon above all the layers in the Timeline) and click the Edit Multiple Frames onion skin option (so that you can select multiple frames). Now select the Modify Onion Markers menu and pick Onion All, as shown in Figure 20.10. Finally, do a Select All (Ctrl+A). With everything now selected, choose Modify, Optimize..., slide the Smoothing scale all the way to the right, and select both option check boxes, as shown in Figure 20.11. Click OK, and you should eventually see a message concerning how much optimizing took place. In my case, I saw that there was a 57% reduction (in the number of curves) .

FIGURE 20.10

To select every frame, choose Onion All after the Edit Multiple Frame option is set.

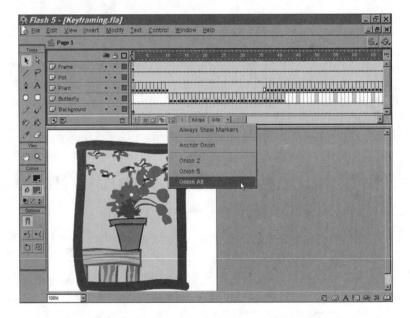

FIGURE 20.11

Using Optimize Curves will reduce the file size by simplifying the shapes.

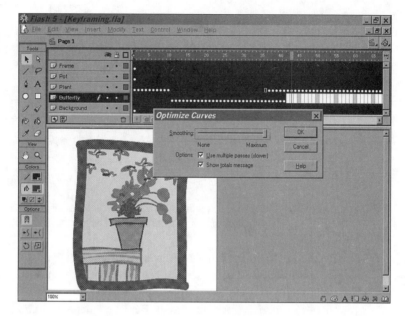

5. Do a Test Movie again and notice the improvement in the file size. I get 22,523 bytes, which is almost 1,000 bytes smaller. Not really a whole lot, but it's something. What's more, the image looks no worse.

Although the big lesson from this task may be that Modify, Optimize can often reduce the file size (simplifying shapes), you're still just in the stage of finding problems. For now, just realize the Bandwidth Profiler helps find the problems, not necessarily fix them. A related feature worth knowing can be found by selecting File, Publish Settings, selecting the tab for Flash, and clicking the option Generate Size Report, as shown in Figure 20.12. The next time you export the movie (just do a Test Movie), you'll see an all-text version of the Bandwidth Profiler appear in the output window. In addition, you'll find a text file (named similarly to your movie's name and in the same folder) with the same contents. This just provides a permanent record of the data you find in the Bandwidth Profiler.

20

FIGURE 20.12

The Publish Settings option Generate Size Report will export a text version of data gathered from the Bandwidth Profiler.

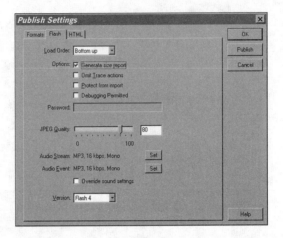

Finally, the Keyframing example still pauses around frame 36 when simulating a 14.4 modem. If this is your target user and you can't find any other way to reduce the file size, you'll have to resort using a preloader, which will load all or part of the movie to your user's hard drive before playing it. Here's a quick way to do just that.

Task: See a Preloader in the Bandwidth Profiler

To get a sense of how the Bandwidth Profiler works, in this task you'll create a basic preloader to pause playback on the first frame until most of the movie is downloaded. Here are the steps:

1. Open the Keyframing sample file (Help, Samples, Keyframing).

2. Because you're going to use a Flash 5–specific feature, select File, Publish Settings... and click the Flash tab. Then select Flash 5 from the version drop-down list. (We'll discuss this feature more in Hour 24.)

3. Select Insert, Scene. Open the Scene panel and rename the new scene Preloader. To rename it, just double-click the current name (Scene 2) and then drag the scene order so that Preloader is on top.

4. Click the first frame of the Preloader scene's Timeline and insert two keyframes (press F6 twice).

5. Select the first keyframe, open the Actions panel, and insert the If Action. Then type **_framesloaded>50** in the Condition parameter. Finally, insert a Go To Action and type **3** in the Frame field. Translated, this means if more than 50 frames have loaded, the user will jump to frame 3.

6. So that the user can see it preloading, place some text on screen. Use the Text Options panel to set the text block as Dynamic Text and type **_framesloaded** into the Variable field. This way the user will see the value of this variable change while the movie downloads.

7. Select frame 2 and insert the script Go To Frame 1 (and select Play).

8. Run Test Movie, and with the Bandwidth Profiler, select View, Show Streaming.

FIGURE 20.13

While the first 50 frames download, the movie is paused on a frame displaying how many frames have downloaded.

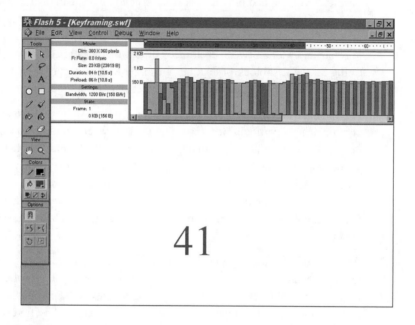

The preloader you built in Hour 18, "Designing Your Website to Be Modular," was more sophisticated. However, this was a good opportunity to use the Bandwidth Profiler. Finally, notice we didn't make our preloader wait for the entire movie to download. By simply waiting for most of the file to download, Flash will likely catch up and download the final frames in time to display them. There's no sense in making the user wait for everything to download.

20

Performance Hits

So far, this hour has covered optimization as it applies to making files smaller (so they download quickly). The other side of optimization involves making your movie play quickly. In other words, ensuring that its performance is consistent and smooth on all users' computers. If you set your frame rate to, say, 12fps, it will never exceed that number. However, on some computers, it may slow to a lower rate. Unfortunately, there isn't a "Performance Profiler" (similar to the Bandwidth Profiler) where you can simulate performance on other machines. There are far too many variables that can affect playback speed. For the rest of this hour, you'll look at ways you can avoid common "performance hits" to ensure the best performance on everyone's machine.

Gratuitous Special Effects

Last hour you learned how unnecessary special effects can distract users from your core message. However, there's another reason to avoid gratuitous special effects: Having too many effects can cause the movie to play slowly. For example, it might not be necessary to rotate and Motion tween each piece of text that appears onscreen. Maybe this is interesting for the first block of text, but it can get tiring to wait for each to do its animation. Plus, if a user's computer slows down for each tween, it's even more disruptive.

Although a Motion tween involving a change in the Alpha effect may be necessary to communicate a particular message, this kind of tween should be used with caution. Not only does the computer need to display the object that's moving, but it needs to display a semitransparent version of the object, which means it must display the graphics underneath the object. Simply put, this means slower machines might not be able to keep up with the desired frame rate. Often, an Alpha effect isn't even needed. For example, if your background is white, a simple Brightness effect will look the same and perform slightly better.

Another significant performance hit that can often be avoided involves tweens that scale, move, or change the Alpha setting of a bitmap. Generally, Flash does not excel in the display of bitmaps. Changing the size of a bitmap makes the computer do a lot of work. Even if you have a fast machine, you can see this behavior by first setting the frame rate to a high value (such as 60fps) and then performing a simple Motion tween on a bitmap. Select Control, Play (not Test Movie) to watch your movie play inside Flash. Then change the scale of the bitmap on either the keyframe of the tween and play it again. You should see the actual frame rate drop during the tween involving scale.

Other special effects can slow performance down, too. The best way to preview such performance hits is by temporarily setting the frame rate very high and then testing different approaches to see how they cause the movie to slow. Keep in mind the suggestion earlier in this section and simply avoid *unnecessary* special effects. If you really need to use an effect, go ahead. Just be careful with those that really cause the movie to slow down, because they might cause your users' computers to slow down even further.

Streaming Sounds

When you place sounds in keyframes, you have a choice between Sync: Event and Sync: Stream. Generally, you should always use Event (or one of the other event-like choices: Start or Stop). These will have the least impact on performance. Stream is useful when you need synchronization maintained. When you use Stream sounds, you can hear the sounds play as you scrub the Timeline. Stream sounds are comparable to Graphic symbols, which also preview their animation when you scrub. The disadvantage to Stream sounds however, is the visual parts of your movie will be sacrificed when a computer can't keep up. That is, Stream sounds are always synchronized, and if the computer can't display the graphics in time, Flash will drop visual frames (to keep up). Therefore, Stream sounds can make the graphics appear to skip and jump. This is simply due to the fact that Flash will never cause the sound to play slowly (it would sound funny if it did).

Event sounds will play as soon as they can. If the computer can keep up, these sounds will play as expected (that is, when the appropriate keyframes are reached). Also, graphics display as soon as they can. However, on slow machines, the graphics may take longer to display, so the sound may not stay in perfect synchronization. That's not to say you can't achieve a decent result with Event sounds. Consider cutting the sound files into shorter bits before importing them. You can place sounds in the Timeline so that they line up closely with graphics. It still won't be perfect, but at least no frames will be dropped. If you don't need critical synchronization, use Event sounds because both the graphics and the sounds will play smoothly—they just might not be perfectly synchronized.

Graphic Issues

Here are a few tips to assure the best performance possible.

Graphic Symbols

Despite all the discussion of the file size–saving attributes of Movie Clips (in Hour 12), nested Graphic symbols tend to perform better. Usually, however, the significant file size increase does not justify the minor performance improvement. You should use Graphic symbols only when you need to scrub (use Movie Clips, otherwise). However, the fact that Graphic symbols can perform slightly better makes them worth considering when you're trying to optimize performance.

Use Optimize Curves

You saw how any drawn shape can be optimized (from the Modify, Optimize menu). Optimize Curves will remove curves from a shape, making it look more streamlined. Sometimes the visual impact is subtle, but the file size reduction is significant.

20

Other times, the visual change is too great to be acceptable, as is the case in Figure 20.14. Consider optimizing any time the visual change is acceptable. In addition to making the file smaller, it often speeds playback performance (yet another reason to use it).

FIGURE 20.14
Two shapes are shown before and after Optimize Curves is applied. Sometimes the results may be unacceptable.

Never Use Modify, Shape, Soften Fill Edges

Never is a strong word, but it applies in this case. It doesn't take more than a few minutes to calculate both the file size difference and the performance difference for a shape drawn and then softened. Try a test where you create a simple Shape tween. Test the movie and note the file size in the Bandwidth Profiler. Play the movie inside Flash and note the actual frame rate. Then individually select the shape at each end of the tween and use Modify, Shape, Soften Fill Edges. You'll see the file size jump and the performance drop. I suppose the one situation when you might consider using this feature is when you're only exporting a static image (that is, if you're using Flash as a drawing tool).

Avoid Line Styles

You saw back in Hour 2, "Drawing and Painting Original Art in Flash," the Stroke panel's drop-down list for stroke style (see Figure 20.15). Try to use only the Solid and Hairline styles. The others tend to make your movies much larger. I can't say that you'll always see the performance drop, but you'll certainly see your file size increase.

FIGURE 20.15

You should try to use only the Hairline and Solid stroke styles.

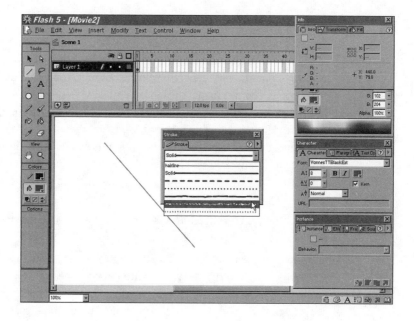

Summary

This hour, you studied two ways to optimize your Flash movies. You should optimize file size to make your movies download faster, and you should optimize performance so that they play more consistently. The Bandwidth Profiler and the Generate Size Report option allow you to analyze your movies in several ways. You can simulate download speeds and identify areas in your movies that need extra attention.

The optimization process was also applied to performance. Even though your movies might consistently play at high frame rates, such as 30fps, on your machine, they may slow down on your users' machines. Although there's no sure way to see how your movies will look (except actually try them on other machines), the basic approach to performance optimization is to simply know what types of effects and techniques tend to slow computers down and try to avoid them.

20

Q&A

Q I've followed all the performance optimization tips and still find my animation appears jumpy. What's wrong?

A It's possible that you're simply trying to move a graphic across a large distance in very few frames. Try extending the total number of frames being used. You can compensate by increasing the frame rate. Provided the computer can keep up with this increased frame rate, you'll see the same motion but in more (smaller, incremented) steps.

Q What's the ideal size for a movie?

A This is a common question but one that's impossible to answer. I think the best answer is "no bigger than it has to be." Consider, too, that you can cover up a long download time in very creative ways. Of course, you could use a "Loading…" message, as you did in one of this hour's tasks. Better than that, you can occupy your users with some small, interactive (or very small file size) content. Make them watch something interesting (but small) while they wait for the bulk of the movie to download. There are many ways to do this successfully. Finally, consider the modular technique of Load Movie (discussed in Hour 18, "Designing Your Website to Be Modular"). That way, users have to wait to download only the portions of your site they request.

Q I used Modify, Optimize, and it sure cut the file size down, but my image doesn't look very good. What should I do?

A Obviously, if the result of Modify, Optimize is unsatisfactory, don't use it. Basically, you should just try this option every time and weigh the file size savings against the sacrifice in the image's quality. Often, an undesirable result isn't as bad as it appears. Consider that in the final movie, the graphic you're judging may only be onscreen for a fraction of a second. The bad quality might not matter in this case.

Workshop

The Workshop consists of quiz questions and answers to help you solidify your understanding of the material covered. Try to answer the questions before checking the answers.

Quiz

1. If you reduce a file to half its file size, how fast will it download?

   A. This is impossible to calculate because everyone's connection speed varies.

   B. Twice as fast as it would otherwise.

   C. This is impossible to calculate because you need to know the movie's dimensions (height and width).

2. Why should gratuitous special effects be avoided?

   A. They can distract the user from your core message.

   B. They can slow down performance and increase download times.

   C. All the above.

3. The Bandwidth Profiler can simulate how a movie will play on a slow computer.

A. True, just set your computer speed in the Debug menu.

B. False, the Bandwidth Profiler only helps you judge a movie's size and how fast it will download.

C. True, but you have to select Simulate Computer from the View menu.

Quiz Answers

1. B. Answer C is just plain false, because Flash movies download just as quickly regardless of their dimensions (vectors scale). Answer A is not entirely false because you really can't say how long a file will take to download. However, if you cut the file size in half, you can certainly say it will go twice as fast. Consider if you ordered a half-sandwich—it would take you half as long to finish it.

2. C. Although special effects are fine when necessary, they can be distracting, increase file size, and slow down performance. These are all good reasons to avoid using them.

3. B. The Bandwidth Profiler simply judges file size and download performance. If the question had referred to a *slow connection* rather than a *slow computer*, answer A would be correct.

20

HOUR **21**

Advanced Animation Techniques

We've studied all the built-in animation tools in Flash. Keyframes, Motion and Shape Tweens, Onion Skinning, masking, and guides—these should all be pretty familiar. What else is there to learn? How to make really effective animations! This hour we'll study some advanced animation techniques that will make your animations more effective, appear more believable, and maybe even take less work to create (though that's not the highest priority). A lot of the material this hour is just an application of traditional animation techniques developed over the years by conventional animators. Nothing we study this hour is new; it's just going to be applied to Flash.

Specifically, this hour you will

- Create animations without tweening
- Learn how to apply traditional animation techniques like anticipation and overkill
- Simulate depth and perspective

There are two different paths Flash users tend to follow: programming or animation. Some people describe the programmers as "technical" and the animators as "artistic." This is a mistake, because programming can be very creative, and visual communication can be very technical. The tendency to specialize isn't necessarily because of a natural aversion to one direction or an inclination in another. It may seem that we're taking a break from technical issues, because in recent hours we've been studying issues like file size and scripting, but this hour will be just as technical—just applied to making animations.

It's the Result, Not the Technology

When you see a magician saw his assistant in half, no one actually gets hurt. He creates an illusion, and you can almost believe the result. Similarly, in animation nothing actually moves. Watching a series of still images can make you believe you're watching something move. In addition to the persistence of vision effect described in Hour 6, "Understanding Animation," animators can use tricks (not unlike a magician) to fool the user into believing he sees something that never happened.

To make someone believe a ball is moving across the screen, for example, it may not be necessary to really move it across the screen. That is, a Motion Tween might display the ball each step along the way—and if the user could slow down the movie, he'd see it actually move. However, if the user *thinks* the ball moved across the screen, it doesn't matter whether it really did. Even if you're trying to communicate a principle of physics, it's not necessary to be completely accurate in your display. It's okay to lie. There's little value in being perfectly accurate if the result doesn't look like you intended.

We're about to look at a few tricks that can be used to enhance your animations. Remember, though, that the techniques are not as important as the result.

Simple Techniques to Use Sparingly

A trick often used in television commercials (especially those played late at night) is to make the screen blink. Sometimes several flashes of white light cause viewers to look at the TV—even if they were not paying attention. This technique is arguably appropriate for TV because people don't tend to give their full attention.

In the case of a Web site, you can rely on the fact that the user is more involved. He is sitting up, maybe even leaning toward the screen—a totally different profile. If you flash the screen, you should do so only sparingly, if at all.

If you want to grab the user's attention, you can use a modified version of flashing the screen—just make a small button or area of the screen blink. For example, if something's about to move, make it blink first. This will draw the user's attention to the blinking object, and then he'll likely be watching when it moves. Technically, this is simply a matter of alternating between filled and blank keyframes (as we learned in Hour 7, "Animation the Old-Fashioned Way").

There are other simple (and potentially annoying) techniques to consider. In the first frame of your movie, instead of starting with the entire interface, animate each element into its final location. If you have an interface with six buttons, you could have each appear, one by one, and move into position. This way you control the order in which the user reads your interface. Be aware, however, that building in such a way can become tedious and bothersome if it's slow or if the user must sit through the same sequence many times. If the home screen builds again every time he returns to it, that's probably too much.

Consider also, that techniques such as blinking and building are ways to resolve potential problems. Sometimes these are good solutions, but the best way would be to simply avoid the problem in the first place. For example, when you find people aren't watching the right part of the screen, don't jump to the blinking solution. Try to first identify if the problem can be resolved—maybe the rest of the screen is too crowded and that's distracting the user. Cleaning up the interface might resolve the issue.

You'll probably discover other tricks to solve problems, but use them sparingly. We'll see some more dependable techniques later this hour, but always ask yourself if the problem you're trying to resolve can be avoided in the first place.

Ways to Fool the User

Unlike magic, where the key to success is often found in the art of distraction, animation doesn't need to overcome any physical limits. The challenges in animation include how to show or imply motion where there isn't any, make things look natural, and exploit the user's expectations (either to help you show something that's not there or to create surprises). Pulling a rabbit out of a hat would be easy in Flash, but making the rabbit look like it's alive is a real challenge. Let's look at a few ways to address these three goals (implying motion, appearing natural, and exploiting expectations). Later this hour we'll apply what we learn.

There are several ways to imply motion. While your eyes never actually see blurred motion, it's quite common in photographs. We can use the fact that people believe a blur to be a symptom of motion to our advantage. For example, you could draw simple lines in the opposite direction of the motion (kind of like exhaust from an airplane). Or, in the frames of an animation where an symbol is supposed to look like it's moving, you can add another instance of the same symbol with an Alpha effect. There are other ways to

21

create a blur. Of course you could create the blur by using the Flash feature Modify, Shape, Soften Fill Edges, but this adds tremendously to your file size. Keep in mind that the blurred version of a moving image should only be shown while it's in motion. It doesn't have to be perfect, because it's only onscreen for a short time.

Making things look natural is possibly the biggest challenge in animation. To animate someone walking is not easy. That's because viewers know how that's supposed to look—if it doesn't look right, they know. There's no button in Flash that will create natural motion. However, you can learn to animate in a way that looks natural. When you are going to animate something from the real world, study the object you're animating. Carefully watch people walking and ask yourself how you know they're walking. Don't watch just the legs and feet, but look at the arms, hands, and head. Try to identify peculiar and subtle movements.

There is one good trick to make animations look natural: Insert elements that would be considered mistakes in traditional media. For example, people sometimes simulate dust and scratches to make an animation look like a conventional film. To make something flicker like an old-fashioned movie, just make a two-frame Movie Clip with a large gray box clip (with an Alpha effect of, say 10%) in the first frame and a blank keyframe in the second frame. It will loop continuously to create a flicker effect. You don't even need this to cover the entire animation; people see flickering, and they think "old movie." Just study what is peculiar in real life and bring attention to these details—this will make your animation more believable.

Finally, you can use the user's expectations in two ways. You can take advantage of their expectations—that is, let them think they saw something because they expected to see it, not necessarily because they did see it. For example, if they see a bowling ball move toward some pins, then they hear the sound of a crash, even if the pins are knocked out of the picture, they'll imagine the pins fell over. You don't have to animate each pin meticulously. Just remove them. The sound and the expectation are enough to make it believable.

You can also use their expectations to add more impact by showing the opposite of what they expect. In the case of the bowling ball, imagine a long and drawn-out tween of the ball moving toward the pins. Then, at the last minute, an elf character appears and stops the ball with a screeching sound. Certainly not what you expect.

These techniques require some imagination on your part. We'll practice in the next section. Just don't be afraid to "lie" to the user. They'll thank you later if you make something more believable.

Conventional Techniques Applied

The information in this section isn't unique to Flash. It's years of traditional, conventional animator's techniques that we will apply to Flash. For each technique, we'll do an exercise.

Anticipation

The blinking technique mentioned earlier this hour is a form of anticipation, drawing the user's attention to something that's about to happen. We can use other forms of anticipation as well. For example, a car with a manual transmission that is stopped facing up a hill drifts back a little bit when it begins to move forward. We can accentuate that effect in our animations, and it will make them more effective. Not only will the user look at the object that's preparing to move (by moving in the opposite direction), but they'll anticipate something's about to happen. Let's try it out in a task.

Task: Use Anticipation to Improve an Animation

In this Task we add a subtle touch of anticipation for a more effective result.

1. In a new file, draw a circle at the bottom of the stage and covert it to a symbol (F8). Name it Circle and leave it in the default Movie Clip.

2. Insert a keyframe at frame 10 (we want the circle to sit still for the first 10 frames). Insert another keyframe in frame 15 and one at frame 25. We're going to squish the circle between frames 10 and 15 and then move it up as it goes to frame 25.

3. In frame 25, hold down the Shift key and then move the instance of Circle close to the top of the stage.

4. In frame 15, use the Scale tool to compress the circle vertically. You'll also want to make the circle a little wider, because when you squish something it has to get wider, too. See Figure 21.1.

21

FIGURE 21.1

When squashing the circle, change both the vertical and horizontal scales (Onion Skin is turned on for easy comparison to the original shape).

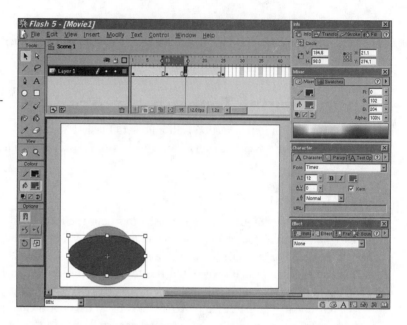

5. We also want the bottom of the circle to remain stationary (only the top squishes down). When you select the Scale tool, it scales it around the center. That's okay, but we should now move the circle down. Turn on Onion Skinning, and you'll be able to position the bottom of the circle to coincide with the bottom of the circle in frame 10. See Figure 21.2.

FIGURE 21.2

After squashing the circle, you want to make sure the base doesn't change location—it's only getting ready to move. It shouldn't move yet.

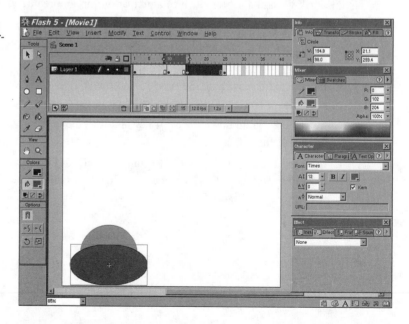

6. Now set a Motion Tween for the keyframe in frame 10 (so it tweens down to its squashed shape) and in frame 15 (so it tweens on its way up to the top).

7. Test the movie. It looks all right, but there's one thing we can add to make it more believable. While the Circle tweens to the top position, it also restores its shape—but it takes 10 frames to do it. Let's make it snap into its normal shape as soon as it starts to move.

8. Go to frame 16 and insert a keyframe (F6). It's good that we set tweening for frame 15 already, because the keyframe we inserted at frame 16 placed the circle in the proper interpolated position. Select the circle in frame 16 and select Modify, Transform, Remove Transform. The circle immediately returns to its unscaled state.

9. Test the movie to see the final result. Save this movie, because in a minute we'll address how to make the endpoint more believable.

The anticipation technique can be used quite extensively and usually means you can get away with using fewer frames (and fewer tweens). You make the user anticipate the movement by including movement in the opposite direction. The exercise we just did involved squishing the circle down because it was about to go up. If you're moving something to the right, adding a slight move to the left can work, too. The anticipation is usually slower than the movement that follows. That is, during the anticipation portion, fewer frames are used or less distance is covered. There are no hard and fast rules for this—you must judge how something looks when you test the movie.

Overkill

While anticipation happens before the animation plays, overkill applies to the end of an animation or after it plays. If you're in a car that comes to a stop, you feel as though you move backward just for a moment after the car comes to a rest. Of course you're not moving backward, but you expect to have this feeling. You can add this effect to your animations, and it will actually make them more believable. Let's try it on the exercise we just completed.

Task: Use Overkill to Make an Animation More Effective

In this Task, we'll add the subtle effect of overkill and make the animation more believable.

1. Ideally you can start with the last exercise. If not, make a simple Motion Tween of an instance called Circle, moving from the bottom of the screen to the top of the screen, ending in frame 25.

21

2. Insert keyframes in frames 26, 27, 28, and 29. (Click in frame 26, and then press F6 three times.)

3. The extra frames will include one frame where the circle goes too far and becomes stretched, one frame where the circle reverberates and actually moves lower than the end frame, and one where the circle ends up in its final resting position (where it happens to be already, so that frame won't need to be adjusted).

4. Vertically stretch the circle in frame 26 so it's extra tall and narrow (as in Figure 21.3). You don't need to make sure the bottom or top line ups with circles in adjacent frames; however, turn on Onion Skin so that you can be sure the stretched circle in frame 26 is positioned a little higher than the one in frame 25.

FIGURE 21.3

To make the circle overshoot its destination, we can stretch it to exaggerate the overkill.

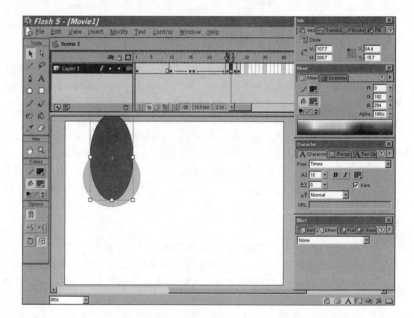

5. In frame 27, simply move the circle down a few pixels.

6. Test the movie. It's pretty amazing that just a touch of overkill can make this animation so much more believable.

It truly is a matter of fooling the user! To prove this, just try an animation with no tweening. Frame 1 has a circle at the bottom of the stage. Frame 10 has a keyframe where the circle is squashed. In frame 11, a normal circle is moved halfway up the stage. By frame 12, it's stretched and past its destination. It's normal (or a little squashed) and a little lower in frame 13. Finally, at frame 14, it's in its normal shape in the destination frame—no tweening, and it looks great. Figure 21.4 shows all the frames with Onion Skinning turned on.

FIGURE 21.4

Just a few keyframes can make an effective animation when you use anticipation and overkill.

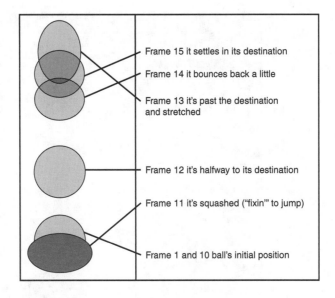

Frame 15 it settles in its destination

Frame 14 it bounces back a little

Frame 13 it's past the destination and stretched

Frame 12 it's halfway to its destination

Frame 11 it's squashed ("fixin'" to jump)

Frame 1 and 10 ball's initial position

Simulating Depth

Despite the fact that Flash is only a two-dimensional program, you can still make the user think your movies have depth. There are many ways to fake it, and we'll just look at a few.

The main way to show depth is with perspective. Simply put, objects appear smaller when they are more distant. When I was a child, I would get scared when I watched an airplane (in which my father was traveling) take off. As it got smaller and smaller in the sky, I thought my father was disappearing.

We'll look at several subtleties related to perspective, but they're all based on the fact that when you see something get smaller, you think it's moving away. Let's try to tween an object and change its size. At first it will look plain, but we'll add to it.

Task: Add Perspective to a Simple Animation

In this Task we add just two lines to make the perspective more apparent.

1. Start by drawing a car and converting it to a Movie Clip symbol. In keyframe 1, place it in the bottom left of the stage. Add a keyframe in frame 40, and move the car to the top right of the stage. Do a simple Motion Tween between the keyframes.

2. Scale the car larger in frame 1 and smaller in frame 40.

3. Test the movie. It probably doesn't look convincing. Now insert a layer and draw two converging lines as if they were the shoulders of a road. The animation looks infinitely better (see Figure 21.5).

21

FIGURE 21.5

The addition of lines can help the user see depth.

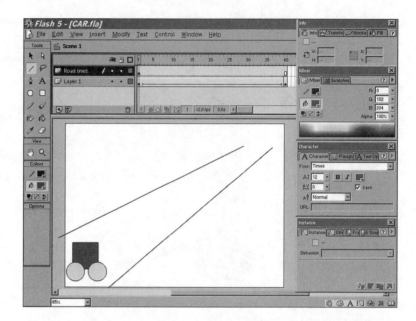

4. To add even more evidence that the car is covering great distances, we can add some mountains or bluffs in the road layer. Draw a horizon line toward the top of the screen and draw a boxy mountain/bluff on the horizon (see Figure 21.6).

FIGURE 21.6

Adding a horizon line and mountain (for scale) makes the depth perception even greater.

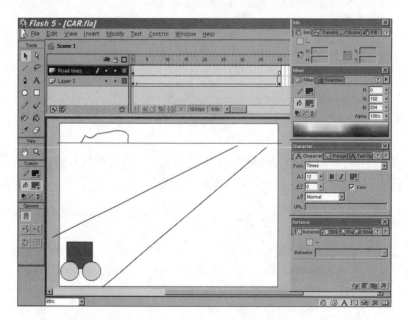

5. Without a reference, the mountain (besides not looking much like a mountain) doesn't have any perspective. Draw another mountain closer (below the horizon) and make it a little bigger. Make an even bigger mountain, partially blocking the road, on the right side. If you fill the close mountain with white (so it blocks the road and the car), the result is even more believable (see Figure 21.7).

FIGURE 21.7

The repeating shape and changing size of the mountains enhance the perspective effect.

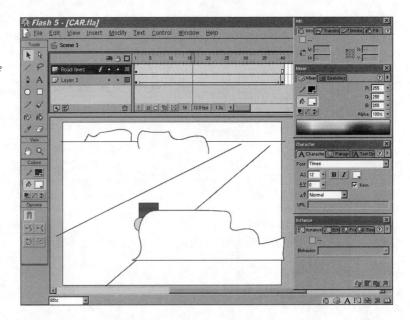

Just imagine how much more believable the previous exercise would be with realistic-looking graphics. We use some simple clues to tell the user there is depth. The road shoulders and horizon are there mainly to explain the surface on which the car is traveling. We add mountains that vary in size according to how far away they are supposed to be. The varying sized mountains actually repeat the converging sense of the lines. Finally, blocking the car with a big mountain leaves little question in the user's brain that the car is going behind the mountain.

We can add even more clues that the car is moving away. Not only do objects get smaller as they move away, but they make smaller and slower movements. If you set Easing to Out, the car would appear to move slower the further away it goes (and that's how a car moving away appears). If you added some bumps in the road (which would have the added benefit of looking more natural), you could make the bumps smaller as the car got farther away. One way to add bumps would be to create a motion guide that gets less jagged toward the end of the car's path. These tricks are just repeating the message that things far away are smaller.

Let's do another exercise that simulates depth. This time we'll travel with a car.

21

Task: Simulate Depth with Size, Layering, and Relative Speed

In this Task we'll travel with a car and create the illusion of depth in several ways.

1. Draw a vertical rectangle to simulate a log. Convert it into a symbol called One Log, copy it, and paste about 15 copies. Space them evenly so they are twice as wide as the stage (zoom out and use the Align panel). Select them all and convert them into a Movie Clip called Logs. See Figure 21.8.

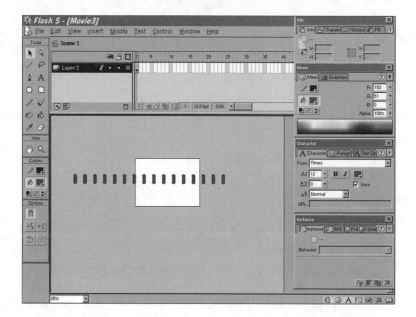

2. Position Logs so that the leftmost log is just touching the left side of the stage. Scale it slightly larger. Copy this instance and paste it into a new layer. Position the copy similarly on the left side of the stage, but scale this version smaller and make sure it's positioned higher (as in Figure 21.9). These will be the posts for the guardrails.

FIGURE 21.9

The two layers for the logs contain the big (close) logs and the smaller (distant) ones.

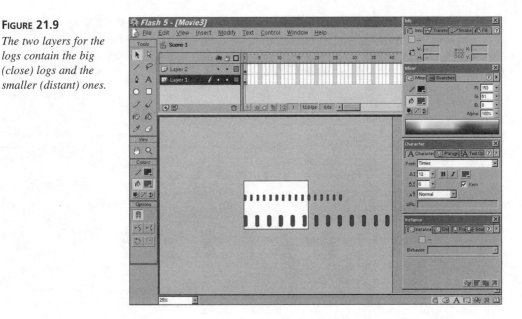

3. In a new layer, draw a very wide rectangle (as the guardrail). Convert it to a symbol called Guardrail and copy it into a new layer. Scale the instance in the second layer appropriately to the smaller logs. Position the two instances of Guardrail in the proper layers, so the smaller one is on top of the small logs and the larger is below the large logs (so that the guardrails are on the inside of the road). (Take a peek at Figure 21.10 to see how it should look.)

4. Insert frames for all the layers at frame 60 (click in frame 60 and press F5). In the two layers with Logs, insert a keyframe at frame 60 (click in frame 60 and press F6). In frame 60 of the layer with the large logs, hold Shift while you move the logs all the way to the left (so that the rightmost log is just touching the right side of the stage). For the layer with the small logs, hold Shift while you move it to the left—but not as far (maybe the middle log will touch the right side of the stage). See Figure 21.10.

5. Set Motion Tween in frame 1 of both Logs layers. You won't need to tween the Guardrail layers, because the motion of the logs will imply that the guardrail is moving.

21

FIGURE 21.10

Don't move the smaller logs quite as far as the larger logs.

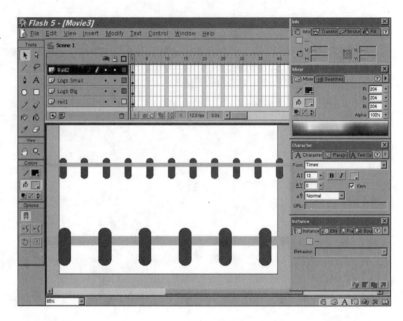

6. Insert another layer for a car. You can draw a car and make it a Movie Clip. You can even go inside the master version of the car and insert rotating wheel clips. But whatever you do, don't tween the car that's in the main Timeline. It will appear in the same position, but the logs passing by at varying speeds will make it appear to be moving constantly to the right.

7. Test the movie. The logs that are close to the screen will appear to move faster because they are closer to the viewer.

8. To add to this Task, you can draw a mountain or other elements near the horizon. If you add trees in the background, you can have them tween to the left as well—but at a much slower rate. You probably don't need to tween the mountain at all, but if you do, only let it move a tiny bit.

Controlling Point of View

The two exercises we just did with cars involved different points of view. In the first, the view didn't change; we just saw the car move. In the second exercise, our view moved with the car, and the foreground and background moved. The first situation was as if a camera was stationary on a tripod as the car moved away. The second case was as if the camera was in a helicopter that was traveling at the same speed as the car. When you watch a movie or animation, you don't often ask exactly where the camera was positioned—but it's very important.

If the camera is shaking, it gives an entirely different feeling than if it's panning slowly. When you watch a movie, try to note exactly where the director has placed the camera.

Of course, in computer animation we're not limited in physical ways. You can use any camera trick you want.

Let's try a simple exercise where the point of view affects the user's experience.

Task: Control Point of View for Visual Effect

In this Task we change the point of view during an animation to imply motion.

1. In a new file, select Window, Common Libraries, Movie Clips. Drag the Biplane symbol onto stage.

2. Insert keyframes (F6) at frames 50 and 60. In frame 60, hold Shift while you drag the instance of Biplane to the right until it's off the screen. Set Motion Tween in the keyframe at frame 50.

3. Test the movie, and you can imagine you're filming this from another airplane that is keeping up with the biplane. At frame 50, your plane stops. It needs something more, though.

4. Insert a new layer (name it Background), and zoom out to 25%. In the new layer, draw a jagged line with the pencil much wider than the stage, as in Figure 21.11. Select the line and covert it to a symbol—call it Mountains. In frame 1 of the Background layer, position Mountains so the left side just touches the left side of the stage.

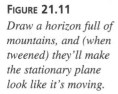

FIGURE 21.11

Draw a horizon full of mountains, and (when tweened) they'll make the stationary plane look like it's moving.

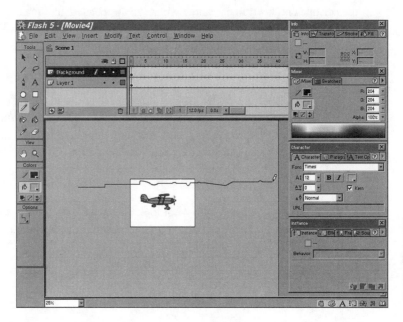

21

5. Insert a keyframe in frame 50 of Background. Move the instance of Mountains in frame 50 all the way to the left so its right side just touches the right side of the stage. In frame 1 of Background, set Motion Tween.

6. Test the movie.

Point of view really drives most animation. When you have a clear sense of where the user's point of view is (that is, where the camera is), the potential is great. You can use camera angle and camera shake—all kinds of tricks that actually become visual elements. Most visual elements are concrete and obvious. Point of view may be the most powerful because it's so subtle.

Watch a few movies and pay attention to the location of the camera. It might ruin the illusion you normally get, but it can be educational. For some really great examples of changing point of view, check out the Flash movies at http://www.bulbo.com.

Begin with the End in Mind

A common approach most animators take is to begin an animation or a tween at the end-point. For example, if you're making a title zoom onto stage, create the end keyframe first, where the title is scaled and positioned in its ending point. Then go back and set up the initial keyframe. It's not so much a technique as an approach.

In this hour's exercises involving anticipation and overkill, we inserted several keyframes (where the circle was not transformed) and then went back to make changes after we had the pristine end keyframes. Know where you're headed, and make plans before you arrive. This may seem ambiguous, but it's so common that it's worth mentioning as an advanced animation technique.

Summary

This hour we saw how just a few touches can make an ordinary animation look rich and believable. Simply giving users a hint that something is about to happen (through anticipation) is enough to make sure they see your animation. Overkill adds a bit of reverberation at the end of an animation to make it more believable. We also studied several ways to create depth and motion.

While some of the examples may not look advanced, with a bit of work they can became realistic. Of course, an artist can add a few finishing touches to make these exercises look great.

Q&A

Q **I want to create an effect in which the entire stage effectively zooms really big and then I can transition into another scene. How do I zoom the stage for the user?**

A Using the Zoom tool to zoom the stage will only affect your workspace. What you need to do is scale everything onstage using a tween. This can be difficult, because you might have several layers. You can solve this a few ways. If you created everything inside one large Movie Clip, you can just scale an instance of that clip in the main scene. If you've already built everything in the main Timeline, you can effectively take a snapshot of the last frame and then place that inside a clip that gets scaled. To do this, go to the last frame and copy everything onstage from all layers at once. Insert a blank keyframe in a new layer, then paste in place. To make sure the clip we're about to make doesn't include any nested looping movie clips, while everything is still selected, use the Instance panel to set everything to Graphic symbol set to Single Frame, 1. While everything is still selected, covert to symbol (and make this a Movie Clip). Then it's just a matter of inserting more frames for the tween where you scale this new clip.

Q **Are there any good resources for more animation techniques in Flash?**

A By now, you have most of the technical skills to execute anything in Flash. Studying other Flash books (of which there are several fine ones) probably won't help you as much as studying traditional animation. With a little refinement, you'll be able to do anything you have clearly defined in mind. If you want some ideas, though, watch animations and movies and study the masters who came long before Flash.

Workshop

The Workshop consists of quiz questions and answers to help you solidify your understanding of the material covered. Try to answer the questions before checking the answers.

Quiz

1. When we stretched the circle using the vertical scale, why did we also compress the horizontal scale?

   A. You can't scale a symbol in just one dimension.

   B. We thought it would look cool.

   C. In real life, compressing a ball in one dimension will cause it to expand in the other direction—the total volume of the ball never changes.

21

2. Why did we add extra reverberation to the circle during the overkill exercise ("Overkill to Make an Animation More Effective")?

   A. We thought it would look cool.

   B. Real balls always exhibit this behavior.

   C. We wanted the ball to act as the user expects.

3. Is it dishonest to use just a few keyframes instead of a long tween?

   A. Yes, it's not accurately demonstrating the physical movement we're animating.

   B. Maybe. But if the effect is more believable, we've succeeded.

   C. No, in real life motion involves only two key points: the beginning and the end.

Quiz Answers

1. C. While it may not be noticeable if you forego this touch, you might be surprised when you can't figure out why something just doesn't look right. Take a rubber ball and push it on the ground. You'll see it get wider as you reduce its height.

2. C. Certainly we shouldn't do something just to make it look cool. A real ball might not settle in such a dramatic way, but the user understands the message, and it looks realistic.

3. B. We're not here to show physical principles accurately, rather to communicate ideas. Remember, it's the result, not how we got to it.

HOUR 22

Working on Large Projects and in Team Environments

So far you've been doing all the work yourself—without any help. Although it's possible to create an entire Flash site by yourself, a team with a variety of skills can usually do a better job. Instead of trying to do everything yourself, build a team in which each person can specialize. One person could create the audio, another person could design the graphics, and still another could do the programming. The roles can be divided even further. Not only does this mean your end product will be better, but you can produce more output in a shorter time period because many people are working simultaneously.

The result of a team effort can be great. However, doing the project well is not easy. There are countless opportunities for conflicts and extra work. (I'm referring to technical conflicts that can cause some components of a project to simply not work.) This hour, you'll study some general ways to work in a team environment and learn many Flash-specific approaches. In this hour you will

- Study traditional production concepts, such as code-data separation
- Create and use shared libraries
- Use Smart Clips as templates
- Develop naming conventions and other productivity-enhancing methodologies

Methodologies

Great work has been produced for many years by creative people working in team environments. Although Flash Web sites have come about only recently, you can learn from more traditional production methodologies. Film production, for example, is not a bad model to follow. Although film is quite a different industry, it has many similarities with Flash. Even more traditional software production can seem quite different from Flash Web site production; however, you can still learn from the knowledge gathered in that field. This hour looks at a few basic concepts and applies them to Flash. These are not original ideas, but how they're applied to Flash is unique.

Role Definition

It's very important that everyone involved in a project has clearly defined responsibilities. Not only does this prevent two people from doing the same work, it actually prevents problems. The entire project should be analyzed as a series of tasks. Then the responsibilities should be divided up among the team members. Each team member can take on more than one task, but each task should only involve one team member. You can even change the roles during the project, but just make sure when you do that the new roles are clear to everyone involved.

Sometimes people think that the purpose of role definition is to help identify who is at fault when problems arise. This is a negative way to look at it. In a way, role definition will help identify the person at fault, but mainly it helps to solve the problem. It's too much to expect that problems can be prevented. Therefore, when one arises, having a clear idea who to address allows you to solve the problem without involving (and distracting) other team members.

Testing the System and Full-Path Reviews

After you've defined roles, the next step you should take is to confirm that all aspects of the system are working. It's amazing how many problems this simple step can uncover. For example, if one person is supposed to record some narration and then send it to the animator, an actual test run should be performed. The test would involve the narrator recording some audio. (It can be anything—it will just be a *placeholder.*) They should make sure it's recorded the same way they will record the real thing. When the animator receives it, they should try to incorporate it. Next, the team can analyze the results. If there's a problem in the process, this is a great time to find a solution. Maybe the audio engineer has emailed the files incorrectly and the animator is having trouble importing them. You'll be glad when you find the problem earlier in the process instead of later. It's almost like a dress rehearsal. Just remember that everyone must act like it's a dress rehearsal—not just a rehearsal—and do everything like they will in the real project.

NEW TERM   A *placeholder* is a piece of media that is used in place of the final media. It doesn't have to be pretty or clean, just representative of the final version. For example, if you plan to have a picture of the president in your movie but the election isn't over, you don't need to wait. Just use a picture of your dog—or anything, as long as it's the same size and placement as the final. When you receive the final picture you can replace the placeholder.

Another similar step you can take early in a project involves a *full-path review*, which is simply a prototype of the entire project, but only a certain portion. It's important to flesh out a "full path" (that is, it's important to go all the way down one representative path). Let's say you're testing the process of preparing 20 envelopes. Each one needs to be addressed, sealed, and stamped. A full-path review would involve addressing, sealing, and stamping one envelope. You wouldn't, for example, address each envelope and then try to make a judgment of your process. Instead, you just use one envelope and take it through the entire process.

In a Flash project, if your site has four sections that each have five subpages, for example, you should build one section all the way through, with its five subpages, instead of building one page for each section. Be sure to select the most representative section. If necessary, use two paths. The point is, you want to go deep, not wide.

Code-Data Separation

This concept is one of the most valuable in any kind of production environment. The idea is that you try your best to keep the code (the scripting and structure) separate from the data (the unique content). The more you can separate code and data, the more you can make changes to either without affecting the other. Imagine a company whose employees install wood siding on new homes. Naturally, they don't paint the wood until after it's installed. They keep the wood (the *code*, if you will) separate from the data (the colored paint). It makes perfect sense in this case, so certainly there's a way to apply code-data separation to Flash.

Suppose you've created a very interesting tween that involves moving text from offstage into the middle of the stage. The code, in this case, could be thought of as the *motion*. The data would be the actual text. In Flash, replacing the data (with no effect on the code) is quite simple. The following task demonstrates one feature that enables this type of separation. After you complete it, you'll learn some more sophisticated techniques.

Task: Use the Swap Symbol Technique as Applied to Code-Data Separation

This Task uses a built-in feature of Flash to demonstrate how the motion of an animation can be separated from the symbol being animated. Here are the steps to follow:

1. Create a block of text and convert it to a symbol called "Holder Text." Create a Motion tween. Add some Easing and scale it at the first keyframe—anything to make the motion obvious.

2. Test the movie. Now, imagine that this is perfect for one section of your site, but you want some other text to follow the same path in another scene. Click the "Layer 1" layer, which should select all the frames of this layer. Now select Edit, Copy Frames.

3. Create a new scene by selecting Insert, Scene. Click the first frame and then select Edit, Paste Frames. You've just copied everything about the first tween into the new scene. However, you want the duplicate frames to animate a different symbol.

4. Create another block of text (it doesn't matter exactly in which frame or layer you create it because you'll trash the instance in a minute). Select the text and convert it to a symbol named "Replacement." Now delete the instance of Replacement onscreen. (Don't worry, it's safe in the Library.)

5. Now swap out the Holder Text symbol. In Frame 1, select the instance of Holder Text and, from the Instance panel, click the Swap Symbol button (as shown in Figure 22.1). This button allows you to exchange the selected instance with a different symbol in your Library.

22

FIGURE 22.1

The Instance panel's Swap Symbol button allows you to exchange the selected instance with a different symbol in your Library.

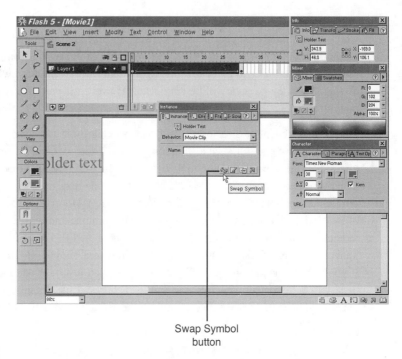

Swap Symbol
button

6. The Swap Symbol dialog box, shown in Figure 22.2, lists all the symbols in your Library and places a dot by the one currently linked to the instance you have selected. Select the Replacement symbol and then click OK. If there are instances of Holder Text in any other keyframes of your animation, you'll have to replace each of them the same way.

FIGURE 22.2

The Swap Symbol dialog box provides a list of all items in the Library and a dot next to the one with which you're currently linked.

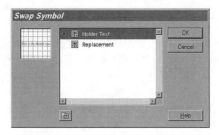

Swap Symbol provides a way to exchange the instance onstage with a replacement master symbol without losing any attributes of that instance. For example, if you had added a tint effect, scale, or anything that would remain applied to the instance onstage, the only difference would be the master symbol to which the instance points.

In the previous example, you could have simply edited the master version of the text, which would have changed the data in every instance in the movie. Instead, the approach you took, as much as possible, separates the code of the tween from the data of the symbol. With planning, you can carry this to any extreme. Eventually, when you deliver your movie, the code and data will be connected. However, if you plan to separate these items, making changes will be easier.

Often when a client or director wants to make a change, it can mean a lot of work for those involved. If you plan for such a situation, you can protect yourself from extra work. Sometimes the extra work won't pay off (in the unlikely event no one makes any changes). However when it pays off, it pays off big. Using code-data separation, you can keep the program as modular as possible. As you'll recall from Hour 18, "Designing Your Website to Be Modular," Load Movie provides a way to combine and reuse .swf files among many movies. For instance, your site could use a separate .swf file containing just a background image. You can include that image (the data) in several movies via Load Movie (the code). If you need to make a change to the background, you just have one file to edit. A change there will be reflected in each movie that loads the .swf file. Imagine the amount of work you would have to do if you had to replace the same image in 10 different movies.

Code-data separation is a great concept to keep in mind as you plan a site. Constantly ask yourself, "Is this content easily separated from the structure?" It's impossible to keep everything completely separated, but the more you can work in this mode, the better off you will be. It's valuable when you're working alone, but the potential productivity is even greater when you're working in a team environment. You can take advantage of Flash's modular features (discussed in Hour 18) to apply code-data separation to your team project.

Applied Techniques

Once you understand some productivity methodologies and their benefits, you'll need a way to apply this knowledge to Flash. For example, exactly how do you allow separate team members to work on the same project? That's what you'll learn in the remainder of this hour. You'll learn to use built-in Flash features as well as some general techniques that are not specific to Flash but are valuable nevertheless.

Shared Libraries

In Hour 18, you saw how Shared Libraries work. One main file's Library items can be shared among many other "user" files. If a change is made to the Library file, that change is seen in all the user files. Visitors to your site only download the items from the Shared Libraries once. You can probably imagine how the productivity of Shared Libraries can help in a team environment.

22

A common issue in Web site creation is that an enormous amount of work is needed to create the artwork for the site. While the principal artist comes up with the graphics, the assembly person (animator or programmer) just sits and waits. Then, when the final graphics are complete, the project must come together in an instant. With Shared Libraries, the assembly people can use a proxy (or *placeholder*) graphic, which allows them to work even while waiting for the graphics from the principal artist. The following task walks you through a scenario so that you can get the idea.

Task: Use Shared Libraries to Start Assembling a Movie Without Final Graphics

In this Task's scenario, you'll use Shared Libraries in order to let the assembly people start working before the artist is finished creating the graphics. Here are the steps to follow:

1. Imagine that the programmer wants to start working, but the graphic artist hasn't finished creating the graphics for the background. The artist can create "holder" graphics that are kept in the Shared Library to be replaced at any time.

2. Create a new file. Draw a box and the text "HOLDER." Select everything and convert it to a symbol. Name the symbol "Background" and leave it as the default Movie Clip.

3. To make registration easy (especially when the final graphics are imported), use the Info panel to set the center to position 0,0 (as shown in Figure 22.3). The programmer will simply need to position this clip at the same location.

FIGURE 22.3

The Info panel is used to specify the x and y positions. In this case, the black square indicates that the center of the object is being used.

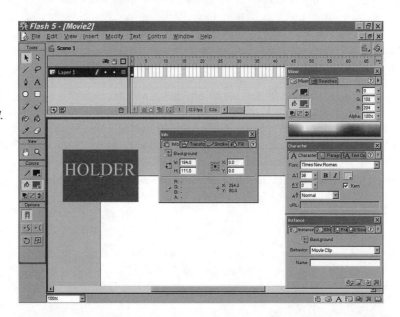

4. Because you've just moved the center point of Background to the top-left corner of the screen, double-click Background so that you can edit the contents of the master symbol. Select everything onscreen and move it to the middle of the screen. Then return to the main scene.

5. Select Background from the file's Library window. Then right-click (Control+click on the Macintosh) and select Linkage.

6. Select Export This Symbol and give the symbol the identifier *Background*. Then click OK (see Figure 22.4) Export This Symbol assures the symbol exports with the movie, regardless of whether it's actually used in the movie. The identifier will be used by the movies that share this item, so that replacing the symbol across all movies is as simple as assigning that identifier to the new symbol.

FIGURE 22.4

Using the Symbol Linkage Properties dialog box, you can ensure that this item will export. You also need to give it a unique identifier.

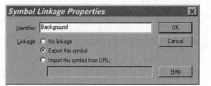

7. In a new folder, save this file with the name `shared.fla`. Make sure you run Test Movie (to create a .swf file).

8. In a new file, the programmer can use this placeholder graphic to start programming. Choose File, Open As Shared Library and select `shared.fla`. Drag Background onto the stage. Then, from the Info panel, specify the center point as 0,0. Lock the layer.

9. The programmer can now continue with his work (he just has to realize that this symbol is temporary).

10. When the graphic artist has a replacement ready, he simply needs to either edit the Background symbol in the Shared Library or create a new symbol. If the artist creates a new symbol, he must remove the old one and ensure that the new one has its Linkage property set the same as in step 6. In any case, he should confirm the background looks properly positioned when it is set to 0,0. That is, when he's done, he should drag an instance of the final version onto the stage and set the center location to 0,0 to confirm that everything looks right. (If not, he must edit the contents of Background to move things around.)

Smart Clips

We used Smart Clips in Hour 16, "Using Smart Clips," to condense complicated script tasking into an easy-to-use format. You explored some of the more advanced and useful

22

Smart Clips that ship with Flash and took baby steps towards creating your own. The value that Smart Clips provide can play a part in team environments as well.

One obvious use for Smart Clips is in the division of responsibility—where one programmer builds a Smart Clip and others use it. But more than that, Smart Clips can provide a consistent template for all the content throughout a site. It doesn't take much effort to make a Smart Clip that simply serves as a template—and you'll do just that in the following task.

Task: Make a Smart Clip That Serves as a Template

In this Task, you'll create a template for each author in your team. Each author can uniquely populate his template while keeping the layout consistent with the other authors' work. Here are the steps:

1. In a new file create two blocks of text. Through the Character panel, make the font of one block fairly large (around 36 points). The other block can be smaller (around 24 points or so).

2. Use the Text Options panel to make each block dynamic. Make sure Selectable is unchecked. Click the Include Entire Font Outline button. Your panel should now look like the one shown in Figure 22.5.

FIGURE 22.5

Both text blocks are made dynamic and non-selectable, and the entire font is embedded.

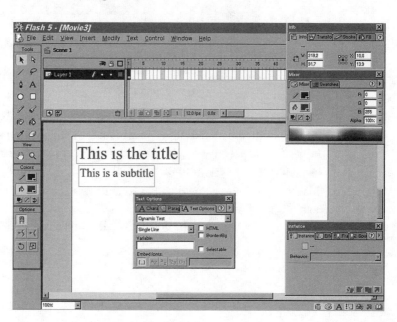

3. Associate the variable name "title" with the large text block and "subtitle" with the small text block.

4. Now set the position of the text blocks so the "title" text is near the top left of the stage and the "subtitle" text is below it. Adjust the margins on both blocks of text so that they're very large (wider than the stage itself). Don't use the Scale tool to adjust the margin; instead, double-click inside one block and drag the margin control box at the bottom right (see Figure 22.6).

FIGURE 22.6

Changing the margin of a text block is different than changing the scale. Drag the margin control box while the text block is being edited.

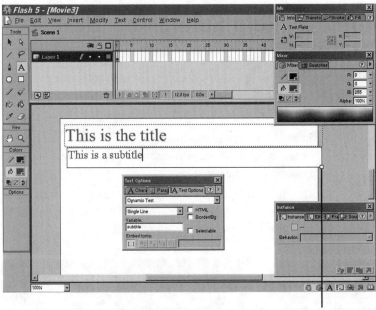

Margin control box

5. The justification of your text boxes is up to you. In this example, I set the Paragraph Align button to Right Justify for the subtitle, but I set the title to Left Justify. The idea is that this layout will be used in several places in your site, so spend the time necessary to make it look the way you want.

6. To convert this into a Smart Clip, you must first convert it to a Movie Clip. Select both blocks of text and then select Insert, Convert to Symbol. Call it "Template" and make sure you leave the default Movie Clip behavior.

7. The layout may be exactly how you want it, but you should make the registration easy for the authors. Select the Template instance you just created and use the Info panel to set the center to position 0,0 (like you did in the last task).

8. Most likely, everything has moved up to the top-left corner of the Stage. Now double-click Template so that you can edit the master symbol. While inside Template, position the text where you want it to appear. Although this may seem like a lot of work, it means that each author will simply need to position this clip in the known position 0,0.

9. To make this a Smart Clip, you need to define clip parameters. Open the Library window, right-click Template, and select Define Clip Parameters. Click the plus button, and in the Name column type `title`. In the corresponding Value column, type `Type Title Here`. Click the plus again and type `subtitle` for the Name column and `Type Subtitle Here` for the Value column. Click OK. This process simply gives the author direct access to change these variables for each clip instance he uses.

10. Now you can distribute this Smart Clip to all your authors. The subsequent steps walk you through how this clip can be used.

11. Return to the main scene. Delete everything onscreen. Drag Template from the Library onto the stage. Use the Info panel to set the center location to 0,0. With Template still selected, access the Clip Parameters panel. Double-click the title field (Type Title Here) and type `This is page one`. For the subtitle, type `…the first page`. Insert a keyframe in frame 2 and change the title and subtitle (via the Clip Parameters panel) to something different. Finally, insert another keyframe and include different text for the third frame.

12. Put a Stop action in the first frame of this layer. Select Insert, Layer and draw a box. Then select Insert, Covert to Symbol call the symbol "Button" (and make sure you select Button). Select the button instance and open the Actions panel. Insert a Go To action. Change the parameter for Type to Next Frame (see Figure 22.7).

13. Test the movie. You'll notice that the text changes but the formatting remains consistent. If any changes are made to the master Smart Clip (perhaps the font or location changes), you'll see that change reflected everywhere else.

FIGURE 22.7
This simple action will let the user click a button to step through the frames. (Don't forget the Stop action in frame 1.)

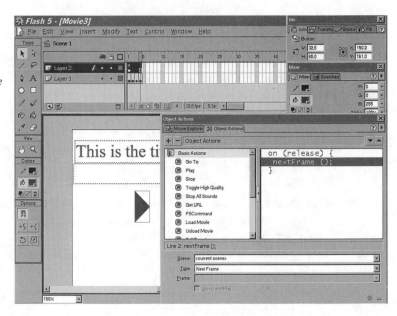

This task makes good use of a fairly simple Smart Clip. You could make it even better by storing the Smart Clip in a Library that would be opened as a Shared Library. This works just as well and has all the added benefits of a Shared Library (only one master version for all the user files). There are still some limits, however. In the example, the authors can't see the onscreen text until they test the movie. They have to constantly view the text by first selecting the clip instance and looking at the clip parameters—not quite as convenient as seeing the text right onstage. There's nothing you can do about this limitation because the parameters specified are only used at runtime.

One other limitation can be addressed, and it only takes a little bit of code. In the preceding task, the author would have to carefully position each instance of Template through the Info panel. You can go inside the master version of Template and eliminate that requirement. In the first keyframe, simply insert an evaluate Action (or press Esc, E, V) and then type **_x=0**. Insert another evaluate Action (Esc, E, V) and type **_y=0**. When the first keyframe of Template is encountered (once every time the instance appears onscreen), the _x and _y properties (of the clip itself) will be moved to the 0,0 position. Now the authors can place the clips anywhere they want—even if they're careless, the clip will automatically reposition itself to the correct location!

Notice that the work and the code invested in this template is pretty minimal. Consider that even if it takes a lot of work to create a template with more features, it may be worth your time investment because the template can be used over and over. Even if it only saves the authors a minute or two each time they use it, that savings is multiplied over time.

Retaining Integrity when Making Drastic Changes

When you intend to extract a significant portion of one file and incorporate it into another, you must follow a few important steps. Perhaps you have one file that works great, and you need another just like it but with all new graphics. Maybe you need to remove the first 20 frames in a particular scene and want everything in the Timeline to shift to the left. There are many reasons you might want to make changes. Unfortunately, there are also many ways these changes can make your project go haywire.

A few techniques for retaining integrity are probably well known to you by now. For example, when you copy or cut an item and want to paste it in the same position from where it was copied, you must use Edit, Paste in Place (Ctrl+Shift+V). Another method related to copying and pasting relates to copying frames. When you want to copy a series of keyframes, including any Frame actions and tween settings, you must select the frames and choose Edit, Copy Frames. Then, when you intend to paste those frames, you must first click a layer and select Edit, Paste Frames. (These options are also available when you right-click.)

You may want to review the timeline-selection techniques covered in Hour 1, "Basics." Click the layer name to select everything in that layer, hold down Ctrl as you drag to select a range of frames, hold down Shift and Ctrl to add to a selection, or simply hold down Shift to add individual frames to the selection. This may seem pretty basic, but it helps to practice these selection techniques. Keep in mind that sometimes you'll select several frames because you want to remove them (not just move them somewhere else). If you select several frames using the Ctrl+drag method, you can remove them by selecting Insert, Remove Frames (or Shift+F5). This way, all the frames later in the timeline shift to the left.

No doubt you use the Library a lot. When copying the contents of one file into another, you need to know a couple interesting facts about instances of symbols. If you create some symbols in one file, you can leave open that file's Library. When you open or create another file, the old file's Library window remains in place, but it turns a dark gray color as an indication that it's from another file (as shown in Figure 22.8). When you drag items from a grayed out (old) Library onto the stage of a new file, Flash copies the symbol into the new file's Library.

FIGURE 22.8

The Library from another file is shown with a gray background.

Current File's Name   Library's File's Name

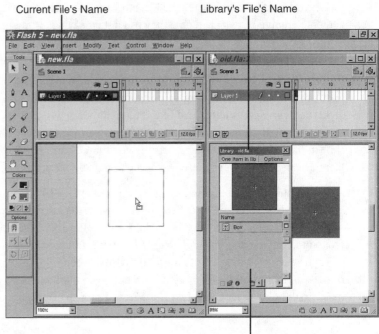

Background Changes to Gray

However, if you continue dragging the same item from an old file's library into a new file, Flash uses the master symbol in the new file's library. This is important, because if you make a change to the contents of the symbol in the new file—for example, you edit a circle to look like a square, and try to drag the original circle symbol from the old file's library—Flash uses the edited symbol from the new file. The bottom line is this: You must be very clear on what's happening; otherwise, you'll lose control and probably feel frustrated.

Documentation and Naming Conventions

As you build a large, complex project, documentation is important. All media elements should be clearly identified and, if necessary, an accompanying paper document should detail how everything works. Think of documentation as the instruction manual. It can be used by any team member to quickly view the entire project. If it's well done, someone outside the project could study the documentation and then begin working on the project.

Not only does a clear paper trail help other team members, but even when you're working solo, documentation can help you sort through your own project if you need to revisit something you built in the past. Documentation doesn't actually need to be on paper either. You can include notes right inside your Flash movie. For example, because Guide layers don't export with the movie, they're a great place to include notes or maybe just a quick explanation of the more-complex features involved in that file. Even the process of creating the documentation will help you sort out how a project works.

Specifically, a basic set of documentation includes a text description of every file used in a project. You could have a folder which, by the name you give it, explains what's contained. For example, a folder's name could be *sounds*. Perhaps it contains .swf files with audio that's loaded into the main movie via Load Movie. Every file dedicated to a project has a purpose (if not, maybe it should be deleted or archived). You just need to explain each file.

A really great project document would also include a description of the process. Although something as vague as "create the animation and be very careful to make it look good" may be too general, you don't need to be really specific either. It's a balance between being clear and being so detailed that you're creating more work for yourself than it's worth. Common sense can help you make this decision. However, realize that if you have to revisit your own work at a later time, you're going to value such a document.

Documentation should be done during the project—not at the end. The incentive to sit down and document a project that's complete is lost because the project is done. When you reach logical milestones, you should document what you just finished. Think of it as protection. Imagine you could be audited and you want everything in order, just in case.

One way to document as you go is by using careful, strict *naming conventions*. Symbol names are important because you can sort libraries alphabetically. If each team member precedes the name of the symbols he creates with his initials, you can quickly sort items based on author. You could also decide to precede symbol names with the section where that asset is used. This is the technique used in the lesson file found under Help, Lessons, 05 Type (as shown in Figure 22.9). All the bitmaps have names starting with "Bitmap-," whereas buttons for navigation start with "Nav button," buttons for close-up screenshots start with "ScrnButton-," and the actual screenshots start with "ScrnSht-." You can use whatever makes sense for your project; it just takes a little bit of organization.

Figure 22.9

A Library is organized automatically when you use a consistent naming convention.

New Term   *Naming conventions* are a set of rules you apply to the names folders and files are given. You can specify the convention without specifying each filename. For example, your naming convention could specify the following: "SectionNumber_SubSection.swf". Then for section 2, subsection 3 the name would be "2_3.swf". This convention can accommodate any numbers that arise.

In addition to the names given to symbols in the Library, the instances used onstage have names, too. Instance names have little benefit for documentation, but naming conventions can still be critical. If, for example, you have three instances of a symbol named "box" initially, the instances don't have unique names. If you name them "box_1," "box_2," and "box_3," you could have a script that sets properties for one box at a time. For example, the following code will set a selected box's x position to 10:

```
function move(boxNum){
    _root["box_"+boxNum]._x=10;
}
```

Naturally, boxNum needs to be either 1, 2, or 3. "box_" + boxNum will dynamically change to "box_1" if boxNum is 1. This issue brings up a lot of scripting issues that are beyond the scope of this hour (instead, you can find them in Appendix B, "Advanced ActionScripting"). However, you should be able to see how naming the instances in this logical manner makes more sense than naming them "boxOne," "boxTwo," and "boxThree," because it would be harder to dynamically change just one of these.

22

Documentation and naming conventions are just good housekeeping. Even if it seems like a lot of work during a project, it can actually save a lot of time, not just when there are problems, but also when you want to make structural changes or track progress. Often you can complete a large project with no regard to documentation or naming conventions—you'll just be more be efficient if you do.

Summary

This hour you saw some general approaches to working on large files and in teams. Adapting the general tips to suit your project productivity and efficiency is a topic worth addressing in every project because time saved, when applied to a large project, is much greater.

In addition to theories and methodologies, you discovered a few built-in features of Flash that can be applied to productivity. You used some features just as they're designed—such as Swap Symbol. Other features were tailored for special purposes—such as using Smart Clips for templates. Often, people tend to get rolling on a project and forget the old proverb "Haste makes waste." Therefore, you should take the extra time to analyze workflow issues, and your project will run more smoothly.

Q&A

Q Is there an alternative to using the Swap Symbol feature individually on each instance in the timeline?

A Well, you can't select several instances and swap them all at once. However, if you are planning to replace an entire tween this way, you can take advantage of a subtle feature of the Library. In one movie, create a symbol called "box." Keep open the first file's Library and create a new file. Drag "box" from the first file's library into the new file. Now, even if you edit the contents of "box" in the new file, Flash thinks the two "box" symbols are the same. Edit the contents of "box" in the new file (maybe change it to a circle). Create a tween in the first file, copy the frames, and then paste the frames into the second file. You'll get the same tween, but you'll be using the newly edited "box" as if you individually swapped each instance.

Q What is the ideal number of people on a Flash team?

A Maybe the easiest situation is when only one person works on the entire project. However, that person will end up doing more work and won't benefit from all the skills others have to offer. Teams as large as 20 people can be very productive. It really doesn't matter—although larger teams usually require more upfront planning and ongoing organization.

Workshop

The Workshop consists of quiz questions and answers to help you solidify your understanding of the material covered. Try to answer the questions before checking the answers.

Quiz

1. Which of the following is *not* a benefit of code-data separation?

    A. Bugs in the code are minimized or eliminated.

    B. Code can be readily used in a new project.

    C. Artwork can be replaced without affecting the code.

2. What's a full-path review?

    A. A situation in which everyone involved in the project is present for a review.

    B. A situation in which you step through the entire project once (going down each path).

    C. A situation in which one path is developed completely.

3. What happens if you click a keyframe and select Edit, Copy?

    A. Nothing, you should select Edit, Copy Frames.

    B. The onscreen contents of that layer are copied to the clipboard.

    C. Flash will quit.

Quiz Answers

1. A. Although good code-data separation practices may tend to make fixing bugs easier, it won't have much impact by itself.

2. C. It probably doesn't hurt to have everyone present, but the idea is to simply go through one path completely.

3. B. You may have wanted to used Copy Frames, but simply selecting Copy will copy the selected items onstage (and clicking the keyframe selects everything in the layer).

HOUR 23

Learning How to Learn Flash

By now you should have a solid foundation in Flash. However, this book is by no means exhaustive. After finishing all the tasks in this book, you'll still need to grow on your own. If you keep repeating the same exercises, they will get easier, but you'll likely want to keep expanding your knowledge, and that's going to mean even more work. This hour looks at techniques used to learn Flash faster and better. I'll provide some resources and suggestions that should prove useful no matter to which level you take your Flash skills.

In this hour you will

- Find valuable learning resources for Flash
- Develop an approach to use as you grow
- Use the Debugger and other techniques to improve your work

Although the main emphasis of this hour is developing good scripting techniques, some material applies to general animation, too. For example, many of the Web resources referenced are good places to learn about animation as well. However, it's the subject of scripting that has the most potential and that this book can't reach. This book has covered practically all the animation tools, so it's up to you to take your knowledge of creating animation to the next level. Regarding scripting, though, this book has just scratched the surface.

Learning from Sample Files

One of the best ways to learn Flash is to snoop through someone else's work. If you can take one look at how something runs and then go "behind the scenes," you can immediately see how that item works. There are lots of places to find sample files, and I'll provide a few tips to help you sift through someone else's work.

Files That Ship with Flash

Some of the best files to learn from are right under your nose! In the Help menu, you'll find several sample files. In particular, the files Calculator, Mosquito Killer, and Puzzle are really well done. There are a few others, but these three exploit some of the new features of Flash 5. The lesson files (under Help, Lessons) have some valuable content, but I wouldn't suggest sifting through how they were made. The lessons are intended for you to step through, not as examples of techniques. All the sample files, however, attempt to show exactly how a particular effect is achieved.

Several interesting files can also be found under Window, Common Libraries. Most of these are simply artwork (such as the Sounds and Graphics Libraries, for example). However, the Smart Clips Library has a few really well-done examples—not only can you learn from them, but you might find them useful in your projects as well. The Learning Interactions Library is nice, but you're not given the source for the custom UI SWF files, so you can't learn as much as you might otherwise. Both Libraries are pretty sophisticated, so there's a lot you can learn.

Later this hour you'll learn how you might step through these files, but for now just pick through them and don't save them when you're done. (You won't even be able to save any files opened through the Samples, Tutorial, or Shared Libraries menus.)

Online Tutorials

Of all the online communities of developers, "Flash heads" seem to be the most open and willing to share. You can find people who've created elaborate projects that they make freely available. Considering the time invested, it's really surprising that people will share so much. In Appendix C, "Resources," you'll find a listing of online tutorials available on the Web.

Most of these sites have articles, forums, and sample files for download. In addition, there are countless email "listservs" to which you can subscribe. Honestly, this book probably wouldn't have been possible without the feedback I received from all the inquiries I made to various listservs. When you face a problem, chances are good someone else has had a related experience. Even if they don't solve your problem, you can usually get some good ideas that can lead you to a solution.

NEW TERM   A *listserv* is an email format that you can subscribe to. Any time you send email to the list, everyone on the list sees your message. Replies made to your inquiries are seen by everyone, too. It's interesting because you can follow a conversation between several people on one topic (called a *thread*) with or without participating. It's a relatively low-tech form of online community.

Many of these Flash community sites include tutorials and actual .fla files you can download and dissect. Often, someone will write a tutorial that shows you exactly how to create a particular effect. You're about to learn some specific techniques you can use while analyzing the work of others; however, you need to keep a couple points in mind while doing so. First, it's best to look at someone else's complete file to learn a technique. Don't just extract the scripting you need and expect it to work within your own project. Often, it will work, but if you don't understand how it's working, you won't be able to make any variations, and you won't be able to fix bugs when they crop up. Second, a lot of tutorials show you how to achieve a particular effect. For example, several tutorials show the effect "mouse trails," in which graphics follow the cursor. Although this effect looks cool, when many sites start using the same effect, it becomes cliché and looks unoriginal. Ideally, when you look at other people's work, you should actually learn and expand on it instead of simply copying it.

How to Extract Knowledge from Finished Work

When you find a finished FLA file from which you want to learn, you simply open it in Flash and start snooping. However, if the file is complex, you might soon feel like you're walking down a winding path into a dark forest without a flashlight—it's easy to get lost! You need to know some techniques to extract just the information you need.

 If you're working on a Macintosh you probably won't be able to simply double-click a .fla file you've downloaded. Open Flash first, then select File, Open and be sure to select "All Files" from the List Files of Type pop-up menu.

Instead of trying to learn everything at once, you should try first to identify a very specific attribute you want to learn. For example, you could deconstruct the sample file Circular Motion. Open it from Help, Samples and do a Test Movie. Naturally, you won't deconstruct the whole thing, but you can try to figure out how to change the cursor and then try to get the line to stretch and follow the cursor. If you just take one little step at a time, you'll be able to better digest the information. The following task walks you through this example and shows you a few techniques.

Task: Learn from a Complex Sample File

In this Task you extract a portion of code from someone else's sample file. Here are the steps to follow:

1. Open the file Help, Samples, Circular Motion and then run Test Movie.

2. Return to the source file and open the Movie Explorer panel (available from the Launcher Bar at the bottom right of the window, as shown in Figure 23.1). The Movie Explorer panel gives you a view of the entire file. You can see the fonts used, every instance, all the actions, and many more details (see Figure 23.2).

FIGURE 23.1

The Movie Explorer button is part of the Launcher Bar at the bottom right of every Flash file.

Movie Explorer

FIGURE 23.2

The Movie Explorer panel provides a hierarchical list of everything in a movie.

Filtering buttons

Search field

Hierarchy of movie content

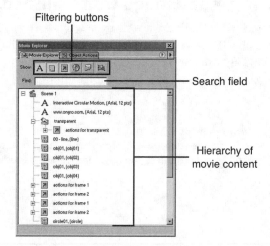

3. You'll now change the filtering setting for the Movie Explorer so that only actions are displayed. From the row of buttons labeled Show, click the last button (see Figure 23.3). The Customize button will give you access to a detailed list of which elements will be shown. From this Movie Explorer dialog box, uncheck every box (in the Show section on top) except ActionScript. Then click OK.

FIGURE 23.3

The last filtering button gives you access to a detailed list of elements that will be shown.

4. You can now quickly sort through all the ActionScript statements in this movie. In the Movie Explorer, click the plus sign next to Scene 1 (which shows or hides the actions for Scene 1). You want to see everything. Try to find the one with the most code. By clicking the plus sign next to it, you can open each action (close the action after you take a peek by clicking the minus sign). Continue snooping until you reach an action with a lot of code. The fourth one—actions for frame 1—has a ton of code, as you can see in Figure 23.4.

FIGURE 23.4

While viewing only ActionScript statements, you can go through each action until you find one with a lot of code.

5. You could print this out and study it, but for now, just copy it. Double-click inside this code and you'll be taken to the Frame Actions panel. (You could have gotten to the same place had you accessed the Actions panel for first frame in the layer code, but this way is easier.)

6. Scroll to the top and see if you can make sense of this code. The first line simply hides the mouse. Notice that the text should be all blue. Any time the text is colored, it means it's part of the built-in ActionScript language (it's not something the programmer created). Copy this first line, create a new file, paste the line into the Script area in the Frame Actions panel for the first frame, and then test the movie. Your mouse should disappear. Good, one thing at a time. Close the movie you're testing (your mouse cursor will return if you move outside the window) and then come back to the Circular Motion file to grab more code.

7. You might be wondering about _root.attachMovie("pointer", "pointer", 10000). This line uses the attachMovie action to create an instance (with the name "pointer") of a symbol from the Library. The Library item must have its Linkage property set to Export and the identifier specified as "pointer." Skip this line for now.

8. Copy the third and fourth lines and paste them into the first frame's action in the new movie you've made (so that it looks like what's shown in Figure 23.5). The only part of this code that's not colored is "pointer." This code will move a clip instance called "pointer" to wherever the mouse happens to move. For this to work, you must have a Movie Clip onstage with the instance name "pointer." In the new file, create a small box, convert it to a symbol, and name it "box." Next, name the instance onstage "pointer" via the Instance panel.

FIGURE 23.5

These three lines of code were copied from the sample file and pasted into a new file's first frame.

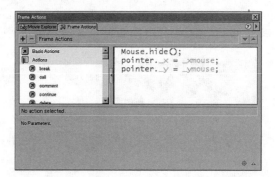

9. Test your movie. It doesn't work! This is perfectly normal, and you should get used to it. However, just think how rewarding it will be when you do get your movie to work. You need to return to the sample movie and see what's different from your movie.

10. Back in the Circular Motion file, notice what's different: It's got two frames. The code in frame 1 executes once, but it will execute again and again (moving the pointer clip each time) every time it loops back to frame 1.

11. Go back to your new file and in frame 2 select Insert, Frame, Test Movie. Although it works, it's not the same as the sample movie. Again, take a look at what's different. The Circular Motion file has a frame rate of 100fps! It will update the location of the pointer more frequently.

12. Change your frame rate to match the Circular Motion file's frame rate and then run Test Movie. The fact is, this example is very complex. Although there are other (arguably better) ways to make a clip move with the mouse, the process you took here was important (not necessarily the detailed tricks you picked up). You've started to rebuild this sample file from scratch.

Going through someone else's code can be frustrating, but when you get the code to work, it can be rewarding, too. Remember that it's the process you're learning—using the Movie Explorer, noticing which scripts are built in (colored green, pink, or blue), and copying as little code as possible at a time, while making sure it works before continuing. As it turns out, although you can learn a lot from this file, the solution to make the pointer follow the cursor is not ideal. Therefore, in the "Activities" section (at the end of this hour) I've provided another solution. Again, when you're exploring the work of others, try not to simply take what they have created verbatim—try to learn from it. There's always more than one way to achieve a result.

Embarking on a Large Project

If you have the goal to create a large, complex Web site, you may feel the tasks you've mastered in this book are too simple to really help. The truth, however, is that these tasks provide a foundation on which you can build. The most complex Flash Web sites ever created are nothing more than an accumulation of lots of small tasks. This may sound simplistic, but as you'll learn in this section, you just have to break up all the large tasks into smaller tasks, protect yourself from going too far in the wrong direction, and always look for better ways to perform tasks.

Breaking Up Tasks

When you deconstructed the Circular Motion file, you took only a single aspect out at a time. First, you looked at the mouse-hiding feature (the `Mouse.hide()` script). Then you extracted the script that moves the pointer clip instance to match the cursor. At this rate, you could reconstruct the entire piece, but it would take a long time. When you embark on a large project, you need to approach it the same way—a little bit at a time.

23

First, envision the finished site in all its glory. Then list all the features you expect to have functioning. Be as detailed as possible. For example, say something like this:

> There will be a glossary accessible from anywhere in the site. When the user selects to view the glossary, it appears on top of the current screen. From the glossary, the user will have an alphabetical list of many terms. When a term is selected, a block of text appears with the definition. Some terms will have additional media, including audio, images, or movie clips. The additional media will always appear in the same location next to the text (not embedded in the text). The user may leave the glossary by clicking a Close button.

This is a detailed description of the features. From this, you can start to break down tasks. If, in comparison, you simply said, "I'm going to build a glossary," it would be premature to start programming until you have a much clearer idea where you're headed.

Once you have specified all the features of your project, you can start to break down tasks. For example, the first thing you could tackle with the glossary feature might be a simple button that, when clicked, causes the glossary to appear on top of the current screen. Then you could create another button to remove the glossary. That's it. Get this part working before you go on to the other tasks. You could achieve this with a movie clip that contains a button on frame 1. Also on frame 1 of the movie clip, you would have a Stop action. Then the button's action could read `gotoAndStop (2)`. Frame 2 could contain a large box for a background (maybe even an instance of a symbol so you can add effects to it like alpha). Another button could appear on frame 2 to serve as the "close" feature, containing the script `gotoAndStop (1)`. You would create this feature and then test it. See if it functions from any place in the movie. Make sure this feature is satisfactory, take a breath, and then move on.

This technique of looking at the entire project, breaking up tasks, and then building one task at a time (and testing after each) is a good approach to take. You can't do everything at once. When you get more experienced, you'll be able to keep in mind the overall goal at hand (and possibly go faster with fewer errors). However, no matter how good you get, you'll always do one task at a time.

Protecting Yourself as You Work

During every great software project, problems are encountered. If you keep this in mind, you'll usually be better prepared when problems arise in your projects. As you assemble a project, there are steps you can take to prepare yourself for—even protect yourself from—the inevitable problems that arise. This is not a bad thing. Instead, think of it as quality assurance.

One specific way you can prepare to succeed in a project is to keep an archive of all your files. If you make a significant change, do a File, Save As and change the filename. One strategy is to include the date in a file's name along with a version number. For example, when you start in the morning, you could name the file `myProject_31oct2000-1.fla`. Every time you make a major revision, increment the last number, like this: `myProject_31oct2000-2.fla`. The latest version is the file with the latest date and highest version number. You can even keep a paper log that specifies the features you've added to each revision. If you find there's a problem—maybe something that used to work is now broken—you can go back to an older file. Even if you need to redo everything you did from that point forward, you can use the log to help. Sometimes it's enough, however, to simply go back to the old file and look at the code and then extract just a certain portion.

Another specific approach you can take is to follow good documentation practices. The previous hour discussed the benefits of documentation as it applies to working in a team. Consider that when a problem arises that needs fixing, it often means you'll need to revisit code that you may have written a long time ago. Nicely documented files are easier to work with as you search for solutions to problems.

Don't Fall in Love with Your Code—Learn to Throw It Away

As a project grows, you build upon the foundation created in the beginning. You keep adding and adding to the same file. In the end, the project may work exactly how you want, but because large portions of the project may have changed significantly, the resulting file could be quite a mess. During a project, sometimes it's valuable to scrap everything you have and start from scratch. It may seem like you'll have to redo everything, but you may find you're more efficient when you take a direct path (you'll know where you're heading after all).

Of course, it's not a good idea to scrap a lot of work for no good reason. Only when the file becomes unmanageable should you consider rebuilding it from scratch. When you do need to rebuild, remember the tips covered in the last hour regarding making drastic changes to a file (things such as Copy Frames). You'll likely get attached to your work and might not want to scrap it. The fact is, a file that has changed many times in its evolution might include unnecessary and even bug-causing elements. Think about how artists create many "studies" of a work before finally making their masterpiece.

You don't have to wait until the end of the project to take advantage of this "trash it" technique. For example, say you've found a bug. Before trying different things to fix it, save the file. When you finally think you've got it fixed, you can use File, Revert (to restore the most recently saved version, as described in the dialog box that appears like Figure 23.6). Then apply the fix you found. This method is better because you'll be much more deliberate and you won't include all those other failed attempts at fixing the problem. A lot of different solutions might have been attempted, and there's a chance you forgot to undo some. Using Revert is a great way to remove all those failed attempts.

FIGURE 23.6

Revert lets you restore your file to its original state—before you started trying lots of fixes.

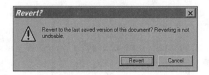

A similar trick is to work out solutions offline. That is, instead of adding each feature (or individual task) to your main file, work out the solution in a new file. When you have something that works, apply the code to the master file. As with working out solutions to bugs (and trying lots of crazy stuff) when you come up with a new element, you'll likely try many different approaches. When you find a solution that works, return to your main file to implement it. The result is that your main file will remain lean and clean.

Finally, if you're doing a repetitive task and think of a more efficient way to perform this task before you're finished, it's often fastest to stop what you're doing and start over. This time, though, do it in the streamlined manner. Often, people get so attached to the process that they're afraid to take another tack. Just as with throwing away old code, be sure you can scrap processes that can be improved.

Never Stop Learning

This may sound depressing, but you'll never learn it all. In one lifetime, it's impossible to be an expert in everything. This isn't to say that you should give up now. In a way, you should be hopeful. Consider that you can become an expert in one narrow area, and you'll always be in demand by those who didn't have time to be an expert in that area. Regardless of how you look at it, you can grow your skills by taking a realistic attitude.

Software Keeps Improving

It's important to only learn what you can use right away. Flash 5 is an amazing product, but it's not the last piece of software you'll ever need to learn. It's more important to learn how to make Flash do what you need than to learn every feature inside Flash.

If you compare the steps necessary to achieve any task with software products from just five years ago, it's almost amusing how much harder things were. The trend of software becoming more powerful will continue. Just a couple years ago, for example, it was critical that you understood palettes because most computers could only display 256 colors. That knowledge is all but forgotten today. The point is that you should only worry about what's important for the immediate future. If you want to prepare for the long term, prepare for change.

You can actually affect the direction that Flash takes! Simply write an email to `wish-flash@macromedia.com`. Although you won't receive replies to your inquiries (as you can expect through Macromedia technical support lines), a real live human really reads emails sent to this address. Macromedia, more than any other software company, really listens to its users' suggestions. You really should consider sending your ideas to make the product better. Because of others in the past, Flash 5 is the product it is today.

Don't Just Learn, Do

You should take the foundational skills you've acquired in this book and try building some challenging sites. Always attempt something just a little outside your reach. Each time you'll have to invest a little time getting up to speed, but this is how you'll grow. You can use the resources listed in Appendix C, the help files, and other books. Use every resource you can, but try to actually build something. Conversely, you could spend all your time preparing and never get around to using the product.

Doing real projects is a great way to learn. Only under the pressure of real life do you encounter challenges you could never imagine otherwise. Another, possibly better way to learn is to try teaching someone else. It's amazing how fast you learn what you don't know when you try to teach someone else. For example, if you think you're an expert with the Motion Tween, try to show a friend or relative how to use it. It may sound corny, but you should find that your knowledge is enhanced.

Basic Exercises to Always Practice

Many of the skills you've picked up in this book should be transferable to other types of software you may encounter. Any time you need to learn a new piece of software, you should attempt to perform a few "foundation exercises." I know that as I've migrated from using Authorware to Director to Flash, I've had to do similar tasks with each. Return to the following exercises periodically or whenever you need to learn a new piece of software (even if you repeat these in a few months, I'll bet you'll find you do them more efficiently):

- *The bouncing ball.* If ever there's a classic animation exercise, this is it. You can spice it up all day long and it will never be perfect. You did this exercise in Hour 11, "Using Layers in Your Animation," but you can always return and try it again. Try adding some of the techniques, such as squash, that were covered in Hour 21, "Advanced Animation Techniques" (see Figure 23.7).

23

FIGURE **23.7**

The classic bouncing ball exercise (with squashing) is a good one to keep revisiting.

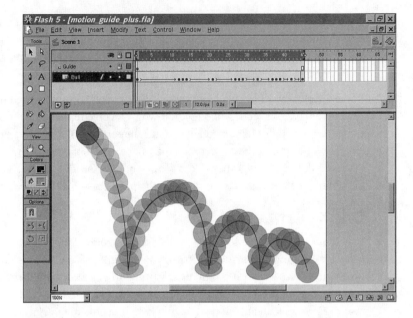

- *It goes up, it goes down.* In this exercise, you create two arrow buttons. One makes the displayed number or the clip instance go up, and the other makes it goes down. You did something similar to this when you increased and decreased the alpha property of a clip in Hour 15, "ActionScripting Applications for Advanced Interactivity."

- *Hello, world.* In this exercise, the user is asked to type in his name, and the computer responds with "Hello, Phillip" (or whatever name is used). This exercise shows that you can store variables and that you can combine a string and a variable in an output string. We actually did this exercise in Hour 15. It was called "Use a Variable to Get the User's Name."

- *Circle, Line, Square.* The idea here is that there are three buttons (labeled Circle, Line, and Square) which, when clicked, show the user a circle, a line, or a square. Since we haven't done this exercise, let's walk through a quick task to see how it can be done. It's important to realize this is just one solution. The idea is that you will be able to return to this task and try to solve it in your own—possibly more efficient—way.

Task: Build "Circle, Line, Square"

1. Draw a large box, remove its fill, then select it and choose Insert, Convert to Symbol. Name the symbol "Content" and leave it as a Movie Clip.

2. Double-click the instance onstage (to edit the contents).

3. Inside the Content Movie Clip, at frame 4 select Insert, Frame (F5). Then create a new layer called "Graphics". Insert a keyframe (F6) in frame 2 of Graphics and draw a circle. Insert a blank keyframe (F7) in frame 3 of Graphics and draw a line. Insert a blank keyframe (F7) in frame 4 of Graphics and draw a square. All three shapes should reside within the confines of the other layer's box. The result should look like Figure 23.8.

FIGURE 23.8

The Movie Clip you build has three frames with the three shapes.

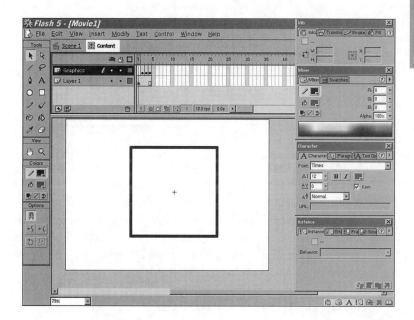

4. In the first frame of the Content Movie Clip, insert a Stop action (it doesn't matter which layer).

5. Return to the main scene and select the clip. Using the Instance panel, give it an instance name of "theContent".

6. Draw a rectangle. Select the rectangle and select Insert, Convert to Symbol. Call it "MyButton" and make sure it's a button.

7. Copy and paste two more instances of MyButton. You can create text blocks to cover each button with the labels "Circle", "Line", and "Square", respectively.

8. Select the button for "Circle" and insert an evaluate Action with the following expression: `theContent.gotoAndStop(2)`. Make sure the uppercase/lowercase matches what is shown. (Incidentally, we could have used the with Action, but since we're only doing one thing—going to a frame—using this one-liner is simpler.)

9. Test the movie. It should work for the Circle button only. Now attach an evaluate Action on the Line button that says `theContent.gotoAndStop(3)`. The Square button should say `theContent.gotoAndStop(4)`.

10. You can enhance the usability of this design by drawing a highlight (such as a non-filled circle) around the currently selected button. Although there are many solutions to this, one way would be to just draw the highlight in frames 2, 3, and 4 of the Content clip.

FIGURE 23.9
Circle, Line, Square is a classic exercise to keep revisiting. Here, a highlight shows the current selection.

Debugging

Hunting down and fixing bugs in your code can be a lot of work. At the time you created the faulty script, you fully intended for it to work, you thought it would work, and you wrote it in a way that made sense to you. Fixing bugs is difficult because it means something you wrote isn't right. If you simply step through your scripts, it is easy to make the same mistakes over again. Luckily, some Flash features and established techniques are available that should help you with the debugging process.

Old-Fashioned Methods

In addition to the brute-force method of simply stepping through a script, there are two simple ways you can find bugs. Often, you might have a script for a button, Movie Clip, or frame that you really think *should* work. The first step is to confirm that the script is even being reached. You can place a Trace action in your script to prove the script is being executed. It's similar to the way you put a message in dynamic text back in Hour 11, but this way is a little quicker. You'll give this method a try in the following task.

Task: Use the Trace Action to Confirm a Script Is Working

This Task simply tests the Trace action. Here are the steps to follow:

1. In a new movie, draw a circle, convert it to a symbol named "Circle", and leave it as a Movie Clip. Give the instance onstage the instance name "ball" via the Instance panel.

2. In the first frame, insert an Evaluate action (Esc, E, V) and then type **ball._x=_xmouse**.

3. Test the movie. You might expect the ball's x property to move as you move the mouse, but it doesn't.

4. Back in the first frame, insert the Trace action and type **moved it** in the Message parameter. Test the movie, and you should see the output window pop up with your message from the Trace action. However, the problem is that you want the ball's _x property to keep changing as the movie plays, but it only happens once (like the Trace function).

5. In the movie, insert a frame at frame 2 (click frame 2 and press F5). Now when you test the movie, you'll see the "moved it" text appear repeatedly in the output window. Actually, when Trace is used in this manner, it becomes distracting, but at least this time you solved the problem.

By the way, you can use Trace to display expressions. For instance, the Trace message could be a combination of characters and numbers. For example, trace("the mouse is at " + _xmouse) will show in the output window "the mouse is at 123.5" (or whatever the mouse position is currently). Just make sure that you click the Expression check box in the Trace action and that you include quotation marks around the string portion of your message (see Figure 23.10).

FIGURE 23.10

The Trace Action's message can be a combination of a string and variable. Just be sure to select the Expression check box on the right.

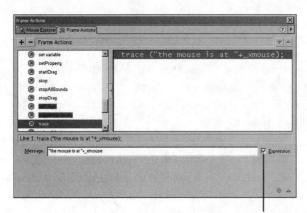

Expression check box

Using the Debugger

Flash's Debugger provides a very convenient way to test your movies. Not only can it fix problems, but it can analyze the movie as it plays. You can find the Debugger under the Window menu, but it only runs while a movie is running in the Flash player.

The following task walks you through a scenario of using the Debugger.

Task: Watch Your Movie with the Debugger

In this Task, you'll use the Debugger to analyze a movie. Here are the steps to follow:

1. Select Help, Samples, Pan Zoom. Then select Control, Debug Movie (Ctrl+Shift+Enter). I have found that sometimes I must close the player (not the Debugger panel), return to the movie, and try Debug Movie a second time before it works right. If your Debugger doesn't have anything listed (like the image on the left side of Figure 23.11), close the .swf file you're testing and try Debug Movie again. Your Debugger should look like the one on right side of Figure 23.11.

FIGURE 23.11

Sometimes the Debugger will appear empty (as shown on the left). Just return to your movie and try Debug Movie again, and you should see something more like the version on the right.

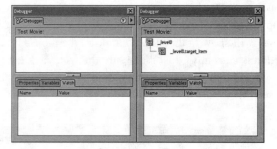

2. In the top area of the Debugger you'll see all the Movie Clips (and any clips inside of clips) used in the file, plus one box for the main movie, labeled _level0. For this movie, just _level0 and the clip _level0.target_item are displayed. Selecting either of these will allow you to investigate the current state of affairs.

3. Click _level0 and then click the tab labeled Properties (see Figure 23.12). You can see all the built-in properties that pertain to the main movie. Only the items in black can be changed by you. Go ahead and double-click 100, in the Value column, next to _xscale. Change this to 200 and notice that, after you click Enter, the entire movie gets wider. (Change this back to 100.)

FIGURE 23.12

When a clip or time-line is selected, the Properties tab displays all the properties of that selection.

4. Click `_level0.target_item` and then set its `_xscale` property to 200. Notice that only the clip changes. (Set it back to 100.)

5. Instead of changing properties from the Debugger, you'll watch them change as the movie plays. Position the Debugger off to the side so that you can see both the Debugger and most of the movie—particularly the flickering clip and the arrow buttons. Make sure that you're still viewing the properties for `_level0.target_item` and that you scroll down to the property `_x`. Watch the value change every time you click either the left or right arrow button in the movie.

6. Properties are built in to Flash. There are only so many, and they're all accessible here. In addition, you may recall that you can create your own custom variables. Click `_level0` and then click the Variables tab. Here, you can view the variables that the author created for this movie (see Figure 23.13).

FIGURE 23.13

The Variables tab displays all user variables present in the selected clip or Timeline.

Just like properties, variables displayed in black can be viewed and changed.

7. Because each variable is unique to each Timeline (almost as if it were a property of each clip instance), it can become tedious to first click the instance (in the top section) and then click each variable you want to monitor. Instead, you can find the variable you want to watch and then select Add Watch. To do this, select _level0, click Variables, and then click once to select x_value (an author-created variable). Now, click the options arrow and select Add Watch. In addition to the blue dot next to x_value, you'll now find that no matter which item you've selected in the top section, when you view the Watch tab, you'll see the current value for the variable in the clip you selected. In this example, there are only two timelines to monitor (the main Timeline and the clip instance's Timeline). In situations when you have many instances, you'll find the Watch feature valuable.

The Debugger is very interesting. You can watch properties and variables, or you can change them. What's really amazing about the Debugger is that you can use it on files you've already uploaded! You must first specify in the Publish settings (Flash tab) the movie in which you want "Debugging Permitted" and then, optionally, provide a password. Next, set the Debugger panel to Enable Remote Debugging via the options arrow (see Figure 23.14). While you're watching the published version of your movie, you'll be able to right-click and select Debugger. By the way, this will be gray if the movie was exported without Debugging Permitted. Additionally, users who've only downloaded the Flash player (that is, they didn't purchase Flash) won't even see the Debugger option listed. All this means is that, if you prepare for it, you can debug movies that are already online.

FIGURE 23.14

The Debugger can be used with finished .swf files on Web sites if the author has selected Debugging Permitted and your debugger is set to Enable Remote Debugging.

Summary

It may seem strange that near the end of this book we discuss how to learn Flash. You have really only started learning about Flash, and I'm confident you'll continue to learn more. If, after reading this book, you stop learning, I will have failed.

In this hour you learned ways to keep growing in your knowledge of Flash. Snooping through sample files is a decent way to do this. Breaking tasks down into steps is a good way to learn and keep from going too far in the wrong direction. Knowing how to face inevitable problems is more important than trying to avoid them because you *will* confront problems. Of course, you want to try to avoid problems, but they'll still crop up. Hunting down bugs is a matter of identifying a problem and then carefully breaking it down into pieces. This hour looked at the Debugger as a way to identify the current state of each and every clip in your movies.

23

Q&A

Q I've copied and pasted every item from a sample file into my file, and it still doesn't work. What could be wrong?

A Most likely you didn't copy every last attribute. In a way, it's good that you have to hunt down the problem. If you simply intended to extract everything from the file, you should review the information from last hour regarding maintaining integrity. However, the only possible cause of problems if you indeed did copy everything is either that the sample movie sends and receives data from a database to which you're not connected (through the Load Variables action or an XML object), or that it's trying to run Load Movie, which doesn't exist. Try typing those actions in the Movie Explorer's Find field. Just remember to clear that field and click Enter again to view everything.

Q When breaking a task down, is it really necessary to break it into tiny steps?

A The smaller, the better! As mentioned, while you work on one task, you can keep in mind the tasks that will come later—even the pros can only do one thing at a time. Do you think a good marathon runner can take just 10 steps to finish a race if he's really good? Of course not—and programming is the same in that you need to take it one step at a time.

Workshop

The Workshop consists of quiz questions and answers to help you solidify your understanding of the material covered. Try to answer the questions before checking the answers.

Quiz

1. To ensure no bugs exist in your movie, you should always run the Debugger before publishing.

   A. False. You need to run the Debugger after each change to prevent bugs.

   B. True. As long as you don't make any changes after running the Debugger, your movie will be free of bugs.

   C. False. The Debugger doesn't prevent bugs. It only lets you view the properties and variables contained in your movie.

2. You build a project one task at a time so you can check your work as you go.

   A. True. There may be other reasons as well, but the idea is to get one thing working before you start something else.

   B. False. Working on one task at a time makes your file smaller, and that's the only reason to work this way.

   C. True. Although this is one reason, the main reason is that your Flash movie will play faster on the end user's machine.

3. Debugging someone else's work online is a great way to learn.

   A. It could be, but only files that have been exported with Debugging Permitted will allow for this.

   B. False. Besides, it's illegal.

   C. True. The first thing you should do is figure out how you can snoop through other people's files in this manner.

Quiz Answers

1. C. The Debugger only provides information; it does not "debug" your movie.

2. A. If, in contrast, you implement two tasks and find neither works, it's difficult to track down the problem. Building in small steps can help.

3. A. Keep in mind that only files exported with Flash 5 have the potential of allowing debugging. Because this is not the default, you'll have a hard time finding many files to debug. Plus, the author could have included a password requirement on the file, so this is practically a nonissue.

Exercise

Here's a better way to make a clip follow the cursor (which will effectively create a custom cursor). In the first frame of your movie, insert the Mouse hide Action (found in the Objects, Mouse, section of the Toolbox list). This will hide the user's mouse cursor.

Create a Movie Clip that will act as the new cursor (it could contain a graphic of a hand, for example). Select the clip and open the Actions panel. Insert an Evaluate action and type **_x=_root._xmouse**. Insert another Evaluate action **_y=_root._ymouse**. Since Actions attached to clips are always inside a clip event, select the first line and change the event (in the parameters area) to Mouse move. Test the movie and you'll see that it will be a bit choppy. You can solve this without increasing the frame rate. Leave the frame rate at the default 12fps. Return to the Actions attached to the clip and insert another Evaluate action at the end, **updateAfterEvent()**. (Make sure you type the upper-case and lowercase exactly as shown.) The updateAfterEvent function will cause the screen to refresh any time this event (the mouse move) happens.

23

HOUR 24

Publishing Your Creation

The final step in any Flash production is publishing. In Hour 17, "Linking Your Movie to the Web," you learned the minimum steps required for publishing, but that was just to quickly get your movies to play in a browser. There's a lot more that Publish can do. In addition to exporting an .swf file and the corresponding HTML file, you can export other media types, such as RealPlayer and QuickTime, plus traditional formats, such as GIF and JPG. All these formats will be discussed.

In this hour you will

- Explore all the publish settings
- Use the templates to publish variations on the default formats
- Publish other media types, such as QuickTime videos

How to Publish

As you'll recall from Hour 17, publishing is as easy as selecting File, Publish. In practice, however, you'll want to first save your files in a known folder and then step trough all the publish settings. You might even want to use Publish Preview as a test and then choose Publish. The following task steps you through a scenario using Publish.

Task: Set Up the Publish Settings and Then Publish a Movie

This Task walks you through using the Publish Settings dialog box. Here are the steps to follow:

1. Either open a movie you've created in the past or create a simple animation. Make sure there's some visual change—maybe a Movie Clip tweens across the screen.

2. Select File, Save As and save this file in a new folder that contains no other files.

3. Select File, Publish Settings. Note that any changes you make in the Publish Settings dialog box will be saved with this file. (That is, you won't be changing the default publish settings.)

4. Select the Formats tab so you can specify which formats will be exported. For every format you select, an additional tab will appear (see Figure 24.1). Each option will be covered in depth later. For now, select Flash, HTML, and GIF. Notice that because the Use Default Names option is selected, each file has the same name as your source file (with a different extension). You can override this setting, but it's probably easiest to leave it—you can always rename files on your hard drive before uploading.

FIGURE 24.1

The Formats tab of Publish Settings allows you to specify which file formats you plan to export.

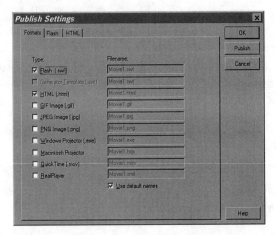

5. Click the Flash tab and take a quick look at the Version option. Which setting you choose for this option is subjective. For this task, suppose you want your movie to work for users who have the Flash 4 plug-in or later. Change the Version drop-down list's setting to Flash 4, as shown in Figure 24.2.

FIGURE 24.2

You can ensure your movie will work with older Flash Players by changing the Version setting from the Flash tab.

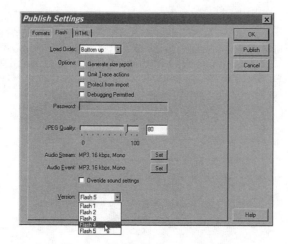

6. Click the HTML tab. From here, you can make some adjustments to the HTML that Flash will create. From the Template drop-down list, select Ad 4 Banner. This particular template will display your Flash movie only if the user has the Flash 4 player installed. Alternatively, users will see a GIF version of the same movie. You can create your own templates (or modify these), as you'll see later this hour.

7. Set the Dimensions option to Percent and then type **100** in both the Width and Height fields. You can come back and make changes to any of these settings. For now, just make sure the check boxes Loop and Display Menu are unchecked. (Unchecking Display Menu prevents users from seeing the extended options when right-clicking your movie.)

8. Click the GIF tab to specify the GIF settings. There are a few things you should note here. For instance, the accompanying GIF that Flash will be exporting can only be an explicit number of pixels because GIF files don't scale like Flash files do. Also, provided your movie has multiple frames, you can select to export an animated GIF. Go ahead and select Animated (and leave Loop Continuously selected). The rest of the options relate to how the image is created. GIF files always have 256 or fewer explicit colors. Flash has to be told exactly how to deal with this fact. Each option has a corresponding visual result that, depending on the nature of the image, will have a positive or negative effect on image quality.

9. Now that you've gone through all the tabs (for the formats you selected), click OK. (The publish settings are saved.) Now, select File, Publish. It may not seem like anything has happened, but all your files have been exported into the folder where the source file resides. Go into that folder and double-click the HTML file. If you have the Flash 4 plug-in (or later), you should be able to play your movie.

24

If you happen to be using a Flash 5–only feature, you'll see a message explaining the issue when you export the movie. If you do plan to export Flash 4 movies, remember to always change the publish settings (under the Flash tab) to Flash 4 before you start. This way, all the Flash 5 features that are "off limits" are highlighted yellow in the Actions panel, as shown in Figure 24.3, and you'll therefore know which features to avoid.

FIGURE 24.3
When you specify an older version of Flash for export, all the unavailable actions for that version are highlighted yellow.

Unsupported actions are highlighted

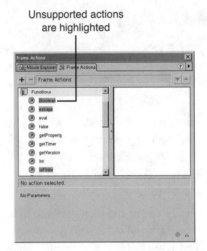

Compared to Test Movie, this was a lot of work. Realize, though, that you get to step through each detail and decide how it should be published. By the way, File, Publish Preview (F12) is the same as Publish, except immediately following the export process your default browser is launched with the HTML file.

The preceding task walked you through each tab, and you made changes as you went. This is the typical approach. Although you may not choose the exact same settings in real life as you did in the task, the process is the same. After a few more details about this particular task, you'll take a look at all the different options (in the section "Selecting Publish Options"). The point is, this was just an exercise. The options chosen are not necessarily the ones you'll always want to use.

A couple interesting things happened behind the scenes in the task you just completed. For instance, the Ad 4 Banner template created a fairly sophisticated HTML document. If the users have the Flash Player, they'll see your movie. If they don't have Flash, they'll see the GIF file instead. Open the HTML document in a text editor and see if you can find the two references to Flash version 4 (one for Netscape and one for Microsoft Internet Explorer). At the end of line 17, you should see >= 4;, and in line 23 you should see `ShockwaveFlash.ShockwaveFlash.4`. You can simulate what users without the plug-in will see if you change both occurrences of 4 to 6. These changes will cause the code to look for version 6 (which doesn't exist yet). This is easier than uninstalling the Flash Player from your browser. When you fool the HTML into thinking you don't have the proper version installed, you'll see the GIF.

> Although changing the HTML will simulate the experience users without the Flash Player will have, this is only a simulation. Ultimately, you'll need to uninstall the Flash Player to most accurately experience what your user will experience. For example, there are other templates that *should* auto-install the player. You'll have to make sure the player is first uninstalled to test this. Macromedia has two technotes that will instruct you on the process of uninstalling the player. From www.macromedia.com, simply search for either technote article number 12727 or 14157 (just type these numbers into the search field at Macromedia.com).

24

Another really powerful aspect of this template is how you can include buttons in your Flash movie. Go ahead and add a button in a new layer of your movie and place the Get URL action on that button (of course, you'll need to provide a URL parameter, as you did in Hour 17). Now when you publish the movie, the HTML will give users without the Flash Player a way to click the GIF! This is a standard HTML feature (called an *image map*), and this particular template creates one for you. Of course, you'll have to change the HTML or remove your Flash plug-in to see the effect, as you did earlier.

Other templates are available in the HTML tab. These correspond to files installed in the HTML folder adjacent to your installed version of Flash 5. You can add to these templates by making your own templates or downloading others. It takes some knowledge of HTML, but instructions are available in the help file "Using Flash," where you'll find "Publishing and Exporting" and then a section titled "Customizing HTML Publishing Templates." (You can also just search "Using Flash" for the section by name.)

You can make minor adjustments to the built-in templates rather easily. We'll do one now.

Task: Customize a Template

In this Task we improve upon one of the built-in templates by removing the natural padding around your Flash movie.

1. Create a movie that includes an animation of a clip instance of a box moving from the top left corner of the Stage to the bottom left corner. Use the Align panel's To Stage option to align the box to the edge of the Stage in both keyframes.

2. Select File, Publish Settings and choose both HTML and Flash. From the HTML tab, select the Template "Flash Only (Default)". Click OK.

3. Press F12 to do a Publish Preview. Notice the square doesn't actually reach the left edge of your browser.

4. Close the browser. Save the movie then close Flash. Next to your installed version of Flash (in Windows, c:\Program Files\Macromedia\Flash 5), you should notice a folder called HTML. Inside this folder copy and paste the file "Default.html".

5. Rename the copied file "myDefault.html" and then open it in a text editor such as Notepad.

6. Change the very first line from $TTFlash Only (Default) to read $TTNo Padding. This will change the template name to No Padding. Just make sure you retain the first three characters.

7. Change the ninth line from <BODY bgcolor="$BG"> to read <BODY bgcolor="$BG" topmargin="0" leftmargin="0" marginwidth="0" marginheight="0">. This changes all the margins to 0 pixels wide.

8. Save and close this file. Restart Flash and open the movie you created earlier this task.

9. Select File, Publish Settings. From the Template dropdown in the HTML tab select the template we just created: "No Padding". Click OK.

10. Press F12 and you should see a preview—this time, with no padding around the movie.

You can make more significant changes to the templates, though you should probably modify the ones provided (as we did) rather than building one from scratch.

Selecting Publishing Options

You can select any options you want when publishing. There's no correct set of options—each case is different. The task you just completed stepped you through the thought process for one possible situation. As you take a look at all the options, you'll become familiar with the range of possibilities. Therefore, the next time you publish something, you should be able to decide for yourself which options to select.

Deciding Which Media Types to Publish

Comparing the different media types available in the Publish Settings dialog box's Formats tab is really a case of comparing apples to oranges. You can export a JPG image or you can export a QuickTime movie. The former is a static image, and the latter is a digital video. This encompasses quite a range of options, making a comparison difficult.

The only two comparable media types are JPG and PNG because they are both static image types. Therefore, instead of comparing the media types, each will be covered individually.

Flash (.swf)

This is the format you'll likely choose every time. It's the reason why you're reading this book—to make scalable vector animations that play well over the Internet. If there's one disadvantage to using this option, it would be the fact that a few potential users don't have the required (but free) Flash Player.

You'll find some interesting options in the Flash tab (see Figure 24.4). Load order affects in what order the layers appear as the movie downloads. Bottom Up, for example, will cause the lower layers to become visible first. In reality, many users won't notice a difference because it only affects the first frame and only becomes apparent on slow connections. Generate Size Report exports a text file that contains the same information we learned when using the Bandwidth Profiler in Hour 20, "Optimizing Your Flash Site." You should also recall, when you're testing a movie that includes the Trace action (as you did last hour), the output window appears with a message parameter you provide. Omit Trace actions won't make any difference if you play the movie in a Web browser because Trace has no effect in a browser. The output window will only pop up in the standalone Flash Player (not a browser). You can prevent this from occurring with the Omit Trace Actions option. The Protect from Import option prevents others from importing the .swf file into their own Flash files. Keep in mind that the .swf file you post on your Website does download to every user's machine (in a folder such as Temporary Internet Files in the Windows folder, for example). In my opinion, the Protect from Import option has limited value. First, when someone imports an .swf file, each frame is imported as a separate keyframe. No ActionScript is retained. Second, just because some users import your file doesn't mean they're allowed to use it. Anyway, you can prevent this from happening. (In the previous hour, the debugging options were discussed.)

FIGURE 24.4

The Flash tab of the Publish Settings dialog box contains all the export settings for the .swf file you're publishing.

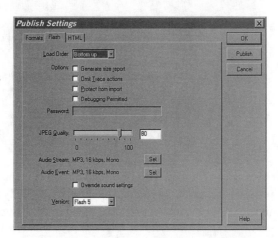

The default compression for both raster graphics and audio can be specified (as discussed in Hours 20, "Optimizing Your Flash Site," and 10, "Including Sound in Your Animation," respectively). You can override compression settings made for individual sounds if you check the Override Sound Settings option.

Finally, unlike most publish settings, which are chosen as the last step, the choice of which version of Flash to export is one you should decide on early in a project. First of all, you can export Flash version 5, and your movie will play in the Flash 4 player; however, any new (previously unsupported) features will fail to execute. If you're not taking advantage of any Flash 5 features, your movie will play fine. If you change this setting to Flash 4 and simply do a Test Movie, you'll see a report of any unsupported features you've included. This is a nice feature because you can fix these problems. However, instead of fixing problems after they're created, you can set the Flash Version option as the first step in a project. This way, as you build, all the unsupported actions will appear in yellow (as you saw earlier in Figure 24.3).

HTML

Although this tab has been discussed several times already, there's additional information you'll find valuable (see Figure 24.5). First of all, realize that every setting in this tab (except for Device Fonts) affects only the HTML file. You can always open the HTML file in a text editor and make edits manually. If nothing else, the Publish Settings dialog box gives you a way to learn all the HTML settings available. To learn them, all you need to do is look at the corresponding HTML files created.

FIGURE 24.5

The HTML tab of Publish Settings contains options, including which HTML template you want to use.

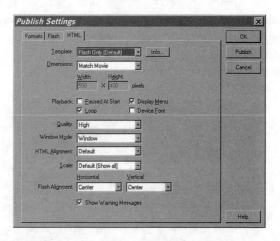

Normally, your users can right-click your movie to display a menu, like the one shown in Figure 24.6 (on the Macintosh, they would Control-click). Only a minimized version of this menu will appear if you deselect Display Menu in the Playback options of the

HTML tab. This menu isn't actually removed; it's just a lot shorter. Keep in mind that the "Debugger" line only appears for users who happen to have Flash installed.

FIGURE 24.6

The menu that appears when a user right-clicks your movie (as shown on the left) can be reduced to the version on the right.

The Device Font check box in the Playback options allows you to globally force the Flash file to use the device font option on all text in the movie. Because this setting actually changes the .swf file, it would make more sense to appear under the Flash tab. As you recall from Hour 15, "ActionScripting Applications for Advanced Interactivity," Device Font will substitute a standard font from the user's machine instead of including the font information in the .swf file, thus making the file a little smaller. However, device font text won't be anti-aliased. When the text is very small, this is desirable, but the resulting rough edges is probably unacceptable for larger text (as you can see in Figure 24.7). However, for small text this the resulting jagged text is actually desirable. In Figure 24.7 you can see small text with anti-aliasing looks fuzzy. Remember, you can set this option individually per block of text from the Text Options panel—doing it here in Publish Settings overrides the individual settings. Also, realize that this option only affects movies viewed on Windows. Macintosh users will not be affected.

24

FIGURE 24.7

Device Font removes the anti-alias effect that's normally desirable, but not when the text appears small.

> # This is regular
> # This is device
> # font...
>
> This is regular... but since it's small, it's hard to read...
> This is device font but it's probably easier to read...

Windows Mode only applies to movies viewed on Windows and through Internet Explorer version 4 or later. Although this is a large audience, it is limited. Also, the other settings in this drop-down list—Opaque Windowless and Transparent Windowless—only affect HTML pages that have elements in layers. As if this weren't enough, the performance drops for these options. Feel free to explore these options, but I'd recommend leaving the default, Window.

Finally, you should always select Show Warning Messages because this will prompt you concerning incompatibility issues every time you publish. For example, if you use select Ad Flash 5 Banner, but then from the Flash tab you select Version Flash 4, you will see a warning dialog box. Because the user never sees this, you should always leave this option set.

GIF, JPG, and PNG

With the exception of GIF, these are all static image formats. (GIF has a sister format called *animated GIF* that is, in fact, an animation format.) All three have their own unique attributes. GIF files always have 256 or fewer discrete colors and tend to be most appropriate for geometric images. JPG is best for photographic or continuous-tone images. JPG can also withstand significant compression with acceptable quality loss. PNG is a high-quality image format that allows for additional types of information to be included. For example, a PNG file created in Macromedia Fireworks has additional options, such as layers and shadow effects. Despite some discussion in the past, PNG does not appear to be a Web standard. However, when you want to export the best-quality image, PNG is a good choice—just don't expect a small file size.

When it comes to Web delivery, your decision for static images is between JPG and GIF. Realize that the question as to which static format to use only arises when you attempt to deliver an alternative image to those users who don't have the Flash Player. For example, every Flash project I've worked on has provided no alternative. The users need the Flash Player; otherwise, they can't see the site—it's that simple.

When you want to provide an alternative to those without the Flash Player (as you did in the first task), you'll need to decide between JPG and GIF. Your decision is based on the nature of the image. Remember, though, that it's not the whole movie that's used; it's only one frame of the movie that you get to use for such static formats. Flash will, by default, use the first frame of your movie for any static image format. The movie's first frame, though, could be entirely black. In order to specify a different frame, simply open the Frame panel and create a label in the chosen frame called #static. It's best to insert a new layer and then a keyframe exactly where you want this label, as shown in Figure 24.8, but this is a relatively simple way to tell Flash which frame to export.

FIGURE 24.8

Labeling a frame with #static *will tell Flash you want this frame to be used (instead of frame 1) when publishing a static image.*

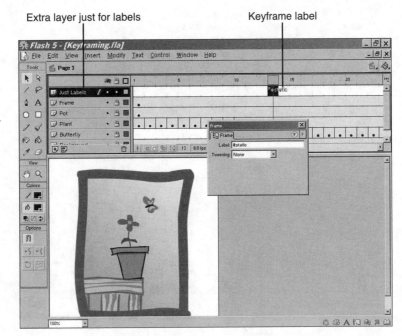

Once you've decided which frame to use, you can decide (based on the contents of that frame) which format to use—GIF or JPG. Remember, photorealistic images are best in JPG format, and geometric shapes in GIF format.

PNG may seem like a useless format since the files are large and browsers don't really support it—but there is some value. Of course you can import PNG files as we saw in Hour 3, "Importing Graphics into Flash," but here we're talking about exporting. If you want to export the highest quality possible, you should use PNG. There may be several reasons to do this. For instance, even though the options available for exporting a GIF file from Flash are extensive, previewing the effects of every slight change is a tedious process of trial and error. You have to make a change, publish, and then view the results. Frankly, there are better tools to create GIF files (as well as JPG files, although this is not quite as obvious). Macromedia Fireworks, for example, lets you change all the output options for a GIF file while watching the image quality change (see Figure 24.9). This fact alone may make the extra steps you're about to learn worth the effort. For the most control over the GIF file you're creating, first use Flash to export a 24-bit PNG file (the export options for PNG are shown in Figure 24.10). Then open that PNG file in another image-editing tool (such as Fireworks) and export the GIF file. You can still use Flash's Publish feature to create the GIF and HTML files—but simply replace the GIF file Flash creates with one you create using a more suitable tool.

FIGURE 24.9

Fireworks is a much better tool than Flash to create static graphics (such as GIFs).

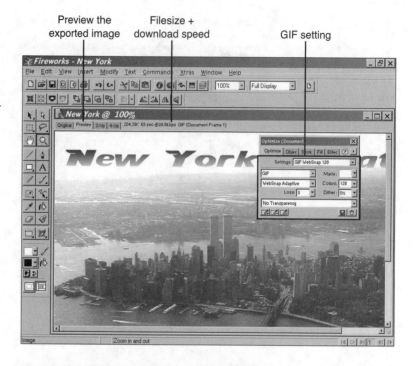

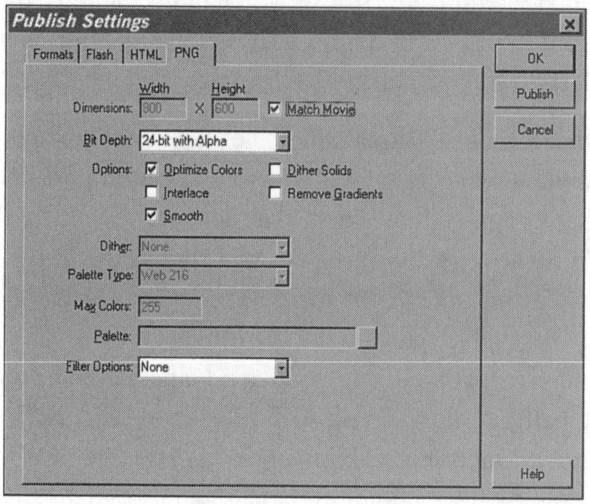

Preview the exported image   Filesize + download speed   GIF setting

FIGURE 24.10

Exporting a PNG file will give you the best-quality static image.

The choice between JPG and GIF might be moot if you want to supply animation to your users who don't have the Flash Player. Only GIF has the Animated Playback option (see Figure 24.11). You have several options when creating an animated GIF. Most are self-explanatory. You won't notice, however, an option to specify the first and last frames—Flash will simply use the first and last frames of your movie. To override this, just label the frame you want to be used first as #first and the last frame as #last. Also, if you'll recall from a previous task, you can let Flash create the HTML image map to be used with your static (or animated) GIF. Flash will create that image map (with all the clickable areas) based on all the buttons that happen to be onscreen in the last frame of your movie. However, you might not have any buttons in the last frame! Just like you can specify which frame is used for static images, you can specify for which frame you want the onscreen buttons to be used in the creation of the image map. Simply label the frame #map. That's it.

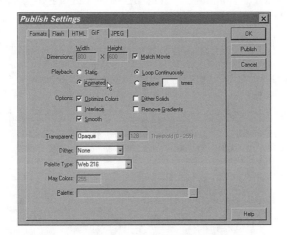

FIGURE 24.11

Of all the traditionally static image formats, only GIF provides the Animated option.

24

Windows Projector and Macintosh Projector

If you put your .swf file in a Web page, users just need the Flash Player to view it. When you installed Flash, it installed the Flash Player, so you can simply double-click any .swf file on your computer and it will run. If you want to send this file to someone (that is, you don't want to publish it in a Web page), you can. The only catch is this: The user has to have the Flash Player installed.

Alternatively, you can create a Projector, which is a standalone executable. Think of a Projector as a modified version of the Flash Player that will only play the .swf file you specify. One way to make a standalone Projector is to open an .swf file with the Flash Player (just double-click an .swf file on your computer). Select File, Create a Projector and then name the file you'd like to create. That's all there is to it. One catch is that your .swf file grows by about 350KB when you convert it to a projector. That's the size of the Flash Player (which you're including in the Projector). The other catch is that the Projector you just made will only run on the platform you're using (Windows or Macintosh). .swf files work on any platform because the user already has the Flash Player unique to that platform installed. Because Projectors have the platform-specific player built in, they can only be played on that platform.

To create a Projector for whichever platform you're not using—Windows or Macintosh—you could repeat the steps just listed on a computer using the target platform. However, you don't have to do this. From the Formats tab of Publish Settings, you can specify for which platforms you want the Projector made (see Figure 24.12). The Projector file that Flash creates can be sent to whomever you want. If you're sending a file from Windows to Macintosh, Flash saves the Projector in a compressed and "bin-hexed" format. Bin-hexing is necessary to allow you to send the file to a Macintosh computer via email (or other method). The Macintosh user must decode the bin-hexed file using software such as Aladdin System's freeware StuffIt Expander for Mac (available at `www.aladdinsys.com`).

FIGURE 24.12

Standalone Projectors can be exported when you publish for both Macintosh and Windows.

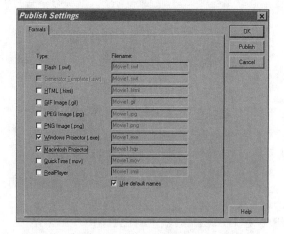

Projectors provide a nice way to use Flash for standalone applications. For example, you might be making a presentation to an audience and want to use Flash to create the "slides." Obviously, you can add a lot of spice to your presentations. The action FSCommand is designed for this purpose. The parameters for FSCommand include FullScreen, Quit, and many others (as you can see in Figure 24.13). For example, you can put an action `fscommand ("fullscreen", "true")` in the very first frame to make your projector fill the screen. Then, in the last frame, you can place a button with the action `fscommand ("quit")` so that you have a way to exit.

Although Projectors are more difficult to distribute than simply posting a Website, they work great for presentations. A lot of people create portfolios of their work that they distribute via CD-ROM. They can include lots of uncompressed audio and high-quality images, for example, and there's no download issues. Just remember that if you use the FullScreen option of FSCommand, you need to give your users an obvious Quit button, too.

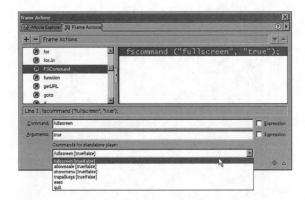

FIGURE 24.13

The FSCommand action includes options to affect standalone Projectors.

QuickTime and RealPlayer

These two options are very exciting. However, fully exploring them is beyond the scope of this hour. The first thing you must realize is this: Flash cannot play video! However, Flash can export to several video formats. Both Apple's QuickTime video player and RealNetworks' RealPlayer allow for a layer of Flash to play on top of their own video formats. Although this is a simplification, consider how a video has multiple tracks—a video track and two tracks of audio (for stereo), for a total of three tracks. You can think of Flash as just another track that can play in sync with the video.

The QuickTime option is really amazing. You can create a QuickTime movie with a special "Flash track," which includes buttons in your Flash movie with the GoTo action so that user can jump to any portion of your movie! However, like most things, there are limitations. QuickTime 4 can only support the Flash track Flash version 3 (so consider first setting the publish setting for Flash to version 3). QuickTime 5 will also support Flash 4. Also, while authoring, you won't hear the sound track for the video. These seemingly funky limitations aside, it's really easy to make a QuickTime video that has an interactive layer of Flash. First, you import a QuickTime video, giving it room in the timeline to play by inserting frames (it will be attached to the main timeline, like a Graphic symbol). Then, in another layer, place two buttons (you can even use the Effect panel to lower the Alpha setting of the buttons so that the movie will show through). Put a simple Stop action on one button and a Play action on the other. Then publish the video (making sure you've selected the QuickTime format option). There are a few more settings you can specify from the QuickTime tab, as shown in Figure 24.14, but most of these are self-explanatory. Just remember, you're exporting a QuickTime video with a Flash layer, not a Flash movie.

24

FIGURE 24.14

The QuickTime tab of Publish Settings provides many details to control an exported QuickTime video.

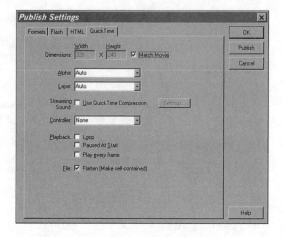

In the case of RealMedia, there's another set of version rules: Flash 2 is widely supported in RealPlayer, but for Flash 3 and 4, you must use RealPlayer 8 (and to stream, RealServer 8). Once you get past these limitations, the RealPlayer tab in Publish Settings makes it a snap to produce all the components to serve RealMedia with Flash (see Figure 24.15). Delivering RealMedia with Flash to your website involves uploading an HTML file in addition to both an .swf and rm file. When you publish a project, you'll find Flash exports an .swf, rm (RealMedia sound file), and SMIL (Synchronized Multimedia Integration Language) file. To learn more about this topic, start by using a text editor to open the SMIL file that's created when you publish with RealMedia. It's equivalent to the HTML file that's published, but the SMIL format (pronounced *smile*) includes tags that specify attributes of the .swf and rm files.

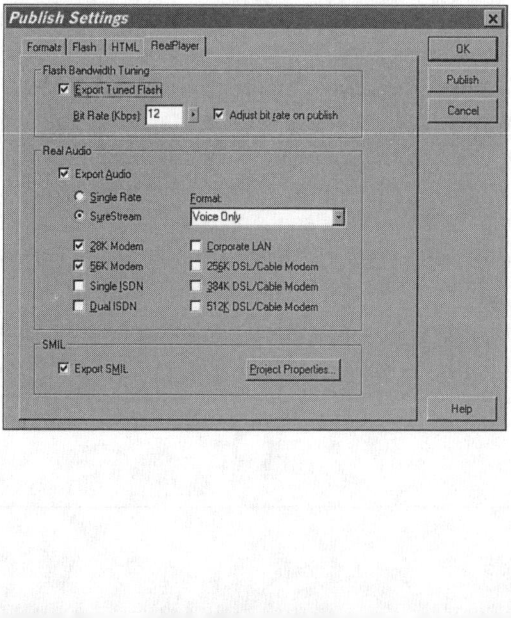

FIGURE 24.15

RealPlayer files can be published, including the "tuned" .swf, RM (RealMedia), and SMIL files necessary.

Once you understand the limits of Flash in QuickTime and Flash in RealMedia, you can deliver some very impressive movies. Remember that unlike animation, video can contain perfectly synchronized audio and images—including people talking. Video is a good choice for teaching and motivating users.

Exporting Other Media Types

Believe it or not, Flash can export even more media types than those listed in the Publish Settings dialog box. Just select File, Export Movie and you'll see a list under Save As Type that's quite long (see Figure 24.16). In addition to the formats listed in Publish Settings, you may see others that interest you. This section covers two formats you might find particularly useful.

FIGURE 24.16

All the formats Flash can export (including those found in Publish Settings) are listed in the Export Movie dialog box.

24

AVI

AVI is another digital video format. Although QuickTime has distinct advantages over AVI (the Flash track for one), if you wish, you can export an AVI file from Flash. There are a few technical details you need to be familiar with (such as compression), but the overall process is pretty straightforward. One thing that's important to realize from the start, however, is that when you're exporting an AVI, Movie Clips won't play. Use Graphic symbols only. (Of course, buttons and actions won't work either because AVI is a noninteractive animation format.)

Image Sequences

Available only from the File, Export Movie menu is a selection of image sequences. A bitmap sequence, for example, will export a static BMP file of each frame in your movie. Several sequence formats are available (as you saw in Figure 24.16). They're all basically the same—only the file format varies. The process is the same for each format. You select File, Export Movie, select the file format, and then name the file. The name you give will be used only as the prefix. That is, if you name the file *myMovie*, the file-name containing frame 1 will be called `myMovie0001.bmp` (or whatever file extension matches the type you're exporting). After you name the file and click Save, you'll be shown a dialog box to specify the details for the selected file type. It's sort of a mini version of the Publish tab. For bitmap sequences, you have to specify details for bitmaps, for example.

You may be intending to create an animation in another software package that can import sequences of static images. For example, if you have an animated GIF–creation tool, you could import a sequence of high-quality bitmaps that Flash exported. You could also use the static images from a QuickTime video inside Flash. Because you can't actually use QuickTime video in an .swf file, you could first import a QuickTime video into Flash, export a sequence of high-quality BMP files, and then delete the QuickTime video from your Flash file and import the BMP files into Flash. What's really convenient is that the numbered BMP files that Flash created upon export will be imported sequentially and placed in separate keyframes, thus saving you what would otherwise be a painstaking task of importing many individual frames.

Similarly to exporting AVI files, when you export image sequences, you can't use Movie Clips (they just don't animate). Obviously, audio won't have any effect either because you're exporting images only. This may seem like the least likely use for Flash; however, you should realize that anytime you see something that *looks* like video in Flash, you're probably just watching a sequence of static images.

Summary

This hour discussed all the common ways to export Flash movies. Other, less traditional applications, such as using Projectors, static images, QuickTime video, and image sequences, were also discussed.

For the traditional .swf in HTML option, Publish gives you a nice interface to select options; then Flash actually creates the files for you. Templates can include code to optionally supply users with an alternative image. Also, other options under Publish Settings let you specify how such an image will be exported.

Less-traditional applications, such as using Projectors and QuickTime video, can give your Flash movies a life beyond the normal Web page application. Some of these technologies are on the edge of innovation, and now you have a better idea where you can take Flash!

Q&A

Q I know I've seen video in Flash. How can I include a QuickTime video in my Flash movie?

A You can't. There are lots of ways to create a nice effect, but if you import a QuickTime video into Flash, you cannot export an .swf file. You can only export a QuickTime video (with a layer of Flash), but it needs to play in the QuickTime player. You can also export a sequence of images (which can be reimported), but realize that you won't get synchronized audio. Likely what you've seen inside Flash is a sequence of static images. Other possible solutions include using Flash's GetURL action to launch another Web page (or window) containing a video. Also, you could put the video in one frame of your HTML and Flash in another. Many other solutions may solve your objective, but Flash 5 doesn't support QuickTime in .swf files. (You can send requests for this feature to be included in later revisions of Flash to `wish-flash@macromedia.com`, but you won't be the first.)

Q I'm working with people who have HTML experience, and we're including Flash within some very sophisticated HTML pages. Is it necessary for the HTML people to make customized templates for this project?

A No. It's probably not worth creating a template unless you plan to use it a lot. You can simply export an .swf file and send it to your HTML people, and they can embed it into the Web pages. You could even send them a sample HTML file that Flash's Publish feature created so they can dissect it. Quite often, the HTML will be worked out long before the Flash portion is done. The Flash movie you're making could already have a space waiting in a larger Web page. Instead of using Publish (which could overwrite an HTML file), you can just use File, Export Movie and export the .swf file. Even faster, if you've set your publish settings for Flash the way you want, you can just run Test Movie, and an .swf file will be exported.

Q Now that I know how to publish, I now know everything about Flash, right?

A Not quite. I think it's fair to say you've got the foundation skills to use Flash effectively, but as you learned last hour, you've only really learned how to *learn* Flash. This book isn't exhaustive, though you're probably exhausted. You now need to go out and get your hands dirty. You can revisit this book if necessary, but this is the point where you *start* your Flash career, not end it.

24

Workshop

The Workshop consists of quiz questions and answers to help you solidify your understanding of the material covered. Try to answer the questions before checking the answers.

Quiz

1. What's the best image format for static images?

   A. JPG.

   B. GIF.

   C. It depends.

2. What happens to users who don't have the Flash Player when they visit your site?

   A. Their machine crashes.

   B. It depends how the HTML handles the situation.

   C. The Flash Player is automatically installed and, with the exception of a short delay for downloading, they experience the site like anyone else.

3. Are all the formats that Flash can export visible under the Publish Settings dialog box's Formats tab?

   A. Yes, this is where you specify details for such exported files.

   B. No, Flash will export other types of files. However, you can't control the export details, so they're not listed here.

   C. No, Flash can export other file types from File, Export Movie (and File, Export Image, for that matter).

4. How do you include a QuickTime video in your published .swf file?

   A. You can't.

   B. Just import a QuickTime file using File, Import.

   C. Import the QuickTime file and be sure to select QuickTime from the Formats tab of Publish Settings.

Quiz Answers

1. C. The best quality and smallest file size depends on the nature of the image. Photographic images usually look best in JPG format, and geometric images are better in GIF format. The best way to compare is to test each (and compare file sizes as well).

2. B. Only if the user has a pretty new browser will he upgrade automatically (provided you use the HTML contained in the appropriate template).

3. C. Other export file types are available. The ones in Publish Settings are, generally, just the Web formats.

4. A. Sorry to repeat this, but Flash .swf files don't support QuickTime. You can include separate static images in Flash. You can also include an .swf file in a QuickTime video (which Flash can export). But, alas, there's no QuickTime support in Flash.

Exercises

Take your best work to date and publish it to your Web site. Send the link to me in an email addressed to `flash5@teleport.com`. I'll thank you for reading the book and provide you with some feedback.

24

APPENDIXES

APPENDIX **A**

Shapes You Can Make Using Selection, Snap, and the Canvas Level

This appendix shows you how several shapes can be created using the unique drawing capabilities of Flash. These are just a few examples of how you can sharpen your drawing skills. They are not necessarily the only ways to achieve the desired results.

Flash has unique drawing capabilities that include selection (anything you can see, you can select), Snap, grouping, and the Canvas level. These were all discussed in Hours 2, "Drawing and Painting Original Art in Flash," and 4, "Applied Advanced Drawing Techniques." You'll now explore these capabilities further by using them in practice. Be sure to have Snap turned on.

Semicircle

1. Make sure Snap is on and draw a circle and a vertical line that is much taller than the circle.

2. Double-click the center of the circle (to select the line and the fill) and then click and drag from the center of the circle (so you get the solid ring near your cursor). Snap the center of the circle to the line.

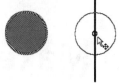

3. Your drawing should now look like the following figure.

4. Click to select just the vertical line at the bottom. Using the arrow keys, nudge the vertical line up.

5. Click away from the line to deselect it. With the Arrow tool, bring your cursor near the top of the line you just moved until you see the cursor type that indicates you'll be dragging the endpoint. Click and start dragging.

6. Don't snap it to the circle. Snap it to the end of the line on top.

7. Click one semicircle to select it. Then delete the fill.

A

8. Click and delete the line portion that corresponds to the fill you just deleted.

9. Click and delete the excess portions of the line.

10. You now have a semicircle!

Spokes on a Wheel

1. Follow the steps for a semicircle through step 6 so that you have a shape that looks like the following.

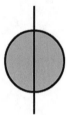

2. Click and delete the fills and the extraneous outside lines.

3. Copy just the vertical line and paste it off to the side.

4. Use the Rotate tool to rotate the line 90 degrees.

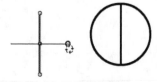

5. Click away from the line (to stop the rotating). Click the line once to select it; then click and drag from the center of the line.

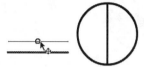

6. Snap your new line to the center of the vertical line.

7. Paste it again for another vertical line—this time just rotate it to the first "snap" (which happens at 15 degrees). Drag this line from its center and snap it to the center of the circle.

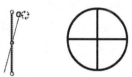

A

8. Continue to increase the rotation on the lines you paste by 15 degrees and snap them to the center of your circle, until it looks like the following figure.

9. Use Shift+click to select all the lines without the circle.

10. Copy and paste the lines off to the side.

11. Select the lines and use the Rotate tool to rotate them 90 degrees.

12. With all the lines selected, you can snap them to the center of the circle.

13. Do you want a quick way to double the spokes used, just like in the previous figure? Just copy and paste the entire "spoked" shape and use Modify, Scale and Rotate… to enter a rotation of exactly 7.5 degrees. Then snap the new image on top of the old one, as shown in the following figure.

Five-Pointed Star

1. Draw a perfectly horizontal line. Then copy and paste it.

2. You'll first make a pentagon (which has five sides). To begin, with the duplicate line selected, access Modify, Transform, Scale and Rotate... (Ctrl+Alt+S). This will open the Scale and Rotate dialog box so that you can specify explicit degrees or percentages. You can figure the inside angle of any shape by dividing 360 (degrees) by the number of lines in the shape. In the case of a pentagon, each inside angle is 72 degrees (360/5 = 72). Therefore, rotate the line 72 degrees.

3. Select the line. Then click and drag the end of the line so that it snaps to the end of your first line.

4. Duplicate the new line.

5. Rotate it by 72 degrees and snap it like before.

A

6. Repeat this process to make a pentagon.

7. Draw a line inside the pentagon that doesn't touch any edges.

8. Grab one endpoint and snap it to the bottom-left corner.

9. Grab the other endpoint and snap it to the top corner.

10. Draw another line in the larger area of the pentagon and connect it to the bottom-right and top corners.

11. After you connect this line, draw a small line in the space shown in the following figure and snap one endpoint to the bottom-right corner.

12. Now, in one motion, drag the other endpoint to the middle-left corner. (If you drag this line partway and stop, it will break where it crosses the other line.)

13. Draw another line in the space shown in the following figure.

A

14. Snap the ends to the middle-left and middle-right corners. As in step 12, if you drag the line partway and stop before snapping it to the corner, the line will break.

15. Draw the last line in the space shown in the following figure.

16. Snap it to the middle-right and bottom-left corners.

17. Remove excess lines.

Oblique Cube

1. Draw a square. Then delete the fill and duplicate it.

2. Move one box on top of the other, positioning it above and to the right.

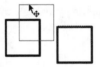

3. Draw four short lines that don't touch either box, as shown in the following figure.

4. Connect one end of one line to a corner of the rear square.

5. Connect the other end of that line to the corresponding corner of the front square.

6. Repeat this process with the second, third, and fourth lines.

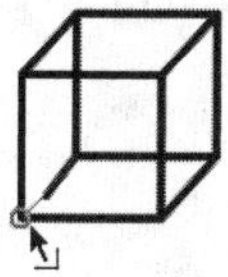

7. If you want a see-through cube, leave the image as is. If not, remove the excess lines, as shown in the following figure. Obviously, if you want a solid cube, the fourth line (the one you removed completely) could have been omitted.

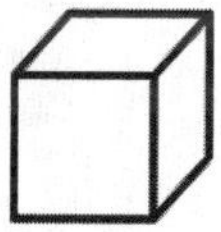

Sine Wave

1. Follow the first six steps in the semicircle exercise to create a circle with a line through it. This time, though, make it a horizontal line.

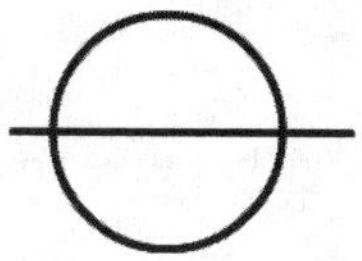

2. Click once to select the bottom half of the circle; then click and drag it away from the line.

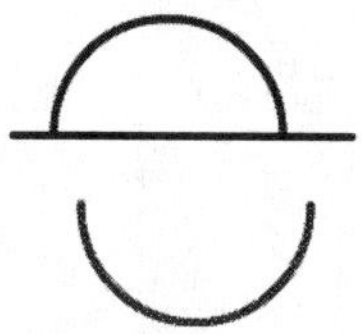

3. Remove the horizontal line.

4. Click once to select the bottom image. Then click and drag from its left endpoint and snap it to the right endpoint of the top image.

5. Copy and paste everything. Then select and drag to extend the cycle. Repeat this process to add as many waves as desired.

6. Once you're finished, you can scale the image however you like.

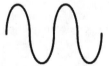

3D Sphere

1. This exercise is really easy—but it looks cool. First, select the Oval tool (no line) and the built-in radial gradation.

2. Draw a circle.

3. Select the Paint Bucket tool and then click the Transform Fill modifier. If you pick up the circle handle in the center of the fill, you can move the center point of the fill up and to the left (where the imaginary light source is on your computer screen).

4. Grab the square handle and move it to the left to change the shape of the radial gradation.

A

5. Grab the bottom circle handle to rotate the shape of the gradation.

6. Grab the circle handle that's between the rotate and shape handles to adjust the fall off.

7. Keep tweaking your image until you've turned the circle into a sphere. Notice that because of the arc in the fall off, the circle has a equator.

Color Wheel

1. You'll first create a triangle. To do this, draw a line and then duplicate it. Rotate the new line by exactly 120 degrees and snap the ends of the two lines together. Now repeat this process with a third line to complete the triangle. Group the triangle so that it doesn't cut away from other shapes when you stack them. Now draw a circle that's noticeably larger than the triangle.

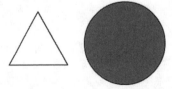

2. Delete the fill of the circle and convert it to a symbol called Hollow.

3. Drag from the middle of the Hollow symbol and snap it to a corner of the triangle. Copy and paste two more Hollows and snap them to the other corners (by grabbing their centers).

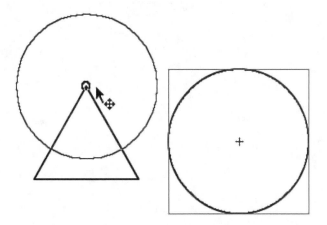

4. Delete the triangle and break apart each Hollow symbol.

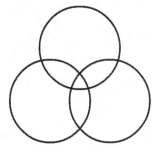

5. Use the Paint Bucket tool to fill in the slices of the image. Then remove the line portions.

APPENDIX B

Advanced ActionScripting

There is so much ActionScript information that if I doubled the length of this book, it wouldn't be enough. Hours 14 through 17 involved some ActionScripting, but this was really just the beginning. This appendix provides an overview of complex scripting.

Basics

You must understand a few basics before you can excel in ActionScripting. Variables and the data types you store in variables are two basics from traditional programming. Flash-specific concepts like targeting are also important, but mostly because this affects a traditional programming concept called scope. Let's look at these critical basic concepts first.

Variables

Variables provide temporary storage for any kind of data. The storage is temporary because the variables only exist while the movie plays. Each variable has a name and a value. If my script reads `username="Phillip"`;, that would mean the variable `username` would be assigned the value "Phillip."

A variable's value can take several forms. Imagine the variable is an envelope. You can put paper in the envelope, you can put flowers in it, you can even fill it with sand. The value (that is, what's inside the envelope) can be many types of material. Flash allows the following data types:

- Numbers
- Strings
- Boolean values
- Objects
- Movie Clips

Here are some examples (note that "`//`" creates a comment, meaning anything that follows it is ignored by Flash—it's just for your reference):

- `currentAge=35; //number`
- `firstName="Phillip"; //string`
- `married=true; //boolean`
- `eyeColor=new Color(); //color object`
- `currentClip=clip_1; //movie clip`

You can hold any of these five types of data in a variable. Actually, you can determine the variable's type with the operator `typeof`. For example, if you use the script `trace(typeof(username));`, the type of the variable `username` would appear in the output window (string, in this case).

I find that the concept of data types is best understood when comparing numbers to strings. For example, you can use `twiceMyAge=currentAge*2;`. This just assigns the variable named `twiceMyAge` a value that is two times the value of `currentAge` (a number). But to say `doubleMyName=firstName*2;` doesn't make any sense because you're trying to use a math operator (multiplication) on a string. This is like comparing apples to oranges—you can't mix numbers and strings.

Finally, a boolean variable contains either true or false—nothing else. You never really have to use boolean however it makes sense for variables containing absolutes.

Pregnant, for example, is either true or false. Other appropriate examples include "newUser," "soundOn," or "passedTest." As for the movie clip type, you'll learn more later in this appendix.

Targeting and Scope

Variables exist only where you use them. The technical term is that a variable's *scope* is limited to the Timeline where it exists. For instance, there can be only one unique age variable within each Timeline. If in the first frame of your movie you place the Action age=35;, then the variable age is part of that Timeline. If that Action were on a frame inside an instance of a clip, the variable would be part of that clip instance's Timeline. You can also put Actions on button instances and clip instances. Attaching age=35; to a button instance is the same as putting it in a frame of the Timeline where the button resides. Placing age=35; on a clip instance is the same as putting that code in a frame inside that clip. If inside one clip you place age=23;, you will only change the age variable for that Timeline.

Some of the applications of scope were covered in Hour 16, "Using Smart Clips," when I equated a variable that's inside a particular clip instance to a property of that clip. It really helps to think of variables inside clips as properties of those clips. Consider how two clips can have different positions using the _x and _y properties. Similarly, they can both have different "age" properties even though age is really just a variable in the clip's Timeline.

You should think of variables as properties of clips because you can access both the same way. Recall that if you want to change a clip's position, you can use code such as clipName._x=100;, where clipName. is the clip you're targeting. If you want to change the age variable (think age *property*), you use the same form: clipName.age=21;. Of course, if the script you're writing targets the clip you're inside, you can forgo the clip name and write simply _x=100; or age=21;. The only time you need to use clipName. is when you're writing an Action from outside the clip.

B

Remember, targeting variables and properties takes the form *Object.property*. If you have two clips (with instance names "clip_1" and "clip_2"), you can target clip_1's age variable by simply writing clip_1.age;. To change its age variable, you could use clip_1.age=21;. For the built-in _x property, you use the same form: clip_1._x=200;. This moves the clip to x position 200. When you have nested clips, the target is extended to clip_1.clipInsideClip.age;.

If it helps, think of this analogy: Every city in Oregon has a mayor. However, I can't just ask "Who's the mayor?"—I must first target the city I'm inquiring about. If I happen to be in Portland, I can indeed say "Who's the mayor?"—and, naturally, I'll get the mayor for Portland. But suppose I'm only inside Oregon. In this case, I'd have to ask, "Who's Portland's mayor?" If I'm simply in the USA, I'd have to ask "Who's the mayor in Portland, Oregon?" Notice in speech the order goes from specific to general. In Flash, the order goes from general to specific. Assuming I had clip instances with names such as "oregon," "portland," and "salem," I could target oregon.portland.mayor and ascertain the mayor for Portland. If I'm in Oregon, I'd only have to use portland.mayor, and so on.

Clip instance names should not have any spaces (although this is not a rule). You'll find a couple more points about this topic in the "Object Referencing" section. Once you understand targeting, you only need to decide what you're targeting and whether you want to change the property you're accessing or simply find out its value.

ActionScripting Foundation Concepts

Although the basics covered so far can be applied to almost all types of programming, the information that follows is specific to Flash. Most of the foundation concepts are intuitive and relatively easy to learn, but some simply need to be accepted as they are. For example, vertical coordinates increase as you move down. It may not be intuitive, but it is a fact and one that you must learn.

Movie Clips for Everything

In addition to all the other reasons to use Movie Clips, only Movie Clips can have their own variables, only Movie Clips can have their properties change at runtime, and only Movie Clips can be named. Neither buttons nor graphic symbols can have their properties changed via scripting at runtime. Actually, I use Movie Clips so much, I often make "invisible" buttons (that is, a button with no graphic except a circle or square in its hit state). I put the invisible button over a Movie Clip and then attach scripts which target the Movie Clip's properties such as _x and _y to the button instance. For example, when the mouse rolls over the invisible button, I make the Movie Clip move down and to the right. When it rolls out, I move the clip back.

Coordinates

On the Stage, Flash considers the x and y coordinates to begin at the top-left corner. The x coordinate increases as you move to the right. The y coordinate increases as you move down. This may be familiar to you, and you just accept that "0, 0" is the top-left corner. In the case of clip instances, position is based on the center registration point of that clip. If you use someClip._x=100, the center of the clip will move to x position 100. Whenever you're inspecting the coordinates of clips on the Stage, use the Info panel and be sure to click the center box (so you're not viewing the top-left corner of the clip).

Similarly, when you are inside a clip, "0, 0" is the center of the clip, as shown in Figure B.1. The best way to understand clip coordinates is to select View, Rulers and edit a symbol by double clicking the symbol item in the Library.

FIGURE B.1

The position of objects on the Stage is based on the top-left corner being 0x 0y. Within Movie Clips, objects are based on the center being 0x 0y.

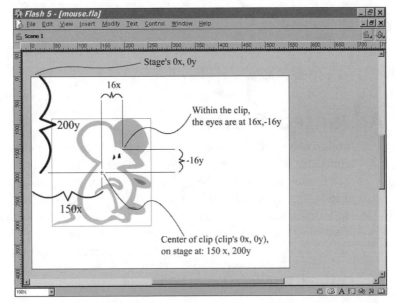

Form

You must follow proper form in several places in your scripts. For example, you should end each line in the code with a semicolon. Also, anything you start you must finish. For example, if you have a quotation mark (to open a quoted portion), you must also have a corresponding end quote. To say this technically, the first quotation mark needs to be *satisfied* with an ending quotation mark. Also, you can't have an open parenthesis without a closing one. Similarly, an open curly bracket ({) must be satisfied with a closing curly bracket (}), and the same applies to straight brackets ([and]). You'll see more about curly brackets in the "Functions" section and straight brackets in the "Object Reference" section.

Arrays Count "0, 1, 2, 3..."

Despite the fact that we count "1, 2, 3...," the first item in an array is always item 0. Although you haven't learned about arrays, this is something you'll want to memorize. For example, January is month 0, February is month 1, and so on. One might assume that "month 1" is January. Here's a code segment of how you might apply this concept (we will explain the syntax later in the appendix):

B

```
now = new Date();
thisMonth = now.getMonth();
trace ("This month is " + thisMonth);
if (thisMonth == 0){
    monthName="January";
}
if (thisMonth == 1){
    monthName="February";
}
//and so on...
trace ("Month name is " + monthName);
```

Advanced Topics

If this hasn't been enough for you, there's more. Most of the material here has to do with referencing. Think of learning to drive. Not only do you need to know the function of each instrument (steering wheel, brakes, gas pedal, etc.), you need to know how to reach them—that you use your left foot for the clutch for example. You can compare this to Flash. If you want to move a movie clip, you have to know how to reach it—that is, how to refer to it. Only then can you determine its properties, move it, or change it otherwise. Precisely how to reference the clip is the next concept we'll cover.

Object Reference

As discussed earlier, targeting properties of clip instances always follows the form `object.property`. If the object is inside another object (as in the case of a nested Movie Clip), you can use the form `object.subobject.property`, where "object" and "subobject" are clip instance names. This form works great if your scripts are all at the main Timeline and they're "talking down" to clips and subclips. However, there are times when your script may be contained inside one clip and needs to refer to another clip, which involves going "up" the hierarchy. Suppose I'm in Portland, Oregon and I want to find out who the mayor in Seattle, Washington is. In what's called a *relative reference*, I can say "go up to Oregon, go up to the USA, then go down to Washington, go down to Seattle." That's a path relative to my target and, in this case, it's quite complex. Even if I'm in Portland, it might have been easier to use an absolute path and say "start at the USA level, go down to Washington, go down to Seattle." This absolute reference starts at the root level of the USA and then drills down. It may sound like a mixed-up idea, but you can actually have such an arrangement of named clip instances as those shown in Figure B.2.

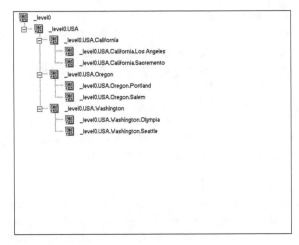

FIGURE B.2

This hierarchy of nested clips uses instance names that match names of cities and states on the West Coast to illustrate targeting.

Relative, Absolute, `_root`, `_parent`, and `this`

In order to apply relative and absolute paths, you need to know three built-in features of Flash: `_root`, `_parent`, and `this`. `_root` is an absolute reference to the main Timeline, which is the starting point for all clips. If the script is in the main Timeline, you could use a relative reference such as `someClip.someProperty`, and Flash knows that you must mean the "someClip" that's sitting in the main Timeline. It's redundant, but you could also use the `_root` absolute reference (`_root.someClip.someProperty`), and there would be no question as to what you meant. If the script happens to be inside another clip, preceding the target path with `_root` would clarify that you intend to refer to the main Timeline absolutely. Therefore, `_root` simply means the main Timeline.

`_parent` is a relative reference that says "go up one level." (This is equivalent to the HTML "`../`" reference.) If I were writing a script *inside* the clip "Portland" (which could be on a keyframe inside the clip or attached to a button instance or another clip inside the Portland clip) and wanted to refer to the clip that contains Portland (Oregon, in this case), I could just use `_parent`. If I use `_parent._name`, I would find the name property, or instance name, of the clip that's one level up from where I am (in this case, Oregon).

If, inside the Portland clip, I want to refer to the Portland clip itself (maybe to ascertain its name property), I'd use the keyword `this`. For example, `this._name` would give me the instance name of the Portland clip. This may seem silly, but consider that you could create a generic clip that could be used many times, each with a different instance name. To see this illustrated, create a button and attach the script `trace(this._name);` (which, of course, gets wrapped in a mouse event). Convert the button to a symbol (F8) with Movie Clip behavior and place several instances of this clip (with the button inside it) on the Stage. Name each instance differently and then test the movie. Each button will cause its host clip's name to appear in the output window.

B

You'll need to make up your mind whether an absolute or relative reference is more appropriate when you apply this knowledge. A good rule of thumb is that when you are only going "up" or only going "down" the hierarchy, it's easy enough to use a relative reference. However, if you are going "up" then need to go back "down," it's often easier to use absolute references. Keep in mind that absolute references can easily break if you change the hierarchy. For example, suppose you decide to put the "USA" clip inside a clip called "World." All of the sudden, your absolute reference `_root.USA.California.Sacramento.Weather;` will be broken (you will need to change it to `_root.World.USA.California.Sacramento.Weather;`).

Dynamic Referencing

Sometimes you may not know the exact name of the clip you want to target. You may intentionally write one script that can be used many different times. For example, you might have one thermometer-type scale for "time remaining" and another for "fuel remaining." Not only can you use the same code to refer to either one dynamically, but each clip can be identical but given a different instance name. The "time remaining" clip can be called "thermo_1," and the "fuel remaining" clip can be called "thermo_2." If you want to move one clip (change its _y property) in *pseudo-code,* you could write `move thermo_x`, where x is either 1 or 2, depending on which clip you want to move.

NEW TERM *Pseudo-code* is a technique programmers use to write scripts initially using only common terms (not the programming language). Instead of worrying about perfect syntax they can concentrate on organizing their ideas. If you can write really good pseudo-code you can probably find a decent programmer to translate it to real code (or do it yourself as it's practically routine to finish). It may seem like extra work but it allows you to separate the programming details from the general task at hand.

First you need to set x=1 or x=2 so that later you can use the variable "x" and its value will be used in its place. If x happens to equal 1 saying `thermo_x._y=100` won't work because Flash will look for a clip with the instance name "thermo_x" (and you want the clip "thermo_1" to be used instead). You might try to separate the "x" from the prefix "thermo_" by writing `thermo_"+x._y=100` but that only creates a string "thermo_1" and you are trying to reference the clip named "thermo_1" (a movie clip data type, rather than a string).

The solution requires that you understand something about arrays. First, an array is a data type stored in a variable that actually contains multiple values. If you think of a normal variable as a house, an array variable would be a large apartment building. When trying to access a normal variable's value you just refer to the variable's name such as x=1. When referring to array variable's value you have to specify which element within the array you are targeting. The basic form is *arrayName[index].* In pseudo-code you could say apartmentBuilding[112] and that might refer to the family in apartment 112. This is important to understand because all the clips onstage are part of a built in array called _root. (You just learned _root as a reference to the main Timeline—it works both ways.) Anyway, back to referencing a clip name dynamically, you can use: _root["thermo_"+x]._y=100. Translated, this means that there's an array called _root and you want to refer to an element in that array (a clip called "thermo_1"). The element is actually the clip itself. We've learned two things here: clips are a data type that are in the built in _root array; and referring to clip names dynamically requires use of this array. You don't have to understand arrays to start using this syntax, but it won't hurt. For now, remember the form *arrayName[index]* syntax.

You may have noticed that a plus sign (+) is used as a concatenation character. You were concatenating a string ("thermo_") with a variable name (x). Suppose the current value for x is 2; the concatenated string is "thermo_2". By using the brackets following an array variable's name, you tell Flash that, even though there are quotation marks, "thermo_"+1 is not a string.

Concept of Self

After all this discussion of relative, absolute, and dynamic referencing, the topic of "self" may seem anticlimatic. The point is, you can often refer to variables and properties without first targeting the clip. Targeting is unnecessary when you're referring to a clip you're inside of. For example, while inside a clip, you can just use age=age+1;. You don't need to use clipname.age=clipname.age+1. When Flash encounters a lack of a clip reference, it figures you must be referring to the current clip—the one where the script resides.

If you recall from Hour 15, "ActionScripting Applications for Advanced Interactivity," you used the startDrag Action without specifying a clip instance name. This worked because the startDrag Action was attached to a button inside a clip. This lack of a clip reference caused Flash to target the clip in which the Action was contained. The point is, you don't have to make this harder than it is. When there's no question what you are referring to, you can leave the target empty. Not only will this be easier, it will also be less specific, which means you can use the same generic code in many places without any hardwiring. The same benefits of code-date separation (discussed in Hour 22, "Working on Large Projects and in Team Environments") apply to generic code.

Functions

A simple definition of a function is "some code that does something." Naturally, we've already used many Actions that—in my mind—are functions. I think of Play and Stop as functions. However, there's an entire section called *Functions* in the Toolbox list of the Actions panel. In addition, there are many Actions that act like functions. Instead of

B

concentrating on the definition of a function, it may be easiest to think of the application for functions and simply learn how to use them. I'm going to separate the discussion of functions into using functions, built-in functions, and homemade functions.

Using Functions

Functions always take the form `functionName()`. Inside the parentheses, some functions allow or require you to provide a parameter (or parameters). Unlike Actions, functions return values. That means, in addition to "doing something," functions provide answers. Let's look at a couple of simplified examples.

Imagine that there's a function called `whatTimeIsIt` (there isn't really one with this name). You'd be able to use the `whatTimeIsIt` function to find out what time it is by simply writing `whatTimeIsIt();`. In this case, the function doesn't require any parameters. However, how the function returns the value is interesting. The "answer" (that is, the value the function returns) needs to go someplace. Consider if you tell someone to think of a number between 1 and 10. Nothing is returned. However, if you say, "Think of a number between 1 and 10 and write it on this piece of paper," the answer would be on the paper. Even though the function will always return an answer, you need to do something with the answer that's returned. For example, `whatTimeIsIt();` doesn't really do anything. However, if you use `currentTime=whatTimeIsIt();`, the value that's returned from this function replaces the function statement on the right side of the equation. Therefore, the variable `currentTime` is assigned that value. It's almost like any time you type the function name (with parentheses), it changes into the answer.

Some functions make use of parameters. This way, the functions can return different answers depending on the parameters provided. For example, maybe you have a function called `convertToUSDollars`. The function will return a dollar amount in U.S. dollars when you provide (as a parameter) a dollar amount in Canadian dollars. For example, if the price is shown in $20.00 Canadian, you could call the function like this: `convertToUSDollars(20);`. Remember, wherever that script is written, the answer will appear. Therefore, you have to do something with the answer—for example, `actualPrice=convertToUSDollars(20);`. When this script executes, `actualPrice` will change to 12.30 (based on current exchange rates). You'll see how the function is created in a minute. For now, just understand the form and usage for functions.

Built-in Functions

For better or worse, there aren't built-in functions called "`convertToUSDollars`" and "`whatTimeIsIt`." However, there are a few very useful ones. For example, the function `getTimer` returns the total number of milliseconds elapsed since a movie started. This is the core technique used in any kind of timing application.

For example, if you want to time how long a user looks at an opening screen before clicking a "continue" button, you could use `getTimer`. In the first frame, you could save the time that the user started in a variable called `startTime`, like this: `startTime=getTimer();`. Then, attached to the continue button, you could write the script `totalTime=getTimer()-startTime;`. If you wanted to retrieve this information you could simply look at the value of totalTime (maybe use it in a dynamic text field). It's as if you wrote down the start time by looking at the clock when the user first started. Then, when he finishes, you look at the clock again and subtract the start time. It doesn't really matter whether the clock is set to the correct time—just that it keeps running the entire time. Also, realize there are 1,000 milliseconds in each second. Therefore, if in the end `totalTime` equals 10,000 (milliseconds), it's the same as 10 seconds.

Another very useful function is `Number`. This function returns a numeric version of any string you provide as a parameter. For example, `Number("2");` tells Flash to treat `"2"` as a number. This is essential when you're extracting the content of Input Text. For example, if you ask the user to type her age into an Input Text field called "userAge," you probably want to convert it to a number before doing any math on her age—you could use `actualAge=Number(userAge);`. The parameter in this case is whatever string the user has typed into the Dynamic Text field userAge, and the function will convert this string to a number before placing the answer in the other variable, `actualAge`.

There are a few more built-in functions, but if you understand the form and usage of the ones in this section, you'll have no problem picking them up.

Homemade Functions

You can create your own functions. Not only does this expand upon the built-in functions, but it means your programming can be modularized and minimized. The time to create a function is when you find yourself typing the same or similar code over and over again. Actually, any time you copy and paste code, an alarm should sound in your head that informs you it's time to consider a creating a homemade function.

The form of a function is almost identical to event scripts on buttons or clip instances:

```
function functionName() {
    //code goes here
}
```

Notice the word "`function`" is always used verbatim, but the word that follows is the function's name. Name it what ever you want using letters (no spaces). The parentheses always appears and can include an argument (which will be used to represent the parameter, if you expect one). The open curly bracket indicates the start of the code (and it's customarily placed at the end of the first line). Following the first curly bracket (and before the ending curly bracket), you place as many lines of code as it takes to create the function. Remember, the "//" merely creates a comment, so anything that follows it is ignored by Flash. An important thing to remember is that functions can only be attached to keyframes.

For example, suppose you have three buttons that each move the same clip 10 pixels to the right. You should consider creating a function because you don't need to place the same code on each button instance. Just write one function and use it many times. Of course, you'll be calling the function from each button, but the bulk of the code will be in one place, where it can be edited and updated at any time. You can write the function in the first keyframe as follows:

```
function moveIt(){
    theClip._x=theClip._x+10;   // could have used theClip._x+=10
}
```

You just need a clip with the instance name "theClip." Then, from each button, you can call this function by using moveIt(); (within a mouse event, of course).

This function does one task, and does it perfectly well. However, it's hard-wired to "theClip." What if you have other clips? You probably wouldn't want to write a new function for each one. However, you can make this function generic by accepting a parameter. Consider this analogy: A server in a restaurant can have several customers. When a customer says "Check, please," the server performs the function of producing a bill. The process is always the same: He looks through all the current bills and finds the correct one—that is, he looks for "a customer's" bill. Consider "Check, please" a function. If I were being very specific (and talking like a computer), I might request the check by saying "Phillip's check, please." In this case, the parameter I'm providing is "Phillip." The server still looks for "a customer's" bill. The argument that he always accepts for his function is "a customer." It just so happens, in this case, "a customer" equals "Phillip." The value for "a customer" happens to be "Phillip," in my case, but it could be something else when another customer requests his check.

If, when calling the function moveIt, the clip that's supposed to move is provided as a parameter, you could move just that clip. For example, if the button calls the function via moveIt(oneClip);, another button could call it via moveIt(otherClip);. You have to modify the function to accept the additional parameter:

```
function moveIt(whichOne){
    whichOne._x=whichOne._x+10;
}
```

In this case, whichOne is called an *argument*. The function expects a parameter to be sent when it's called. Once inside the function, Flash needs a name for the parameter (whatever its value). For the sake of argument, suppose it just calls the parameter whichOne.

Later in the function, it can refer to whichOne, and that's the same as referring to oneClip, otherClip, or whatever is sent as a parameter. So to actually use this function, you could place the following script attached to a button: moveIt(ball). Then the clip called ball would move 10 pixels to the right. This might not sound easy, but that's all there is to it.

So far in this section, you've only seen how to create functions that perform tasks. Functions can also return values. They're easy to create but a little harder to apply. Basically, within your function, you include a line that begins with "return" and follow that by the value you want returned. Usually "return" appears as the last line in the function. Check out the following example of a currency exchange function (just so you know, while I was writing of this book, the exchange rate from Canadian to U.S. dollars was .615):

```
function convertToUS(valueInCAD){
    answer= valueInCAD * .615;
    return answer;
}
```

The only parts that have to be used verbatim are the words function and return (plus all the parentheses and curly brackets). I could have written one line of code instead of two as return valueInCAD * .615; but doing it in two lines (that is, first setting the variable "answer" then returning the variable) might be easier to read. To use this function, you can simply write convertToUS(20);. But remember, with functions that return values, you should probably do something with the answer that's returned. For example, you could write priceInUS=convertToUS(20); and then possibly view priceInUS in a Dynamic Text field.

Functions As Methods

Without going into a lot of detail, I think it's important that you understand how methods work before going further. A *method* is just like a regular function, except it's assigned to an object (in this case, the object is a Movie Clip instance). Recall how you can reference a clip's properties with dot syntax—for example, someClip._alpha=50;. You can also reference a clip's variables (which, in effect, are just homemade properties) with someClip.someVar=100;. Functions can work similarly. Functions can only be written in keyframe scripts. However, a function could appear inside a clip if the script is in a keyframe within a Movie Clip. If you're writing a script inside this clip, you just call the function like normal: functionName();. However, if you're writing a script outside the clip, you must call the function specifically for one clip instance. Because, after all, if you have several instances of the clip, the function is repeated in each.

B

The way you call a function specific to another clip should look familiar because you use the same dot syntax: `clipName.functionName();`. Notice the parentheses after the function's name. For example, you can cause a clip instance to jump to frame 10 with this: `clipName.gotoAndStop(10);`. If you had your own function called "birthday" on a keyframe inside the Movie Clip, you could call it for just one clip instance by writing `clipName.birthday();`. Applying this takes some creativity. However, I wanted to point it out because, in this case, the function is acting like a method.

Objects

In Flash, there are both built-in functions and homemade functions. Similarly, although several objects are "built in," you can also create your own. This appendix only covers how to use built-in objects. Quite simply, an object is a data type that can have multiple properties. You've already seen a lot of the functionality of objects, because clip instances, which can have multiple properties, are objects. Properties of objects are accessed with the simple dot syntax you've seen so many times before. Additionally, objects can have functions assigned (called *methods*, as just discussed). In addition to clip instances, there are some other interesting built-in objects.

The basic approach to using objects is that you create a new instance of an object, put it in a variable, and then refer to that variable as if it were an object (which its value is). For example, there's a built-in object called `Date`. Suppose you want to display the time onscreen. Simply make up a variable named `now` and put an entire `Date` object in it. The form is `now = new Date();`. Translated, this means "give me a new `Date` object and put it in the variable now." With any object you must do this step first (it's called "instantiating" the object). Once an object is instantiated you can use it and modify it. If you have a Dynamic Text field onscreen associated with the variable `now`, you'd see a very detailed description of the time. (You might have to make the Dynamic Text field wide enough to see it all.) If you only want to see the minutes, you could make another variable, `minutes`, and use the `getMinutes` method on your `now` variable: `minutes=now.getMinutes();`. Finally, you'll probably find that this works fine except for the fact the time will be displayed once and then appear to freeze, because it won't change. If you put the Dynamic Fields "minutes" and "seconds" inside a clip, you can then attach the following script to make the variables update more frequently:

```
onClipEvent (enterFrame) {
    now=new Date();
    seconds=now.getSeconds();
    minutes=now.getMinutes();
}
```

The idea is that you have to keep getting a new `Date` object so that it's fresh.

Other objects are available, and they follow the same form: Use new to create a new instance of the object, put it in a variable, and then you can use methods on the variable.

Smart Clips

Finally, here are some suggestions for when you want to attack the programming aspect of creating a Smart Clip. First, make a plain-old Movie Clip that works great when you hard-wire properties. Then figure out which properties will need to be adjusted by the author. Only "extract" those properties to become the *clip parameters*. All the properties you want the user to have access to must be properties of the clip itself. That's not to say you can't have other variables or properties inside the clip, but the ones the using author can change have to be on the surface of (attached to) the Movie Clip. If you can keep that straight—as well as all the related targeting issues—then the process isn't too bad.

Creating Custom User Interfaces

Creating a custom user interface (UI) to replace the Clip Parameters panel can involve a lot of work. To see how the Clip Parameters dialog can be replaced look at the examples provided when you select Window, Common Libraries, Learning Interactions. Drag an instance of "DragAndDrop" and access the Clip Parameters panel. This example is good because it walks the using author through all the steps to populate an instance. If you want to create a custom user interface just to make the standard dialog box more graphic, you're going to invest a lot of time for something of limited value. After all, the standard Clip Parameters panel works fine. However, if you want to save the using author the effort of calculating parameters, which would otherwise be a lot of work for him, then creating a custom UI might be worth the effort.

To create a custom UI, you start with a plain .fla file. You need to create a Movie Clip with the instance name, "xch." Target this clip and its properties as though it were the clip instance the using author has dragged into his file. For example, if the clip parameter you're allowing the using author to populate is speed, you'll want to set the value for xch's speed parameter (xch.speed=100, for example). For all intents and purposes, the xch clip is the clip the user has dragged into his file.

Finally, the trickiest part is restoring for the using author the most recent values for all the parameters. Each instance the using author creates will maintain unique values for each parameter—it's not like the values are lost. But you want to make sure the user can see the values. If you use Dynamic Text fields to contain the parameters (that is, properties of the xch clip), there's nothing extra for you to do—the fields will restore themselves. However, you can use clip instances to represent parameters by changing their position or other visual properties—such as a slider the using author can move left and right. If you use clips to represent parameter values, you'll want the clips to reposition

B

automatically any time the using author inspects with the Clip Parameters dialog box. You'll need a "kick start" script to do this. The only catch is that it doesn't seem to work unless you put several frames (at least five) in front of such a script. For example, suppose your custom UI has three buttons, named small, medium, and large. Normally, when the user is interacting with the Clip Parameters UI, you have a script under each button to move a clip that represents the currently selected button. Like in Figure B.3.

FIGURE B.3

A custom UI to replace clip parameters can be created in Flash.

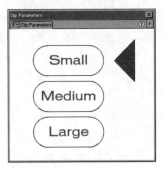

The "small" button might have this code:

```
on (release) {
    current=1;
    highlightClip._y=100;
}
```

The "medium" button could have the following code:

```
on (release) {
    current=2
    highlightClip._y=200;
}
```

Of course, you could probably abstract a function out of this, but the problem at hand is that when the using author returns to edit the clip parameters, the "highlightClip" _y position won't restore itself to the old location. However, in frame 5, you could have a script that reads highlightClip._y=current*100;. This effectively kick starts highlightClip so it appears in a location based on the old value for current. Like I said, this is not an issue when you use Input Text fields to display variables.

One Step at a Time

This appendix covered way more material than a new user will need right away. Don't try to digest it in one sitting. It's good to browse this appendix once and then return to it as you use some of its material. You'll still need other resources, but hopefully this has provided a good overview of basic ActionScript.

APPENDIX C

Resources

Tutorials and Online Resources

Macromedia

http://www.macromedia.com/support/flash/

You can't beat going straight to the source.

Moock.Org

http://www.moock.org

General resource not only for Flash but for all things Web.

Colin Moock's site is a great resource because it not only makes information on Flash easy to understand, but he puts it in the context of the whole Web. This is the site to check out if you have any technical issues related to publishing your Flash movie, JavaScript, or HTML.

The Flash Academy

http://www.enetserve.com/tutorials/

This site offers intermediate-to-advanced tutorials in the form of Flash player movies. They're easy to click through and follow along with.

Flash Kit

http://www.flashkit.com

This site offers downloadable tutorials so that you can see the .fla source files as well as click through the tutorials. It offers sounds as well.

Virtual-FX

http://www.virtual-fx.net/

Tutorials on all levels, from beginner to advanced action scripting, are offered at this site. There also is a library of open source .fla files, articles, and links to other Flash sites.

Flashlite

http://www.flashlite.net/

Good source for tutorials and Flash news.

Flazoom.com

http://www.flazoom.com/

Good source for links to Flash sites and Flash news.

Flash Magazine

http://www.flashmagazine.com

Articles and news about Flash.

We're Here

http://www.were-here.com

Probably the most active Web forums on Flash.

Content Sites

Generally, creating custom graphics and sounds will provide the closest match to the message you want to convey. However, there are plenty of sites with clip media that you can use in your practice files.

Keep in mind that there really is "no free lunch." Some clip media that may appear free often isn't. Copyright laws are no joke either. Consider that if you are using any kind of artwork or sound in a movie that you make money creating it's important to pay for it. Often, the value an artist brings to a project will easily offset their cost. Sometimes the cheapest route it the one that appears most expensive.

Audio/Sound Sites

Music 4 Flash

http://www.music4flash.com/

This is a good resource. It offers free sounds and has some high-end options (if you want to pay for them). It's a thorough site so those who are unfamiliar with the use of sound can get a lot of info. It also has a lot of links to other resources.

ACIDplanet.com™

http://www.acidplanet.com/

ACID™ is a loop-based music creation tool made by Sonic Foundry (http://www.sonicfoundry.com). At ACIDplanet.com, you can download a free version of the software, ACID XPress, download free music loops that change frequently, and buy loop collections on CD.

Winamp

http://www.winamp.com/

Primarily a site with shareware software, where you'll also find clip sounds.

Wavcentral

http://www.wavcentral.com/

This offers wave files and so much more. It's a good place to find sound (WAV only) as well as miscellaneous effects.

C

Images/Photos

Clip Art

http://www.clip-art.com/

This site offers a variety of bitmap clip art in cartoon style. It also offers tutorials on image optimization as well as free downloads.

Clip Art Connection

http://www.clipartconnection.com/

Site for free clip art.

GettyOne

http://www.gettyone.com/

GettyOne is an umbrella site that offers a host of sites from high-end (expensive) to low-end (cheap) image options. It's a powerful resource, but you can't legally get free images. Images are divided into royalty-free and licensed images. Keep in mind that royalty-free is not actually free; it means you pay only once, as opposed to a licensed image, which you have to pay for every time you use it. Artville and Photodisc are good low-cost options.

Artville

http://www.artville.com/

Artville, as mentioned before, can be accessed from GettyOne. It has both illustrations and photos.

Photodisc

http://photodisc.com

Another site accessible from GettyOne, Photodisc is a searchable site that offers low-cost, low-resolution files.

Fonts and Miscellaneous

T-26

http://www.t26font.com/

This site is a digital type foundry started by Carlos Segura, an internationally known designer who lives in Chicago. It's not free, but the fonts are beyond compare.

GS Homepage

http://nebula.spaceports.com/~huge/

This Website offers a selection of free fonts.

Émigré

http://www.emigre.com/

Émigré is a great source for fonts. Keep in mind that they're not free.

Inspirational Sites

Of course "inspirational" is subjective. Also, sites that are an inspiration to many can often become cliché when everyone copies them. The sites included here either include links to other award winning sites or they provide source Flash files from which you may learn.

Pray Station

http://www.praystation.com

This is a site from a group working out of the MIT media lab. Joshua Davis is the mastermind behind this site and many others, such as barneys.com. The site is created with Flash and features a calendar in which to access daily projects. You can also download .fla source files.

Flash Challenge

http://www.flashchallenge.com/

This site includes links to many other sites—most very well done.

Flash Film Festival

http://www.flashfilmfestival.com/

This site provides links to the winners of a Flash conference (FlashForward2000) previously held in San Francisco and New York.

Spooky & The Bandit

http://www.spookyandthebandit.com

In addition to a few amazing games created in Flash, this site has a Flash Object for Dreamweaver and other downloads.

C

Communication Arts

http://www.commarts.com/interactive/

Communication Arts is a magazine that covers the graphic/ad and design community. The interactive section of their Web site always has a site of the week, and often it's a Flash site. Every year they publish an "Interactive Design Annual". I'm proud to say a Flash site I programmed was included in the Annual for 2000.

Statistics

Macromedia

http://www.macromedia.com/software/player_census/

This page on the Macromedia site gives a running census of how many people have the Flash and Shockwave players installed. This is especially useful if you need to report to a third party, such as a client, how compatible a Flash piece is with the general public.

Glossary

Symbols

.fla file   An editable Flash file.

.swf file   A Flash file meant only for distribution—it can be watched, but not edited.

.swt file   A Flash template file for use with the product Macromedia Generator.

A

ActionScript   The computer language Flash uses.

Animated graphics   Moving images of any type. Often, Flash graphics and animated GIFs are image types seen on the Web.

Aspect ratio   The ratio of height to width. Like a television or movie screen, the shape of a Flash animation remains the same—no matter its size.

B

Bitmapped graphic   *See* Raster graphic.

Blank keyframe   A keyframe that causes nothing to appear on stage. *See also* Keyframe.

Button   An item that a user can click that causes an action.

Button state   A visual version of a button. For example, during clicking, the button is in its *down* state; when dormant, it is in its *up* state. When the mouse is hovered over the button, the button is in its *over* state.

Button symbol   A symbol used to create interactive buttons that respond to mouse events. *See also* Symbol.

C–F

Coordinates   Numbers signifying a place in a Cartesian plane, represented by (*x,y*). The top-left pixel in Flash, for instance, is written (0,0) or (0x,0y).

Down state   A button state that occurs when the user clicks the button with his mouse.

Export   To move a file or object from a Flash file. Often, the term is used to discuss the creation of distributable Flash files (.swf).

Focus   The state of being active. Usually the last object clicked currently has focus. In Flash, a dark line indicates which option has focus in a Timeline. *See also* Timeline.

Framerate   The rate, stated in frames per second (fps), at which each frame in an animation is played back for the user.

Frame-by-frame animation   Animation using a series of keyframes with no tweening that creates a flipbook-like animation Flash file.

G

Graphic symbol   Used for animated symbols which need to be previewed inside Flash. Graphic symbols should only be used for situations requiring this such as lip syncing.

Grid   Like grid paper, a grid is used for precise placement of objects in a Flash file. *See also* Ruler.

Guide layer   A special layer that does not export when you export a Flash file. This layer can be used to help registration of various elements of a Flash file.

H

Hit state   The clickable area of a button.

Hyperlink   Text or an object (such as an image) that can be *clicked* to take a user to related information, as used on the World Wide Web.

Hypertext Markup Language (HTML)   The language read by Web browsers to present information on the Internet.

I

Import   To bring a file or object into a Flash file.

Instance   An occurrence of a symbol used from the Library—especially helpful because, although more than one instance can exist, only the master symbol must be saved; thus, file sizes are kept small. *See also* Library *and* Symbol.

Interface   The design with which users interact.

J–K

Keyframe   A frame in which you establish exactly what should appear on stage at that particular time.

L

Layer   Aptly named, one of a stack of media in a Flash file Timeline. This is especially useful in animation because only one object can be tweened per layer.

Library   A storage facility for all media elements used in a Flash file.

Library item   Each media element in the Library is called an item. *See also* Symbol.

M

Masking   A kind of layer property with at least two layers: one for the Mask and one that is Masked (like Motion Guide and Guided). The graphical contents of the Mask layer will determine which parts of the Masked layer will show through.

Morph   A kind of animation that transitions one shape to another. *See also* Shape Tween.

Motion Guide   A Guide layer that has an adjacent layer (below it) that is set to Guided. Tweened objects in the Guided layer will follow a path in the Guide layer.

Movie Clip symbol   A symbol that contains interactive controls, sounds, and even other Movie Clips. Movie Clips can be placed in the Timeline of Button symbols to create animated buttons. Movie Clips follow their own internal Timeline, independent of the main Timeline. *See also* Symbol.

N–O

Onion Skin tools   Tools that enable you to edit one keyframe while viewing (dimly) other frames before or after the current frame.

Over state   A button state that occurs when the user passes his mouse over a button.

P

Panning   An effect that makes a sound seem to move from left to right (or right to left).

Parameter   A specifier used in ActionScript.

Q

QuickTime   A video format created by Apple. A common file format found on the Internet.

R

Raster graphic   An image file format that contains the color information for each pixel. Raster graphics' file sizes are relatively large.

RealPlayer   A streaming video player created by Real Networks. RealMedia (RealPlayer files) is a common format to find on the Internet.

Registration   The process of making sure screen components are properly aligned (often from one frame to another). *See also* Guide layer.

Rollover sound   A sound effect that plays any time a user places his cursor over a button.

Ruler   Like a physical ruler for Flash, a ruler is used for precise measurement of objects in a Flash file. Also, the Rulers must be visible in order to create dragable guides. *See also* Grid.

Runtime   The point at which the user is watching your movie (as well as when you're testing the movie).

S

Scale   To resize as necessary.

Scene   A component part of a Timeline in a Flash file.

Scrub   A technique to preview your animation by dragging the red current frame marker back and forth in the Timeline.

Shape Tween   A utility to create a fluid motion between two objects. *See also* Tween.

Smart Clip   A movie clip with parameters unique to each instance. In addition, Smart Clips can include a custom user interface to populate the parameters.

Stage   The large, white rectangle in the middle of the Flash workspace where a file is created. What is on stage is what the user will see when he plays your Flash file.

Statement   A single line of code in a script. *See also* ActionScript.

Static graphics   Graphics with no animation or interactivity. The computer-image equivalent of a photograph or a painting.

Symbol   A graphic, Movie Clip, or button that is stored in the Library. This is especially useful because no matter how many instances of a symbol are used, it only has to download once, and changes made to the master symbol are immediately reflected in all instances already used. *See also* Button symbol; Graphic symbol; Library; Movie Clip symbol.

Sync   The timing between an animation and a corresponding sound. You choose sync settings in the Sound panel.

T

Tile effect   A raster graphic used as the fill color in any shape you draw.

Timeline   An object on the Flash workspace that contains the sequence of frames, layers, and scenes composing an animation.

Tween   Used as a verb, "to tween" is to have a change made between two objects. For example, you can use a Shape Tween to morph a solid circle into a doughnut.

U–Z

Up state   Normally a button's default state, which occurs when the user has not clicked or passed over the button with his mouse.

Vector graphic   A vector graphic file contains all the calculations to redraw an image onscreen. A vector graphic's file size remains small, and the image can be scaled to any size without any degradation to image quality. Flash .swf files are saved as vector graphics.

INDEX